ON BECOMING
A COUNSELOR

ON BECOMING A COUNSELOR

A Basic Guide
for Nonprofessional Counselors
and Other Helpers

New Expanded and Revised Edition

**EUGENE KENNEDY AND
SARA C. CHARLES, M.D.**

A Crossroad Book
The Crossroad Publishing Company
New York

The Crossroad Publishing Company
481 Eighth Avenue, New York, NY 10001

Printed in the United States of America

Library of Congress Cataloging-in-Publication Data

Kennedy, Eugene C.
    On becoming a counselor : a basic guide for nonprofessional
counselors and other helpers / Eugene Kennedy and Sara C.
Charles. – 3rd expanded and rev. ed.
        p. cm.
    Includes bibliographical references and index.
    ISBN 0-8245-1913-2 (alk. paper)
    1. Counseling. 2. Psychology, Pathological. I. Charles, Sara C.
II. Title.
BF637.C6 K46 2001
158′.3 – dc21

                                                2001003819

6 7 8 9 10 11 12 13   13 12 11 10 09 08 07

CONTENTS

Preface: A Changed Book for a Changed Time vii

PART ONE

1. Guiding Principles 3
2. Emotional Involvement 11
3. Hard-Bought Wisdom 20
4. What Other People Do to Us 29
5. What We Do in Relationship with Others 40
6. Revelations about Ourselves in Relationships with Others 48
7. What Is It Like to Be Real? 57
8. The Self as Instrument in Helping Others 65
9. Are We Friends or Counselors? 73

PART TWO

10. How Do We Interview? 85
11. This Wasn't My Idea 101
12. I Won't Dance, You Can't Make Me 111
13. Plotting Our Course 121
14. Diagnosis: Goals and Resources 134
15. Listening to the Lives of Others 142
16. To Whom Shall We Go? 149
17. When Can I Say What I Feel? 159
18. Supportive Psychotherapy 167

PART THREE

19. Reading the Signs / Working with Families   175

20. Drugs: Use and Abuse   180

21. Drink, Drank, Drunk   192

22. The Language of the Seriously Disturbed   202

23. Everyperson's Illness: Depression   215

24. Stressed Out and Anxious   232

25. The Problems of Healthy People   247

26. Introductory Notes on Personality Disorders   255

27. Personality Disorders: Cluster A   261

28. Personality Disorders: Cluster B   275

29. Personality Disorders: Cluster C   295

PART FOUR

30. Marriage Counseling   311

31. Counseling Persons with Sexual Problems   327

32. Counseling the HIV/AIDS Patient   340

33. Suicide: Weighing the Risk   352

34. Death in Our Culture   361

35. Suffering Our Losses   372

36. Emergencies: Being a Steady Presence   386

37. Taking Counsel with Ourselves   401

Notes   409

Index   419

– Preface –

A CHANGED BOOK
FOR A CHANGED TIME

O NE EVENING AT HARVARD UNIVERSITY several years ago, a member of the audience of distinguished mental health professionals rose immediately after a talk by advice columnist Ann Landers with a pointed question, "Just what credentials do you have for advising others?" She did not hesitate. "None," she responded, "except common sense."

The extraordinary advances in medication in psychiatry in the last decade tell us that times have changed greatly. The recent embrace of religious faith as a significant factor in life resembles calling a great spirit, like the Russian writer Solzhenitsyn, out of a long, cold, and unjust exile. The transformation of care through Health Maintenance Organizations has compelled professional helpers to work according to an economic model that limits the length of therapy. As a result, treatment modes, their timing, and the training for them have all been altered. A more refined vocabulary for identifying the troubled states of persons has been carefully developed and published by the American Psychiatric Association in the *Diagnostic and Statistical Manual of Mental Disorders,* now in its fourth revision.[1]

One qualification, however, remains unchanged in this greatly changed universe for all counselors: that common sense and understanding of the human condition are inseparable elements of true helping.

Who Does the Helping?

The nameless legions of ordinary people who do most of the counseling every day and everywhere in this greatly altered world remain effective if they possess this compound ability to listen to and lessen the woes of the world. A lack of professional training does not make them unfit or unable to respond effectively to the anxious and the troubled people

vii

who turn to them for assistance. Graduate schools do not offer credit for the common sense that is the not uncommon characteristic of those whose human credentials are bestowed invisibly on them by the needy people who intuitively come to them with their troubles.

"We are all much more simply human," psychiatrist Harry Stack Sullivan once observed, "than anything else." An acceptance and appreciation of our shared foibles remains the greatest strength of those with the common sense, if not the formal training, to be counselors. That special account within themselves can never be overdrawn by the teachers, pastors, managers, supervisors, lawyers, doctors, architects, beauticians, funeral directors, and, not least among many others, bartenders, in whom people by the thousands are confiding their troubles even as you read these words.

This is a book for all these persons who, without extensive psychological training, must deal in their lives and in their regular work with people who can be troubled as much by trifling as by titanic life events. Those in whom they confide must respond in difficult and often far from ideal circumstances because they cannot screen those who approach them or control the situation in which they do. An emotionally distressed person may make an appointment to see the teacher, pastor, or lawyer in a structured setting. The disquieted, however, may also turn someone into a designated counselor by surprise and in unlikely surroundings.

The stranger in front of you on the Will Call line at the drugstore may open life and worry to you, "The doctor just changed my medication and I don't understand it, I thought I was getting better...." Or the student who never says much in class may wait in the hallway with a worry she can no longer contain, "I wonder if I could speak to you for a few moments...." The person next to you on the plane may never tell you his name but will tell you his life story, "I thought we were in love, I thought it would last...." Sometimes the professional you consult — the physician, the lawyer, the architect — makes you into a consultant, "Sorry I'm a little late but my mother called. She has this knack for calling at just the wrong moment...." You may be called up to serve, basic training or not, in the helping army at any moment and in almost any circumstances. You do not select them; they select you, ready or not.

You may never know whether they chose you because you are a member of the clergy, a professor, a nurse, or somebody who reminds them of a favorite relative. Human woe turns, as flowers do to the spring sun, to those nearby who seem capable of offering some understanding and good sense. The first murmurs of emotional pain, often disguised but ever recognizable, are almost always whispered first to such ordinary people.

If such nonprofessionals are the primary resource for our everyday troubles, what can they do to prepare themselves better to respond in such unpredictable situations? How can they, without extensive training, improve their ability to tap into the energy of their common sense and human understanding in order to respond effectively to those who come for assistance?

What Helpers Can Do

The inborn common sense of such persons tells them that they cannot and should not attempt to treat deep and long-standing emotional difficulties. They may, in fact, have only a few minutes, or the remaining hours of the plane trip, to spend with those who seek their counsel. But even in an exchange that consumes but a few seconds, they can be truly helpful to others. They help by simply being human with the troubled others, by marshaling their own resources of the spirit and capitalizing on the strength of their best instincts, in short, their common sense, to reply to them. It is also important for helpers to listen to themselves with this powerful combination of understanding and common sense to sort out their inner sources of static and interference and to manage the stress that arises from dealing with the stress of others. Helpers must monitor and identify their own reactions so that they will not be hijacked and held for ransom by them. Helping yourself goes apace with helping others.

The late Mayor Richard J. Daley of Chicago once said about the lawyers who advised him, "They're always telling me what I *can't* do. I want them to tell me what I *can* do." His words speak to the cautions often expressed to nonprofessional helpers. If there is much that they *cannot* do because they lack training, there is even more that they *can* do because they have healthy human qualities. This book is designed to assist counselors qualified by their human nature to help other persons.

Such helpers need not feel inferior because they are not experts. Neither should they judge their own good sense to be less sound than the often facile lesser celebrity gods of self-help. Men do not come from Mars and women have not parachuted in from Venus. What is healthy in the helper is usually more reliable than what is flashy in such therapists-at-large. If these chapters are not intended to transcend the humanity of counselors, neither will they challenge or attempt to modify their basic professional identity. Teachers should remain teachers, ministers need not doff their robes, bartenders continue to serve customers, everybody remains who and what they are. Changing their identity is not the purpose of this book.

Being Yourself, Being a Helper

Common sense tells us that our first line of response to troubled people cannot be provided by the relatively limited numbers of fully trained psychiatrists, psychologists, psychiatric social workers, marriage counselors, or kindred specialists. It must come from the persons who stand on that front line in whatever profession they find themselves. It is all very well to speak about making referrals, but what do lawyers, priests, and others, what, indeed, do *you* do in the meantime? And what can such persons do when there is no possibility of a referral or when the problem is one, like the death of a spouse or a child, for which there is no easy reassurance and perhaps no cure?

It is our experience that nonpsychological professionals — nurses, general physicians, and lawyers, as well as those many others previously mentioned — end up doing most of the counseling that actually goes on every day. They have no choice about it because their commitments are not just to aching body parts, conflicted wills, or mortgages, but to the whole living persons who have emotional connections as tangled as computer cords to these and all the other ordinary snags in the human situation.

Problems never exist in a pure state; there is always a human being attached to them. That is what makes them problems. As long as those who meet most of the troubled persons in the world are without psychiatric training, they need to know something more than how to say "Stop worrying." They need constructive ways to do what they can humanly do as they draw on their very real strengths to assist those with whom they work with their emotional problems. We have written this book to provide some positive assistance to those paraprofessionals, to these ordinary people who are neighbors and friends, who must, by necessity, do the bulk of psychological counseling during their regular work and everyday lives.

The Democratization of Counseling

Partly because of a growing distrust of professionals, we are deep into the era of the nonprofessional in many fields of endeavor. People are working out their own taxes, mortgages, wills, and even their divorces without the help of lawyers. They represent themselves in court, and an increasing number even design their own weddings and funerals without the help of the clergy, dressmaker, or florist. They also try to treat themselves through following the libraries filled with self-help books, twelve-step programs, and a twelve-course menu of diets. We have also witnessed what we might term the "democratization" of therapy through programs that reduce or reject outright the role of the trained professional in assisting others.

This is a political rather than a psychological conclusion, the replacement of knowledge by ideology. These enthusiasts are not interested in learning more about themselves or how they may focus their efforts as they establish themselves as therapists of one kind or another. They look on training as recent antitrust lawyers did Microsoft: a function of professionals conspiring to monopolize control over mental health practices. These helpers may be sincere, but that does not help them to recognize their own motivation in their own need to involve themselves in the intimate lives of other persons. This book is not written for them or for other independently established amateurs who do not wish to acquire learning in a disciplined or systematic way. They fly on what they judge to be their good therapeutic instincts, and on what the late pianist Oscar Levant called "a smattering of ignorance."

The Human Assets of Helpers

This book is designed to be a source of encouragement and practical help to the paraprofessional counselors who want to improve their ability to work effectively with others. It is not a how-to-do-it book but one that recognizes both their nonprofessional standing and also their basic strengths of common sense, good judgment, and their available humanity. This is a book for those persons, some of them professionals in other fields, who appreciate the need for some discipline and, far from wanting merely to indulge their own needs, want also to acquire enough skill to be able to respond to emotional problems with a genuine concern for others and a respect for their own limitations. Such persons deserve encouragement as well as resources against which to check themselves as they refine their counseling abilities. This work is an effort to make the power of disciplined understanding — the art of helping without hurting — available to them so that they can read and respond to the complex language of emotional distress.

Therefore, the book offers reflections on the nature of counseling

as well as treatments of the typical problems whose meaning is found
only in the life context of those experiencing them. Addressing itself to
persons who are professionals in some field other than counseling, it
does not treat problems and difficulties in the same depth that would
be found in a text for psychologists or psychiatrists, but rather it deals
with information and attitudes that fit the typical work situations of
such readers. The choice of topics for this book, however, was made
on the basis of years of experience in teaching and working with the
kinds of professionals to whom the book is addressed.

The clear aim is to reinforce the common sense and fundamental
identity of those who use it. It is written to make these great national
assets — commonsense people who counsel others — be more comfortable by deepening their simple but powerful human capacity to
recognize and respond to the emotional dimensions of the problems,
all of which are personal or have a personal reference, that they meet
every day.

An increased ability to rely on their own strengths enables these
paraprofessionals to work with greater integrity and self-possession.
This dissolves the feeling that they are under siege by totally mysterious forces all the time. It should also relieve them of feeling that they
must completely solve everybody's problem perfectly. Sometimes the
little they do is the most anybody could do in the situation. One of
their objectives lies in assisting persons to take greater responsibility
for themselves. This is no small gift to bestow on others.

Emotional Involvement

The insights they develop into themselves are important windows
through which to see and modulate their own investment in their work
with others. With a little help they can better maintain their own balance and feel free from the demands of one of the great changes that
has taken place in the therapeutic culture and, indeed, in the general
American culture during the last twenty years. Once, amateur counselors were warned against the cold remoteness that was supposedly
demanded by professional relationships in what now seems a long ago
time. Now they need to be on guard against the inappropriately informal and warm relationships that have become the style more recently.
One need not be artificially distant or falsely close to others in order
to help them. Indeed, the recent trend to abandon any formalities —
the immediate use of first names, for example, even by professionals
with those they help — may, as the book will discuss, harm rather than

help the relationship. This pretend-intimacy is a further example of the political democratization of counseling that undermines professional standards and insights.

Incidental but highly significant to the process of helping is the term employed to describe the person the counselor is helping. They are variously referred to in the helping professions as "patients," "clients," or, in a term adopted in the 1970s by the American Psychological Association in its Ethical Standards, as "consumers." This last designation makes helping into a business, an economic exchange, and, despite its use, implies that people can buy mental health like any commodity in the market place. Most of the persons for whom this book is written should continue to refer to these they help according to the positions that brought their relationship into being. Thus the minister sees a parishioner, the chaplain talks to inmates, the teacher helps pupils, while many others, including lawyers, architects, and tax-preparers, see clients. In order to underscore the emphasis of this work, we will use the term "person" to identify the one seeking or receiving help.

Challenges of emotional involvement with those we help are problematic enough without promoting them by blithely erasing the boundaries that make good counselors as Frost's good fences made good neighbors. Yet helpers who want to observe sensible formalities may be prey to emotional involvements. Indeed, nothing may be more discouraging to paraprofessionals' willingness to help people than the stinging tangle of emotions, engaged but unidentified, of the trapped absorption with others that destroys their own composure and severely limits their ability to help. They are frequently glad to escape such entanglements, vowing that they will never again get so closely involved with other peoples' personal problems. This book offers a resource for reflection and self-evaluation that helps counselors to remain personal and involved without fearing that they will inevitably be lost in the process.

What Can We Really Do for Others?

What can we really do for others? That is a question at the very heart of all the helping professions, and those who counsel in conjunction with other responsibilities ask it of themselves all the time. They want to be constructively helpful, yet they are often puzzled as to how they can best achieve this ideal. It is important to realize that in most emotional problems a little help is a lot of help. A modest enough notion, yet one that many, ambitious that they can deliver more, hesitate to espouse, with the result that they frequently end up delivering considerably less. Paraprofessionals need honest and reasonable expectations about what they can accomplish in their counseling; there is no disgrace in not being able to remake people, for very few fully trained therapists ever come close to this. There is every honor, however, in helping persons to move even a few inches closer to self-responsibility, in assisting them to turn in a new and healthier direction in life. The curse in the soul of "amateur" therapists is their determination to change people at all costs, and they frequently blunder, trampling on the sacred places of others' personalities in the process. Paraprofessionals without such ill-starred notions about their capabilities can both avoid the gross errors of these amateurs and deliver a service that is solid and lasting even though it is modest in scope.

Understanding is at the heart of all good therapy. It is, interestingly enough, a quality that cannot possibly harm others, and it is also something of which all humans are capable. Understanding transmitted through the discipline of counseling skills helps bewildered people to see themselves in better perspective. And all individuals, no matter the primary identity of their profession, can convey it. It is hoped that this book will help counselors use the energy of their own common sense and understanding in a measured but powerfully effective manner.

EUGENE KENNEDY, PH.D.   SARA C. CHARLES, M.D.
Professor Emeritus of Psychology   Professor of Psychiatry (Emerita)
Loyola University of Chicago   University of Illinois at Chicago
                                        School of Medicine

PART ONE

– 1 –

GUIDING PRINCIPLES

A S LIFE DEMANDS growth and transformation, so books seek, almost of themselves, to be revised. The most obvious reason for
recasting a book such as this is to include new insights and developments in the field of counseling of which even nonprofessional
counselors should be aware. It is just as important to enlarge and bring
up to date the references to which those who use the book may turn for
more extended and timely information about the subjects of concern
to them.

For example, the *Diagnostic and Statistical Manual of Mental
Disorders* (fourth edition, text revision), referred to in professional
shorthand as *DSM-IV-TR*, is a landmark achievement in developing
a common language to describe and assess psychological problems.
Although nonprofessionals may never use it in the same manner as
psychiatrists and other specialists, it is a volume of which they should
be aware. Some working acquaintance with its carefully delineated behavioral signs will help them understand better those people who seek
them out for help.

It also opens helpers to a store of information from which they can
fashion an accurate and timely sense of the psychological burdens of
others. This not only increases their own confidence but may also be
crucial to their making a well-timed referral of those who need more intensive treatment the helpers can provide. Familiarity with its contents
also allows helpers to comprehend and speak the special language of
emotional disorder with greater ease and conviction.

Designated Counselors

Unlike highly trained therapists, that hardy, widely deployed force of
nonprofessionals who, on any given day, actually carry out most of the
counseling done in the world work in life as it is with people as they
are, at the blood-smeared accident site rather than in the sterile surgical suite. They resemble medics more than specialists and, as such,

they cannot be selective about those they are called upon to help. The armies wandering through dark nights in their souls huddle outside their doors, the mendicants of the spirit whose numbers never dwindle crouch in wait for them at the unlikely hours of real time and real life conditions. The clergy, general physicians, teachers, lawyers, funeral directors, law enforcement personnel, even you, the tired air traveler who finds the passenger in the next seat suddenly pouring out a troubled life story, lack what Americans prize and professionals enjoy, the freedom to choose which persons they feel competent to help. Counselors are designated as such by circumstances. They earn battlefield promotions.

From the challenges related by nonprofessionals themselves, we learn that more specific distinctions serve them well in understanding and implementing the limits and possibilities of the help they may offer. This third edition of *On Becoming a Counselor* has been extensively modified and new chapters have been introduced to clarify the difference between the approaches and responses appropriate for professionals and those who are designated counselors by the undifferentiated needs of others. This hardly makes nonprofessional counselors into second-class helpers. What they do in the intense but often mottled light of everyday life is often extraordinarily helpful, frequently life-saving or at least life-renewing for the varied legions of the troubled who would otherwise have no help at all. The good that they do, however, is a function of their sensible perception of the chalk lines within which they respond to persons whose need anoints them as designated counselors. Their greatest strengths are their own common sense and what we may term psychological mindedness.

Self-Confidence and Psychological Mindedness

Nonprofessional counselors should, in the first place, have confidence in their own identity and not apologize for or try to obscure it. Whatever their role, it represents achievement and hard-earned wisdom about a number of theoretical and practical matters. As with the military that, in centuries of dealing with human beings, has learned, without any psychological insight or sophistication, a great deal about the pragmatic management of their strengths and weaknesses, so ministers, lawyers, and countless others designated as counselors by the distress of others have also acquired, without any deep psychological self-consciousness, estimable stores of practical ways of helping people get through difficult incidents in their lives. Nonprofessionals, somewhat like mothers who have never read the books of experts, often have healthy intuitions about how to draw on this information — as well as on the reserves, as with the clergy, of their own specific traditions — in order to help those who seek them out.

Failing to use their own well-developed identity casts a vote of limited confidence in those very things that nonprofessionals are already good at. In the wake of a sudden death, for example, bereaved persons depend on the knowledge of the undertaker, the lawyer, the doctor, and the minister, leaning on them for what they know how to do in these painful intervals and looking to them for cues as well as support. Such experience within a particular field, along with the hard-earned good sense that usually accompanies it, are hardly to be disowned. These are extremely valuable, not to say indispensable and irreplaceable, strengths in nonprofessionals.

Psychological mindedness is the unself-conscious characteristic that draws others to pastors, professors, and even police officers for advice. Teachers do not get the reputation of being "very understanding" unless they possess this capacity to appreciate the emotional pillars of life and to enter the world of others, to walk, as the familiar Indian saying puts it, in their moccasins for a while. Being psychologically minded is not everybody's gift. Many bottom-line oriented business executives are strangers to introspection and are puzzled by noneconomic factors in human relations. They are unaware of their own impact on other people, inclined to make judgments and decisions without taking psychological factors into account, and are often surprised that a psychologically minded person can quickly identify problems whose nature, because it is psychological, has baffled them.

Everybody, however, has the capacity to grasp the critical significance of emotions and to read and to follow them as reliable signposts along the path to the underlying, or real, causes of the behavior and events that are otherwise difficult to fathom. If we possess at least some feeling for the human factor in life, we can focus and sharpen our capacity for *empathy,* the ability to understand what another is feeling without necessarily feeling the emotion ourselves. It differs from *sympathy,* which means "to feel *with*" another person, and connotes our experiencing their sadness, joy, or dejection within ourselves. Sympathy is no small gift, but it depletes and distracts helpers by leaving them open to the emotional tempests and tides that it welcomes.

Empathy enables counselors to help by providing them with a breakwater perspective that permits them to measure the currents sweeping through other persons without being swamped by them. One of the first and most important lessons lifeguards must master is how to keep drowning persons from pulling them under in their panic so that the guards can use their strength to help the others survive rather than exhaust it in an entanglement with them. That is the basic lesson for nonprofessional counselors as well. Their capacity for empathy, rather than their expressions of sympathy, preserves their own strength to keep others afloat and get them safely to shore. You need not experience drowning to be a good lifeguard.

It follows that what designated counselors do should match and flow from their already well-defined occupational roles. Ministers, for example, do not abandon their calling and its spiritual insights and denominational traditions to act as neutral and secular therapists without laying waste to the fundamental identity that, like swimming for the lifeguard, is the greatest strength they bring to their counseling.

Being Who You Are / Being Supportive

For most nonprofessional counselors, an easy security in their function should be coupled with a disciplined commitment to be *supportive* rather than *uncovering* in their psychological interventions. Helpers who stay within the boundaries of sensible supportive assistance not only avoid entangling and unforeseen complications but they guarantee that they will be doing both the *most* and the *best* for the persons with whom they work.

What do we mean by being supportive rather than uncovering in responding to others? The core principle of healthy supportive assistance is that we focus ever and always on the *current conscious life situation* of the persons seeking help. As supportive counselors, we consciously choose not to dig beneath others' consciousness of what ails them. We deliberately and carefully avoid any psychological archeological expeditions to excavate levels beneath their everyday awareness of problems. We do not deny but neither do we disturb the active unconscious life of the others by, for example, offering interpretations that may pierce the membrane enclosing the unconscious. The overall strategy of support is implemented through tactics that confine the conversation to those events of which the person is immediately aware or which he or she can readily recall.

As nonprofessional counselors, we respond as the emergency technician does who aims to stop the bleeding without repairing the underlying defect. Our principal tactic is to focus on what the persons are aware of — that they wound easily at the slights of others —

rather than delve into the unconscious determinants that make them susceptible to being so easily hurt.

As in immediate medical treatment, supportive counseling is *limited* in goal, to the point, and ordinarily *brief,* that is, as a rule of thumb, not extending beyond a semester at school or a season of the year. Supportive therapy is *active,* as applying a tourniquet is. It is not passive as treatment aimed at uncovering unconscious determinants is when the therapist withholds responses in order to force the person to dig deeper within the self.

We implement this array of tactics by carefully centering the discussions on subject matter that the persons can, with relative ease, draw out of their immediate consciousness. Not only do we actively shepherd them along this fairly well-lighted path of awareness but we also carefully avoid doing anything, by chance or design, that would divert them from, or darken, it. We are not interested in Robert Frost's musings on the "road not taken." As supportive counselors, we want our conversation to be conducted in prose rather than in poetry.

We therefore consciously avoid techniques, such as *free association, dream analysis,* or remaining achingly *neutral,* that may rupture the defenses that the person has erected against dealing with the unconscious conflicts beneath his or her current difficulties. Helping is not a place for experimenting with approaches, often superficially presented in a variety of media, that may get both the designated helper and the person to be helped in over their heads psychologically. Here, as the legends once read at the corners of ancient maps, be dragons.

Supportive Tactics

Designated helpers may use any of several common techniques of support without violating the borders of the unconscious:

Ventilation is the simple expression, perhaps long put off, of what is bothering the other person. We allow him, give him permission, in a sense, to tell us, from his point of view, who or what is troubling him on the conscious level.

The *exploration of problems* not only allows the person to describe problems spontaneously but by gentle prompting, where called for, elicits details that are easily retrievable from memory.

Clarification, through careful responses, is designed to catch the feeling beneath what the other may be struggling to describe, and by which he is helped to recognize and acknowledge what he is trying to express. It resembles handing a jigsaw piece to a player across the table

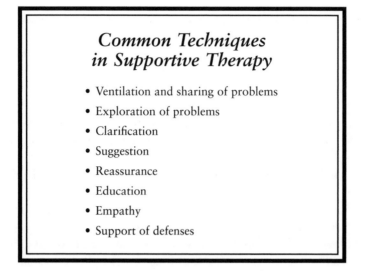

Common Techniques in Supportive Therapy

- Ventilation and sharing of problems
- Exploration of problems
- Clarification
- Suggestion
- Reassurance
- Education
- Empathy
- Support of defenses

who has been searching for it. Once she sees it, she immediately put it where it belongs, taking another step in illustrating what she sees as her problem.

Suggestion, not the kind used by fake mediums, magicians, or other manipulators of people's perceptions, but straightforward prompting, is often in the mode of a question, of a topic or reaction that is within the realm of consciousness but, for the moment, beyond the reach of the other. A suggestion cannot go beyond this boundary without running the risk of probing the unconscious. Rightly matched in content and tone to the person's rummaging for the right expression, suggestion can be very helpful in supportive counseling.

Reassurance is familiar from everyday life. We all feel better and more confident that we are on the right track when someone we respect — a teacher, a pastor, a judge — agrees with and endorses what we have done or the way we are proceeding in some endeavor. It is simple, direct, and very helpful in motivating people as they sort out their feelings.

By *education,* we consciously inform others about some subject or approach relevant to their situation. We teach effectively when, without imposing meaning that they are not ready to accept, we explain something they do not understand well, or misunderstand completely, such as the objectives of counseling, the usefulness of identifying emotions, or a truth they misunderstand about a law, for example, or a religious or an ethical issue. A helper may constructively teach others an approach to exploring their emotions.

Empathy has already been described. The *support of defenses* is a tactic so critical to the success of supportive counseling that it must be explored in some detail.

Identifying and Reinforcing Defenses

The supportive counselor understands and selectively reinforces the *psychological defenses* of the other in order to keep the focus on the present as well as on the strong points in the person's emotional resources.[1] Defenses are largely *unconscious* mechanisms, that is, they are put in place, as a foundation might be laid under the cover of darkness, out of the sight or control of the person using them. Their purpose is to *maintain self-esteem* by controlling the *anxiety* that flows from the *threat* perceived in events that contradict or challenge one's *self-image,* or accepted idea of oneself. The defense serves, imperfectly but effectively, to resolve the threatening conflict, thereby reducing the anxiety that, along with stress, are its twin offspring. Defenses, like self-sealing tires, allow the person to go forward without facing the full truth of the blowout or the implications of neglect of the tires that brought it about. We readily recognize *rationalization* as giving a good reason, although not the real reason, for what we do.

Defenses may be healthy, as with sublimation and anticipation or the use of irony and good humor. They can also be unhealthy, as in outright denial, distortion, or fantasy. These will be discussed later in specific situations. For now, designated counselors need only understand and carefully second those defenses that serve needy persons well in keeping their problems inside the chalk lines of their conscious lives.

Nonprofessional counselors can identify and strengthen the healthy defenses, or psychological resources, of those who want their help. These may take the form of revered ascetic practices, for example, such as "avoiding the occasion of sin." These can be practically and usefully applied in the lives of those troubled by continually falling into the same discouraging life traps over and over again. They assist such persons on the *conscious* level, seal the unconscious conflicts safely away, and, coupled with understanding, are often an enormous and successful source of support for them. Forcing individuals to confront and dismantle the defenses that are the very structures that are holding them together is an ever and always dangerous tactic to employ, for, as in dynamiting a building instead of allowing its builder to take it down floor by floor, it may wreak havoc and cause such persons to regress, to become worse instead of better. Untimely assaults on the defenses of others are a hallmark of counselors who have taken small sips, if they have drunk at all, from the deep springs that nourish commonsense helping.

These basic notions are the cornerstones of the work of designated counselors who may have little or no professional training. Maintaining one's own identity, staying out of the unconscious, and strengthening the person's best defenses: helpers will not err very much by keeping these in mind as they draw upon what is healthy and sensible in themselves in their work with others, the strengths that nonprofessional counselors already possess in such abundance.

– 2 –

EMOTIONAL INVOLVEMENT

S TRESS IS A REALITY — like love or electricity — unmistakable in
experience yet difficult to define. Stress, however, much like these
phenomena, touches everybody sooner or later, and for members of
certain occupations, it is a daily companion. A person whose chief responsibility, indeed, whose sense of calling, is to help others is the most
vulnerable to its strains because, unlike other professionals who do
not hear groans or imprecations from their balance sheets, test tubes,
or dockets, counselors work face to face if not *mano a mano* with
the greatest stress-producers we know — other people. And ordinarily
the helping person is alone in this situation, sometimes out of range
of supportive colleagues, reference books, or computer files just when
they would be most useful. Stress seems to be a dignified and acceptable burden for dedicated persons, something they discount as part of
the personal price of serving others; often it is shrugged off or even
denied altogether. After all, does not the goal of assisting others justify
emotional sacrifices?

No helping individual can escape the special stress that goes with
concentrating on others' problems. There are no analogs for the ster-
ilized gowns and instruments of the surgical theater available to the
counselor, the pastoral worker, or any other kind of therapist. They
must learn to manage the stress associated with their work in a constructive manner or it will deal with them in a very harsh way. Too
often, generous helpers fail to realize how many *Gs* of interpersonal
stress have been pulling at them until the relationship comes to an end.
This is particularly true with the most common problem that helping
persons must learn to understand and oversee successfully: *their own
emotional investment and involvement in the lives of those with whom
they work.*

Few people with even a little experience in responding to the needs of
others manage to escape the sting of emotional involvement. It causes
an invisible wound whose nature people may not easily talk about even
to themselves because it smarts too much with hurt and confusion. This

vulnerability is for counselors what black lung is for coal miners — a significant risk that cannot be separated from descending beneath the surface of life every day. While working with people in trouble, we come to like them, to feel deeply about their problems and their own efforts to do something about their difficulties. Caring about them, time, circumstances, or the people themselves ultimately pull loose some of the timbers of our hearts.

Sometimes, however, helpers discover that they have cared more than the one they are helping, and they are left with servings of churned-up feelings too hot for holding and too delicate for putting down. Small wonder that after we pull or are pulled away from an overheated and overinvolving relationship, we mutter something equivalent to "Never again!" It hurts too much, we announce to ourselves, to get so involved in such a personal way with other people.

As helpers nursing such emotional wounds, we may shift into a defensive mode and begin to handle stress in a manner that saves something of ourselves. Individuals may affect a cynical attitude, for example, and turn away from humankind with the familiar protestation that "people are no damned good." Or we may be more urbane and, following a tested and quite acceptable route, adopt an impersonal posture that creates a saving emotional distance between ourselves and those we help. "You cannot afford to get involved" is the cooling advice sometimes passed out to doctors, nurses, teachers, counselors, and men and women in church work, as routinely as aspirin is given for headaches. A professional stance is not wholly to be scorned, of course, and in recent years its place as a state of saving grace has been neglected by those who plunge into the emotional sea as confidently as General MacArthur did the Pacific on his way back to the Philippines in World War II. Indeed, an interval of restraint at the beginning of a relationship allows us to assess where we are and what we can do to assist others without losing ourselves in the process. Such a disciplined period can be warm and cordial and yet provide an emotionally neutral zone in which to gather necessary information, fill out forms, and carry out efficiently the information gathering that has increased with the advent of managed care and limitations on the hours of help that may be available. There is no intrinsic antagonism between being professional and personal at the same time. It can be a sensible first step in monitoring our emotional investment so that our warmth and concern will be present but that our account will never become blindly and destructively overdrawn.

Experience and research demonstrate that, no matter what school of training or personality theory we choose to follow, two facts of life must be acknowledged by all helpers: First, we must be in *relationship* to the persons we assist; and second, it helps if we like them but do not try to *possess* them just for ourselves. Techniques come and go but these two realities abide. We need not become overinvolved to guarantee the presence of these values.

Unmodulated and ill-observed emotional involvement is one of the chief sources of stress for helpers. The very thing that makes counseling or good advice work — that it is done in a personal, caring way — is also the reason that it may be hazardous to the emotional health of the helper. "If I could just figure out why I get so hung up on my clients," a typical young psychologist said, speaking for countless others, "I'd be a better therapist and a calmer person." Fair enough, but how do we accomplish this? How do we walk the tightrope that seems to be anchored in our hearts?

We begin with ourselves. We can deal with this "close-quarters stress," not by erecting defenses against an invasion of our emotional lives by those we are helping, but by reducing our own defensiveness — by standing down from a high alert — so that we can see and hear ourselves better in the midst of our helping activity. If effective interpersonal helping is always tied to the relationship with the other person — a student, a parishioner, a patient — then we must focus on ourselves as we are when we are with that person. Often we think that it works the other way around and that if we concentrate totally on the other, getting together as much information about him or her as possible, we have done our work well. Nobody will deny the importance of understanding the other; we must, however, also take ourselves and our own reactions into account at the same time. This is the demanding double focus that is essential for being a good helper as much to ourselves as to other people.

We must, therefore, know what is taking place inside ourselves at the same time that we are trying to grasp what is taking place inside others. After all, these feelings and emotions occur simultaneously, and they are often significantly interrelated. We cannot draw close to others without beginning to affect and be affected by them; this is the nature of human relationships. We cannot operate from a protective position. Counseling work takes place out in the open where we are defenseless. This is precisely why the potential stress of unrecognized and unmanaged emotional involvement is so great; it is dangerous out in the open unless we know who we are and why we react as we do.

Helping is rooted in a human equation in which there should be

no unknown term. The unknown term is all too often the person of
helpers who, because they are not sufficiently sensitive to themselves,
do not know what is happening to them as the course of the helping, no matter how short or long, progresses. Such persons easily get
lost, not because the one they help has such complicated problems,
but because they have not learned to take their own problems into
account.

It is clear that the somewhat cold but presumably prudent injunc-
tion not to get involved is simply not good enough in this situation.
If we remain uninvolved, nothing much will happen, and the potential stress of emotional engagement will be transformed into a different
kind of difficulty not unknown by reluctant or defensive counselors.
Such helpers experience the problems of others as burdens or down-
right impositions; they struggle through relationships like a downed
airman crossing a swamp with a parachute dragging behind him. There
is nothing sadder than helpers who steel themselves against their tasks,
who speak of "having to see all these mixed-up people," and who seem
more grimly dutiful than interested in their work. The stress associated
with self-imposed noninvolvement is not very dramatic, but it is steady
and relentless. It resembles being caught between two great grindstones
that crush us slowly into a fine, dry powder. Few things are worse than
working with people and not enjoying it.

It is wise, then, to face directly the challenge of being present to and
with other people and to know firsthand the dynamic consequences of
being close. This requires a balance between our sense of ourselves and
our sense of the other person; it begins, however, with that previously
mentioned willingness to listen to what is taking place inside ourselves.
Of course, we cannot do this if we are preoccupied with other things or
if we so fill the relationship with noise — the sound of our own voice,
perhaps — that we cannot hear the other at all. What is required?

What We Should Do?

As noted, we must first develop a sense of what it means to be in relationship *to* someone else. This is not the same as just waiting for
another person to stop talking so that we can talk. Nor does it mean
indulging in our own daydreams while the other tells us what we consider an all-too-familiar story. To be in relationship demands, at the
very least, that we give up our own thoughts and interests for a while
so that we may give our complete attention to the other person.

There is an invisible sacrifice involved in this, a readiness to empty

> ## *Do's and Don'ts of Counseling*
>
> Do:
>
> - Learn what it means to be in relationship with others
> - Recognize signs of a developing relationship
> - Recognize signs of transference and counter-transference
>
> Don't:
>
> - Panic
> - Misinterpret
> - Force our own or other's reactions

ourselves of our own concerns in order to make room for those of others. Being in relationship with another calls for a positive effort on our part to inhabit the same life-space as the person speaking with us. This is easy with someone we love; it may take a little practice with those we are just getting to know.

Second, we recognize that what stirs in that shared life-space — whatever feelings others express toward us and whatever we experience in feelings toward them — is never just accidental or incidental. What we begin to experience reciprocally constitutes the life signs of relationship; such feelings tell us *that* something is going on, and they also give us major clues as to *what* is going on. If we do not feel anything, then we are probably not close enough to make any difference to the other anyway.

Third, what occurs between ourselves and others — even when this is difficult to listen to — provides us with codes to understand two things: whether we are going to be of any help to the other, and whether we are going to grow ourselves. Unless we can sense the human outlines of the developing relationship we will never be able to understand it or to possess ourselves strongly enough not to be finally absorbed by it. This is true because helping others implicates us in something that is live, not prerecorded or simply intellectual, but in an honest-to-God *you-and-me* relationship. We must touch at some level or we will never make any difference to each other at all; we might just as well be on tape or have our lines written beforehand. The strength and vulnerability of what

16   *Emotional Involvement*

we mean to each other depends to a large extent on our continuing capacity for spontaneity.

These considerations lead us to the questions of *transference* and *countertransference*, notions that are very important yet not very complicated. They describe some of the feelings that take place in helping relationships.

Transference refers to those feelings the person we are helping seems to have toward us in this relationship. They are, however, feelings appropriate to previous, significant persons in their lives, such as parents or those who took their place. These feelings get transferred to the counselor or helper, and they may be either positive or negative in tone. Helpers must be aware that this can happen and not construe them as feelings the person is having toward them as individuals. It is at this point that self-monitoring allows us to balance sensitive closeness and sensible objectivity. When we naively get involved in responding as though we were the direct object of these feelings, complications and confusion tumble upon us.

Example: the priest-counselor working with the adolescent who is in conflict with his own father. The clergyman, already titled "Father," should not be surprised if feelings that are really meant for the boy's true parent get directed at him. These are ordinarily mixed and, if the priest cannot maintain some perspective on what is taking place, he will soon be confused and quite unsure of what is happening. He may, for instance, try to correct the boy's attitude and only reenact an attitude typical of the real father, thus stepping into the quicksand that pulls us down very fast in these situations.

Countertransference, on the other hand, refers to feelings (again potentially positive or negative) that we as helpers feel toward those we are counseling; they grow, however, not out of this relationship but from our own past history and needs. These reactions may include feelings of being strongly attracted or unattracted to the other; these feelings are ours and say something about us that we must understand before we proceed further. There is nothing wrong with reacting to other people in this way; a problem arises only when we neither attend to nor try to understand the reaction because it disturbs, surprises, or shames us in some way. This feeling is ours at the moment and, rather than turning away from it or denying it, we should gently listen to it and identify it as clearly as possible. Only then can we impose understanding that gives rise to the freer and unconflicted control we experience; otherwise, the feelings will remain alive, dominating and controlling our responses even when we are not aware of it.

Example: the man who finds himself strongly attracted to a young woman who comes for help. This is not uncommon. Defensive about himself, he does not admit these reactions and expresses them only indirectly. He may defensively treat the woman harshly, antagonizing her frequently, not because of anything she may have said or done but in response to his own less-than-conscious feelings of attraction to her. He has established distance in a destructive manner in order to handle his own countertransference feelings. Although he does not acknowledge them, they dominate the relationship anyway.

What Should We Not Do?

We should not panic; we are not really in danger if we remain calm. The more self-possessed we are, the better we will hear, and be able to distinguish, the signals coming from the other person's feelings as well as from our own. The key to being close to others without being destroyed depends on getting these messages straight right from the beginning. This requires self-acceptance, patience, and a willingness to suspend action until we have a fairly good idea of the sources and nature of the emotions involved.

We should not misinterpret; that, we might observe, is the easiest thing to do in such a situation. This only makes the experience more dreadful; it may even be a symptom of our need to master a situation prematurely. We have to let these things come to term; let the fog and the sound dissipate and the outlines of meaning will emerge.

We should not try artificially or dutifully (by force, as it were) to change either our own reactions or those of the other person. This will garble meanings immediately and destroy some of the important foundations of our helping work. Instead of covering our emotional tracks, we should read and learn from them. We may not always react the way we would like or in the manner we would consider ideal, but the way we react defines us, and we look away from it at our own peril. We may not be perfect, but we are what we are and we cannot grow unless we can get our complex imperfection into reasonable focus. The beginning of a helping relationship is precisely one of those moments of mutual self-revelation through which we can lay hold of our identity more firmly. This is essential in maintaining ourselves in the kind of balance necessary for avoiding the ravages of unobserved overinvolvement; only when we do not face and label our reactions properly do we have to worry about such overinvolvement. We get lost, not only when we do not know the way but, more often, when we do not know ourselves.

A Checklist for Counselors

✓ What is behind my more-than-average interest in this person?

✓ What am I trying to get out of this relationship that I would not like to admit to myself?

✓ Am I always ready to argue with this person ... or always ready to agree?

✓ Am I beginning to feel more sympathy for this person?

✓ Do I think about him or her between sessions? Do I daydream about this person? If so, why?

✓ Do I feel bored when I am with him or her? Who makes it so, I or the other?

✓ Do I overreact to statements the other person makes?

✓ Is there a reason that either of us is always late?

✓ Is there a reason that either of us wants more time together than we agreed upon?

✓ Why do I say this is the best (or the worst) person I ever worked with?

✓ Do I find myself wanting to end this relationship or to hold on to it even though it should come to an end?

As helpers, we constitute our own most important counseling instrument. What we know and possess of ourselves makes a crucial difference in whether we help others effectively or not. It also makes the difference in whether we can actually be close to these people without losing ourselves in the process. To remain separate as we draw close is fundamental in avoiding the kind of identification with the other that may finally snag and bring us close to emotional ruin. Yet being separate does not mean being cool or distant; it depends on whether we recognize and respect our own individuality as well as that of the person we are helping. It involves a knowledge of the kinds of reactions — transference and countertransference — that may arise and the sensitive discipline of the self that is required to sort these out appropriately. It demands that we trace down the sources of these feelings without experiencing guilt over having the feelings in the first place. Respecting ourselves begins with respecting our feelings and being able to distinguish between them.

Being a separate individual who can move unafraid into an intimate relationship with persons who want our help provides the human energy in our being of assistance to them. When we know who we are and can tolerate and deal with ourselves without impatience or excessive fantasy, we can also see other persons as separate individuals. We can learn to respect and care for them without fearing that every spontaneous concern will draw us closer to the pit of agonized emotional overinvolvement. But this is where we begin: in learning to be separate and in allowing others to be separate from us.

As we pay more attention to the silent stress generated by working closely with people, we may build up a preliminary checklist that will enable us to keep our relationships in healthy perspective. We need to be able to recognize the signals that inform us about our emotional steps and missteps and add items and insights as we proceed. We should move ahead with less belief in old saws like "Don't get involved" and more belief in ourselves and our ability to be close and helpful without being overwhelmed at the same time.

– 3 –

HARD-BOUGHT WISDOM

T HERE ARE THINGS we learn only after we have had some actual experience in counseling other persons. In fact, we are not ready to learn them until we have made some mistakes and, while reassembling our self-confidence, we begin to wonder what has happened to us. Helpers who reflect on the emotional scars they have collected begin to understand things about themselves and their approach to others that they could never learn if they performed like an errorless or unconscious machine. Counselors have no monopoly on learning from experience, of course, but it is one of their most important methods for improving themselves and dealing constructively with the stress that is intensified in relationships where things do not seem to be going just right.

The following notions have been learned the hard way; they summarize truths you can read in textbooks but that you get to know only in life itself. While they are framed in terms of laws, they are not intended to be commandments nor are they intended to be a shorthand version of how to be a counselor. They provide a useful framework for our continuing efforts to develop ourselves as persons wise in the ways of helping other persons.

Listen to the Person

People, in distinctive and unmistakable ways, are always trying to make better counselors out of us. Indeed, the word "patient," borrowed from a larger world of helping, is rich in connotations to which we should attend. Patients are often tolerant of helpers and their sometimes uncertain efforts to grasp what they are trying to tell them. The fact is that, whether we can hear them or not, the persons who come to us for assistance work very hard telling us — concretely or symbolically — what it is that is bothering them. They cannot do this with complete clarity nor can they explain it, yet in most instances, patients do not hide the truth about themselves from us.

It is a source of wonder that human beings can be so determinedly honest about their lives even when they catch us on a bad day and we cannot seem to grasp their messages fully. They continue on, giving us as many hints as possible in an effort to help us understand them. In ordinary circumstances, the person has not come to outwit or to humiliate us — and even when people can do nothing but this, raising the colors under which they sail, they are transmitting clear signals about themselves. Most persons, even in quite brief encounters, want to tell us where or how life is hurting them at the moment. Many of our problems as helpers arise simply because we cannot or do not listen to what they so doggedly try to get across to us.

Whether we call them clients, pupils, or parishioners, those persons seated opposite us are really trying to be helpful to us. They correct us, for example, telling us, perhaps with a fresh example, that we have missed what they are saying. This is done in a variety of ways but none of them is obscure. The person may interrupt quite directly and say something like, "No, that's not what I mean at all," or, making a smaller correction for us, "That's close to what I mean, but it isn't quite it." These phrases are familiar to anybody who has ever listened seriously to others.

Sometimes they let us know when we are wrong in our understanding of them by not saying anything at all. This is not necessarily a conscious or deliberate move on their part as much as it is the normal feedback from people who feel that their message has not been received. They stop dead in their tracks because, in the face of misinterpretation of their meaning, they have no place to go with their narrative. They cannot move forward because we have erected a barrier or cut the ground from beneath them. Generally, they move back, regroup their forces, and try again to tell us what we have just missed or misunderstood.

What are some signs that they are doing this? They may switch examples, moving to a different illustration in order to try to clarify their previous point. If we listen carefully to these transitions we begin to realize just how helpful these persons are to us, how, in a very real sense, they are trying to make good counselors out of us. Let us examine the case of Mr. R. for a moment.

Mr. R., a businessman in his forties, tells us that there is something wrong with him, something he would like to correct:

MR. R.: *Well, I don't know what to make of it exactly and I'm not very pleased with it but . . . well, it's like in the morning. I get up and want to have a good day, I want to do my best. Then I get down to breakfast and, before I know what's happening, I'm having a quarrel with my wife.*

COUNSELOR: I guess you're upset because you've been having trouble with your wife.

MR. R.: (Pause) *No, it's not that. That's not why I'm upset. (Pause) It's more that I can't seem to avoid these squabbles; it's got something to do with me. It's the same way with the car pool I ride in. I want to be pleasant but, well, we don't go a mile before I react to something one of the other guys says....*

It is clear that Mr. R. is attempting to communicate his puzzlement and discomfort about his argumentative reactions. He doesn't know why these are occurring, and he doesn't know what to do about them. He says this fairly clearly, but the counselor, alerted by the example which Mr. R. uses to try to explain himself, responds in terms of this specific relationship. Mr. R. corrects him immediately in a way that makes it clear that his wife is not the focus of the difficulties. What more, we might ask, could a counselor want? Mr. R. apparently understands this, so he shifts to another illustration, compressing the same difficulty into a new setting. All the counselor needs to do is listen carefully to get all the information needed to recalibrate a response. The one being helped, in a very real sense, is trying to make a better helper out of the counselor.

How is it that, despite the clear testimony of the other person, the counselor can miss the point so easily? This can happen to veteran as well as to novice helpers and, because it piles up a sense of dissatisfaction with one's performance, it not only causes stress but it is discouraging as well. Helpers may not hear well because they are listening to something else, something like their own expectations of what the other person's problem must be. This happens easily, for example, when we feel that we have heard this kind of story before or when something within us — akin to football game announcers gazing down at an injured player — self-confidently diagnoses the situation on fragmentary and unconnected evidence.

When, as helpers, we find that we are frequently being corrected by the person or that we are running into roadblocks of frustrating silence, it is a good idea not to berate ourselves but to shift our attitude so that we can discover why we cannot hear what is being stated so lucidly to us. Obviously, not all those we help will be as directly helpful in return as Mr. R., but if we listen more carefully, if we are less preoccupied with

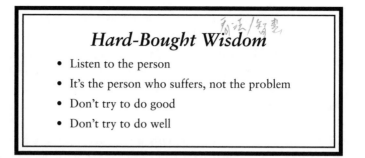

our own expectations, we can read the signals — even the symbolic ones — more assuredly and, at one and the same time, decrease our stress and become more helpful to others.

One of the chief indications that we are not hearing the other person may be found through an examination of the whole counseling session, whether it is ten minutes or an hour long. If the person is still trying to say at the conclusion of the period the very thing he was trying to say at its beginning, we must examine our hearing rather than the person's messages. If we can shake ourselves loose from the course we are set on pursuing, we free ourselves as if we had our hearing and vision restored so we can hear and see everything persons say or do, sometimes in gestures, to help us understand them.

Forget about Problems

Closely related to our difficulties in catching what other people are plainly and patiently communicating to us is the difficulty of over-focusing on *problems* rather than on the *persons* who experience them. Although we frequently refer to them this way, problems do not exist in some raw and unprocessed state.

For example, a counselor might muse inwardly, "I have *another* alcohol case this afternoon," or, searching for a psychological cookbook, might ask, "How do you *handle* alcoholism?" There are, of course, useful things to learn about alcoholism and other human difficulties, but it is also important to remember that the problems do not exist independently of the people who have them. There are only *persons with problems,* and our response must always be to them rather than to some disembodied state. Even in the application of behavioral modification techniques, persons remain the vital variable; their perceptions and reactions remain central and powerful factors in any course of treatment or approach to helping them.

Helpers who concentrate too much on the *problem* run the risk of missing the *person* who is troubled or of distorting the situation by emphasizing the problem excessively. That can bend the whole helping relationship out of shape. This occurs, for example, if we perceive the problem as separate or even separable from its possessor's reactions to it. In these circumstances we treat it as a package the person places on our desk for our wise examination and prescription. That is the kind of emphasis we give when we ask too many questions about the problem, or when we feel, for some reason or other, that it must be solved as swiftly as possible.

Actually, we do not have to solve problems; we only have to help other persons accept that responsibility for themselves. To isolate a problem so that we cannot see its organic relationship to the person experiencing it resembles doing surgery on an organ without understanding its function or relationship to the whole body and the whole person of its possessor. All we have to deal with are human beings and their reactions to the particular stressors of their lives; unless we can manage to see the situations they describe, we won't even get a good view of the phenomena that they call problems.

The problem — whether it is alcoholism, school failure, or infidelity — can be understood only in the context of the person who experiences it. If we get the individual into proper focus, we will automatically get the problem into the right perspective. The less counselors feel that it is their responsibility to solve the problems of others, the more freely they can communicate to others the strength and support they need in order to begin finding solutions for themselves.

It is a great relief for many counselors when they realize that they need not solve every problem or have the answer to every difficulty. This does not lessen the challenge of understanding people with problems, but it factors out of a counselor's life a considerable amount of unnecessary stress.

Don't Try to Do Good

The suggestion — to avoid trying to do good — grows naturally from our awareness that we need not be the world's greatest problem solvers. It also builds on the realization of how much harm has been done all through history by resolute do-gooders — that sturdy tribe whose heavy-handedness with human beings cannot be compensated for by the virtuous gleam in their eyes. Do-gooders are defined as those persons who act on others in response to their own needs. It is clear, therefore, that doing good is not to be avoided as much as setting out purposefully to inflict good on others at all costs.

In any helping situation we hope that the outcome of our efforts will be the good of other persons. This is most often accomplished as a by-product of our sincere interest and effective understanding of them. Trouble arises, however, when we directly — and sometimes uni-laterally — decide what must be done and how best to achieve our preplanned outcome.

Thus, for example, we have the college mathematics teacher who believes that the junior class member seeking counsel must avoid, at all costs, dropping out of college for a semester. The good end is decided by the teacher who is now personally involved in accomplishing this goal and so may even move outside the counseling session's boundaries to push this resolution. Such a teacher may talk to the student's other teachers, get one of them to arrange a special makeup exam, follow this up with inquiries at the dean's office about the student's chances, and begin coaching sessions in the math course. Massive energies are engaged, in other words, in trying to get the student to do something that has been preordained by the teacher's own judgment and coincidental emotional stake in the project.

This scenario can be rewritten with a dozen different settings and as many leading characters, but the basic dynamics are always similar. The helper suffers from what psychologists call a rescue fantasy — a deep need to rearrange people's lives and to provide them with happy endings designed by the counselor herself. Several questions immediately arise: Whose needs are being met in this situation, those of the helper or those of the person helped? What do we accomplish for others when we decide what they should or should not do and then exert massive pressure on them to conform? How much lasting good is achieved by this common but makeshift arrangement that depends so much on the almost muscular intervention of the helping person?

These are hard but good questions for every counselor to ask, if only to avoid the enormous stress and lopsided emotional consequences of such an arrangement. Not every helping person is inclined to do good in this rather blundering and hardly insightful way, but even old hands at the work may find themselves tempted at times to take over and work out the life problems of another. The reasons can be varied: a need to show a little power; an unconscious response to the attractiveness of the other; a need for self-enhancement. All of these can interfere with responding effectively to the person whose needs presumably come first, the one who comes for help in the first place. The impulse to do good —

and to get involved beyond the helping situation in doing it — is one that needs careful periodic examination by every person who works closely with others.

The central difficulty is that the predominance of the do-gooder's needs may make it more difficult for other persons to take serious responsibility for their own decisions. It is no favor to others to shield them from the consequences of their actions or to deny them the opportunity to fail. The overprotected child is the classic example of this; although such children are spared many of the hazards that others must suffer in growing up, they are necessarily made more vulnerable because of this situation. The capacity of such children to cope with unexpected difficulties or even to be able to stand on their own two feet may be impaired. This was illustrated by the kind of doing good in which the college math teacher became involved. Such persons may feel better that the counselee makes it through to the end of the year, but there is no guarantee that lasting good has been done.

The object of helping others through counseling or other similar work is to assist them in marshaling their own strengths so that they can confront and deal with their lives effectively. This requires understanding and other skills, but it does not need the overkill of doing good through imposing on others decisions and strategies to accomplish them. One element that every good relationship requires — whether in love or counseling — is the kind of self-restraint that acknowledges and respects the potential of others to begin to put order into the confusion of their life. We can give others our time, our understanding, and our honest selves, but what we do beyond that may be quite harmful if it proceeds from our need to do good.

It is an enormous gift to make ourselves present in a responsive and understanding way in the lives of others without trampling all over them. As psychologist Carl Rogers once noted, it takes a lot of discipline to do what we can for others and then, literally, let them *be*, that is, let them take responsibility for their own existence. They, indeed, all of us, must answer Hamlet's question — to be or not to be — or miss life altogether.

The real good that we accomplish flows from those relationships in which we have come to terms with our own needs to redesign the lives and plans of others. Self-conscious do-gooding may be one of the signs that we should inspect our own emotional lives more carefully and face honestly any need we may have that could interfere with helping others to take care of their own lives. The people we help will be freer and so will we.

Don't Try to Do Well

If doing good can interfere with helping other persons while increasing the counselor's own experience of stress, then the urge *to do well* is almost equally destructive. It is common enough, especially in bright people who are afflicted with obsessive-compulsive tendencies. They like to get things straight and carry them out according to the wishes of authority as promptly and effectively as possible. They are easy to recognize in class, for example, because they take their notes and themselves rather seriously. The questions these people ask are endless and all in the service of the need to do well, which is as American as apple pie.

These observations are not meant to degrade the practical desire to achieve; they are, however, intended to emphasize how much that desire can interfere with what is involved in helping other persons effectively. It is, therefore, something with which we must come to terms before we can become good counselors. What are the elements of this attitude toward life?

Persons who want to do well at all costs are handicapped because this motivation clouds their vision of life and contributes to their perception of human beings as opportunities for achievement rather than as individuals in themselves. Persons for whom doing well is a strong incentive find that it is very difficult to look at life without the feeling that they must produce and earn gold stars or else they will be found unworthy. The reward of approval by parents and teachers seems to be very important to these persons. Worth for them is not something intrinsic; it is always in danger and they must keep earning it. Mix this attitude with an obsessive style and it is easy to understand why, in helping others, these achievers have special difficulties.

Persons who want to do well find it difficult to be part of a relationship with someone who comes for help because they are excessively focused on their own performance and concerned beyond measure about the endorsement of invisible authorities to whom they feel that they must prove themselves. Sometimes counselors begin to compare themselves with some expert they know or whom they have heard on a tape or seen on video; if emulating that expert's technique becomes too important, it can be very hard to be spontaneous and unself-conscious with the person seeking help. The major obstacle remains their handicapped vision of other people. As long as they look on others as tasks or tests they will never see them clearly as persons.

Most of this is unconscious on the counselor's part; many have never examined their need to excel or to be approved, and they are terribly frustrated at meeting a challenge in which these familiar approaches do not work anymore. They learned this combination for success at some previous time and it is a serious and stressful blow to their adjustment when it no longer opens the way to honor and applause.

Successful helping is an unself-conscious phenomenon, and it shrivels when it is seen as a polished performance after which judges will raise cards with their score. It is hard to help when you are trying for a perfect "Ten." Good counseling demands less and more at the same time: less of the self-regarding attention to the way one counsels, and more of the simple humanity that is considered too ordinary to be impressive. The personality of counselors remains their chief asset, and the more they can liberate it from the grip of the twin needs of doing good and doing well, the more they will be able to respond to others just for their own sake. In the bargain, counselors will feel better about their work and, although they may not think about it so much, they will also be more effective at it.

– 4 –

WHAT OTHER PEOPLE
DO TO US

MANY, PERHAPS MOST, HELPERS occasionally find themselves unsure of where they are in a counseling relationship. They may as well be in an alien forest as in the midst of helping someone. Uncertain of where they are or when they will come upon a clearing, they hack their way forward as best they can. Their somewhat random search is frequently accompanied by rising confusion and frustration, two leading producers of stress. To manage this pressure, counselors, like veteran guides, must read the signs in the jungle closing in on them rather than wait for good luck or deliverance from outside sources. Like the guide who pauses to take his bearings beneath the unfamiliar circle of trees, studying the fall of the light and deciphering the messages in the vegetative growth, lost counselors may also pause to read the signals found as clearly in the helping relationship as they are in the filtered sun and leaves of the forest. Taking the measure of where we are is the right first step in completing our journey. This strategy makes the situation understandable, resets our compass to the way out, and relieves our stress all at the same time.

Failing to read accurately the signals in a stalled relationship, counselors may only increase their own frustration and bewilderment. They become discouraged and irritated at the other person, at themselves, or just at life in general. They may also suffer a loss of self-confidence because they seem to have lost control of the expedition they are supposed to be leading. How and where did I get off track here? Shaken self-confidence betrays counselors, undercutting their ability to help other persons. Such uncertain guides may begin to feel helpless and puzzled when the techniques with which they are familiar no longer seem to work. They cannot find the trail of a counseling experience when its direction is being set by conflicting emotional forces within the person they are trying to help. As with the animals and birds busy in the dark

around them, they sense their powerful and confusing presence but they
cannot identify them.

Counselors may also blunder badly under the stress of the moment,
reacting to their own bewilderment by pushing or pulling the person
in unhelpful directions. At times, helpers do not even realize that they
are contributing to the breakdown of the relationship. They resemble
the motorists who make dangerous maneuvers and then drive off quite
unaware of the pileup collisions they have set off in the line of cars
behind them.

It is equally possible that, while counselors may do the right thing in
the relationship, they will not understand why they did it or, for that
matter, why it proved to be effective. The trouble with these experiences
is that counselors, like amateur home repairmen who sometimes get
results even when they do not know what they are doing, may take
the wrong lessons away from the experience. This learning can be very
subtle, something we step into without being quite aware of what we
are doing, as ballplayers or golfers absorb extra and harmful motions
into their swing. It is difficult to know how or when it was learned,
and it is even more difficult to correct it. The helper can easily confuse
association with causation in these circumstances. I once observed a
harried man who, having failed to turn the ignition key far enough,
could not start his car. He tried twice, shook his head, removed the key
and got out of the car. He then climbed back in, slammed the door with
special vigor, inserted the key, turned it and, of course, promptly started
the car. "Son of a gun!" he said. "Slamming that door does it every
time." Learning the wrong responses causes us to misread ourselves
and the situation, ultimately adding to rather than relieving our sense
of being under stress.

Another Way of Listening

Clearing up our confusion in certain relationships cannot be left to
kindly fate or a favorable arrangement of the stars. It requires a willingness to work sensitively at understanding what is taking place and
why we are uncertain or troubled in some particular way. There is a
library full of literature about learning how to listen to other persons,
detailing even the symbolic language of the body. All of this is fine and
indispensable for the counselor's professional development. For the moment, however, we want to learn to listen in a new and indirect manner
to the person with whom we are working. This is one of the most help-

ful ways of locating where we are by sorting out the relationships that seem to confuse or dismay us.

When we are lost and cannot find our way, we should ask ourselves, "What is this other person doing to me?" We begin to listen, not to what the other says, but to what we can hear of that person in our own reactions. One may perceive a train in many ways, by riding on it, looking at it from the platform, or feeling its power reverberating in the window sill as it passes. Counselors use the latter method by attending to the resonations that others send through their own personalities. This is a very special but very real language; being able to understand it allows us to get the relationship into perspective and protects us from inaccurate learnings as well as from self-destructive reactions.

There are many ways to sense and read the world and other persons and, although we may have some idea about this, that is, we may be aware of the array of confused messages, we may lack the patience or the disciplined sensitivity to clear the interference from the signal so that it will register truly within us and we may hear it correctly. This is a valid way of learning, especially in those relationships in which even the other person does not fully know what meanings he or she is conveying. It resembles staying overnight in the rooms of others: their things surround and whisper of them to us — their photographs, clothes, the things they like to read, even their toothpaste. We can feel their presence in this array of inanimate objects; the absent persons are not absent at all but speak to us in a special casual language that is completely silent but very powerful in its significance and impact. We have been at close quarters with the intimate world of others and, even though all the communication is indirect, it is nonetheless clear and unmistakable.

We are at close quarters in counseling as well, and the same kind of messages — often unopened or untranslated by us — are delivered to us throughout the relationship. Something of who the other persons are comes across in style, in the sometimes quiet but symbolic way in which they present themselves to us. That communication is as important as the words that others speak. We listen for the splash as others drop souvenirs of themselves into the well of our own personalities. What we hear helps us to understand why we are uncertain or troubled, outlining the path we may now follow to right the relationship and start it moving again.

This style of listening for the messages of the other in our own reactions does not lead us to tortured or brooding introspection as much as it does to a feeling of understanding and mastering the forces and pressure we could previously feel but could not identify. Hearing these messages, we can put names on our experiences; this both relieves our stress and increases our understanding of the one with whom we are working. Some examples will make this clearer.

Reverberations of Others in Us

Later in this volume we will survey in greater detail the diagnostic criteria from *DSM-IV-TR* as well as the description of the traits associated with what are termed "personality disorders." For our purposes here, we cull and apply some of the material from this source that enables us to hear and understand the messages that other persons deliver to us in a variety of ways during counseling.

I Feel Helpless

Feeling helpless may begin as a rather vague but discomforting feeling to which we ordinarily respond by searching ourselves for possible explanations. What have we done wrong here? Have we been careless or are we lacking sufficient knowledge or training? These and similar questions are initially appropriate. When, however, we ask them and there is no returning echo — when they do not seem to fit the situation — we may shift and listen to the other person in the indirect manner that has been described. The question becomes: What is this person doing to me? Are my feelings the result of something that is being communicated to me by the general mood or attitude of the individual I am trying to help? Is he or she, in other words, giving me a firsthand experience of what others regularly feel in relationship to this person? Are we feeling the weather they bring to all relationships? Our answer resides in our own reactions and, until we can read it there, we may be puzzled about why things are not going better.

We may feel helpless because the other views us as magically omnipotent, as able to solve all of the other's problems as if by magic. We are viewed as a surrogate for a good parent, and we are therefore expected to take care of the other, to assume all responsibility for that person's helpless condition. This is the message sent to us by what is termed the "dependent personality." The dependent person exhibits traits of submissiveness, timidity, passivity, and clinginess. On the positive side, these same individuals manifest an unusual degree of agreeableness and friendliness. Michael Stone sketches a picture of one feature of persons who so present themselves:

Patients who are particularly clingy must be taught the terrible Catch-22 inherent in this tendency: that excessive demands on the attention of others almost invariably drive away — and evoke abandonment by — the very persons on which they have so tenaciously clung. . . . Inevitably the therapist *gets caught up in the clinginess* (demands for extra time, nighttime calls, symptom outbreaks before vacation). . . . *This may elicit counter transference annoyance, riddance wishes, and the like.*[1]

A transaction, at once vintage and common, of this sort may be observed in persons who fulfill their description as passive and dependent by acting out, despite verbal protestations to the contrary, a helpless role with everybody, including their doctor, clergyman, or counselor. We are particularly vulnerable to this psychological tactic if we are already under pressure from other commitments, or if we have not as yet learned to read and reflect on our own emotional reactions. This is not to say that other persons deliberately and consciously generate a sense of helplessness and then, by a process of psychological osmosis, finally pass it along to us.

Rather, as noted by Stone above, these persons reveal their whole style of relating with the world in the way they relate to us. Far from hiding it, they display it so that we can hardly miss it when we examine their arrows in flight and the bull's eye they strike in us as targets. They provide in their behavior with us a good sample of their style of clinging expectation and turning away from accepting much responsibility for themselves or their actions. The helplessness of such persons is infectious until and unless we can immunize ourselves successfully through becoming aware of just how this process can and does operate. They transfer their helplessness to us, making us feel helpless through invisibly arraying us, as if we were pack animals, with all their burdens, and letting us bear them up the trail for them. If we do not recognize them when they hand their baggage to us, we can identify them in the ways we respond to them.

I Feel Angry

Here again, after searching ourselves honestly but without finding cause for our rising hostility, we may discover that our anger is the end product of the personality structure of the individual we are trying to help. Helpers are notoriously open game for this kind of transfer because they generally involve themselves fairly openly and with a genuine desire to assist. The frustration and irritation that builds inside us can be our best information about the person whose difficulty is passive aggression or negativism.

In the current *DSM-IV-TR* this characteristic way of relating, once thought clearly and crisply defined, is thought more complex, and its description is found only in the appendix. This syndrome needs further research even though it is referred to, in familiar terms, as the passive aggressive or negativistic personality disorder:

> Its essential nature is a pervasive pattern of negativistic attitudes and passive resistance to demands for adequate performance in social and occupational situations that begin in early adulthood and that occurs in a variety of contexts.... These individuals habitually resent, oppose, and resist demands to function at a level expected by others ... expressed by procrastination, forgetfulness, stubbornness, and intentional inefficiency, especially in response to tasks assigned by authority figures.[2]

This personality disorder, like a knot in a tree, is part of the lifelong flow of growth. People who experience this problem may not understand why they have difficulties in their relationships or at work. The problem is best read in the reactions of others and, of course, in our own reactions because what we experience from such persons is exactly what everybody else experiences. Their style communicates hostility in an indirect and seemingly nonassaultive manner. Such persons hurt others, not by doing things but by failing to do them; their psychological satisfactions from behaving this way are delivered at personality levels of which they are not aware.

For example, the person who fails to show up at an important meeting commits an aggressive action toward everybody who does; the individual who agrees to support a certain motion and then remains neutral when the votes are taken is a familiar disturber of the peace. This condition is no longer considered the common cold or most frequent of the personality disorders, a category that we will explore in detail later. Nor, as mentioned previously, is it recognized as a diagnosable personality in the *DSM-IV-TR,* but it is considered an entity that needs more study. Its elimination from the tables of the *DSM-IV-TR* does not mean that this condition no longer exists. Its apparent frequency is attributed rather to a more sophisticated understanding of personality disorders and to the fact that passive aggression is present in individuals experiencing a wide range of other personality disorders, including those who suffer from borderline, histrionic, paranoid, dependent, antisocial, and avoidant disorders.[3] Helpers who identify this negativistic behavior in those seeking their assistance should be alerted not to take this part for the whole but to consider it as a feature of a more general condition, such as depression or some other disorder. This reading of a potentially complex syndrome suggests that the non-professional may wisely seek consultation with a specialist or a referral for a second opinion. In other words, what we may be experiencing is not the larger anchoring problem but rather the defense that the persons are using against recognizing and dealing with it.

Individuals who exhibit such negativistic behavior are often referred for counseling because of the problems they experience in their work or their marriage. Their boss or their spouse sends them. We can learn a great deal from the extremely subtle way in which such persons reveal the basic difficulty. As observed, it shows up in what they cause us to feel — through signs that are sometimes almost too small to measure — as in being just a few minutes late or canceling an appointment at the last minute. These persons are masters of timing, sensing how to be uncooperative at just those moments when it will do the most harm. We cannot help being affected by this style of relationship. Indeed, one of the chief hazards of helping others is the often confusing and upsetting effects of so often encountering such behavior.

Unless helpers can listen and understand that the anger that flames up in them is kindled by the invisible negativism of the one they are trying to help, they may be confounded by it or they may even express their own hostility in ways that are harmful to them and to the relationship. The treatment of those suffering from this complex feature of personality is difficult and will be explored later on. For the moment, our concern lies in turning our attention to the profile gradually etched out on the screen of our own emotions by these persons. Once we perceive this correctly we can identify the source of and deal with our own mounting anger and see the entire relationship in a much clearer perspective.

I Feel Frightened

Although feeling frightened may not occur as often as anger, it is just as true an indicator of what is really going on in the helping relationship. When we cannot find the source of our uneasiness in our own experience, it is helpful to pause and listen again to the dynamics of the other person as they resonate inside ourselves. Paranoid patients, who are afraid themselves, can transplant their own fear into us, making us restive and uneasy and crippling our capacity to be helpful. Such persons do not cast a spell on us, but their influence is transmitted

along wavelengths that defy conscious or rational analysis. Such paranoid persons may be very difficult to detect except by paying attention
to what they manage to do to us in the context of our relationship
with them.

One clever paranoid person can disrupt a whole school or a whole
community, her destructive achievements easily read in the reactions
of those all around her. Such persons are frequently intelligent and
charming, and they seem to be deeply concerned about the problem
they transmit from levels deep within themselves. The fear they generate in us may lead us to do things we would not otherwise consider;
they get us to act inconsistently and, of course, then they have us just
where they want us. These individuals often get us to doubt our own
good judgment. They are extremely difficult to deal with and, in fact,
may require referral for other professional help. This cannot be accomplished, however, if we do not recognize what is happening to us, if we
do not read their fearful messages in our own emotional responses.

I Feel Depressed

Feeling depressed is a reaction in ourselves we should read unhurriedly
and carefully. When we have ruled out causes from extrinsic sources
we should gently inspect the helping relationship in which we are now
working. Often, when we feel depressed in the relationship, it is because
the person we are helping is depressed.

Counselors may feel depressed as a reaction to the subtle put-downs
and frustrations those being helped build into the relationship in order
to maintain their defense of seeming mastery or superiority. These function, like the engines deep in a great ship, at a level that is at first
difficult to identify, especially by counselors who have not had much
experience or opportunity for training. Others may goad them, but the
energy of this transaction is discharged at remote strata of consciousness. Helpers may not know what is happening to them, except that
they feel quite discouraged and depressed. This depression is actually
their way of managing the anger that is being generated inside them
at an unconscious level. Counselors can feel very down but, precisely
because the basic emotional transaction between them and the other
person is outside immediate awareness, it is vexing that they cannot
identify the source.

In a role-playing episode in a graduate class, for example, the person playing the one seeking help, who admitted that he had some real
things he wanted to discuss, projected all his unresolved and complex
problems onto the person who was taking the role of the counselor.

Because the latter was just learning something about the process of helping others, the subtle but powerful attack hit him very hard. He was depressed and very dissatisfied with himself for several days. It was not until he played back the tape of that session and was able to reflect on what was happening to him that he recognized his own deep reactive anger at the situation — the very substance he was experiencing as depression. He quickly dealt with the situation more constructively.

Many of our other reactions are also powerful clues to the difficulty at the heart of the relationship with which we are working. We can, for example, feel bored because the other person is boring us just as he bores everybody else in his life-space. The list of possibilities is almost endless but the important principle remains the same: when we feel lost or perplexed and can find no reason in our own attitudes, we may explore how the other may be at the bottom of our own reaction.

The Benefits of Listening

High on the list of the benefits of listening is the increased sense of self-confidence that flows from getting a more fully developed picture of what is taking place in the counseling relationship. Helpers have a surer possession of themselves when the reactions they experience no longer constitute a mystery but rather a significant clue to what the other person is, however indirectly, communicating. There is an immediate reduction in the pressure that can mount on counselors who are unsure of themselves or who are thrown off their ordinary stride by persons who communicate such subtle and disturbing messages.

It is very reassuring for counselors to understand that their feelings are not all their own fault — indeed, that fault is a wholly inappropriate category — and that their confusion is not just a product of their own shortcomings in these situations. While it takes practiced sensitivity — and perhaps a helpful consultation with a knowledgeable professional — helpers who learn to listen to the other through their own reactions are bound to feel more competent and to perform more effectively.

The capacity to pick up the clues that are scattered inside ourselves also increases our ability to respond more purposefully and helpfully to the other person. As long as we are trapped in our own confusion or depression we remain crippled in our efforts to be of service, no matter how well-intentioned we may be. Breaking through to the truth of our own reactions is a very freeing experience, and we can then immediately use our insights and skills in a far more integrated and

successful manner. In other words, we can begin to deal with the issues
that are really at stake and, even if we come to realize that we cannot
take away all the other person's problems or that somebody else may be
able to assist them more than we can, we will have made real progress.
All too often when these situations arise, counselors slog along, feeling
the burden grow heavier all the time, but never really getting anywhere,
and they sometimes become, in effect, just another part of the disturbed
person's world, an aspect of symptomatic self-expression rather than
any real help to the other. These relationships sometimes stagger on for
months, much to the discouragement of counselors and not much to
the improvement of those seeking help from them.

Perhaps the most important learning associated with this way of
listening to others is the insight it provides into the meaning of human
relationships. If we can sense the meaning of another in the mix of
our own reactions, we can also grasp more clearly what goes on in life
between persons all the time. We are forever registering our messages
on each other in many ways and at various levels of consciousness.
Helpers begin to understand that the core of their work consists, not in
doing something *to* or *for* another but in experiencing something *with*
the other. Counselors thereby deepen their understanding not only of
counseling but of life itself.

When we are in the midst of a relationship, receiving and sending
communications at close range with another person, we are no longer
in the abstract, diagnostic realm. We are part of what is going on; what
we do and what we experience as done to us are not just random or
accidental occurrences. These reactions are profoundly significant in
the living give-and-take context of the helping relationship. This is not
just talking about the other person's problem or analyzing it imperson-
ally from afar. Counselors who work closely with others get a ringside
seat, an inside experiential view of the way others place themselves in
relationship to the rest of the world.

What these persons do to us is just a sample of what they do all the
time to the people in their everyday environment. They not only tell us
about themselves or their problems. They give us free samples; they let
us experience these things firsthand. When counselors become sensitive
to this reality, they can read the signs in themselves far more easily and
profitably. Suddenly their bewilderment, anger, or discouragement take
on a new and positive significance.

At this stage counselors begin to be what in the professional literature is termed "participant-observers" in their helping others. Through
observing what they are participating in, they can sort out their own

countertransference feelings from the transference feelings of those who come for help. The ability to refine our skill at this frees us to understand others better as they come to understand themselves more completely. Helpers with this skill can be of much greater assistance because they understand that the static inside themselves is more than meaningless interference with communication. It is *the* communication that, when grasped properly, breaks the deadlocks that can interfere with effective counseling.

– 5 –

WHAT WE DO IN RELATIONSHIP
WITH OTHERS

I F THOSE WE HELP often send messages that even they do not fully comprehend, so too we helpers communicate a variety of instructions and judgments to them in return. This other side of the coin finds us quite actively engaged in doing things *to* the person seeking help, often enough without any clear idea of what we are doing. We may assume a neutral or seemingly distant pose in order, as we say, "not to take sides" or "to avoid emotional involvement," but such an antiseptic presentation of the self in a therapeutic role is both unlikely and unrealistic. We need not be consciously aware of any feelings toward the person we are helping in order to have these feelings and, in subtle ways, to get them across to the other. We are never devoid of reactions — the sterile knife of the surgeon is a misleading analog for the helping person — and we cannot help but transmit some of these reactions to the other individual. Of such human exchanges is counseling made. If effective, it is not as an exchange of thoughts purged of all feeling but as a deeply rooted mixture of human reactions that tells us that people are in contact with each other.

The problem of emotional involvement, as previously observed, is not solved by placing an embargo on our feelings but by becoming more aware of them so that we can better understand what is happening to us — and between us and the other person — during the time of counseling. Unless we can hear all the messages, including those we send ourselves, we may find our effectiveness limited and the stress of such work needlessly increased. Even in those presumably less personally involving helping efforts that come under the heading of "behavior modification," the qualities of the relationship between the helper and the one helped — and their reciprocal messages — are crucial to the outcome. An examination of the complete file of our own attitudes helps us to appreciate how central these are to effective helping.

The Styles of Helping Relationships

Relationship is an idea many presume to understand fully even when they grasp only portions of it. Many persons do understand this notion quite well even though they never think about it at all. The capacity to be in relationship to others unself-consciously is, in fact, a sign of good psychological health. People become friends or fall in love without necessarily describing their experience in psychological terms; they don't *theorize* about it, they *do* it. Being in relationship for these persons is demonstrated in their practical human response rather than in an abstract philosophical statement.

The Analyzer

Certain counselors are analyzers by nature and may be accustomed to, as well as adept at, the intellectual description and classification of personal problems. They may, without quite thinking about it, live with an abstract view of helping relationships rather than with an inside experience of them. Because they can talk about them clearly, they may not notice how removed from them they can become. It is not easy to be in intense relationships with many people at the same time, the very challenge that pastors, counselors, and educators must meet every day.

The retreat into a more stylized mode of dealing with others can be slow — hardly noticeable at first but gradually hardening into a settled trend that leaves some busy counselors on the outside of many of their relationships. At times, this subtle distancing via abstraction signals an unconscious effort to reduce the stress that is associated with many hours of close interpersonal counseling. It is also an occupational hazard for the individual who is intelligent and whose education may have emphasized logical thinking and rational analysis over a grasp of the significance of feelings.

When helpers retreat from relationships through intellectualizing them, they lose something that may be difficult to recover — the sense of freshness and presence that is the hallmark of living human relationships. Being in relationship is more like being in love than it is like solving a murder mystery or a complicated chess problem. It may take some reflection to discover why or how we have forgotten the way this works, but it is vitally important that we do so. Perhaps the best metaphor here is marriage, the essence of which consists in man and woman remaining in lively relationship to each other. When couples somehow slip out of this relationship, they can no longer see or hear each other very well; the marriage relationship becomes a source of stress rather than of refreshment. So, too, with helpers who, for whatever reason, let something die between themselves and those with whom they work. Helping relationships become burdensome when they become extrinsic to our own personalities. Then we have to drag them and ourselves along and, although we may complain a lot, we may never suspect what happened to us or that we had a role in it.

The Neutralizer

Human relationships are interactions in which there is no neutral corner. Counselors learn to recognize their own emotional reactions — as, for example, when they are deeply moved by the wife's story in marriage counseling and are thereby quickly but subtly enlisted on her side even before the husband speaks — and to take these into account so that prejudice and partisanship do not rule the day. Unless helpers can hear their inner voices, they will not understand why things happen as they do nor why the helping situation can become such a confusing chore.

Helpers must see the whole relationship, not just one term of it. Counselors respond more freely and effectively when they include themselves in the picture and can understand, accept, and deal sensibly with everything that is going on in their personal exchanges with others. It is something like a parent's reaction to a child; this is simply not a one-way street and, until we grasp the transactional essence of the relationship, we remain outside it. We tend sometimes to overemphasize the parent's effect on the infant, thinking of the latter as almost totally plastic and impressionable. Wise observers, however, know that the very young child also has an effect on parents that may have a powerful long-range influence on the mother's and father's ongoing responses to them. The laughing child gets the loving response.

It is never too early to assess what is going on inside us in a relationship — and it is never too early in a helping relationship for some characteristic of the person seeking help to shape strongly the nature and degree of our continuing responses. The immediately attractive or unattractive person may, in other words, set up responses in us that determine early the course of the subsequent counseling. There is nothing wrong with spontaneous reactions to people; they are instructive in themselves. Problems arise only when, unaware of our own responses to these inner promptings, we end up maneuvering the counseling to accommodate ourselves more than to assist others. Seeing all the aspects of the relationship enables us to take everything about ourselves and the other into account so that such invisible factors do not become the fixed and guiding star for the counseling journey.

Wise counselors may learn from the relational nature of healthy human sexuality. Although many factors in popular culture emphasize a self-centered attitude toward sexual gratification, in which "having sex" is a consumer's activity in which one does something *for oneself* and *to* someone else, this misses its human significance and leaves the person in melancholy isolation. Another viewpoint perceives "having sex" as a service, as doing something *for* another person. True maturity of relationship comes about, however, when men and women understand that sexuality is something they experience *with* each other.

The Doers

These are fair if approximate categories that allow us to examine how we really relate to those whom we help. It is not unusual for counselors to consider themselves in a class with surgeons or other professionals who, in the main, actively *do* something *to* others in carrying out their services. As we become more sensitive to the psychological factors closely associated with surgery, this is not the best attitude for its practitioners to assume either. It is certainly not the relationship style of choice for those who want to be effective helpers.

This approach makes the counselor the center of gravity, thereby destroying the reciprocal nature of the relationship. Endowed with great power, helpers may use this position of doing something *to* others to make all the important decisions about the goals and content of the counseling process. This is a dangerous and excessive load of responsibility to assume, and it not only makes the relationship hopelessly one-sided but adds considerably to the emotional burden experienced by the counselor.

Why do some counselors unconsciously assume this position in their work with others? Everybody's life history is expressed in the way they relate to others, a style that has developed gradually over the years. It is possible, for example, that helpers who, in effect, take charge of counseling the way a dentist takes charge of teeth thereby protect their own emotions. We can stay somewhat clear of others when our focus is on doing something *to* them; they do not need to get close to us, and our need to reveal ourselves is minimal. In other words, helpers who use this approach relate to others and defend themselves at the same time.

Such self-protection may ward off the kind of excessive emotional involvement they experienced in some previous relationship. The price for this is high because the helper's own personality — one of his or her chief assets — is thereby obscured. This diminishes their capacity to enjoy their work with other people, making it more onerous in the name of saving them from unwanted hurt. This reaction resembles the bizarre surgery that took place many years ago in Vietnam after a soldier came to the hospital with a live shell embedded in his back. The operating theater was sandbagged, a wall of shatterproof glass was erected, the surgeon donned heavy protective garb and used specially constructed elongated tools to perform the delicate surgery. Understandable in these circumstances, one might say, because the patient was literally a threat to the doctor and everyone else around. Unfortunately, some counselors don psychological armor and operate from excessive distance in their helping relationships out of fear that they may explode. The attitude of *doing* something *to* others is often accompanied by such defensive maneuvers.

Working for *Others*

Counseling as a service *for* others also deserves careful examination because its true motives may powerfully affect the counseling process. Individuals determined to do something *for* other people may actually be doing something through them *for themselves*. In other words, counselors with this approach are not in relationship with others as much as they are with themselves. They may counsel to meet their own needs or to fulfill some set of expectations they have set up for themselves.

Helpers who must do something *for* others may not feel worthy or productive — or lovable for that matter — unless they are constantly assisting others in this manner. The difficulty is that such helpers frequently respond to their own inner needs and do not perceive others as separate persons. Although the thought would horrify them, they are, in effect, using others to satisfy themselves. This style of counseling is wearing and its effectiveness is ultimately lessened because these helpers have not yet identified or learned to deal with their own feelings. Such counselors find themselves impounded by their own emotions and cannot easily understand much less actually enter into the free flow of relationship that is essential to good counseling.

Working with *Others*

As with friendship, love, or good sexual relationships, the essence of helping lies in experiencing something *with* another person. This is a different realm as well as a different range of experience from that in which the emphasis is on doing things to or for others. It is far freer and is, therefore, less stressful in the long run than any other approach. This is not to say that it is easy or without its problematic moments, as we understand about the best of love and friendship as well. However, helpers who begin to understand their work as sharing rather than performing both decrease the pressure they experience and increase self-confidence and a sense of more significant participation in life itself.

Counselors who can let go of themselves more freely in counseling find that the list of appointments on the desk calendar no longer looms like the labors of Hercules at the edge of the day. Helpers who experience things *with* others lessen the demands on themselves because they no longer need to know exactly what the next step will be or what lurks around the next bend in the counseling process. One of the greatest sources of a sense of decreased stress for counselors is the realization that they are not taking an exam and that they need not prove anything. They are liberated to employ the instrumentality of their own personalities, to let the truth of themselves show through more honestly and with a largely muted need to explain or defend themselves.

Such counselors enjoy their day's work because it is no longer an occasion for defensiveness or for self-justification. Aware of greater inner freedom, these helpers can go more deeply into the relationship itself. It becomes a deeper experience of life itself as the exchange with the person becomes one of reciprocal and creative discovery. These fancy words have a down-to-earth significance for counselors. The "Blue Collar Blues" may exist on assembly lines because of the boredom generated by doing the same thing over and over again, but this is not the problem for liberated counselors. These helpers possess the closest thing we will ever get to a boredom-proof job by the fact that they are constantly in relatively deep contact with the most interesting of all phenomena, the human person. Each relationship is different, and, as helpers see them that way, they also see others in all their wonder.

Counselors who see everybody the same need to examine the reasons for this unfortunate stereotyping. They miss what is truly refreshing and genuinely re-creative of their own energies. In such counseling, helpers can freely receive as well as give. Until they can free themselves enough to experience at least some of the spontaneous rewards of counseling-as-experience-with-others, they will bear a steady increase in the pressures that spring from doing things *to* or *for* others.

It is no secret that the strain that accumulates in the lives of some helpers comes from their conviction that they have the responsibility for the success of the counseling as well as for improvement in the behavior of their counselees and the increased maturity in their goal-setting and decision-making. Enormous energy is expended by some in trying to solve the problem that needy persons cause by coming to see them in the first place. These and other considerations — sometimes it is just the volume of people that a counselor must see — make it difficult to ask the simple question we all must answer honestly for ourselves: *What can I really accomplish with others?*

The stress in many helpers' lives is made worse by unrealistic answers to this question, or perhaps from their failure ever to ask it seriously of themselves. We cannot change people's parents or their experiences; neither can we cry or grieve for them, much as we sometimes might yearn to do so. We cannot even keep them from making mistakes or bad decisions. And we cannot provide guaranteed happy endings for them the way the movies used to do.

A more modest and realistic approach to the possibilities of accomplishing something with others that will truly help them not only keeps the responsibility for their lives with them, where it belongs, but it also frees counselors from being the superperson or savior to everyone who enters their lives. Such "rescue fantasies," as such romantic notions are described, help neither party to the counseling relationship.

The capacity to be there with another person without letting our own needs intrude or determine the course of the counseling; the willingness to experience with others their own patient and sometimes painful exploration of their lives; the improvement of our ability to move with them in their inner lives without trampling all over them: these are not small gifts and they are extremely important ones in counseling. In order to give them freely and generously we must get to know our own selves very well so that we avoid spoiling the best things we have to share with others. Sometimes when we think that we can or must do more for others, we end up frustrated because we have set goals for ourselves that are unrealistically high, and, failing to achieve these goals, we may abandon our efforts to offer others the far simpler but substantial wealth of our presence and understanding.

One of the most difficult lessons for most of us to learn is when to let go, that is, when to give other persons enough freedom and trust to move forward without us, even when they have previously made a miserable botch of their lives. We may think, as mythical stage mothers do, that we still know best and that we must keep such persons and their choices fairly well under our control. Giving up control, however, does not mean giving up interest or turning away; it does mean that we permit others to be the center of the stage in their own lives. Can we or should we really try to prevent or control that? Can we, in fact, ever successfully or for very long maintain a guiding control over the destiny of other persons? When we find out why we are at times reluctant to give people this operational freedom, we discover the secrets about our own needs that free us from their domination.

REVELATIONS ABOUT OURSELVES IN RELATIONSHIPS WITH OTHERS

W E HAVE BEEN EXPLORING the living nature of our relationships in counseling, underscoring the importance of seeing them as dynamic experiences rather than as rigid exercises in applied science. As we look at and listen to our relationships, we learn far more than we expect to, finding in them what we can never discover in textbooks — images, as filled with revelation as those of a master photographer, of ourselves in action with other people.

The more we perceive ourselves as living although imperfect persons — and the more we can accept ourselves that way — the more we can let go of falseness and self-consciousness, or the stylized elements of imitating others or striving to meet some abstract role-expectations of being good counselors. The latter situation deprives counselors of the freedom and spontaneity through which they best express their strengths. As we become freer of affectation as counselors, our work with others becomes less a burdensome chore and more personally re-creative for ourselves. We also become better helpers.

Some persons examine themselves rather harshly out of motives that are a mixture of fearfulness and a need never to be found wanting, a demand from within themselves always to get it right. It is not difficult to raise guilt feelings in people, as most preachers and fund-raisers know, and it is not hard to make us feel bad about the shortcomings that can be found in our counseling work. Progress, however, is not a function of feeling guilty or of unrealistic striving to be the supercounselor with magical powers always to do the right thing. Planting its seeds and then ever harvesting unnecessary guilt makes self-examination almost unbearable and explains why so many people shun it or postpone it and, therefore, never realize its values.

There is, however, another way to look at ourselves. It resembles the way professionals do it, whether doctors or athletes: accepting a particular discipline of self-review to improve their performance. Healthy

48

professionals consult supervisors or review the films with the coach, not to punish themselves for the imperfections these identify but to understand and eliminate them in the future.

If professionals become too self-conscious or uptight, it is difficult for them to assay their performances. They tend to defend rather than learn from them. A more relaxed approach allows them to observe themselves in action, to note the false moves or the extra steps they have unconsciously incorporated into their behavior, and to deal constructively with these discoveries. There are no exceptions to the need to explore the self in view of improving performance; this means bringing forth the best blend of natural ability and acquired skill. We help ourselves if we approach this with confidence and a willingness to accept our imperfect selves. Dodging such self-examination only sentences us to an increased experience of stress.

The need to keep refining ourselves, even as counselors, is expressed well in the old saying, "If you have always done it that way, it is probably wrong." The following questions are offered to stimulate the examination of our approaches to other persons to learn more about ourselves and to improve our ability to help them.

Do We Want Others to Like Us?

Of course we do. That is natural and can certainly express itself in our looking for a positive response from people who come for help. Although this may be hard to admit, few if any of us are truly indifferent to the way other people feel about us. This human need for approval becomes a problem only when it becomes the chief determinant of who and how we are in the helping relationship. Getting on good terms with the other may, in fact, be overemphasized in those books and guides that put excessive importance on what they call "creating rapport."

Ordinarily, this understanding of "rapport" means that the person and the counselor should, right from the start, work at becoming comfortable in each other's presence. On the face of it, this is not a bad idea; it turns into a problem when our efforts to create rapport are artificial. Then we do more harm than good. Good rapport arises, not out of studied efforts to get along well with others, but out of a simple and sincere effort to listen and hear accurately what they have to say.

Rapport automatically exists when we are concerned enough about others not to worry about whether they like us or not. Efforts to find out where they went to school, or if you know somebody in common, or whether they are interested in sports or art merely interfere with a

warm to people

process that is immediately initiated by placing ourselves, insofar as we can, directly and sincerely in relationship to others.

Do We Judge Others?

Received counseling wisdom suggests that our tendency to evaluate others is so much a part of ourselves that we hardly realize that it is present. It is understandable that we pass judgment on the world and people around us, but this finding for or against others may interfere with our effectiveness as counselors and increases rather than relieves the pressures we experience in our helping relationships.

In reflecting on our inclination to referee the behavior of others, we do not dispute the need for accurate diagnosis, nor do we condemn our own need to put rational order and meaning into life as we observe it. The penchant to pass judgment refers rather to our deeper and less conscious need to compare ourselves to others, to give a grade to our performance or to their behavior and, in general, to preoccupy ourselves with ratings that may keep us on the outside of relationships when we really belong on the inside.

To stand in judgment on others means to evaluate — to place a value on — persons or events based on our own special point of view. For most of us, this is a near automatic reflex after a life spent giving our opinions on classes, movies, candidates, and marketsful of merchandise: the first question seems inborn, "What did you think of that?" The question is not, "What was the director, lecturer, or office seeker trying to communicate?" Rather, it is the inquiry of critics, those who look out on life and reflexively judge it in terms of their own perhaps limited experience, education, and tradition. Such judgments, as we know, may also be affected by our prejudices and unconscious motivations. Automatically assuming the role of evaluating everything and everybody from our own necessarily limited viewpoint may dig a moat around us so that we live in the castle and always look from its towers on the world. Evaluating others too quickly creates a subtle distance that may interfere with our ever really getting into relationship with others seeking help. Pasting labels on jars without opening them and testing their contents is a risky undertaking.

If we are to be good helpers, we must suspend our own judgments for a while in order to get others into accurate focus. Judging others forecloses on their telling us about themselves and leaves us listening only to ourselves. The signals of excessive evaluation are found in our own remarks. It takes a great deal of self-assurance even to say things like, "It's too bad that you did that," or "It's good that you can tell me these things." How we can be sure, from our viewpoint and limited information, about the correct courses of action for others is a mystery. If we find that we are inclined to be moralistic or that we lead others by reinforcing certain of their statements, the jury within us convicts us of passing judgments too quickly on too little evidence.

Do We Ask Too Many Questions?

This exploration might be subtitled: "What to do when we don't know what else to do." Approaching others through asking them for information, through saying to them, in other words, "Tell me more about this or that," is very common, especially among counselors not seasoned by much experience. We know, however, that nothing frustrates us more than being interrupted by off-the-point questions that distract us and interfere with our effort to tell somebody else about what is bothering us.

Being peppered with such inquiries resembles being required to fill out a long medical inquiry at a desk in an emergency room when we have a sick child for whom we want immediate attention. Questionnaires and forms of inquiry have become staples in American culture, however, and some people think that nothing, including entrance to the afterlife, can be done validly unless documents in triplicate are filled out in advance. Something similar occurs whenever counselors, determined to get information they want, break the continuity of what others are trying hard to tell them. Misplaced or excessive questions may, in fact, suggest a style through which we keep control over our work with others.

Obviously, counseling cannot proceed without any questions. They are sometimes very important to clarify certain points the person makes or to check that we have really heard correctly what the other has said. Although sensible questioning obviously has a place, any approach that depends too much on soliciting information may be rooted in our own curiosity or in the simple fact that we do not know what else to do.

Learning how and when to ask questions is an important element in the art of counseling. Observations by MacKinnon and Michels in a medical context put this into perspective:

> The tendency of the novice is to interrupt the person in order
> to hammer him with questions. With more experience, he learns
> when a person has completed his answer to a question or if he

merely requires slight encouragement to continue his story. As his competence grows, it becomes possible to hear the content of what the patient is saying, and at the same time to consider how he feels and what he is telling about himself through inference or omission. For example, if the person spontaneously reports several experiences in the past in which he felt that he was mistreated by the medical profession, the interviewer could remark, "No wonder you're uneasy with doctors." The interview is most effectively organized around the clues provided by the person and not around the outline for psychiatric examination.[1]

Or, we might add, the counselor's own agenda.

Even a little experience teaches us that when people come to talk, they usually do not need to be questioned very much. All we need do is make it possible for them to tell us their story and to clarify their own perceptions of it as they do. When we cannot follow what they are trying to say, or when we still lack sufficient skill to infer it from their statements, we may find ourselves at sea, using questions as we would flotsam and jetsam to keep ourselves afloat. This does not help the other person very much, and it also disorients us and increases our experience of stress.

We sometimes ask questions because we are uncomfortable when the person is silent for a while. This common problem in counseling is a source of stress for many helpers. Silence can have many meanings; it can be the embarrassed fruit of noncommunication, but it can also be the sign that something meaningful is going on in the relationship. Good friends need not talk to each other all the time, and lovers share many silences that are signs of the depths of their relationship. When persons pause and seem to be thoughtful, they may be absorbing what they have been able to discover about themselves. They are, in short, working on themselves. Good counselors understand this and tolerate these fruitful interludes without anxiety. We need to learn to live with the significant silence that follows on genuine self-exploration. To break the purposeful reverie with unnecessary questions destroys the mood and meaning of counseling itself.

Do We Rush to Interpret?

A chapter on pressured interpretations might be entitled: "How to be wrong even when you are right." Some counselors, especially neophytes, feel that the art of helping others consists in weaving some interpretation of their behavior out of a smattering of Freudian principles and overconfidence in their own powers of analysis. Is it ironic or revealing that persons given to interpreting too much often give the same or a very similar interpretation all the time? Such counselors-savant may, for example, always tell people that they have not resolved the oedipal situation, or they constantly find the diagnosis that is currently getting a great deal of attention in the professional literature. This one-size-fits-all allows us to hear what is going on inside the counselor better than what is going on in the person being counseled.

What do we mean by "interpretation"? This may refer in counseling to a good understanding response to what the other is struggling to say, a reply that matches the other's tone, depth, and meaning. Interpretation has a more sophisticated meaning as it is employed in the *uncovering* therapy that we have contrasted with the *supportive* approach we recommend for nonprofessional helpers.

In uncovering therapy, helpers want the person to enter the domain of the unconscious. In supportive therapy, helpers want the person to remain on the conscious level. Classic interpretation that builds on unconscious dynamics is, therefore, not used by helpers who want to maintain the conscious frame of reference for those they help. Interpretation is used in the latter to filter out unconscious motivations and to strengthen the defenses of the person in conflict.

Interpretation is a valid and crucial aspect of skilled counseling, but the helper who understands it knows that it cannot be used carelessly, out of some desire for mastery or as a demonstration of cleverness. Brash interpreters, however, are out to teach others about their behavior and to add meanings that the others may not be ready yet to recognize. Persons skilled in interpretation know that they must time their interpretive statement to that moment when the other individual is prepared to see, accept, and profit from this kind of response. Good interpretations are characterized by understanding rather than mystery.

Counselors who define their work as searching for the right psychological analysis to apply to the other person's conflicts may badly misunderstand the nature of interpretation and retard their own development as competent counselors. The risk involved in premature interpretation is that, even though we may be right, we may be wrong because of our poor timing. Most of us resent having our behavior interpreted. We are defensive on this matter, and interpretations work only when we are quite close to accepting and making them for ourselves. Otherwise we can be threatening and increase the defensiveness, if not the total withdrawal, of the person we are trying to help. Interpretations may display our cleverness or they may help us to feel powerful because we seem to know more about others than they seem to know about themselves. This approach to dealing with others is filled with dangers, and if we find that we are indulging in it, or excessively insisting upon our judgment of things, then it is time for a careful self-examination on this matter and, on occasion, consultation with a skilled psychotherapist.

Partial interpretations may be used in supportive counseling, but they require skill, judgment, and a mastery of the art of responding. In a partial interpretation a counselor chooses only some elements in the larger view of the person and the relevant circumstances and structures it carefully so that it does not undermine but rather supports a conscious defense that the person is using. As Dewald expresses it:

> In this way, he may be offering the person an opportunity to use mechanisms of displacement and rationalization and to continue the repression by focusing on the person's attention to an aspect of the problem which is less anxiety provoking and more acceptable. The same might be true in the use of interpretation to reinforce the intellectualization by providing the patient with an explanation of the content of a conflict while strengthening defenses against its emotional impact and fostering the use of further isolation of affect.[2]

In other words, counselors give the person a breather by reinforcing a defense that is keeping the unconscious secure ("continue the repression") while allowing him to pull himself together. A good example is found in the individual who experienced the symptoms of a panic attack when brought to an intensive care unit in which there were only other male patients. Instead of exploring the unconscious dynamics activated by finding oneself in a same-sex environment, helpers would focus on the conscious elements — the isolation of the setting, the unfamiliarity of the monitors, the worry about the outcome of his surgery — that bolstered his conscious ability to cope and get through the experience without being overwhelmed.

Do We Like to Reassure People?

We have defined the counseling done by nonprofessionals as *supportive* rather than *uncovering*. Being supportive requires insight and skill and a mastery of the tactics that maintain the conversation on the conscious level. What, we may ask now, is the foundation of support in the counseling process? It flows from simple sources: our healthy contact with the person seeking help and our communicating our understanding of that person's view of the world. Persons experience an immediate infusion of support when they are taken seriously as individuals. Great strength flowers out of our acceptance and understanding of others.

Sometimes counselors take a different approach to support. They stress reassurance rather than the simple and solid exchange of understanding. We can appear to reassure people, however, in ways that are not at all supportive. We do this whenever, in effect, we tell others that they need not feel the way they are feeling. To say, "You shouldn't be upset by this," when they are very upset by it denies their true experience. This writing off of their testimony is, of course, the very opposite of acceptance and understanding and, in the long run, may be discouraging or destructive.

Falsely supportive reassurance can be overheard in the movie dialogue of clergy and counselors. They are demeaned when they are portrayed as having nothing really to say to persons who are in trouble. The phrases, "It isn't as bad as you think," or "You'll feel better tomorrow," or "You shouldn't feel so upset about this," are run-of-the-mill reassurances that discourage rather than help others. Perhaps we have all overheard well-meaning persons gently telling a weeping widow not to cry. What they are really saying is, "If you don't cry, I won't feel so bad because I don't know what to say to you." Studies of grief and mourning show that "jollying" people along during periods in which they are experiencing deep feelings of sadness is not at all helpful.

Real support exists when we enter into the experience of other persons, stand there with them as they explore themselves, and do not back away when the experience threatens to become hard on us. Reassuring another falsely opens an escape hatch for ourselves that may isolate us from our counseling work and leave us empty and puzzled that we are not getting anywhere. In such efforts to avoid stress, counselors increase the pressure on themselves. They may not realize that such strain is a measure and a model of their whole approach to other persons. It may keep them on the outside of the wrenching experience but it also nullifies understanding and may provoke great anxiety in the other.

A good example of the latter is found in the obviously edgy parishioner who approached his pastor in the church to tell him that he could see angels in the sanctuary. The priest, thinking to be reassuring, put his arm around the man's shoulder and said soothingly, "Yes, I can see them, too." This well-meant response deepened rather than lessened the man's anxiety. He was not looking for this affirmation of his experience that did not reassure him but only disturbed him more. The man did not keep the appointment he made to see the priest that evening.

Do We Try to Be Understanding?

Understanding is an essential aspect in all healthy human relationships and is indispensable in any work that comes under the heading of counseling. It is central in all schools of psychotherapy and in all techniques or applications of counseling principles. When understanding is lacking, nothing very effective can take place. It is the single most important aspect of our approach to others and, even when we fail to be completely understanding, the very effort to grasp even partially the experience of others is helpful both to them and to us.

The effort to understand puts aside a tendency to evaluate or to pass judgments from some distant authoritarian vantage point. Understanding does not mean that we agree or disagree with persons as they try to tell us about their feelings or experiences. Genuine understanding does not condemn those seeking help but neither does it condone or enlist itself needlessly on their side of an issue.

Accurate understanding begins with an effort to get out of ourselves and to empty ourselves of our own narrow viewpoints, prejudices, and traditions. It begins with and grows from the simple effort to see from the viewpoint of others. It demands that we suspend our tendency to impose our own meanings or judgments on them. Through understanding we are able to enter the world of others and to view it without trampling on or confusing them or the meanings they attach to people and events.

This approach to others requires great sensitivity and plain hard work on the part of the helper. It is as powerful as it is essential if we want to improve our counseling and control our own experience of stress. The willingness to understand and to work consistently from this point of view strengthens our capacity to be helpful, frees us of a need to prove ourselves or demonstrate our mastery, and increases our sense of lively participation in the deep and meaningful work of counseling.

– 7 –

WHAT IS IT LIKE
TO BE REAL?

A SPECIAL STRESS may be associated, for at least some of us, with anticipating the role demands of counseling. Being a counselor may mean donning the raiment of the counselor, as a police officer does a uniform, and taking on official behaviors and attitudes. In other words, we may think that being counselors means being different through adopting positions and protocols that are not natural for us. We may imagine that a conflict exists between acquiring disciplined skills and just being ourselves, between trying to do something correctly and doing the right thing spontaneously.

It is as if counselors had to play a part that makes them sacrifice their own reactions in favor of those prescribed by their texts, teachers, or supervisors. As a beginning counselor once reported, "It seems that everything I do on my own is wrong and that everything I'm supposed to do as a counselor makes me feel artificial."

Our growth as helpers may be observed in the way we handle this common challenge. It flows from our developing a sense of unity about ourselves that incorporates what we learn with what we are. The continuing task resembles many others in life, including becoming parents, in which we integrate our learned skills with our own personal identity. There is no necessary conflict between what a good counselor does and what a good person does.

The discipline of counseling does not engage us in activities that are antagonistic to the truths we understand about ourselves. The discipline requires us to concentrate on and refine more fully our genuine human strengths; it offers a systematic way of tapping the healthy resources of understanding and concern that are hardly foreign to the best side of ourselves. Maturing counselors appreciate the fact that what they do in counseling does not ask them to change themselves as much as it invites them to come closer to their best but frequently unrealized selves.

What Goes into Being Real?

Being ourselves does not, we recall, mean saying or doing anything we feel like at any moment in the counseling process. This erroneous interpretation of what it means to be natural — that is, responding to one's impulses without reflection — echoes a general misunderstanding about achieving our individuality. "Being my own man" not only rings of male chauvinism but it is a prime cliché that sums up one of our lesser national illusions: it is far easier to proclaim we are our own person than it is to be our own person. Being our own person involves us, not in repeating contemporary aphorisms or behaviors that supposedly confer identity on us, but in straightforward growing as truly and as fully as we can. This demands that we take ourselves and our talents seriously and that we live deeply enough to grasp at least some of the meaning and possibilities of existence itself.

These, of course, are precisely the opportunities that are available in counseling work. Reflecting on meaning and existence is unavoidable whenever we take others seriously enough to listen carefully to their efforts to give us an account of their experience of life. When we are in a relationship of serious purpose, when what we and the other do and say has real effects, we experience a kind of meaning that others can only talk about. The necessary and sufficient condition for this is that we be ourselves.

Being oneself suggests that we do not live on the skim of life but that we respect ourselves and our gifts and make the most of them as we gradually enter the depths of responsible relationships with others. In a way, this is a different version of Sigmund Freud's statement that the purpose of life is "to love and to work." Being serious about our lives, of course, is much different from being solemn. We achieve this seriousness only by refining our abilities, by honing them and using them — wisely. This means ridding ourselves of the defenses or habits that interfere with our coming more completely alive and expressing ourselves more fully in our work.

Counseling does not ask us to be startlingly different but to be more genuinely ourselves in our work. Only counselors can take care of this side of the counseling relationship. They do it with less strain as they realize how, within counseling, they have the opportunity to bring their best disciplined performance — the best of themselves, in other words — to their understanding of other persons.

As we become more comfortable with this realization, artificiality drops away and the atmosphere and the exchange become less studied and more genuine. Stress decreases and the experience becomes, so to speak, more intensely real for both ourselves and those we counsel. We may not be self-conscious about it, but our best responses begin to match our best potential as human beings. This developing sense of oneness about ourselves and our counseling resolves the anxiety that builds up when we are too concerned about how well we will perform. This effortless being who we are improves the therapeutic environment and is the natural medium for progress by the other. As the counseling loses its staginess and becomes more spontaneous, we experience not only greater personal ease but also a deeper sense of contentment in our work. It is no longer a burden or a test of our laboriously acquired techniques. Counseling becomes a truly re-creative experience because we are more fully and freely involved in it. This builds a sense of security that makes the counselor's person more available and, without trying, lessens the stress of the work.

Some Reality Principles

There are certain perennial truths associated with helping others. Allowing these to become second nature to us allows us to consolidate our sense of ourselves both as human beings and as counselors. As we enter counseling, we feel less as if we are changing roles and more as if we are entering at a deeper level into an important human relationship. Among these bedrock stress-reducing reality principles are the following:

People Are Always Trying to Tell the Truth about Themselves

It is helpful to understand this because so many people who find themselves involved in counseling perceive what others are doing in quite a different fashion. It is understandable in a world dominated by the "spin" of the public relations ethic to presume that human beings naturally try to hide the truth about themselves. If we accept that, counseling becomes a contest, sometimes muted and sometimes intense, between helper and the one helped. Counselors who feel that they are engaged in a battle of wits, a power struggle, or a demonstration of their own cleverness clearly increase their chances of experiencing stress during their therapeutic work.

Everybody in our culture has some awareness of the "Freudian slip." In *The Psychopathology of Everyday Life*, Freud tells us that apparent mistakes in what we say are actually signals about our real intentions.[1]

Reality Principles

- People are always trying to tell the truth about themselves.

- The things about people that drive us crazy are the things that are keeping them sane.

- We should not try to open people up.

- We should respond to the person instead of trying to make a good response.

Thus, the man who says, "I now close this meeting," instead of "I now open it," tells us what he really feels about the gathering. This understanding of the meaning of slips of the tongue is closely associated with the reality principle we are discussing.

However, for some persons Freudian slips have become clues in a detective story in which they try to discover a culprit rather than be an aid to a subtler and more penetrating understanding of another human being. Catching a person in a Freudian slip, in other words, has become a triumph, a way of exercising higher wisdom, reassuring oneself, and possibly even putting other persons down. This gamelike quality of interpreting Freudian slips diminishes rather than enlarges human relationships. The work of counseling is not to get the goods on others or to demonstrate that we know more about them than they know about themselves.

When we say that *people are always trying to tell the truth about themselves* we refer to the totality of their communication. Most persons really do want to get the truth out even though they are sometimes confused or deceived about it themselves. They do this through many styles of communication, some of which are direct but many more of which are symbolic and proceed from unconscious levels of their personalities. Even as people express one thing verbally, they are often communicating just the opposite by their tone, their gestures, or by other behavior. It is the counselor's task to read with an ever-increasing sensitivity the many languages in which we speak to each other so that the message being delivered can be correctly received. The problem is not that the message is not sent; it is that we miss it.

Sensitivity of this sort demands a high level of skill as well as an accepting attitude that tries to understand people rather than to snare them in their inconsistencies. Inconsistencies, after all, are part of the language we all use in expressing and revealing ourselves. When we use our sensitivity to Freudian slips against the person we may obscure rather than get closer to the truth. We may also separate ourselves from the other, accenting the relationship as one of competition rather than cooperation.

Some examples may be helpful in assisting us to unravel how other persons are actually trying to tell us the truth about themselves. Persons who verbally attack us, saying that as therapists we are not helpful or that we do not seem to be very experienced or that they would like to end the counseling, can certainly upset or make us uneasy. As we become more sensitive, we begin to understand what they are doing more clearly. We know that the other person is actually saying something like, "I'm getting involved in this counseling relationship and it makes me uncomfortable. The only way I can respond to my discomfort is by trying to put some distance between us through these attacking statements."

Individuals who use defenses extensively in counseling, intellectualizing about the process or about psychological difficulties, reveal something of the truth about their inability to deal with their own inner problems. They are saying, in effect: "This is the best I can do, the only language I know in which I can feel safe telling you about my anxieties and about the sense of threat I experience when I try to talk about what is bothering me."

People who attempt to manipulate us by getting us to do extra things, such as granting additional time, make us uncomfortable but they also reveal a good deal about their own style. They are saying: "This is the way I handle people. I'm showing my style to you, trying it out on you, displaying to you exactly the manner in which I relate to people in the rest of my life." Counselors who understand that people are really trying to get the truth of themselves across feel less combative toward such persons and are able to read their behavior with much greater accuracy. They catch the meaning of the whole person, and this both increases their effectiveness and decreases the experience of stress in their counseling work.

The Things about People That Drive Us Crazy Are the Things That Are Keeping Them Sane

This is merely a commonsense way of understanding the functional nature of the symptoms and complaints people bring to us. It also heightens our awareness of the fact that the rough edges of the sample

just showing their pattern's difficulty
problem to us. ✓ good.

62   *What Is It Like to Be Real?*

of behavior people offer us during a counseling session provide a pro-file of their painful and difficult adjustment. The things they do wrong, the defeats they inflict on themselves, the trouble they get into — the things that bother both them and us — reflect their inadequate attempts to solve their life problems and to keep themselves going. 不胜胜任

A pattern is embedded in this behavior and, if we sense its outlines, we develop a feeling for the fuller dimensions of the other's psycholog-ical motivations; we get a look deep down beneath the surface activity. This enables us to see persons in better perspective and to appreciate the functional nature of the defenses they employ. Their defenses work, maybe not very well, but they work nonetheless. Looking at the situ-ation this way enables us to factor out the annoyance we sometimes experience at the kinds of problems some of those we help repeatedly manage to get themselves into. Remembering this enables us to pos-sess ourselves more easily and to be more understanding of them as total persons. It also gives us a fresh way of dealing with the stress of transference and countertransference.

We Should Not Try to Open People Up
(acting

There are strong cultural and personal reasons that sometimes make the objectives of friendship or counseling converge in the phenomenon of "getting the other person to open up." Counselors or overhelpful friends occasionally perceive themselves as psychological safecrackers, spinning the emotional dials sensitively and urgently in order to have the doors swing open on the presumed treasures within.

It is almost an accepted principle that the objective of a good talk or a good counseling session is to open up the person in distress. Perceiv-ing this as an objective leads certain helpers to invest great energies in bringing this outcome about. They decide beforehand, in other words, that the revelation of the inner life of the person seeking help is the sign that all is going well. They are frustrated when this does not easily come about, and they shift from tactic to tactic in an effort to find the precise one that will get people to talk about what is really bothering them.

Working intensely from their own outside point of view leads some counselors to miss the important things that are going on inside the person who has come for help. These counselors are so anxious to get the person to open up — and are consequently so disappointed if the person does not meet their expectations — that they easily miss a great deal of what is significant. They are playing hard, but they are heading for the wrong goal.

Persons do not come to a counselor to be opened up. They come to open themselves up, a process that is successfully accomplished only from within. The objective of the counseling relationship, or even of a friendly talk, is not to get others to drop their defenses quickly. This is something they will do if they experience the qualities that seem to be indispensable for good counseling; they need to be accepted and understood in a relationship where they are respected and prized as persons capable of taking more responsibility for their own lives. Counselors must periodically reflect on whether they have been caught up in the cultural tide that can make opening up seem the unquestioned ideal in counseling work.

This is simply not the goal of counseling. Once we understand that, we lessen our own stress because we are willing to wait for things to happen instead of deciding when and how they should. One among many Chinese proverbs tells us that we can chase butterflies all day long, but only when we finally sit still will one come and light on our shoulder. Waiting is more important in counseling than pushing hard.

Counselors who have not learned to wait compound the experience of stress for themselves and never know quite why. Clearly, some gentle listening to themselves will help them track down the sources of their own impatience. It also gives them some clues about why it is sometimes difficult for them to see things from any perspective but their own.

We Should Respond to the Person Instead of Trying to Make a Good Response

This may be the most basic of all the reality principles of counseling, the common thread that runs through friendship, love, and any kind of relationship in which individuals reach out to enlarge each other's lives. The more we actually see each other as persons — the more, in other words, we perceive each other as distinct individuals rather than as extensions of ourselves — the more freely we can respond to each other. We then see each other less as cases, as psychological burdens, or annoying time occupiers. However, when we do not see those who seek help as persons they quickly get pigeonholed into one of these categories. Counseling becomes harder work when people are seen this way; the stress we experience multiplies in exact relationship to our failure to appreciate the individuality of those with whom we work.

We identify this difficulty as our own when we find that much of our counseling effort is going into making good responses rather than in responding to the person. It seems like an oversimplification to remind ourselves of this, and yet, in their efforts to do well, many counselors find it difficult to disengage themselves from the process of making artful-sounding responses. They get self-conscious because they want to sound like accomplished therapists.

The only way to avoid this syndrome is to concentrate on others and to pull the spotlight away from ourselves. When we respond directly to others, we lose the studied and contrived quality that creeps into so many of the things we say when we are trying to sound like experts. When we put others first, always asking what their experience is in telling us about themselves, then our responses take care of themselves. They may be ragged and incomplete at times but, catching the core — the point, we might say — of what the person is telling us, compensates for all that is unfinished about them.

All the effort that goes into sounding good only makes counselors excessively conscious of themselves, and this cannot help but make them less aware of others. Persons do come first, but it is a lifelong task to learn to respect them practically and genuinely in this way in our counseling work. The more we do this, however, the more effective and free we become in counseling because it is less a role we assume and more an identity we inhabit. Our responses then reflect our best attention and concern.

8

THE SELF AS INSTRUMENT
IN HELPING OTHERS

W HILE SURGEONS TRANSMIT their healing art through their scalpels and writers express their enlightening sensibilities through pens or word processors, counselors are themselves the instruments through which they help other persons. Attuning ourselves to our own resonations — those of who and how we are with others — is a crucial task for every counselor. While this prospect may rise before us with the restrained appeal of a tour through the mist-laden Stonehenge of our consciences, listening to and learning about ourselves can also be an exhilarating and freeing experience.

Examining ourselves at the same time that we are counseling others requires us to listen, as it has been expressed, "with the third ear." This monitoring of ourselves as we attempt to understand others may seem as cumbersome as being a one-person band, but it is far closer to the matching of personality and art in a virtuoso musical performance. Such memorable occasions begin, however, in artists' coming to terms with themselves, accepting both their endowments and their liabilities and the discipline of practice sweetened by new depths of self-understanding.

Being Human, Being Imperfect

If aspiring writers find their unique voices when they stop trying to sound like Hemingway, those who counsel express understanding best when they stop trying to do it perfectly. Helping other persons to grow is a function of operating as best we can within the limitations of the human condition. We may never sound as wise as Freud or Jung, but we do fine by being true to ourselves. These limitations include a realistic sense of how much we can really do for others. Some helpers feel uncomfortable at first in accepting that, in the last analysis, we may never do as much as we long to do for others. Varied feelings arise because of the inevitable intersection of counselors' desires to be helpful with the realistic possibilities of actually being helpful. What we yearn to do may be the *Titanic;* life's iceberg teaches us what we can do. And what we do, as noted in chapter 5, is never something that we do *to* them but always *with* them.

Answering the question about our limits — or at least asking it honestly — about how much we can do, is a big first step in managing our assisting others at close range. For our own good and theirs, we need to develop simple and reliable estimates of our range of the possible help we give *to* others as we work closely *with* them.

Our need to do good has been discussed sufficiently in a previous chapter. It is clearly operative when we pose the question about our capacity to help others. There is no reason to deny the impulse to do good shared by so many people who do counseling on a full- or part-time basis. It is a strong motive that is associated with the great religious and humanitarian achievements of history. That it can be overbalanced in favor of meeting the counselor's need *to* help, rather than the need of others *for* help, does not mean that it is unworthy or should be regarded as a bad habit. It is a factor that influences persons in every profession that delivers service to the community. It is central in the motivation for many of these, such as medicine and ministry.

We grow with an adult grasp of our own need to do good and an awareness of this motive's at times sly strength in the choices we make while helping others. We need not deny the need to help, but we must understand it — tame or socialize it, if you will — in order to integrate it successfully into our personalities and our counseling work. This demands that we keep the refining factory of our self-understanding open at all hours. We continually process our impulse to do good, blending it with the truths about our own abilities to help others with their capacity to be helped. That will prevent us from pursuing, much less forcing on others, what are termed "rescue fantasies."

Optimism is an important strength in counselors; we can never do much if we are plagued with a negative and unhopeful approach to people in need. Adult optimism, however, is not the same as the dangerously naive expectation that we can remake successfully all the persons who come to us. This latter attitude calls for special effects transformations that we cannot fabricate or deliver. Trying remakes on those who cannot easily be remade causes counselors bewilderment and guilt when the goal is not achieved. Sometimes, counselors unconsciously design their own defeats. Most of us, however, want to succeed in reasonably human fashion with a becomingly modest sense of our therapeutic powers.

Practical Themes

The following notions may help us as we learn more about ourselves and what we can and cannot do for and with others.

Every Therapist Is Limited

That applies to all of us, no matter how many degrees or how professionally advanced we may be. No one therapist can do everything, can work effectively with every kind of person, or can guarantee cures for every problem. There is an obvious quality to this statement that is often forgotten, especially by counselors who are always comparing themselves to some therapist whose skills they admire and may even try to imitate. The perfect therapist is like the perfect wave. The quest in search of this kind of perfection would carry us throughout the world and leave us unsatisfied. Some therapists are clearly more experienced and far more skillful than others; part of the reason for this may lie in the fact that they do understand their limitations, that they have, in other words, answered for themselves in a practical way the question of how much good they can do for others.

Counselors who acknowledge their limitations no longer *need* to prove anything about themselves. They need not win the power game with others or get them to like them, or even impress their colleagues. Counselors liberate themselves through making a pact of truth with life. They are thereby freer to be effective because their defenses are automatically minimized. They do what they can with integrity and do not feel guilty about it. They are less conflicted and, therefore, interfere less with the dynamics of successful therapy. They can understand and manage the challenges of countertransference honestly and cleanly because they have learned, in a real sense, to be counselors to themselves. This relieves them of unnecessary stress and permits them to achieve a deeper involvement in their relationships with those they are counseling.

Nobody Is Expected to Succeed All the Time

Success is one of the great American obsessions. It is generally defined in concepts of "more" rather than "better." In counseling, success can only be understood as a continuous improvement of our performance. It is unrelated to seeing more people, making more money, or having more people impressed by us. Therapy, like growth and life in general, is a series of approximations. It is never magic, and it is difficult to observe when it is going on. Counseling works because, like life, it matches and builds on the imperfect way in which we come to terms with the truth about ourselves. Therapy is built on the basic stuff of human experience that underlines the personal growth that, by its very nature, is limited and never takes place overnight.

If We Cannot Accept Limitations and Defeats, We Are Probably in the Wrong Work

To expect that we can always provide the right answer at the right time is self-enhancing in theory but it is never found in real life. Counselors suffering from a "savior complex" only multiply their own experiences of stress by insisting on total therapeutic victories that they cannot possibly achieve.

interested that we seems have to do multi-task work work load more as deal "y both....

We Need to Be Counselors to Ourselves

This is a necessary aspect of our growth as helpers. Often, the counselor's self is left behind as though it could safely be overlooked or disregarded in view of fulfilling an ideal of service to others. A failure to listen to what is going on inside ourselves, under the banner of heroic self-forgetfulness, may increase our experience of stress and place a heavy mortgage on our effectiveness. It may also make us vulnerable to being slowly consumed by our own unrecognized needs. The reverse of the golden rule applies here: counselors should do unto themselves what they try to do unto others. This means that they should listen carefully to their own feelings in an accepting and nonjudgmental manner.

We should try to understand and forgive ourselves for our share of human fallibility. Unfortunately, many counselors are hard on themselves and uncomfortable with their own humanity. The understanding they can share with others they curiously deny to themselves. Until we can open ourselves to our own experience we will be caught up in the tension between our ideals and our ideas about counseling.

Revisions of counselors' self-ideals follow automatically from a more realistic perception of themselves. The key to answering the question about how much we can help other persons is found in the realism with which we look upon ourselves, our talents, and our expectations about life. Our self-concept can be revised, of course, but only as we lay aside our habitual defenses against the truth about ourselves. As defenses harden to preserve a distorted self-understanding, it becomes increasingly difficult for us to process the truth about ourselves. We become rigid, dogmatic, and unyielding because we must insist on the view that we have of our own personalities.

Once we can modify all this — call anger or longing by their right names, and not feel undone because we have a surprisingly rich capacity for emotional reactions — we can more easily be ourselves. This step toward assessing and accepting our own personalities allows us to define our ideals more realistically. There is a correlation, so to speak, between a truthful sense of oneself and an appropriate and attainable set of professional and personal ideals. Our personal ideals of helping everyone are tempered sensibly by a good grasp of the facts about ourselves.

The less we know ourselves in depth, the less appropriate will be the expectations we place on our performance. People feel guilty when they perceive themselves habitually falling short of their ideal. This leads to stressful recriminations and regrets, the twin killers of many persons who engage in counseling. An honest appraisal of ourselves necessarily leads to a modified and more attainable counseling ideal.

The central question that enables us continually to review our own potential in a realistic manner comes to this: What do I think I can actually *do* for people? Can I undo the compounded experience of years? Can I change their childhoods or eliminate their realistic griefs? Can I compensate them for their bad breaks, their lack of love from others, or their own genetic disadvantages? Can anybody remove the obstacles that are found in everyone's life?

A philosophical theme resonates in these questions that takes us slightly beyond what we might term the mechanics of counseling. We cannot forge an answer about our own capacity to help others unless we are philosophical about the many things we cannot change. Hard as it is to admit, there are some people we simply cannot help, some people for whom we will not be well fitted as counselors, some people with whom we can never establish a helping relationship. Being honest in this context is the beginning of wisdom for counselors. This implies some common sense about human nature as well as some humility about ourselves.

Counselors also need informed realism about themselves for their own professional work with others. However, they are also shapers of public opinion, mediators who are asked to translate the issues connected with mental health for the understanding of the general community. Even if counseling is not a full-time activity, nonpsychological professionals have an obligation to be well-informed about the major psychological questions that are relevant to the community. This cannot be done without reading and reflecting on these important questions.

These concerns cover a broad range of issues, including the legal rights of patients, the nature of psychiatric hospitalization, the problem of the homeless, and the conditions of penal institutions.

What Do We Do with People We Cannot Help?

As counselors, we must come to terms with the fact that we cannot assist everybody and that we cannot solve every problem even imperfectly. In many instances, our primary work will be to secure an appropriate referral for individuals and/or their families. Such options will be discussed in greater detail later in this book. Beyond this, however, the community is concerned — sometimes because it has not been properly informed — about the implications of the inability of even an array of professionals to be successful in treating some persons.

Strong feelings can accompany these discussions when persons can cite news accounts of recently released psychiatric patients who commit crimes, especially if these are crimes of violence. It remains true that most crimes are committed by persons who have not been hospitalized. This does not lessen the horror that spreads across a community in the face of some shocking murder committed by someone who is receiving psychological treatment or who has been dismissed from a hospital. All persons who engage in counseling have a responsibility to clarify and to help people face and deal with the strong emotions that can block a mature discussion of the various issues involved here. These are perennial sore spots in every community. The fact that we cannot treat everyone successfully is a problem that the community shares. And the community can deal with the problem only if it is helped to understand the facts about psychiatric treatment, hospitalization, and the need to rehabilitate many psychiatric patients in the environment of the community rather than in an institution.

Associated issues center on the heavy attacks that have been launched against the very idea of psychiatric hospitalization. These have been spearheaded by lawyers who make the case that the patient's civil rights are frequently violated in these circumstances. The increasing number of legal challenges to psychiatric hospitalization cause medical authorities to be understandably defensive about the possibilities of civil suits or lengthy courtroom wrangles over the clinical judgments associated with hospitalization.

The issues are important, of course, but this discussion sometimes obscures the fact that hospitalization is oftentimes absolutely necessary. The perfect solution for preserving patients' rights while providing them with the environment necessary for treatment and control has not been found as yet. It is a major public question to which there is no fully satisfactory answer. The answer must be worked out every day in each concerned community. Counselors can assist in this, not only through their input of up-to-date information but also through their sensitivity to the emotional issues that surround such questions. They can be effective in clarifying and mediating the discussion of these problems.

The counselor's sense of realism about what can be achieved in a reasonable balance of the medical, legal, and ethical issues connected with community psychiatry has no cut-and-dried formula. Counselors contribute to the continuing resolution of our understanding of these issues if they avoid committing themselves to related causes. Ideologues are impassioned in their demands for hospital and prison reform and for a general renewal of community psychiatric practice. Heightened personal emotions do not help the community arrive at reasonable answers about improving its response to emotional problems.

Counselors to the Community

Counselors can respond better to their communities when they have struggled with some of these questions in their own professional work. They develop and can provide the seasoned view that enables steady and mature progress in the community's quest for improved mental health. The notion of being counselors to the community is hardly a new one. It is as old as the idea of priesthood and ministry. The need for professionals with emotional sensitivity to take on this function is one that may be appreciated fully only by the very professionals involved.

Oftentimes, members of the community look toward those who do counseling as possessors of solutions and turn to them for answers in times of crisis. This is frequently very unrealistic; it is the product of a set of commonly held expectations about professional counselors — that they know everything and should be able to handle anything. The inversion of counselors' unrealistic view of themselves is found in the community that makes magicians out of counselors and mental health workers.

Magic is, of course, hard to resist because it confers a special kind of power on those who are presumed to have it. One of the best ways to lessen our own stress and to help our communities is by refusing to don the wizard's robes even when others urge us to don them.

This is particularly so in relationship to the growing problem of the homeless, especially those who are mentally ill. The counselor will sometimes be contacted to aid in evaluating or in helping to find solutions to the problem. Such individuals, by virtue of their homelessness, may no longer receive their social security checks or be able to comply with prescribed medications for their medical or psychological illnesses. In these instances, familiarity with community resources is especially helpful.

Everyone with counseling responsibilities shares in the obligation to help the community understand and utilize counselors in a realistic and timely way. This is one practical way in which counselors can lessen the stressful demands made on them by communities or colleagues who do not appreciate what they can do — and what they cannot do.

9

ARE WE FRIENDS OR COUNSELORS?

S OONER OR LATER every person involved in helping others comes up against a question that looms like the Monument Valley massif in John Ford Westerns: Can a counselor be a friend and can a friend be a counselor?

In what seems a double inquiry, we see two aspects of one question about the relationship between friendship and counseling. It is not easily answered and certainly cannot be dismissed. Here we pause, stepping out of the sound and fury of a filled schedule, to survey our inner lives to understand who and where we are as helpers to other persons. Such an examination is particularly relevant for counselors who manage heavy workloads or whose main occupation, as a pastor or teacher, for example, necessarily entails counseling responsibilities. Counselors may be so busy that they cannot easily find the time to reflect, as a baseball player must, on the stance that they have assumed when they are, so to speak, at bat in their relationships with others. Like hitters, helpers come to understand that these periodic self-investigations are boon rather than burden. They are carried out outside the pressures of game-time performance and allow helpers to observe whether they have made subtle shifts in their counseling relationships, to understand why, and to make healthy adjustments in their stance.

The questions raised in the previous chapter tighten the focus of counselors on their own personalities as influences in the helping process. Counselors answer by refining their perception of the impact of their personal and professional attitudes on their lives both in and out of counseling.

For many years the model for therapy — one still to be found in the professional work of many psychiatrists and other therapists — defined the helping relationship in a highly specific way. It is described in a nationwide study of psychotherapists in this fashion:

The unique nature of a therapeutic relationship undoubtedly contributed to the therapist's ability to distinguish between intimate personal and intimate professional relationships. Unlike close personal relations, a therapeutic relationship is affect-laden but asymmetrical. That is, only the patient is supposed to reveal the intimate details of his life. The psychotherapist is not only free to determine what he will reveal and conceal about himself, but also to choose how to react to what the patient is saying, if indeed he decides to respond at all. The relationship is also asymmetrical in that only the therapist is supposed to interpret and impute meaning to what the patient is saying and only the therapist can evaluate the degree to which therapeutic objectives are being achieved in the relationship. In sum, the therapeutic relationship is a highly circumscribed, personal relationship conducted in accordance with the ground rules laid down by the therapist. These rules result in relationships in which the therapist comes to know all about the patient as a person while the patient never comes to know the therapist as anything but a therapist. Thus, from the therapist's standpoint, the therapeutic transaction provides intimacy in close personal familiarity without, at the same time, involving the risks entailed in revealing one's inner thoughts and feelings to another.[1]

As most counselors realize, this traditional view has been questioned sharply over the last generation. Inspired by the personalistic emphasis of figures like Carl Rogers, Everett Shostrom, and many others, counseling has been domesticated and, to some extent, deprofessionalized and democratized. This characteristically American development reflects the nation's deepest habits of mind and faith in democratic institutions as solutions for everybody.

Under the democratic paradigm, counseling is described more in terms of friendship and as an equal relationship between the helper and the one seeking help. Indeed, so transformed from its professional roots is therapy that it is defined operationally by some as that which a therapist judges to be therapy. Such nondiscriminating attitudes led researcher Hans Strupp to observe that "in many respects the field must be characterized as chaotic."[2]

American culture, with its optimism and faith in democratic forms and equal opportunity, has been welcoming soil for the seeds of counseling in which all participants, including therapists, are equals. This has been reinforced by the generalized suspicion of authority that flows from confusing *controlling authoritarianism* with *generative authority*. This also underlies the widespread rejection of professionalism and an outright denial of the therapeutic value of professional training and skills. A generation and more ago, we entered the age of the naive but confident psychotherapist. In extreme, indeed in occasionally bizarre forms, these attitudes may be translated as advocating that the sole condition for being called a therapist is a claim to sincerity. This all but dissolves the boundary between counseling and friendship.

Common Ground

It is, of course, true that therapy and friendship contain many qualities in common. This appreciation of this shared human foundation has, even in more disciplined therapies, encouraged a greater emphasis on the characteristics of genuineness, openness, and equality in the relationship. These qualities of ordinary friendship became the basis for describing the elements that are important in any counseling relationship.

Powerfully influential, in the half century that followed World War II, in shaping this thinking were Carl Rogers's famous reflections, "The Necessary and Sufficient Conditions for Therapeutic Personality Change," first published in 1957 and later incorporated in his book *On Becoming a Person*.[3] Rogers hypothesized explicitly the similarity between good therapeutic relationships and good personal relationships in general, noting that the formal qualities of therapy permitted a more intense and consistent experience of these. The publication of William Schofield's *Psychotherapy: The Purchase of Friendship* symbolized this understanding of therapy as a specialized form of friendship.[4]

A subsequent massive review of the research inspired by Rogers and others led to the isolation of certain common qualities as characteristic of a wide variety of therapeutic relationships. These included genuineness, a capacity for empathy, and the expression of "unconditional positive regard."[5] Indeed, "unconditional love," a hybrid of this, has entered the general American vocabulary.

The subsequent distortion of therapy into a way of life among equals may be observed in scores of therapy-like television programs in which untrained hosts are regularly paired with untreated guests with the confidence that every participant would be better off as a result. E. M. Forster's famous phrase, "Only connect," was easily appropriated but not deeply examined as a slogan for this American obsession with successful relationships. The therapeutic theme was blended into the New

Age religions that took water from many wells, some shallow, some tainted, some beyond their depth, to provide a "feeling of being spiritual" for those for whom the ascetics of true spiritual growth proved too onerous. This therapeutic amalgam became a campaign tool and a broad feature of the presidency of Bill Clinton (1993–2001), who affected therapeutic attitudes and responses, including the famous "I feel your pain," to great short-run political advantage.

The narcissistic overflow of much of this development was criticized in many books, especially those by Christopher Lasch, in the latter decades of the century. One of the earliest critics of this pan-therapeutic approach within psychology was Hans Strupp, who sharply questioned the friendship model of therapy. He stresses the helping relationship as resembling that of a good parent to a child rather than that of a friend to a friend. Good therapy, he suggests, is analogous to good child-rearing practices. He writes:

> The problem of how our external controls are transformed into internal controls is one of the most basic issues of psychotherapy as well as child rearing, and the two are indeed analogous in very important respects. . . . Psychotherapy . . . resembles child rearing . . . and makes use of the psychological mechanisms although in more refined and self-conscious forms.[6]

The debate about which model is appropriate for understanding effective counseling continues in what has been termed "The Therapeutic Society." It is important for counselors to understand these background factors and the widespread simplifications of counseling as motives for honing their own skills in helping others. It is, therefore, important for counselors to find out exactly how they conceptualize their counseling work. This is especially true for counselors who do their work in the context and under the heading of other professional responsibilities or who work in smaller settings where they cannot help but know socially many of the people they also see in counseling.

Counseling as a Different *Relationship*

Such advice does not mean that counselors should take back anything they sincerely understand about the utilization of their own personalities in therapy. This is still important. As Richard Felder wrote many years ago: "It is appropriate to use the Self in psychotherapy because it is the Self which is doing the psychotherapy anyway, and it works out best to recognize this."[7]

John M. Reismann and Tom Yamakoski explore the kind of communication that goes on between friends. It does not, in fact, very closely resemble the communication that takes place in therapeutic relationships. While this is only the beginning of much needed careful research in this area, the article does suggest some very practical ways in which counselors may explore the manner in which they handle themselves in their personal and professional relationships.[8]

Resolving our stance obviously requires balance and judgment. Dewald frames the issue with sound advice for all counselors:

> Most nontherapeutic relationships occur on a give-and-take basis in which each participant is expected to be interested in the welfare and concerns of the other, and neither is permitted for long to exploit or claim exclusive attention to his own problems or desires. The psychotherapeutic situation, however, is different in that by mutual agreement, reached in the establishment of the therapeutic contract and relationship, the major (if not exclusive) area of interest is the patient and his difficulties and problems, and aside from the financial obligation, the therapist does not make personal requests or demands of his own on the patient. The luxury of having someone to listen to all that is said and treat it with regard, respect and interest is in itself a relatively unique phenomenon, and provides a significant gratification to the patient which is rarely offered in other human relationships.[9]

On the Lookout for Dangers

One of the chief dangers, especially for those just starting on their counseling work, is not that they will be friends with those who seek help but that they will act like therapists with their friends. This illustrates how counselors may submerge their true selves in a role that not only destroys their spontaneity but generally distresses their friends as well. It is not uncommon, however, for certain therapists to transfer their counseling attitudes to their social activity. They look solemn, pause, use reflections or interpretations in place of ordinary conversation, and quickly give the impression that they are not being themselves with others.

Such reactions, whatever their source, lead to a falsification of the counselor's personality and thus to a destruction of the mature use of the self that is so essential to effective therapy. Persons who find that they are changing into therapists in all their relationships need to look carefully at why this is happening. They will feel relieved — as will their friends — when they free themselves from assuming the therapeutic stance in social activities.

Common sense also validates something professionals have understood for a long time. Neither doctors, lawyers, nor clergy should take family members or close friends for patients or clients. The unconscious factors, the overlapping areas of relationship, all create a stress that cannot be handled easily even by mature therapists. Clear thinking and self-discipline remain essential even in this era of freewheeling therapeutic styles.

Counselors may rely, in a judgment that reflects both common sense and sensible therapy, on understanding their helping relationships as fundamentally *different* from friendship, even though they share many common elements with it. This gives them a healthy perspective from which to monitor the character of their work with other persons. Sorting out the demands of professional expectations from the clamor of their own personal needs is critical to the effectiveness and, indeed, the survival of the counselor as a helper. They must often serve as their own supervisors until they can review their work with a mentor.

A significant question for helpers is this: Am I leading my emotional life in my counseling? Do I harvest so much emotional reward there that I limit or otherwise contain, consciously or not, my emotional reactions in other areas of my life? Research has suggested that some psychotherapists lead most of their emotional lives in their offices and that little remains for their family setting. Is an overinvestment in work draining off responses to those family members who have a legitimate claim on the emotional reserves of such therapists? In these circumstances, it is clear that therapy becomes not just *like* friendship; it is *the operational friendship* in the helper's life.

It is of no small consequence to find out whether the counselor is leading a balanced emotional life. The pressure of work is often invoked as an excuse for letting one's emotional life become distorted. The *need to respond* to those in distress has legitimated or rationalized many needy adjustments on the part of helpers. If therapists do not work at maintaining a balanced life, they may find that their own needs predominate whether they want them to or not. The resulting emotional confusion constitutes a major source of stress for practicing therapists. This situation never takes care of itself.

Several years ago, a series of reflections was developed to assist helpers to examine the style of their therapeutic relationships. These include unconscious possibilities that may strongly affect the way counselors place themselves into relationship with others:

Counselors may need to *dominate* others and often very subtly assume stances that enable them to do this. They may need the emotional response of others to such an extent that they find themselves in competition with other figures in the person's life to get it. Such counselors want those they help to listen to them and, at times, seem to be anxious that others may also be important and influential in other aspects of their lives. Counselors may shower excessive love and attention, too much concerned treatment, on others in an effort to make the bonds of this *counseling-become-friendship* more secure. This is a common danger in almost every profession that involves people giving help to people needing help.

Some counselors suffer from the "My Fair Lady" or "Pygmalion" complex, in which they wish to remake others, especially those for whom they may have some deep but unverbalized feeling. Counselors should note, for example, if they become resentful of certain seeming demands made by others. A further flag for self-examination is raised when the counselor fears possible hostility; this often leads counselors to try to appease these persons at every stage of their work together.

Seduction as a Reciprocal Process

The emotional *pas de deux* between the parties in a counseling relationship is as old as any tale we have to tell of it. While the possibilities of emotional involvement may seem remote to nonprofessional counselors, they are ever-present and need calm, reflective monitoring. "Seduction" is an explosive term, yet nothing else describes quite so well the dynamics of the situation in which many helpers find themselves.

Obvious seductive moves by persons seeking assistance ordinarily symbolize a resistance to therapy. The moves may often be overtly sexual and, unfortunately for ethics and professionalism, some therapists have suggested sexual relations as an important part of the treatment process.

Research underscores the relativistic vacuum in which sexual relationships occur between those helping and those helped. Thus, it has been reported that 10 percent of psychiatrists responding to a survey — 7 percent male and 3 percent female — acknowledged having sexual or inappropriately intimate relationships with their patients.[10] Further evidence about this problem may be found in work done by the same researchers in which almost 5 percent of resident psychiatrist trainees reported that they had been sexually involved with their teachers and about 1 percent reported such involvement with their patients.[11] The influence of permissive teachers on their trainees in this delicate area of professional behavior cannot easily be discounted. In response to such reports, the American Psychiatric Association not only prohibits sexual activities with patients but also recently endorsed an addendum to its *Code of Ethics* prohibiting such involvement with patients and with former patients.[12]

Boundary Issues

Thomas Gutheil and Glen Gabbard speak of the significance of *boundary issues* in therapy.[13] If Robert Frost tells us that "good fences make good neighbors," these researchers argue that sensible boundaries make good treatment. Lines of demarcation are necessary in treatment to signal that it is, indeed, a *different* relationship than that of friendship or marriage. A shift, they suggest, has occurred from that period that might be termed "boundaryless" in clinical practice in which easy transgression of the invisible wall between doctor and patient was too easily rationalized with predictable results of sexual involvement.

Since that period, they have observed the other extreme of rigid over-reaction. The poet's wisdom — that it is "good to know what you're fencing in and what you're fencing out" — is applied to establish a "middle way of boundaries," termed the "edge" as a space of acceptable behavior. The "edge" creates "an atmosphere of safety and predictability within which treatment can thrive" without license or rigidity.

Such boundaries have conditions and behaviors appropriate within them: these preclude sexual contact but allow for many necessary transactions such as making the fee arrangements and setting the length of the sessions. There is an understanding that patients are expected to disclose more than the therapist about themselves. A distinction is made between "boundary crossing" and "boundary violation." A *boundary crossing* occurs when a truly appropriate human response to unusual events might involve or even invite physical contact. When a therapist touches, as with a hug, a person who has suffered a grievous loss, the boundary is crossed in a healthy way. A *boundary violation,* on the other hand, occurs when the passage is a clearly harmful exploitive action that may, in fact, inflict severe trauma to the person's psychological equilibrium.

To clarify these distinctions, the authors discuss the critical role of "context" in which these exchanges occur. Mental health staff members who drive clients to a supermarket to help them learn to shop relate to them in a close manner. That is a boundary crossing that is central to achieving the goals of their work. That same behavior on the part of a psychoanalyst who sees a patient four times a week in psychotherapy that focuses on unconscious issues would be totally inappropriate and could be characterized as a boundary violation even though it does not include overt sexual behavior.

An important dimension of this same area concerns the controversial issue of self-disclosure. Again, the role of the counselor and the goal of the interaction determine the appropriateness of self-disclosure, that is, when talking about one's own experience is acceptable and when it is unacceptable and may well constitute a boundary violation. As the authors note: "The key issue is what the therapist self-discloses and whether the therapist burdens the patient with personal problems in a manner that reverses the dyad." The disclosure may enhance the goals of the therapy, as when a shy young man who hesitates to talk to his therapist responds to the therapist's revealing his own great interest in baseball. If, however, the therapist begins to discuss his own sexual attraction to the patient, that revelation may be an advertisement for the self that does not serve the goals of therapy as much as the selfish goals of the therapist.

Another related issue is extratherapeutic contact between the counselor and the person seeking help. In general, chance encounters are the risk of living in close proximity with one another. Planned meetings outside of therapy that are unrelated to therapeutic goals are clear boundary violations. Nothing improves on the authors' citation of a dictum of the late Karl Menninger, "When in doubt, be human."

These thoughts merely suggest certain areas where self-examination can be extremely profitable for counselors who take themselves and their work with others seriously. The greatest stress occurs when strong potential sources of conflict exist about which the counselor is uninformed. These are generally unconscious aspects of the transference-countertransference phenomenon and the questions help us to examine the complexities of such issues. Counselors who neglect this self-supervision almost certainly sentence themselves to problems that will generate great stress in their lives.

PART TWO

10

HOW DO WE INTERVIEW?

A S WE APPLY OUR THEORY about relationships and the art of counseling, we come upon what seem commonplace but are, in fact,
critical aspects of the typical helping interview. Explorations of these
seemingly incidental questions throw us and our work into better relief.
Sometimes the stress that we helpers experience is related directly to —
possibly even compounded by — these apparently peripheral attitudes
and behaviors.

As in life itself, some of our most important communication takes
place not in the core but at the edges of our meetings with each other. In
the counseling interview we may overhear revelations — no less important for their being coded and simplified, in the clutter and adjustments
like those of tuning a radio — in the opening and closing moments
of the interview. These disclosures resemble the compressed data of
computers, for, despite their tightly packed and quickly transmitted
character, they are filled with helpful information.

Such messages are delivered while people are hanging up their coats
or still settling into their chairs or, later, as the hands of the clock close
in on the session's ending and talk turns to the time of the next meeting.
Unless counselors learn to read the messages delivered and received in
these moments that seem but preludes and afterwords, they may miss
the unveiling of the conflicted dynamics of the person's life. It is not that
the person has not told us; it is that we have not heard. Our not hearing
others may increase their frustration and our stress at not hauling in
the catch they have set swimming before our eyes.

In reflecting on our style of interviewing, we must be, like an ath-
lete ready for the game, trim but not tight, loose enough to play
unself-consciously instead of awkwardly trying to follow a chalkboard
diagram. Trying to implement an abstract plan may cause us to fall into
the trap of trying "to do well" as if to impress some invisible observer
or ourselves. Blind dependence on game plans for counseling, even if
they are sensible, may rob us of our best strength, our own free and
available personality.

The themes in these chapters that concern interviewing are not prescriptions to help the obsessive counselor become perfect in a stiff and therefore self-defeating manner. They are, rather, to be pondered in the perspective of the overall helping relationship, especially as they help us understand and deal positively with the many levels of communication that crowd every interview, indeed, every contact between persons. Helpers who want to be more at ease with themselves as they counsel gradually, rather than breathlessly, absorb fresh insights about interviewing and integrate them into their approach. Insights applied in too studied a fashion increase rather than decrease the lost chances and wrong turns that can occur in interviewing.

The Telephone

The telephone has become an important factor — and sometimes a source of considerable stress — in the lives of many counselors. It is their first point of contact with many of those who want their help. Many of these are first a voice and only later a full presence, so this exchange is a highly specialized but increasingly common beginning for many counseling relationships.

If we understand the many positive possibilities of these phone contacts, we immediately decrease their own sense of stress. The phone, now carried by Americans as commonly as six-shooters were in the Old West, presents an array of opportunities when we employ it in a sensitive and therapeutic way to initiate and lay the foundation for a continuing relationship with the caller.

The realization that help begins in the initial phone call makes it an interview of special possibilities. Even though the call may come at a difficult time or find us unprepared, it can still be developed as a brief but substantial encounter. We need depth more than duration to make the conversation into a fruitful meeting with the other person. We begin to build a relationship with unseen callers by taking them seriously rather than by dealing with them routinely and by structuring important elements of their possible future relationship in the time that is available.

When we receive a call from someone who wants help from us we should, in ordinary circumstances, use the call as a bridge to a face-to-face meeting. Although this is sometimes impossible in the lives of certain people who do a great deal of counseling — clergy and teachers, for example — it is still the preferred goal. Anyone who gets many calls for help is vulnerable to the "let's settle this on the phone" attitude, a not uncommon response from the far end of the counseling spectrum. At the near ends sits the person sitting by the phone, waiting for calls for help to come, like the emotionally needy professor who once told us that he would not go out at night for fear of missing a call from a student with a problem.

Humanly effective uses of the phone are actually much simpler and more constructive; they center on gathering essential information about callers and why they want our help. Our imagination can run wild when we only hear someone else's voice and we imagine what that person looks like, indeed, what that person *is* like, sight unseen. Reducing the vagueness changes others from a phantasm into themselves. We do that by getting some facts about their age, marital status, and occupation, and why they called.

Second, we should not get into a long and involved discussion on the phone of a specific problem with someone we have yet to meet face to face. We may gently provide a framework for a personal meeting by displaying interest while indicating that a detailed discussion should wait for an appointment. We should also explain to callers something of our way of functioning as counselors. It is helpful to make ourselves less vague, less mysterious, and less liable to the distortions their own needs may introduce. We can also explain in simple language something of our approach and what the face-to-face meeting will be like and where it will be held. It is usually helpful to construe the initial meeting as one in which a mutual decision is to be made about whether we and the prospective counselee can work effectively together. Promises that seem routine to us may sound grandiose to people on the other end of the conversation. We want to avoid saying anything that would mislead others or cause them to expect what we cannot deliver in counseling. We are professional if we restrain ourselves from setting out treatment goals before we really have our bearings or a good sense of direction about the relationship.

The telephone is frequently the instrument of emergency calls, the not so uncommon events to which counselors must also react sensibly and without panic. Not every fire alarm means that a fire is burning. We should calmly get a name, an address, and a phone number in case the emergency is of such a nature that someone else must be notified. We may, for example, need to notify some emergency squad if the caller announces that he or she has just taken "a lot of pills." Such incidents may be relatively rare, but we should be prepared in advance to respond with practical courses of action.

Many calls are not quite the emergencies that callers may make them seem, so a measured response that does not require us to alter our own schedule immediately is more sensible than rushing out before we understand whether an emergency exists. Our phone number is not 911. Do *they* need us to come, we might ask, or do *we* really need to go? We must restrain our potential for melodrama in order to lessen our own stress and be of real service to others. This can be done, even within the limitations of a phone call, quite simply and effectively.

Appointments

Although one would not expect any great difficulty connected with something as uncomplicated as making an appointment, important questions do arise about the way appointments are arranged and kept. Most professional counselors or therapists, for example, try to make as clear as possible to clients the conditions under which they will meet. This also applies to a range of other persons as well. Doctors, funeral directors, educators, and pastors should also be clear about the time and circumstances of a projected meeting with someone who needs their help. It only takes a few minutes to do this, and it usually involves nothing more than stating the time, place, and duration of the appointment. It may also involve other simple matters, such as explaining how to get to the office or some other routine procedure, to eliminate unnecessary mystery and confusion. These are straightforward matters.

The time of making an appointment is also a good occasion for a brief structuring of the helping relationship. This does not take much time either; if it is not done, however, it may consume a great deal of time in straightening it out later on in the counseling. For example, counselors — whether identified as psychotherapists or as nonprofessional counselors whose principal identity lies in some other profession — may well take this moment to state their understanding of why the appointment is being made. Informing callers about the typical length of the session helps them to mobilize themselves to organize their thoughts and prepare to discuss their problems. This decreases the possibility of unhelpful fantasizing by callers by placing the relationship into a real world context in which counselors see other persons and have a separate life of their own.

"I'll see you in my office, then, at nine o'clock. We'll be meeting for an hour to discuss this problem you've been having at home." In a few sentences both the time, duration, and nature of the discussion are helpfully recapitulated. The time of setting this appointment is, in other words, an occasion for clarifying some of the contractual issues connected with the counseling relationship. In the interest of clearing up ambiguity, the counselor may even wish to add something about what the counseling experience itself will be like. This makes clear to others the counselor's perception of the service that is being offered and permits them to question it so that they will not misinterpret or expect something else.

Helpers may, for example, say something like this: "When people come to see me about questions like this I usually just try to listen while they explore their feelings. They usually find that helpful. I don't give a lot of advice or tell them what to do. I try to help them deal more constructively with their problems." There are many possible variations of this, each one appropriate to the counselor's style or purpose. Such statements reveal something of the counselor's approach and describe briefly the clients' accountability for examining and taking responsibility for their own personal problems. Such brief structuring statements are honest commitments by helpers and not an effort to manipulate or control others. Obviously, it would not be helpful to offer structuring unless it reflected the true nature of the experience that people are about to undergo.

It is sometimes surprising to find that people who do extensive counseling operate on an approximate or somewhat vague basis. Instead of making a precise appointment, they feel that it is adequate to say that the person should "drop in after supper on Tuesday." This may seem to preserve an easy informality, but it also leaves the boundaries of the interview in shadows. This may lead to expectations on the part of those seeking help that will not be realized but will almost certainly complicate the relationship itself. If we hesitate to make definite statements about the projected counseling session and its length, we might well examine ourselves to uncover the source of this attitude. Rationalizations abound to support this strategy: "Making appointments is too official sounding," sounds good but such approximations may really reflect a general uncertainty on our part about what we do, how we do it, and perhaps about our capacity to function as counselors at all.

A prime source of stress for many counselors who find reasons for not making definite appointments springs from how, like movies that don't know how to end, their counseling sessions drag out. Some helpers claim that they would rather spend the time and get something settled in one evening than see the person over a long period. Prolonged sessions of counseling do not necessarily mean more effective counseling and may exhaust both the individual and the counselor.

Some helpers need to exhaust themselves in pursuit of what they think is helpful to others, but such stances may be self-serving and, in the ordinary course of events, a reasonable amount of structure helps rather than interferes with effective counseling. Counselors who feel that they cannot set an end point for their helping may reveal something about their own psychological needs, such as their inability to say no or some similar inner dynamic. It suits such counselors to court severe stress and to complain about the long hours for which, in fact, they themselves are responsible.

Even the most sensible plans are sometimes changed by circumstances. For example, the person seeking help may have problems that demand immediate or, as it were, emergency attention. Others may be so defensive and potentially unsettled that we end the session early to allow the person to "ease into" the issues that might otherwise be overwhelming. Others may begin to weep, or to evidence other discomfort that may require spending a few more moments with them before they leave the session. If, however, some find ways to get extra time out of helpers and this becomes a pattern, this tactic and its possible meaning should be explored with them.

Suppose that the person has been clearly informed about the time and duration of the session and yet arrives very late for the first meeting. Some understanding or empathic comment may be used after the reasons for the tardiness are acknowledged. It is never useful to say, "Well, that's okay," or "No problem." What is the person saying to us by arriving late? Since such behavior, unless related to a traffic accident or some other such contingency, may suggest later problems, it should not be sloughed off but, if repeated, explored with the individual.

Every coin has two sides, of course, and if, as counselors, *we* are the ones who are always late or always finding reasons to end early, then we must examine ourselves, or get help to do so, if this suggests that we resist working with certain persons.

The Physical Arrangements

Most professionals take great care in seeing that their offices provide the environment that will minimize unnecessary stress both for themselves and those seeing them. The surroundings and general arrangements for counseling immediately say something about a helper's sensitivity to these issues. We are always delivering messages and, if we ignore or think unimportant how much we write our signatures and our attitudes toward others into our surroundings, we should find out why. The

Now, interruption is so important

answers may not be immediately apparent, but that suggests our need to retrieve them from the level at which they are operating.

For example: Is the office soundproof so that one is shielded from outside noises and feels secure against being overheard by others? Are precautions taken against unnecessary interruptions, such as phone calls, or someone's knocking on the door with a message, a delivery, or a request for help? If these disrupt counseling, they also reveal carelessness on the part of helpers about the nature of their work and the seriousness of their commitment to those who come to see them. Helpers who tolerate interruptions convey very clearly to others that, during the time they are together, they are not as important as intrusions from the outside world. Allowing unrestricted interruptions may also reflect a distracted and ill-organized person whose counseling will be characterized by similar chaos. If we cannot anticipate and make arrangements to minimize or eliminate altogether these interruptions, we have reasons — that need investigation — to create jarring and stressful conditions to frustrate and complicate our helping work.

The place of counseling need not be luxurious, but it should be reasonably comfortable and devoid of any harsh or distracting stimuli. The counseling room, in other words, is not the place where we display the model airplanes we may make as a hobby. Neither do we exhibit photographs of our family, travels, or the famous people we know. The counseling room is not a place for unnecessary "conversation pieces" placed strategically to give the person and counselor something to talk about when they cannot seem to get going.

Most counselors know that the seating arrangement in their offices can also sharply define the relationship to others right from the start. They pick up, at some level, that helpers who feel that they must sit behind imposing desks may protect themselves from others or need to impress them in some way or other. The excessively casual counselor — the barefoot guru or the one who appears to have just pulled away from an interesting football game on television — also sends a message, and it is not always one about the joys of informality. Underscoring the unconventional may reveal the reluctance of certain counselors to be disciplined or their need to project a sense of inner freedom. Such self-referent signals are not necessarily helpful to others, and they may well reflect unresolved stresses in the life of the counselor.

The way that the chairs are arranged can also be instructive. Counselors may, for example, choose the chair that puts them always in an elevated position. This is hardly a subtle signal. It is surprising that we may at times do this without realizing how much we thereby reveal about ourselves. Obviously, the chairs used should be reasonably comfortable and not positioned to give the helper any psychological advantage over the one being helped. As we examine such features of our work, we may also learn a lot about ourselves.

We may also learn something about others from the mode and manner of their choosing a place to sit. We do not do this to "get" something on them but to learn from all aspects of their interview behavior to understand them as well as possible. Persons who sit as far away as possible may, in fact, be distancing themselves from us just as they do from everyone else in life. Persons who cannot decide where to sit and who force the choice onto us may reflect a habit of dependence and indecision that is also found in their relationships with other persons. We cannot, of course, jump quickly to conclusions on samples of such behavior. They should be judged in relationship to other verbal clues or symbolic gestures through which others reveal themselves and their concerns to us. Nonetheless, as an old song goes, every little movement has a meaning all its own and we must observe and understand each of them.

If there are to be any charges, even minimal ones, connected with the counseling, it is crucial to deal with them right away. Sometimes finance is the first concern expressed and people may need the opportunity to explore why they are so uneasy about it. This may have no direct bearing on their capacity to pay, but it does tell something about their general style and the level of their personality development. Payment is not an issue to be left in a vague or ambiguous state, nor something to be put off until a later meeting. It does not take long to clear this up or to arrange for payment of whatever cost is involved.

At this time, payment for services to many professional counselors is determined by the insurer or the health plan of the persons seeking assistance. We must be clear about these from the very start of the relationship. At times, individuals, out of privacy concerns, do not want to claim insurance coverage provided by their employers. Any counselors who accept reimbursement for services need to inform themselves about the parameters, including legal considerations, of making alternative compensation arrangements with such persons.

If we are careless or hesitant to deal with payment issues when their discussion is appropriate or expected, we must search ourselves to find the reasons for such behavior. Do we value the work we do? Do we feel that we are sufficiently trained or experienced to provide this service? Are we really helping the other? Are we the best resource available to help this person with this problem? Would we feel better if someone else were seeing this person? Our valuation of money and our anxiety about what we are doing are quickly communicated to others, who will respond accordingly, even if the entire exchange is at the unconscious level.

While there are many counseling situations — such as those with the clergy — where this is generally not an urgent issue, the symbolism of compensation may be quite significant. For example, a person may tell a member of the clergy, "I was going to see a psychiatrist about this, but I thought it would be better to see you because it wouldn't cost any money...." This statement is awash in implications, and counselors should be ready to deal with them even if no financial charges are going to be involved. Such a statement may reflect the way others perceive the value, the professional competence, or the manipulable qualities of the counselor.

What Do I Call the Person?

How to address the person seeking help seems a simple enough problem, one that professionals can ordinarily solve on the basis of their healthy instincts about a situation. The titles employed, however, do advertise something about our relationships with other persons and deserve close examination. Some counselors do not make much of the question of titles, allowing themselves to be called by their proper designation and referring to the other in a formal way. It is far more usual to call adolescents and children by their first names than it is to address others whom we have not previously met in this informal way. As relationships develop, it may seem appropriate to call adults by their first names; the best judgment on this can flow only from the counselor's mature sense of what is fitting as the relationship grows.

How others are addressed may also be a function of their previous relationship. A pastor or a funeral director who has known a person for many years by that person's first name may not want suddenly to formalize the interaction. Nonetheless, and despite the cultural tide that seems to endorse unearned intimacy in modes of address, using first names from the start does not make for a promising beginning.

Some helpers, on the other hand, may want to display a certain informality or easiness of relationship by addressing others by their first names right from the start. Here again, counselors may profitably serve their own motives in doing such a thing. If it is an easy and spontaneous approach, something that reflects the helper's own personality, it is probably the right thing to do. If, on the other hand, such informality is forced, it may be perceived incorrectly and misinterpreted by the other person. This is particularly true of certain persons who, consciously or unconsciously, attempt to manipulate the counselor right from the start.

The corollary of this concerns the manner in which the person refers to the helper. If there is a premature effort to reduce professionalism in the name of friendliness, the counselor may wish to explore what the individual is attempting to do through this mode of address. Helpers need not make a big deal of it and may, in fact, merely restructure the situation by saying something like, "Most people call me Dr. Smith or Mrs. Jones or Father Brown...." The point is that there is some significance to the way the person and the counselor address each other even at the early stages of their interviews. This issue is not to be ignored nor is it to be seized upon with excessive zeal. It is a signal to be noted and gradually understood correctly in the context of a developing relationship.

Great Expectations

Expectations of one sort or another are shared by both counselors and those seeking help. Factors operate even before the first interview to shape it and sharply affect the way the parties perceive each other and the goals that they try to achieve together.

Individuals may, for example, come to a counselor with the uneasiness that arises from misunderstanding the nature of counseling itself. They may expect that they will be diagnosed by a person of superior intellect and professional competence who will know more about themselves than they possibly could. This is a part of an abiding cultural mystique about various types of counseling assistance.

For example, persons whose opening statement is, "I guess you're the kind of doctor who can tell if I'm crazy or not," may be making a joke to handle uneasiness but this still says something about their expectations. This is obviously an issue that individuals bring into counseling, and it should be perceived as such and dealt with as soon as possible. Counselors should not get involved in long explanations of their work. They should respond to the uneasiness of such persons and make it possible for them to work the issue through on their own. Straightforwardness also dispels the fog of mystique that obscures or makes counseling seem magical.

In the same way, persons who go to religious figures for counseling may have expectations based on a confusion of psychological counseling and religious ministry. This is a difficult area, one to which counselors who are also religious figures must be particularly sensitive. Otherwise, they may find that individuals expect absolution or a guarantee of salvation rather than an opportunity to explore themselves and their own behavior. Counselors who allow themselves to be perceived in a confused way hamper the counseling and multiply their own experience of stress.

Counselors must also be aware that they are almost always perceived as authority figures. The expectations that persons, quite silently and often unconsciously, bring to the relationship provide counselors with a good firsthand experience of the challenge of transference. Other people, in other words, react emotionally toward counselors as they have toward previous authority figures in their lives. It is clearly important to sort out these expectations and not to confuse the experience of transference with any direct feelings of the person toward the counselor. Such challenges are commonplace in the work of counseling. The sooner counselors learn to understand and appropriately incorporate them into their awareness, the more fully and easily they possess themselves and the more effectively they carry out their work. While opening themselves to the range of expectations that may be brought by others, counselors need to check off their own expectations and the role they may play in giving form to the counseling activity.

It is possible for counselors, even against their best intentions or firm acts of their will, to look on people who darken their doors as problems they must solve so that they can get back to other work. To perceive others as interruptions in one's otherwise busy schedule is an attitude that can drastically affect the course of counseling. Counselors who find themselves looking at a person as "just another case" have abundant material for exploring their own inner attitudes. Such counselors may be overtaxed by a larger number of clients or patients than they can effectively handle. Admitting this may be difficult, but it is also therapeutic.

Some counselors, laboring under the urge to save everybody, diminish their capacity to assist anybody when they are worn down or worn out by the excessive burdens they pile onto themselves. They should investigate the expectations they make on themselves in the work of counseling. Until these expectations are understood, the helpers will be affected by them without understanding why. A failure to admit our own expectations may be a prime source of stress for us in our counseling work. A prudent modification of schedule — even though it seems to admit some partial defeat or at least a lack of omnipotence —

is far more sensible than losing our footing because of the unbalanced burdens we heap upon ourselves. Helpers should examine their own expectations if, for example, they are surprised or thrown off balance by the person who comes for help. If they find that the person is not at all what they expected, counselors should wonder why. This may lead them to a healthy survey of the role of their own expectations and how these affect their attitudes in the counseling process. By such reflection, helpers can free themselves from much of the unnecessary stress that builds up when factors, generated from within themselves, remain unnoticed and unremedied.

Hostile Persons

Counselors should prepare in advance for the highly likely possibility that some persons will test out their reactions right from the start. The opening moves of such a tactic are usually very revealing, and helpers should not automatically disregard or dismiss such statements or symbolic actions. Hostile clients may, for example, act aggressively as soon as the curtain rises on the interview. How counselors handle what constitutes an attack may have a marked influence on the effectiveness of the subsequent counseling.

Persons who enter the room and seat themselves in the chair that is obviously meant for the counselor give a clear message that cannot be ignored. What would the helper do in such a situation? This outright challenge may come from levels of consciousness of which the person is not aware. It is conceivable that the counselor could become defensive, as people do when they are attacked symbolically. When people try to pick a fight — and they can do this in many ways besides sitting in the counselor's chair — helpers must place this provocation into a larger frame of reference. This meaningful gesture telegraphs a person's typical style of dealing with everybody. Counselors should deepen their sensitivity to the possible meanings of the assault while maintaining self-composure and avoiding overreaction.

Counselors must steadily learn from such interview experiences. To take the bait by becoming angry in such a situation signifies a surrender to the manipulation of the person who is only revealing to us a fair sample of typical behavior. Few things increase counselors' stress more rapidly than being drawn almost naively into a power contest at the very beginning of a relationship.

A variant of such aggressive testing of helpers is found in the individuals who inquire, in skeptical tones, about whether the counselor really has the training or the experience to help them. This direct challenge to their competence to participate in the interview can unbalance helpers unprepared to deal with it, especially if, as it often does, it touches some nerve ending of their own insecurity. "Where did you go to school?" or "What special training have you got to help me with this problem?" can both irritate counselors and increase their stress. "How long have you been doing this kind of work?" or "You haven't had much experience, have you?" are very similar inquiries. These questions can upset even experienced counselors, so helpers, of whatever background, must be at peace with whatever training or experience they possess.

Counselors may find themselves suddenly caught up in a lengthy explanation of their training or justification of their competence. It is always a mistake to enter this quicksand of accepting and operating from a defensive and explanatory role. The important issue is to understand the significance of these questions and to respond to what motivates the inquiries rather than to their factual content. The meaning of these questions is found at a level beneath their conscious utterance. They should then be accepted and not responded to directly or responded to by keying the answer to the feelings beneath the question. This can be done simply and even gently with a statement that reflects a capacity to accept and understand the attack without responding in kind. Counselors may, for example, say, "You really want to get some information about me, don't you?" or "It seems important for you to examine my credentials."

The first moments of an interview, even when they are not marked by a subtle attack from a hostile client, still constitute a time of reciprocal stress. It is hard for persons to come and talk about their problems; it is also difficult for busy counselors constantly to readjust their emotional reactions in order to be open, accepting, and understanding toward the latest in the long line of people waiting for help. It is not unusual to detect some awkwardness in a situation that is not only novel for a client but also stressful for the counselor.

Instead of small talk, as has been noted before, it is always sensible to start with something that is real, with feelings that flow out of the context in which the counselor and the person have met each other, even if they do not know each other very well. The counselor must read the beginning of each interview with understanding and as much naturalness as possible.

If, for example, the person has been referred by another teacher in the school, the counselor may begin with some sentence that sets the stage for the interview very easily. "Your teacher tells me you have had some problems lately," is a sentence rooted in the reality of how this person got to the counselor's office. It is not imaginary or based on some effort to please or persuade the person to talk. This response recognizes the other's situation and recapitulates very briefly the manner in which the individual has been referred.

At times counselors have very little information about the person. They may have only the name of a stranger who finds it difficult to open up. Such a person may often ask, "How do I begin?" This inquiry can have many meanings and counselors find the correct one in the tones in which it is asked rather than in its literal content. It can be an expression of dependence or a declaration of genuine bewilderment about what to do in this new and unusual situation.

The counselor should respond to the emotional coloring of the statement, realizing that not all those coming for assistance are trying to test the counselor's skills and directly acknowledging the difficulty they express. It is simple enough, for example, to accept the uneasiness of others with some statement like, "Sometimes it is hard to talk about yourself, isn't it?" This puts both the person and the counselor more at ease, especially if the beginning problem is not rooted in some conflict in the other. Experience helps counselors tell the difference between those who are uneasy and those who use their uneasiness in a provocative way. They read others in their expressive language — in their feeling tone and in their facial expressions and bodily movements and gestures. The issues of resistance and reluctance will be treated in depth in later chapters. For the present, we are concerned with the garden-variety problem of how hard it is for people to talk about their own emotions.

Counselors may here be tempted by two extremes. At one pole they feel that they may never say anything, that they must never break the silence or communicate a sympathetic or understanding response until the other person takes the responsibility for the first remark. This "stone-face syndrome" is too rigid a posture for effective counseling. Not shaping itself to the practical, real-life situation, this martyrdom to an uninvoked principle often does more mischief than good. Counselors should never hesitate, if the emotional climate seems appropriate, to ask something as simple as this: "Can you tell me something about why you came?"

At the other extreme, helpers may be so overanxious to help the faltering person that they supply a bewildering number of possible leads or topics for them to discuss. This ends up confusing both the person and the counselor. If you post too many notices on a wall, it is hard to read any of them. Both extremes increase the stress of beginning a counseling relationship. This is, however, a stress that observant counselors can do something about for themselves.

As counselors develop experience, they trust their own reactions more, sensing that they can communicate interest and understanding in a human manner without needing to prove anything or to win any contest with the client at the beginning of counseling. Self-confident counselors avoid stereotypes or theoretical imperatives and let their own spontaneous reactions lead the way.

Endings

Since the counselor has arranged to see the person for a specified length of time (an hour, for example), there need be no unnecessary concern about reminding the person of this arrangement. This arrangement should be adhered to carefully, and the counselor should avoid unnecessarily shortening or lengthening the initial interview. The beginning interview sets the pace for those that follow, and very few individuals express much difficulty if the length of the appointments is handled in a prompt and straightforward manner.

Counselors may profitably remind the person near the end of the interview that a certain number of minutes remain in their meeting together. This can be done very gently and to good effect: "We have about five minutes left." This enables a person to bring things together and avoids the abruptness of suddenly stopping someone in the middle of an important statement. As noted earlier, it is not unusual for persons to produce important material near the end of the interview precisely because they know that the end is in sight. Indeed, some of their most significant self-explorations may be reserved for these closing moments. This possibility should not cause counselors to prolong the interview, but they should be prepared to deal in summary fashion with important closing statements and indicate that they can be talked about more at the next meeting.

The counselor, in other words, should try to bring together any loose ends in the closing moments. This can be done briefly, effectively, and with due respect for the feelings of the person seeking help. To bring an interview to an end is merely to place a relationship in the context of a broader reality. This is a healthy thing for both the person and the counselor. If it becomes a source of stress or struggle, helpers have an occasion to study their own reactions. They may discover evidence of an emotional involvement with the person that needs monitoring in order to keep the relationship in balance. It may also suggest conflicts that have not yet surfaced. These possibilities point to the helpfulness of reviewing each counseling interview at its conclusion and of making some notes about its significant dynamic movement.

It may also be helpful to write down questions about one's own re-actions. Self-reflection can frequently answer most of these inquiries, but it may at times be necessary to talk these things over with a col-league or with someone who can serve as a psychological supervisor. As counselors learn to take advantage of the difficulties they encounter in their work, they gain a freedom from such problems that enables them to be more effective with others.

In conclusion, the counselor should make clear arrangements for the next meeting and not leave it up to some chance arrangement by saying, "Call me about this," or "I'll be in touch with you about this." These are not casual let's-do-lunch matters, and few experienced counselors would ever give such vague signals. In the lives of busy ed-ucators or other professionals for whom counseling is not the whole of the day's activities, these somewhat amorphous arrangements are not uncommon. They can become prime sources of stress because they in-dicate that something is always left up in the air. The counselor who links one concluded interview with the time and place for the next one indicates a good sense of managing and minimizing the possibilities of misunderstanding and stress.

THIS WASN'T MY IDEA

S TRESS MULTIPLIES, especially for persons who must blend counseling with other professional work, when people do not seem to
want help after they ask for it. Such persons, by no means uncommon,
either quickly withdraw from counseling as if it were an ocean too
cold for swimming, or never get off the beach and into the water at
all. Such behavior can be confusing and frustrating because it strikes at
the heart of counseling and at the counselor's heart at the same time.
A twofold importance attaches to the issues connected with this phenomenon: such reactions have implications for the meaning and extent
of the help that may be given, and it may also affect the counselor's
own self-confidence and self-esteem. When people reject the counseling
they requested, some counselors automatically assume that it is *their*
fault. Quickly finding oneself guilty is usually as unnecessary as it is
destructive for conscientious helpers.

All persons who engage in counseling, on either a full-time or a part-
time basis, assist themselves and others by understanding the nature and
source of these derailments of the helping process. First, we distinguish
between two very different situations in which all counselors, sooner
or later, find themselves. These are *resistance* and *reluctance*, separate
realities that have the common result of blocking the progress of therapy. Exactly who come reluctantly for help, and how do they differ
from the resistant individuals?

In general, they are people who are sitting across your desk not
because they want to be there but because somebody else thinks that
they should. These individuals are present to reject rather than to avow
their need for counseling. Somebody else, with sufficient authority or
influence over them, has cast them in a role that they would never have
signed on for on their own.

A good sense of these persons emerges from examining the root
of the word *reluctant*. It comes from the Latin *reluctari*: "To struggle
against." Back in this stem's family of meanings their dynamic beats
like a pulse: "To wriggle." Like fish who did not seek the bait, these

people wriggle against being landed. Two important elements must be remembered in any discussion of the challenge they present to us.

First, reluctance is as common a problem for counselors as low back pain is for general physicians. Far from being an unusual phenomenon, reluctance may, in certain situations, be the rule rather than the exception. Dr. William Glasser, author of *Reality Therapy*, has described the universal experience in telling of his work as a school counselor. "They put you in a small room, about six by eight, and then they throw a kid at you and close the door."[1] The counselor is expected to take things from there and to return the student in improved shape to the school environment.

Second, reluctance on the part of individuals does not necessarily mean that there is something wrong. It is not necessarily the same kind of signal as *resistance* to therapy, which indicates a need to maintain repression in place, that is to say, the lid on inner conflicts. Not wanting to be in the presence of a counselor can be a natural and understandable response to a situation of which the individual is not the author. On the conscious level, it is understandable that persons who are not self-motivated — that is, not convinced that they need help — should present themselves as reluctant witnesses to what seems an unnecessary trial. When individuals do not want help, why should we be surprised when they express this sentiment in word and behavior?

This combination of features makes the reluctant person one of the most formidable sources of stress for counselors of every stripe and theoretical persuasion. The armies of the reluctant are found in many encampments, from schools to jails, but the emotional context of their appearance in the helper's office is frequently similar. Counselors, whether formally designated as such or not, are expected by others to "cure," "adjust," or otherwise "solve" a problem person. This weight of expectation from the sources of referral can be very great and can seem almost a test, as if they hadn't had enough already, of counselors' skills and resources. It is as if other people were implicitly saying, "You're supposed to be able to help others. Okay, prove it."

Added to these external expectations are those counselors may make on their own performance. Many counselors feel that they should be able to reach and change most of the persons who come to them. This is because they have high ideals, humanistic value systems, and optimistic outlooks from their training and reading that make them feel that they can constructively transform most of the persons who come to them. These, of course, are classic American ideas and ideals. These confident assumptions can lead to trouble for counselors just as surely as the unrealistic assumptions of diplomats lead to war. Reluctance resides primarily in the referred person, but counselors would help themselves by inspecting their own expectations about their work. Until they can come to terms with a semi-messianic conviction that they can help everyone, they may increase their own stress in ways not fair to themselves. Counselors may also have to retranslate the notion of help into a more modest and sensible concept. A little real help is a great deal of help. When counselors can accept that, they lessen their experience of stress and increase their chances of assisting other people in a positive way.

Meet the Reluctant

The reluctant may be described in terms of the settings in which they are found. For example, counselors who work in or with a school may find many young people coming routinely to their offices at the suggestion or command of someone else. Their appearance may be a function of various situations, ranging from academic counseling about appropriate courses to disciplinary cases in which the individual's behavior has caused a teacher or supervisor to "send" them to the counselor.

These referrals frequently solve the problem of those who recommend counseling by relieving them of a difficult item on their agenda through substituting presumed therapeutic counseling for some kind of punishment. Counselors in school also see students who puzzle administrative officials because of their poor attendance record, because of their failure in certain subjects, or because they are suspected of such behaviors as drug use. Students in danger of dropping out are often referred to the counselor's office along with those who are not living up to their potential in class performance. It has been suggested that a very high percentage of school counseling is nonvoluntary, that is, with decidedly reluctant students. The latter knock on the counselor's door because somebody else thinks this is a good idea. Some counselors spend most of their days dealing with students whose common sentiment is "This wasn't my idea."

There are many other settings in which enforced counseling is common. Those in ministry often find persons in their offices sent there by frustrated parents or relatives who hope that the religious counselor may be able to straighten out the behavior or attitudes of the one sent. The clergy are particularly exposed in this regard because they cannot, like members of other professions, pick and choose the persons with whom they feel they can be effective. Their ideals commit them not only to see everybody hauled up in the day's catch but to try to help them too. The jaws of this vise of commitment place enormous pressure on them. Many other counselors, because of institutional or societal regulations, find themselves in a similar position.

Is Forced Counseling an Oxymoron?

Counselors who work in community agencies, for example, must see persons referred by the courts, no matter what the motivation or attitude of these referred people may be. Judges, feeling themselves enlightened in the matter, dictate that prisoners, as a part of their sentence, must seek psychological assistance for their personal problems. Sometimes the possibility of parole is contingent upon the prisoner's complying with this regulation. It is obvious that such referrals may run a high risk of being pro forma arrangements. These individuals, with minimal, if any, internal commitment to change, must show up because of external motivation.

In recent years, legislators in many states have endorsed mandatory counseling for psychiatric patients — usually suffering from psychosis — who do not cooperate in their outpatient treatment and may, in fact, pose some risk to the community. An increasing number of states allow for outpatient "commitment," so to speak, for these individuals. This forces them to "accept" treatment at an outpatient mental health center.[2]

Certain states and other jurisdictions demand that married couples contemplating a separation or divorce must see a marriage counselor for a prescribed number of visits before taking any further steps. As the century turned, legislation was introduced in Colorado requiring all those applying for divorce to undergo a year of marriage counseling before the divorce could be granted.[3] Some religious denominations require people below the age of twenty-one to accept a specified term of marriage counseling before approving their marriage plans.

All these people, who may be very different in background, interests, and personality features, share reluctance-to-referral in common. They are not asking for counseling; they are sentenced to it.

Counselors who deal with such unwilling persons come to recognize a wide variety of behaviors that tell the same story and offer the same challenges. These against-their-will seekers of help may, for example, express themselves eloquently in silence. This silent communication can be unmistakable and may register on counselors unprepared for it in an intense way. Such periods of silence include expressive gestures, such as shrugs of the shoulder, and other messages telegraphed through body language. Sometimes the reluctant, by doing something as simple as fiddling with a loose button on a jacket, express their genuine removal from the counseling situation. They are there, but they make us feel that they are really somewhere else.

Hostility has many vocabularies besides silence. "This wasn't my idea," the person says, and the room fills with the imagined sounds of forces engaged on a field of battle. This hostility can be raw and unprocessed, but it can also be subtle, as when the person senses just how to tease the counselor or how to go through the motions of counseling while frustrating it at the same time. Some of the reluctant have been referred so frequently for help that they are wise to the system and perceive each succeeding counselor the way a scarred old bull may regard a young matador. They know how to lead the counselor by telling colorful stories that are more fiction than fact. They play the role of productive and cooperative clients on the surface while withholding or shutting themselves down completely within, much to the exasperation and frustration of the counselor. One is reminded of the famous cartoon, drawn when America was just beginning its romance with psychoanalytic concepts, of the young prisoner being led from an interrogation room. He turns to speak to another young prisoner just being led into it. "Tell them your mother beat you," he says with a knowing smile.

Others make it clear that they do not want to be there by distracting behavior that gets silly at times in a self-conscious way but that, nevertheless, achieves the goal typical of the reluctant armies: it foils or defeats the helping process itself.

Beneath Reluctance

Nonvoluntary referrals may share many motives in common with all persons who are not motivated to deal with their problems or to change themselves. The only difference, of course, is that they find themselves where they do not want to be, in the helping situation. It is helpful to explore some possible explanations of why people balk at counseling.

The reluctant resist the idea of facing things that they do not wish to examine or admit about themselves. These may not be causing them enough subjective anxiety to move them to seek help; in fact, their behavior may be getting them some secondary gains that tend to reinforce it and therefore they are reluctant to deal with it. We recall our notion that the things that drive us crazy about others are the things that are keeping them sane.

Talking to a counselor frequently involves a loss of self-esteem — which may already be a basic aspect of the individual's problem — because it seems tantamount to admitting that they cannot handle it on their own, that, in some way, they have failed. America's culture, for example, still endorses an aging masculine ideal of keeping one's problems to oneself. In certain institutional settings, seeing the counselor is what you do when there is something wrong with your head. Going to see the doctor becomes an advertisement for one's painful failure.

Some individuals are referred for counseling as a result of their being against-the-establishment-in-general. As they act out against their setting — or against any symbols of authority — they become annoying to the institution or the enterprise and are referred with the admonition that "You'd better get your thinking straightened out on this." The counselor's office may merely provide an extended and well-lighted stage on which the individual can act out even further, employing dramatized reluctance as a new weapon against the expectations of the uncongenial establishment.

This creates circumstances in which counseling failure is easy. This is especially true for new counselors who bring to their work high expectations on their performance. They are vulnerable, therefore, to reluctant individuals who will not cooperate and who may, by their behavior, slowly pick apart the substance of the counselor's self-confidence. Inexperienced counselors frequently try too hard to do good or to do well, investing too much in succeeding and not enough in understanding the underlying dynamics of the counseling relationship. They sometimes live with the fear of meeting a noncooperative person because, having been taken two out of three falls by one, they are not eager to go to the mat with another.

Sometimes counselors, whether experienced or not, encounter difficulties when they project the person's reluctance onto themselves personally and feel it as rejection. They then blame themselves for the counseling's not succeeding and, taking too much responsibility for its being positive or negative, they do not sort out the elements of the relationship's emotional exchange; they feel trapped or engulfed by the experience.

It is very helpful for counselors dealing with such persons to accept them as reluctant or as uninterested in counseling. The key to any kind of success in counseling is our capacity to let people be exactly who and what they are in our presence. If we try to transform them into cooperative seekers of help when they are constitutionally the opposite, we impose a demand that interferes with the counseling's ever getting started. We treat feelings of reluctance, in other words, in the same way we would treat any other emotions expressed by those who come for help. It is useless and unnecessary to get into a psychological wrestling match with nonvoluntary persons or to present ourselves as extensions of the environment or the "system," as they see it, that propelled them into our offices in the first place. It may be easy to fail, but it is not difficult to succeed if we keep clearly in mind the notion of accepting them as *persons* rather than as cases we must solve or converts we must make. If we cannot see that acceptance is the response of choice, we may well explore the reasons for this attitude and for our outlook on reluctant individuals in general.

The pressure involved in dealing with these reluctant persons is often associated with the context in which counselors work with them. Counselors who are part of a larger institution, like a school or a prison, may find that their function is presumed to serve institutional ends as much as individual needs. No one thinks this out clearly or writes regulations about it; it is the accepted organizational imperative in almost any institutional setting. All helpers who have institutional affiliations must be aware of this situation-specific condition in order to survive and work effectively. Institutions, in other words, process all experience to fit their own contours; they need to accomplish their ends and this becomes, through no one's fault, a compelling and consuming but impersonal exercise. Institutions, whether they are universities or churches, expect other people to adjust to them, and this includes counselors. This fact creates an immediate stress for the helpers whose philosophy of counseling commits them to serving the individual rather than to implementing institutional policies in regard to other persons.

This individual-versus-institution dilemma creates an abiding tension in the life and work of a variety of helpers. It cannot be totally eliminated any more than institutions can be persuaded to transform themselves so that the individual good is always the goal of their functioning. Counselors must try to view this difficulty in perspective in order to meet their own expectations as well as those of the encompassing institution.

Such challenges are also ethical dilemmas. When a counselor is a double agent, in a sense, because of a commitment both to the institution and to the individual, which loyalty has the higher priority? This issue has become more complex in recent years because of the intensified constraints from administrative and financial demands of the institution with which the helper is affiliated. The sensible rule of thumb is always to consider the welfare of the individual as primary and, in circumstances in which this cannot be implemented, to inform the person with whom one is working of the competing interest and conflict.

Sometimes, just or unjust, right or wrong, there are situations and relationships in which we cannot effectively change other things or other people. The only thing we can do is change something about ourselves; if that is all we can do constructively, then that is what we should do. It may be a very small change but one that allows more fresh air and sunshine into the situation than it would otherwise enjoy. Small, positive changes in ourselves can be significant when nothing else can be done to alter circumstances or reality.

It is a much better alternative than getting angry at uncooperative persons or dialing out those who give us nothing but static. It is certainly better than backing away from the people whose presenting hostility makes us defensive. Counselors who deal with reluctant clients by trying to win them over only add to an already difficult problem. Neither is it helpful to attempt to transform negative feelings rather than to explore them with those possessing them. Such reactions will not really work but will increase the stress of the situation.

Many counselors have simply not had sufficient training to deal easily or skillfully with reluctant individuals. They may seek additional training or supervision, or at least read and reflect on this problem if only to avoid some of the pitfalls common in these commanded relationships.

What to Do When Others Don't Want to Do Anything

Counselors may begin by examining themselves, not punitively but with some understanding. They may ask without histrionics, "What is this person doing to me?" and "What am I doing in response or perhaps in retaliation?" We need a *feel* for the flow of the relationship so that we may judge whether we are allowing ourselves to be trapped or if we are provoking added reluctant behavior by what we are doing. We may well focus on the source of reluctance to see if we are rewarding it in some way and therefore strengthening and extending it.

The primary task is, of course, to deal with others' reluctant feelings instead of merely getting angry or attempting to coax or cajole them out of having them in the first place. Fundamentally, we must accept the individual as unwilling or uninterested in seeing us. When we can catch and convey an understanding of the way the reluctant others perceive the situation, we may relieve at least some of the distress we experience with them. This also reveals more of our own wholeness — for nothing can be faked here — and of our capacity to understand them while remaining separate from them. This also permits individuals to experience themselves in relationship to a concerned person rather than to a functionary of a remote bureaucracy.

It may be such persons' first such experience of being recognized and accepted as individuals with feelings and rights that are completely their own. This defuses the situation, takes the reward out of any behavior that may be designed to bait or to defeat the counselor, and may open up the possibility of such individuals' exploring their own previously unexamined reluctance. If we are not defensive, individuals may learn that they need not be defensive either. As their now less necessary defenses collapse, these persons can take a closer look at the reluctance within themselves.

The emphasis is on dealing with the reluctance as a mutual exploration of a serious matter. The counselor takes others seriously and does not engage in trying to win them over or in other such unproductive behavior. If nothing more is accomplished than that the parties to the counseling perceive each other in a more personal and less official way, small but substantial progress has been made, making further progress possible.

Counselors should explain the process of counseling so that it does not seem strange or mysterious to others. The reluctant may never have allowed themselves to learn anything about the way counseling ordinarily works. As it is explained to them — especially when they feel they are being taken seriously — they may feel a lessening of their own reluctance to participate.

We may also set up a brief contractual arrangement with reluctant individuals, offering them a series of appointments at a certain time in order to explore whether they wish to go on or not. We may find it helpful to explain to reluctant persons some of the various aids to self-knowledge that we can give them. These persons may become interested in taking certain psychological tests that may provide helpful information about themselves and may assist them in dealing with the roots of behavior that brought them to the counselor's office in the first place.

Reluctant clients must be recognized for exactly what they are: people who do not want to be in our office and who need to be accepted and understood as such before any real progress can be made.

Envoi

Dewald sounds a positive note after acknowledging that some people cannot benefit from counseling: "Such a relationship frequently represents the first sustained experience the person has ever had with a consistently accepting, helpful, emotionally stable, and effective person who is himself capable of adapting to life's stresses. By his active interest, concern, participation, and if necessary, environmental interventions in the problems the patient faces, the therapist presents himself as a model for problem solving."[4]

– 12 –

I WON'T DANCE,
YOU CAN'T MAKE ME

W E HAVE ALREADY EXAMINED RELUCTANCE and here we explore resistance and strategies with which to deal with it. "Resistance" describes an attitude on the part of the person that seems to fight the treatment. It is the motive for the famous line ascribed to fictional doctors, "You're fighting me." People resist treatment in order to stay the same, that is, to maintain their repressive defenses so that they need not look at the truth about themselves and can therefore keep anxiety at bay.

The Faces of Resistance

Resistance, as psychoanalyst Paul Dewald describes it, includes "those psychic functions within the patient which are actively opposed to the therapeutic task of bringing unconscious material to conscious awareness, and of modifying old behavior patterns in favor of newer and more appropriate patterns of integration."[1] Resistance arises as a heckler does to interrupt the speaker who is getting too close to a threatening truth. This protest against progress is usually carried out without any conscious planning on the part of the person and is expressed in symbolic ways that the alert counselors should be able to recognize.

Resistant individuals are not necessarily directly resisting the counselor; they are not even necessarily consciously resisting the idea of getting well. Resistant individuals do not want *any* changes to occur; they do not want *any* rearrangement of the dynamics within themselves. They attempt to preserve and hold on to ways of acting that, even if obviously full of shortcomings, nevertheless manage to satisfy them and help them to adjust to life even if in a psychologically crippling way. The symptoms exhibited by these people do not constitute

111

Types of Resistance

- Repression resistance: prevents awareness of the conflict
- Transference resistance: identifies with the counselor instead of resolving the conflict
- Secondary-gain resistance: fails to relinquish the benefits of the illness
- Repetition-compulsion resistance: needs to unconsciously reinforce punishment

---

an ideal solution to their problems, but they at least enable them to hold themselves together and ward off anxiety.

Nor should we perceive resistance as something bad or morally deficient. As Dewald observes, "Earlier...the concept of resistance was equated with the patient being uncooperative, and resistances were seen as something bad, to be removed as soon as possible so that treatment could continue. The recognition that resistances chiefly occur unconsciously was one of the major pieces of clinical data which forced the reorganization of psychoanalytic theory."[2]

Freud discussed several types of resistance besides this main one in which the central feature is the effort to maintain *repressive* defenses in place. He mentioned, for example, the *transference resistance*, through which persons identify with the counselor instead of resolving their inner conflicts. Such individuals may be looking for the counselor's affection or, in certain situations, may even be trying to compete in some subtle way with the therapist.

Another form of resistance occurs when people are unwilling to give up what psychiatry describes as the *secondary gains* of being sick. These include attention, freedom from ordinary occupations, and other benefits that sometimes accompany affliction. Still another variety is found in those who resist positive treatment because, at an unconscious level, *they wish to continue to punish themselves.* They do this by refusing to give up their painful symptoms.

The Sounds of Silence

Resistance ordinarily manifests itself in the person's style of communicating. One of the most common ways in which this occurs is through *silence.* A person who comes for help and who does not or will not talk can raise the stress level of a counseling interview considerably. Even experienced counselors may find it difficult to tolerate this, especially if they are unfamiliar with the deeper meanings of resistance.

What do counselors do in this situation? Do they make the relationship into a tug-of-war by waiting out the person grimly? Or do counselors try to coax or manipulate the person into speaking, often thereby getting themselves into an impossible position in the relationship? It is easy enough for counselors to react in these ways. The most effective response, however, and one that is consistent with the best professional counseling attitudes, is to make an effort to hear the person in the silence itself. Many feeling tones may be communicated even when there are no sounds from the voice of the other person. Many messages are delivered to our senses during and through the other's resistant communication. The feelings are there and, as some people say, one can almost touch them or cut them with a knife in certain situations. It is better to try to sense what these may be rather than to enter into a combat mode with the other because they make us angry.

Listening carefully, counselors may pick up the tones of hostility in the very presence and nonverbal gestures of the person. The counselor may also hear other things, such as confusion and uncertainty. Our response should be to this predominant tone. For example, if the tone is one of confusion, we may ask, "It seems very hard for you to get your bearings in here." If the individual bristles or otherwise seems hostile, we may appropriately say something like this: "You seem to be mad at the very idea of being here." The advantage of such statements is that they are directed at the feelings rather than at the person. They make it possible for the other to take a look at these feelings along with the counselor. That can provide the beginning of more positive counseling.

Recognizing and responding to resistance requires sensitivity and skill. Inexperienced counselors, quite like rookie ballplayers flustered into errors by the tough old professionals around them, sometimes make mistakes that only add to their own subjective experience of stress. This happens, for example, when counselors make a direct attack on the resistance, especially if they take it personally or if they think that the other person is deliberately and consciously trying to circumvent them. To ask something directly like, "What's the matter with you that you can't say anything to me now that you're here?" illustrates the kind of response that may deepen rather than resolve the silence. Attempting to understand and to respond to the other individual is demanding work and remains the most significant aspect of

the counseling. Counselors help themselves in doing this by seeing the silence within the context of the individual's overall personality.

At times, overeager counselors, wanting the other person to be able to participate at least minimally in the counseling, begin to ask questions that demand only a yes or no answer. This strategy is also dangerous because it implies clearly that such counselors are taking responsibility for the success of the counseling on their own shoulders. Whenever we take unto ourselves major responsibility for progress we encourage passivity in the other. If we do the work, the other person does not have to. This complicates the problem because it rewards the person for being resistant.

It is also a mistake to trample all over the communication in some effort to improve it. This happens when counselors, for whatever motivation, begin to talk about themselves or to interrupt the silence prematurely. When there is a direct attack on the silence rather than an effort to understand it, this is almost certain to create more silence and, therefore, more discomfort and distress for both participants in the counseling.

Other styles of resistance that a counselor may meet in the course of a day's work include the following:

The Laugher

This person treats everything lightly, staying on the surface of even the counseling relationship in order to stay away from the material that would multiply anxiety if it were ever discussed more clearly. Such laughing individuals never light down for very long on any subject and the smiles and jokes are not substantial or rooted in genuine experience. The laughter is a defensive distraction.

The Talker

This individual talks constantly, the verbal barrage achieving the same purpose as the laughter described above. Both the laughers and the talkers keep at a safe distance, protecting their emotions from involvement, and escaping any serious commitment to the counseling process. What are we to do when such resistance emerges?

The principle to be applied remains the same: We should attempt to understand the persons beneath the laughter or the excessive talking. How can we reach them so that they may be able to lower these defenses just a little bit? In order to do this we must make some genuine commitment of ourselves to them, one that recognizes their difficulty and that does not threaten them by judging them as consciously uncooperative. We may say, for example, "I wonder why you are making it so hard for us to really meet each other, or to talk seriously to each other" or some other statement that directs the other's attention *to the process* and at the same time does not indict the other too severely *as a person*. It is an effort at a mutual recognition of a difficulty.

The same approach may be used with persons who, in small and sometimes undetectable ways, hesitate, stop, interrupt themselves, or shift the emphasis of their remarks whenever they get close to emotional pay dirt. Our task as counselors is not to trap them, pointing out what they are doing and thereby making them more defensive. It is better for us to sense the struggle that is going on and to respond to this by saying something like, "You seem all tied up," or "You don't seem to feel free to talk about yourself very easily."

The Intellectualizer

The defense of intellectualization is a natural for a therapeutic process that is built on verbal communication. It is almost an occupational hazard. "Intellectualization" refers to the manner in which some persons talk about their problems with apparent clarity and in great detail but without much emotion. They drain away their emotions by abstracting their problems. They do not sound like resisters because they are speaking about serious personal subjects. They are doing it from a distance, however, and the most important clue is the fact that their feelings do not seem to be present.

When we are new at counseling we may have difficulty in recognizing such intellectualization and responding to it effectively. It must be dealt with without destroying the other person, who is, after all, not indulging in it as a matter of conscious choice. We can communicate understanding by saying something like, "We seem to talk and talk but not really get anywhere." Understanding counselors also remember not to encourage intellectualization by indulging in it themselves. It is very easy, and at times tempting, to use jargon or to retreat into psychological abstractions for reasons of our own. We should not be surprised if the other person picks up our style and examples and uses them against us.

An effective way to discourage the use of intellectualization is to refrain from asking questions that begin with the word and interrogative thrust of "Why?" Often, people do not know *why* something happened or why they behaved as they did on some occasion. They may respond to this probing style by becoming more defensive, especially if they think that we expect them to be able to answer *why* they feel a certain way or *why* they did or did not do something else. We do better to ask, "How did this happen?" or "What was going on when this event took place?" Such inquiries diminish defensiveness and allow other persons to explore the details of the significant event or feelings in their lives.

The Generalizer

This very effective form of resistance is displayed by individuals who avoid tying their feelings down to any specific subject or person. As long as they can continue in general terms, they can approach their emotions without making them concrete or associating them too closely with their real lives. This is not the time — it probably never is — to use a variation on that familiar line, "You're fighting me." Any such statement is always taken as an attack. It is much better to try to react with an appreciation for the other's difficulty by saying something like this: "You seem to talk in general about your job — or your wife, or your children...."

If we can point to the area in which persons are generalizing, we demonstrate our understanding of the difficulty that others experience and make it possible for them to break through themselves. Counselors who speak only in generalizations can expect to get this same abstract style back from other persons. We also want to avoid getting caught in the traps that resistant persons can spring when they finish a sentence by saying, "You know what I mean." It is always better to say that we do *not* know what the other means rather than to give the false impression that we do. We can never get that ground back once we have surrendered it.

The Scene Maker

Persons have no more clever or effective way to interfere with the progress of counseling than through making an emotional scene. Like a lawyer with more bravado than facts, individuals can sometimes weep, pound their fists, or get wrathfully indignant in order to keep away from the kind of material that might make them change. Making a scene is a way of getting attention, but it is also a way of avoiding something else, something that would be more painful by far. Persons who get angry in counseling may, for example, be covering shattered internal feelings that they strongly resist examining. We cannot afford to become angry when others do this to create a diversionary action. Here our counseling skills are tested, for we must understand others at levels deeper than those of the dramatic scenes that they engineer. The response must not be to the anger or indignation but to the inner reason that makes the person choose the noisy demonstration as a defense.

The Seducer

Seductive behavior by those seeking help can be disturbing, especially if we are inexperienced and, therefore, it can easily achieve its desired effect of slowing down progress. Seductive behavior that is intended to be disturbing can have many meanings. It suggests that the other, quite unconsciously, may be trying to flatter us (and we can be flattered by it) to get our attention or care. This may also be a maneuver to seize power in the situation by changing the relationship and taking charge of its dynamics. In either case this resistance strategy can be very effective and very stressful, especially for counselors who are unfamiliar with it and who may dangerously misread it. They should recognize it as a form of resistance and not take it personally at all. That is to say, they should not conceive of themselves as suddenly sexually attractive, or imagine that the greatest crisis of their counseling career has suddenly arrived. It is a tale of resistance told many times in the lore of counseling.

As with the other resistance strategies, seduction is understood best in terms of the total personality of the other. Such persons say, in a dramatic way, "I do not want to go ahead with the real business that I should be taking care of in therapy." Such persons are definitely not saying, "I find you irresistible," or "I want to spend the rest of my life with you." It is deflating in a healthy way for counselors to face the reality of such situations.

Acting Out

Sometimes others engage in "acting out" and attempt to mitigate the influence of the counselor by talking to other people about their problems. If they talk to others, they need not talk deeply or directly about their difficulties to us as their counselor. That is one of the reasons that bartenders sometimes hear so much of other people's troubles. It also explains why some people go to their parish priest or their internist and talk about difficulties they should be discussing with their counselor or vice versa. All possible parties to this kind of resistance should be aware of its existence and be ready to deal with it therapeutically in their own experience. It is quite easy for some persons to enlist the support of outsiders by saying that their psychiatrist or other counselor is unsympathetic and that they need a new kind of help. If they try this on us, our proper response is to avoid being manipulated by their story and to refer them back to discuss their problems with their original therapist. The original therapist must also recognize what is going on and not become so irritated that he or she cannot respond with the kind of sensitive understanding that such a maneuver deserves.

The Counselor's Involvement

Many other subtle behaviors exist that spring from or are functions of the relationship — and some aspect of transference — between us and those we see. These may quietly slow down the progress of therapy if we counselors are unaware of how they embody these styles of resistance.

Individuals who switch appointment times frequently may have a good reason for this. On the other hand, we should examine this behavior, which is always explained to us in terms of external factors. We, the counselors, may be more involved than we at first think. We need to review all behavior related to making, breaking, or arriving late for appointments. If we try to feel our way into what is really going on, we ask, without any quick readiness to retaliate in kind, whether such persons are trying to avoid moving ahead or whether they are trying to seize control of the therapeutic situation itself. In both cases we are involved because the person is doing something to us in order to modify the pace of the counseling. This phenomenon obviously needs careful reflection and exploration if we are to avoid becoming victims of it.

At times the individual may unconsciously attempt to compete with the therapist. If we counselors find others trying to "one-up" us or "put us down," we may safely suspect that subtle resistant behavior is present. We need to take a hard but sensitive look at such incidents to catch the emotions behind them that arise from the unconscious levels of the other's personality.

It is a part of wisdom to acknowledge that some people are not good candidates for counseling or therapy. This is so because of their personality structure. People who were once called "psychopaths" and are now termed "antisocial personalities" seem to have great difficulty in establishing any kind of meaningful relationships with other persons. Such persons quickly manifest their resistance when, for whatever reason, they meet with a therapist for counseling. Counselors who are unaware of such personality difficulties may feel that they have failed personally when they cannot reach persons who are psychologically inoculated against relationships. That is to take too much responsibility for a situation that is intrinsically self-defeating.

To sum up these reflections, it is clear that the therapist must work with those who come for help in order to explore the nature of resistance. Sensitively working through the resistance may be the first step to a deeper, more effective, and longer lasting therapeutic change. If the resistance is misunderstood or mishandled, counseling may be sidetracked and its purpose completely defeated. It is important, then, to listen to the whole person and not to respond to the fact that the resistant behavior irritates us. We counselors need to recognize resistance as a form of defense that cannot immediately or easily be torn down or eliminated. Such defenses have important purposes in the lives of troubled people; they employ them in order to avoid a deeper and more truthful look at themselves. Counselors who see whole persons and respect their defenses will manage quite effectively the stress of the inevitable resistant behavior.

Supportive Counseling and Uncovering Therapy

In general, nonprofessional counselors operate in the supportive mode, an immensely helpful realm that they manage by not prying the lid off the unconscious or, as the technical manuals put it, "allowing the repression to remain in place." In uncovering, or insight-directed, therapy, the objective is to enter the unconscious and to bring its contents into the open. Can we maintain these distinctions as we deal with the various forms of resistance?

Dewald answers the question for us in this way:

During the course of insight-directed treatment, if the patient were to become restless part way through a session and suggest that he wished to leave, the immediate tactical maneuver might be an attempt to oppose his leaving through an interpretation of the wish to leave as resistance. During the course of a supportive treatment relationship, if the same thing were to occur, the therapist would not oppose the patient's wish to leave as firmly, and might even support it by an intervention such as, "If there is nothing else you feel like talking about today, perhaps we should stop early."[3]

If, in supportive therapy, this behavior should become repetitive and, therefore, threaten the counseling altogether, we should, with the care of a person listening to the tumblers fall inside a lock, explore the meaning of the behavior without throwing the door to the unconscious completely open. This can be discussed in terms of the patient's conscious frame of reference even if the deepest reasons for it are not uncovered.

– 13 –

PLOTTING OUR COURSE

W E LIVE IN AN ERA, it may one day be written, in which a passion
to locate *where* we are came to rival our curiosity about *who* we
are. Postmodern devices, named after premodern points of reference,
such as North Star and On Star, and guided by satellites, were built into
automobiles while others, termed Global Positioning Devices, could be
carried in the hands of travelers. In counseling and psychotherapy, we
avoid becoming lost and wandering away from our goal not by catching
a satellite beam from outer space but by exploring the inner space of
those with whom we work.

To be truly helpful, we need a good "fix" on the other person's
functioning. "Diagnosis," a sometimes formidable term, comes from
the Greek *gignasein*, to perceive, and *dia*, apart, and means, in familiar
synonyms, to discern or to distinguish. By diagnosing, we try to see
others clearly and apart from everyone else, so that we may better grasp
who and *where* they are and decide *what* we can do to keep them on
course to a helpful goal.

At times counselors think of diagnosis as an activity appropriate
to medicine or to some other specialty such as clinical psychology or
psychiatric social work. While professionals in these fields have special
training and tools to identify and classify the problems of others, we
all need some sense of the dynamics beneath the behavior of those
we help. Whether they aver to it or not, most helpers, especially if
counseling is incidental to other responsibilities, make "working" or
informal diagnoses of those with whom they work. They do not want
the person to be lost, and they do not want to become lost themselves.
Overworked counselors may not have the time for careful evaluation or diagnosis according to the classical model of the textbooks.
Occasionally they also lack the skills or the experience to deliver a
complete or sophisticated discernment of the other's problem. Nonetheless, we are not easily excused from plotting the other's position if
we are committed to being of real assistance.

Thou Shalt Not Judge

Afloat unexamined for many years on the nation's cultural updrafts is a vague principle that we should never judge anybody else, that we should let others make their choices, whatever they are, without evaluating them morally or psychologically. This romantic democratization of social perception cannot, however, be so generalized as to rule out common sense in helping other people. While counselors wisely hesitate to evaluate the moral quality or desirability of the behavior or motivations of those with whom they work, this does not rule out intelligent and informed reflection about how others, given their difficulties, may best be helped.

To forge sensitive judgments about these individuals without condemning them as persons is a serious obligation for the mature counselor. We have much to decide: Do we have the capacity and resources to help these other persons, and what assets and liabilities do they possess to manage themselves through life in general and this crisis in particular? The answers to these questions are eventually given, sometimes in the shipwreck of overambitious and underdiagnosed counseling, so we are wiser to find them before proceeding with our counseling.

The combination of overapplied democratic ideals, misapplied scientific objectivity, and half-applied political contentions that the problem lies in society or the "system" rather than in individuals also clouds the need for even a tentative diagnosis in helping others. Indeed, a sharpened sense of the way and the why of the function of others may be critical to the effective management of supportive treatment in which we strive to keep deeper dynamics from surfacing. One cannot easily do this without a good knowledge of what these dynamics are and how they are manifesting themselves in the life of the other.

No theoretical or practical approach can be safely applied to others without some understanding of their psychological structure. One size does not fit all. Proceeding without a sense of our true position in relationship to the actual position of others may involve us in serious miscues, as, for example, in behaving in a manner that seems friendly to us but may be perceived as highly threatening to someone with paranoid features. Counselors who, with good will, press a demand for closeness that the other cannot handle may lead to a blowup, as the person violently rejects the closeness, resulting in damage, not easily reversed, for both parties. Only amateurs who do not appreciate the subtleties of human behavior or the potential for harm move forward without the navigational aid of at least a tentative discernment of the functioning of others.

Nonprofessional counselors must meet and respond to many persons each week. What are the practical issues connected with diagnosis that we must explore in order to help others intelligently and responsibly?

When Diagnosis May Not Help...

Diagnosis does not help if it ends up placing distance between the helper and the one seeking help. This can occur when diagnosis is really an intellectual exercise played largely within the confines of the counselor's own personality. It happens in the amateur's approach in which a detective-story excitement of "figuring somebody else out" dominates the intention to help. The Hercule Poirot approach is not, of course, genuine diagnosis in any therapeutic sense, but rather is a response to the counselor's own need to keep people from getting too close. The intellectual assaying of another's strengths and weaknesses serves counselors who use it far more than those they are supposed to be helping. It gives them a false sense of where they are and how to proceed.

Diagnosis does not help if it becomes a formalized and self-conscious activity that robs counselors of the very qualities that are most important in assisting others: warmth, true acceptance, and a healthy spontaneity. Genuine diagnosis never comes out of a "cookbook style." The latter approach does more harm than good both to the person and the counselor.

This may occur when, to "save time," counselors employ structured interview protocols or questionnaires instead of interviewing the person. Such aids are meant to inform, not replace, the interview. Anything that gets between us and the other — that abstracts us or intellectualizes the conversation — leaves us outside the life of others, increasing our stress, and perhaps even making us gun shy because of diminished self-confidence.

It is very frustrating for well-motivated helpers to sense that they are not getting through to others even though they believe they know what is wrong with them. When diagnosis is awkwardly attempted, it has the classic bad effects that go with anything that is done poorly despite good intentions. From our own experience, we know that we are made uncomfortable by someone who seems to categorize rather than understand us.

...*and When It May*

Although there are times when attempting a diagnosis seems undesirable, it is clear that no counselor can fly blind; indeed, no conscientious helper wishes to do so. There are theoreticians who claim that even the most elaborate diagnosis does not change the person or the counselor very much, and that, in the long run, the course of the relationship will be determined by the capacity of both to experience it in a reasonably deep way together. There is something almost admirably open in this stance, but it is romantically naive to insist that a sensible diagnosis of the other's condition is of little or no value. Just as those who insist that no counseling can occur until diagnosis is complete exaggerate their claims in the face of life's practical demands, so those who make a principle of avoiding diagnostic inferences exaggerate in another direction. Responsible helpers need to have some sense of what is going on inside other persons in order to place themselves in an appropriate and helpful relationship.

This is important because of the manner in which certain disturbed or extremely anxious persons may distort or misinterpret our interest in them or our responses to them. One of the more important reasons for a diagnostic sense about others flows from our need to calibrate our responses in accord with this information. This can be done without sacrificing any genuineness and without becoming involved in manipulation. For example, counselors who sense that individuals have a paranoid flavor to their reactions may wisely temper their own natural friendliness to avoid its being misperceived by them.

As observed, paranoid individuals may become suspicious and uneasy with persons who appear to be assaulting their own inner castles by what healthy people would describe as openness. The counselors who do not monitor their interventions on the basis of sensible diagnosis only invite problems into what is already a highly stressful work. More detailed examples of how we may have prudent reasons to modify our behavior in the presence of certain kinds of emotional problems will be discussed in later chapters.

How Deep Is the Ocean?

Developing a feeling for the processes or dynamics that govern the behavior of others is not solely an intellectual problem; indeed, in a certain sense, honing such a feeling into a trustworthy instrument in counseling is an art in itself. It demands an intellectual understanding of psychological processes but it also requires our developing our sensitivity to emotional messages even when they come in whispers or half gestures. One need not be a poet to possess this capacity to sense the stirrings inside others and to use them to form reliable clinical judgments. Many things go into that hazy phenomenon we term clinical judgment; it is hazy, however, precisely because it is human and consists of a blend of reactions, intellectual information, and the kind of responses that are refined by experience and that cannot be easily or exactly specified.

This sounding board for the inner experience is like radar, receiving and echoing information that enables us to appreciate the quality and intensity of the process taking place in those transmitting the information to us. This capacity allows counselors to catch the live dynamics of others and to translate them with accuracy and sensitivity. The *depth* of their emotions is of crucial importance to us. It is possible to listen to the emotions of another person and to tune them, as one might a radio, too softly or too loudly. Every individual resonates at a certain pitch and, when we hear it without distorting it, we have a direct line to the dynamics to which we must respond.

Our best guide in this exploration of the internal life of the other person is the feedback we constantly receive in our steady relationship to them. In other words, as we react to the person as understood by us, we send out impulses that induce further responses from the other. In the waves that flood back to us, we find our best sense of how others not only function currently but how they structure their private worlds. As we sit closely with others we are permitted a view of their universe otherwise denied to us. This fundamentally nonverbal communication permits us to respond to others in ways that match who and where they are. This practical and artful form of diagnosis must become second nature to the counselor.

Obviously, we cannot assist others unless we are in contact with their real personalities, that is, with the dynamic factors that govern their behavior. These are not necessarily the same as the reasons they offer to explain their attitudes or actions. Neither are they the same as some notions we may have formed from previous experience or because we once worked with another person with remarkably similar difficulties. Diagnosis need not be understood as an elaborate and distancing method of assigning persons to psychological categories; it is simply getting as true and clear a picture of them as we can manage. It is getting them, as a great photographer does, in a pose in which their true personality is revealed. Doing this does not turn them into

objects but rather allows us to see them as subjects, as individuals in
their own right.

Such diagnosis improves our work with others, indeed, it makes it
possible. It is also helpful if we must decide whether they should be
referred to some other helping resource. An accurate diagnosis enables
us to balance our feeling for others with our own abilities to help them.
A crucial judgment with long-range implications is in order here. It can
never be made if we lack this feeling for the nature and depth of the
other's true psychological difficulty.

We can best help people — and ourselves — by getting them to the
right sources of help as soon as we make a judgment about their needs
and our own relative ability to respond to them. Sometimes counselors
regard a referral as an indictment of themselves; more often than not it
is an example of good judgment exercised at an appropriate moment,
a responsible professional decision.

Who May Be Diagnosed?

Many helpers never meet anyone whom they would classify as seriously
disturbed or in need of a different and more specialized kind of treatment than they can provide. This is partly because so many problems
are subtle and difficult to detect with a high degree of confidence; it is
also partly due to the fact that many individuals who need counseling
simply cannot be put very neatly into any diagnostic category. They
experience difficulty in adjustment or in coping with life — they may
drink too much or bicker with their spouses — but their basic problem
seems no greater or no less than that of the average person. These, in a
profound sense, are residents of the human condition: the people who
from time to time require some understanding assistance to regain their
composure and to take charge of their lives once more.

Persons in this category — and perhaps there should be a special
classification for the ordinary syndrome of facing life — do not fit into
textbook pigeonholes. They do not have hallucinations, nor do they
suppose themselves to be great historical figures. They have the garden
variety of human problems and deserve to be understood accordingly.
These people come to talk to old friends — their clergy, former teachers,
perhaps even bartenders — in their quest for a better grasp of themselves. That they are not classically diagnosable does not mean that we
should not try to understand them as sensitively as we can.

To realize the way individuals feel when they are caught in the web of
the human situation is a great and appropriate diagnostic gift to offer.

This is built on the same foundations of intellectual understanding and emotional sensitivity as are more elaborate diagnostic formulations. They feel — and we counselors may also feel — more like persons because of our effort to understand them simply but thoroughly.

Sensing the Spirit

Specialists tend to view others through their own profession's categories. Dentists may interpret our moods in terms of our teeth, internists in the vocabulary of our metabolism, and clergy in terms of our prayer life and religious tradition. There may be no area in which a sense of diagnosis is more appropriate than in sifting out emotional problems from those that may be termed spiritual. Confusion has existed in this area for a long time and, despite good intentions, it is not easily resolved. The need to explore this distinction, however, is real and illustrates a seldom cited but important justification for the process of diagnosis.

Spiritual problems do exist; one needs only to consult the daily papers or magazines for documentation of a widespread spiritual malaise that is complicated rather than abated by progress or affluence. In recent years, a renewed interest in, and practice of, spiritual direction has boomed in many countries. Spiritual problems, however, do not exist independent of human personality; they do not grow without roots in the person. A significant difficulty with sexual problems arises from their being discussed as if they existed in a world of their own, a planet we can chart and visit, that is independent of human personality. This is commonly referred to as "sex out of context" — sex, as it were, dis-integrated from the person who is sexual.

Spiritual problems may also be discussed in this disembodied or extrapersonality fashion. They, too, are, as we humans are, of the earth earthy, ever rooted in the same human soil from which all our difficulties grow. Spiritual illnesses cannot be spoken about out of context any more than sexual problems can. Diagnosis aims at understanding all the longings — whether for meaning or as a result of unresolved conflict — in the human situation that spring from this common ground of our being.

Sensible counselors will not quickly apply purely spiritual solutions — such as prayer and fasting — to problems that usually have deeper and more complicated origins. Diagnosis aims at understanding personality — including its spiritual and sexual dimensions — and makes sense only when these dimensions are seen in true and full perspective. Counselors cannot ignore a person's spiritual nature any more than the clergy can ignore a person's sexual nature. It is the person who suffers in these various areas and the person who needs to be understood in all his or her complexity. There is no great help in encouraging sexual behavior as a solution to spiritual pain, and there is certainly no lasting assistance in recommending spiritual remedies alone for sexual conflicts. A balanced and healthy diagnostic sense permits us to see the interrelated aspects of personality and to respond with the sensitivity that acknowledges and illumines the person's search of the self. A healthy attitude toward diagnosis always transforms people from numbers and categories into unique individuals.

Practical Issues

Making room for some diagnosis does not demand that we quickly probe deeply into the psychological wounds of other persons. Asking a great many questions from our own viewpoint may, in fact, interfere with our hearing the message that tells us best what we should know about other persons. Most anxious people want to talk when they first see us; they want to get their feelings out into the light and the air as best they can. To block the flow of these initial communications by inappropriate or ill-timed questions may interfere with counseling and with our best chance of diagnosing wisely.

Let other persons start where they wish; they will lead us in the right direction if we pay attention to what is being said. Diagnosis as discernment draws on all our capacities as we develop a pervasive human understanding of others. This is very different from harshly judging or yoking them with a psychiatric label from which they will never be free. Diagnosis is a living, interactional process whose strength depends on our awareness of how others struggle to deal with their conflicts and problems.

We listen first for the reason others give us for coming. The story of how other people get to our offices generally includes important information about their previous experience and the way others have reacted to them. An appropriate question to ask ourselves as we listen in an initial interview is, "Where do we hear the pain?" Closely related is, "What do they feel about this painful area?" How, in other words, do they see and experience their problem? We can then see their presenting problem — the reason they came — in the context of their own personalities and their ongoing lives. Here we get a sense of the general sweep of the others' psychological experience; this allows us to glimpse

Practical Historical Information

- Description of the current problem
- History of the problem
- Personal information — age, marital status, children
- Social history — family and nonfamily relationships, current living circumstances
- Occupational history — current occupation, education, job history
- Physical health
- Drug and alcohol use
- Previous counseling or psychiatric treatment

them in depth rather than just in cross-sections. Permit others to speak, and even in their silences and hesitations they will say much to help us understand them and their current functioning.

The counselor who wants to understand others is well-advised to count to ten before asking any questions at all. This restrains over-eagerness, curiosity, or the use of a question to cover up for not knowing what else to do. Questioning can back already anxious persons against the wall, making them raise their defenses against us so that it becomes more difficult to understand them. The manner of asking questions, and the sensitivity with which they are shaped and placed, not only carries a message of respect for them but also brings forth information vital to understanding their current functioning. Our inquiries, phrased in gentle tones, should be directed toward those parts of the other's story where the flares of hurt are burning. There is obviously a message in how we approach these sore points, and doing this gently but clearly assists others to clarify their problems both for themselves and for us. The best diagnosis arises in those moments in which both the counselor and the client learn together.

While we need not distract persons who are anxious to talk by asking them unnecessary or ill-timed questions about their life histories, there are basic items of information we should try to secure during or close to our first interview.

Many of these emerge naturally in the context of the story the person tells. If these do not surface in this fashion, however, the counselor should try to elicit the information in as warm and genuine a manner as possible. This information is not usually hard to get, especially if we match our questions to similar material in people's stories. These include their age, their marital status, and something about their family life and children. It may be helpful to know something about their parents, job history, current living circumstances, and whether they have had previous treatment or are having concurrent treatment. These provide the framework for a rich appreciation of the other's life.

Counselors are neither prosecuting attorneys nor members of senate committees; they are not trying to expose guilt but to understand the texture of the other's experience. In framing our questions there is hardly ever any need to ask *why*. This is asking for an explanation that most persons seeking help are unable to give in a rational or completely logical manner. They come for help in order to be able to answer this question for themselves. It is better to frame our inquiries in an open-ended fashion that decreases threat and allows others enough room to develop their answers in their own way. Our questions should be more like invitations to search themselves rather than subpoenas to produce evidence.

Counselors also need the opportunity to reflect on what they have heard and on their own manner of reacting to it. To reduce their own experience of stress they should try to build some time into their schedule in order to integrate the experiences they have with individual persons. This helps the diagnostic process. Counselors, in other words, need some perspective on their work in order to perceive those with whom they work distinctly and not have them fuse into some overall mass emotional impression.

To maintain the balance needed for healthy diagnosis, counselors often find a checklist of their own reactions helpful. Is this an emergency? That is a fair question if the evidence of the interview has revealed behavior on the part of the other that is increasingly agitated and destructive. In the light of this, for example, must some judgment be made about the place and number of future appointments or even the possibility of an early referral to other facilities?

One of the most important elements in a good referral is its timing. If counselors sense that others need more help than they can provide, the manner and moment of arranging for them to see somebody else becomes an important function of timely diagnosis. The referral should be made when counselors reach reasonable certainty about the seriousness of the psychological difficulty. The manner of referral should be gentle and constructive rather than a response that expresses the counselor's own anxiety about the other person's behavior.

It is also possible for some counselors to refer in an excited and premature fashion out of a sense of romantic emergency. This may well bewilder persons who come for help and make them feel worse about themselves; it may also be a kind of disowning response through which we make them feel that they are too sick for us to have anything to do with them.

An Extension of Understanding

The strong egalitarian emphasis of American and similar democratic cultures makes suspect any diagnosis that involves a presumed "expert" passing judgment on the behavior of another person. To presume so to diagnose seems a function of authoritarianism and a generally depersonalized attitude toward others. As previously mentioned, however, this need not be the case at all, and an appropriate effort to grasp the significance of another's symptoms can and should be an exercise in treating people with dignity and respect for their individuality.

Helpers sincerely committed to the good of those with whom they work are not trying to "get something" on their clients or to dominate them through categorization. Their attitude is best described as an effort to broaden and extend their understanding of others. When diagnosis is understood as an aspect of understanding another person, it reflects an appreciative closeness that is concerned and positive. The more deeply counselors understand the private world of others the less they need to distance themselves out of fear of them and the more easily will the relationship develop. Diagnosis and its recommendations are never threatening when they are offered in the context of concerned personal understanding. The healthy use of diagnosis is truly up to the counselor.

The steady effort to extend our understanding of others so that we have a feeling for them and their needs requires hard work and the self-awareness that keeps us free of emotional entanglement. Our commitment to increasing the freedom of others takes concentration, self-knowledge, and professionalism. In the long run, however, this intense approach is far less stressful for counselors than the uninformed groping in the dark that often characterizes imprecise relationships. Sensitive diagnosis makes us work harder at developing the practical understanding that is at the heart of effective counseling.

It is axiomatic that the counselor must be alert to the attitudes and behavior exhibited by individuals during interviews. These contain powerful signals about their condition. Even small gestures or statements — things we might not ordinarily pay much attention to — can contain big truths about how others view themselves. We need not jump at the first small revelation but make our judgments only when sufficient, consistent clues are gathered and integrated.

Some counselors may miss other manifestations of disturbance, or they may misread the ones they do observe, because of a lack of experience or a failure to integrate for themselves the impressions they gather in their relationships with others. Among the items the counselor should note are these: Are patients so deeply depressed that it is difficult to make contact with them? Is it difficult for them to speak about their problems? Such hints of depression need to be examined more closely. How deep is it and what overt behavior does it give rise to in their lives? Is the other person able to report the situation in a coherent way, with reasonable continuity and with some satisfactory sense of time or place? Where there is some interference with these aspects of their communication, counselors should take the possibility of major disturbance more seriously.

This is also true if there are obvious abnormalities in the way people talk about their lives or experiences. Persons who derail their narrative with a flight of ideas, one association leading in wild distraction to another, exhibit symptoms that demand careful evaluation. The same is true of persons who perseverate, that is, who cling to one concrete and inappropriate part of their narrative and cannot seem to get away from it.

A counselor must also ask if the emotions displayed by the other are appropriate to the events described. Any gap here prompts the counselor to listen more carefully to what the other is attempting to describe. No counselor should read things into the statements or the behavior of others that are really not there, but we cannot ignore indications of possible major difficulties. Questions of diagnostic judgment and prognosis are not answered facilely. We do not reduce another's stress or make progress in handling major symptoms by ignoring them; neither can we help if we pay no attention to our own informative reactions. Our diagnosis may need to be provisional, a working hypothesis in need of more evidence or confirmation by the judgment of somebody else. The tentative nature of a diagnosis does not lessen its significance, nor should it make a counselor hesitant to follow healthy instincts in developing it further.

Once counselors have a general feeling for others, they must ask: Am I the best qualified person to assist in this situation? Or am I unnecessarily taking over what might be done better by some other professional person? Am I well acquainted with the referral resources in my community? Do I want to get rid of this person because I am afraid? The answers to these serious questions come only from the counselor's willingness to pursue the possibilities of sensible diagnosis.

Counselors should develop some communication with the professional resources of their community. Too often this is done only under the pressure of making a referral and on the tardily sought word of someone else. Some preliminary relationship with other resources would increase self-confidence, lessen stress, and make the process of referral much easier on both the person and the counselor.

Counselors should learn to speak the professional language of diagnosis; the best road to this is through studying the descriptions in the *Diagnostic and Statistical Manual of Mental Disorders (DSM-IV-TR)*. Counselors can also expand their appreciation for diagnosis by making use of supervision when this is possible or through continuing education and reading.

– 14 –

DIAGNOSIS:
GOALS AND RESOURCES

THE AMERICAN DEMOCRATIZATION and popularization of therapy, or therapy-like experiences, has led to some blurring of professional identities as well as an equalizing of the relationship between professionals and those they serve. Despite the growing impression, spread more widely every day on television, that anybody can treat anybody else, the role of knowledge and experience remains central in counseling. Descendants of the French Revolution and capable of creating just as much chaos, many claim the title Citizen Therapist, but only the knowing may safely carry it away.

Well-informed diagnosis remains indispensable, however, as a deepening and refining of our efforts to understand other persons. It is, in fact, a way of taking them and their complaints seriously, of valuing and respecting them enough to be sure that we choose a course of treatment that matches their needs. Indeed, those who treat diagnosis casually dehumanize others by not making the effort to appreciate them individually, by eliminating diagnosis or using a prefabricated diagnosis and responding to everyone in some generalized fashion. Nonprofessional counselors can only profit, and those they help only benefit, from their developing their diagnostic skills. There are many reasons that this is of practical importance for them.

Speaking a Common Language

Over the past generation, the American Psychiatric Association has developed a manual of diagnosis that allows people from differing orientations and clinical settings to bridge their differences through using the same vocabulary to describe mental states. Its current version is the *Diagnostic and Statistical Manual IV-TR,* ordinarily referred to as the *DSM-IV-TR.*

The use of this manual for diagnosis accomplishes several purposes.

It provides a shared language for a wide spectrum of clinicians and researchers in a rich variety of disciplines, orientations, and settings. Among these professionals, we identify psychiatrists, other physicians, psychologists, social workers, nurses, counselors of various kinds, occupational and rehabilitation specialists, and public health statisticians. Any one of these can speak to any other in a mode that allows them to view the person being assessed as if through the same lens of conceptualization and understanding. Recently, this diagnostic system has also been used in the determination of insurance reimbursements for various professional services.

This common nomenclature allows professionals to study and conduct research on individuals in terms of these specific diagnostic categories. The results serve as the basis for what are called "evidence based" treatment decisions. These latter, sensible protocols are good fits, so to speak, for persons experiencing this or that disorder.

For most mental problems, the cause, or *etiology*, is unknown. The numerous theories about the origins of specific disorders usually depend on the observer's theoretical orientation. In this book, we describe these disorders from the psychodynamic or psychoanalytic viewpoint. This views psychological reality as a living, influential, interactive universe, a lively world that we enter through understanding the underlying influences on a person's observed behavior. This vantage point on human function does not see this observed behavior as random or meaningless but links it to its psychological roots.

Defining Mental Disorder

In the *Diagnostic and Statistical Manual IV-TR* we read:

> Each of the mental disorders is conceptualized as a clinically significant behavioral or psychological syndrome or pattern that occurs in an individual and that is associated with present distress (a painful symptom) or disability (impairment in one or more important areas of functioning), or with a significantly increased risk of suffering death, pain, disability, or an important loss of freedom. In addition, this syndrome or pattern must not be merely an expectable and culturally sanctioned response to a particular event, for example, the death of a loved one. Whatever its original cause, it must currently be considered a manifestation of a behavioral, psychological, or biological dysfunction in the individual. Neither deviant behavior (e.g., political, religious, or sexual) nor

conflicts that are primarily between the individual and society are mental disorders unless the deviance or conflict is a symptom of a dysfunction in the individual as described above.[1]

In deepening our appreciation of diagnosis and in facilitating at least our occasional use of this basic work, we understand that the categories of illness are not distinct, that there is considerable overlap of symptoms between categories, and that individuals with the same disorder may vary considerably in the way that they manifest their illness. We will now examine some of the basic principles and methods of this standard reference work for the classification of mental illness.

Current Classification: DSM-IV-TR

This system uses a descriptive approach toward problems in mental health and strives to be neutral regarding theories of causation (etiology). No assumption is made that all individuals described as having the same mental disorder are alike in all important ways. They are members of a heterogeneous group who share the defining features of a disorder. It is recognized that as descriptive analysis is more carefully refined, new disorders will emerge while some problems presented by individuals to therapists will not fit easily into any of these recognized clusters.

Most clinicians and researchers can agree on the descriptive terms for specific signs and symptoms. This behavioral emphasis is therefore atheoretical and defines disorders in terms of what we observe in our experience with troubled individuals. Using these agreed-upon descriptions enables clinicians to apply their own theoretical tradition in developing an appropriate and consistent treatment plan.

A certain amount of training and experience is required to employ and apply these guidelines effectively in diagnosis. They should not be used as a cookbook but more as an aid to inform a judgment about an individual's current status. It equally important to recognize that, even after intensive contact with an individual, counselors may not be able to assign a final diagnosis but must work with a "provisional" diagnosis instead.

An innovative dimension of the *DSM-IV-TR* is its multiaxial approach. In this system, several different domains of information, assumed to be of high clinical value, are examined for each person. Considered together they offer a more comprehensive view of the person than an evaluation limited only to the symptoms of mental disorder. This is organized around five axes:

Axis I: *Clinical disorders and other conditions that may be a focus of clinical attention.* This lists the principal diagnosis and other major diagnoses in the classification — except for the personality disorders and mental retardation (reported on Axis II).

Axis II: *Personality disorders and mental retardation.* This axis is used for reporting personality disorders, mental retardation, and other prominent maladaptive personality features and defense mechanisms.

Axis III: *General medical conditions.* This axis is used to report current general medical conditions that may be relevant to the understanding or management of the person's disorder.

Axis IV: *Psychosocial and environmental problems.* This axis is employed to report psychosocial and environmental problems that may affect the diagnosis, treatment, and prognosis of Axis I and II disorders. This range of stressors includes such incidents as the loss of a parent or family member, change in occupation, educational or housing problems, economic or legal problems, or any of a wide variety of positive or negative events that may stress an individual.

Axis V: *Global assessment of functioning.* This axis is utilized to report the assessment of the individual's overall level of functioning. A useful instrument for accomplishing this is the Global Assessment of Functioning (GAF) Scale that is divided into ten levels of functioning and is included in the diagnostic manual.

Nonprofessional counselors should have some knowledge of the *DSM-IV-TR* classifications for adults and children. We note here only some of those relating to adults.

1. Delirium, Dementia, and Amnestic and Other Cognitive Disorders

The main feature of these disorders is a clinically significant deficit in cognition that represents a significant change from a previous level of functioning. For each disorder in this section, the cause is either an identified (or unidentified) general medical condition or a finding of a substance that is abused, such as alcohol, cocaine, a medication, or a toxin or a combination of these factors. Depending on a variety of other factors, this may either permanently or transiently affect brain function. These disorders and other medical- and substance-related conditions were previously described as "organic mental disorders." This has been changed since this former designation incorrectly implied that "nonorganic" mental disorders do not have a biological basis.

Counselors may have direct contact with individuals suffering from such problems in their early stages but are more likely to be consulted by friends or family members of those so afflicted. It is useful, therefore, to be familiar with the nature of these disorders in order to provide needed and informed support and to be of practical and sensible assistance in obtaining resources for the suffering person. In working with the families of affected individuals, counselors should also become familiar with resources within the community, such as the Alzheimer's Association, that provide support and educational information for family members.

If a counselor, on the basis of comparing behavior to the list of signs and symptoms, feels that an individual — or a person described by a friend or relative — may be suffering from such a disorder, an appropriate and prompt referral to a psychiatrist is indicated. Such serious problems need effective medical evaluation and management and cannot be dealt with wisely through any time-buying improvisation or through the use of unproven remedies. The use of the latter may visit an even greater cruelty on afflicted individuals and on those around them.

2. Mental Disorders Due to a General Medical Condition

This section delineates conditions characterized by mental symptoms that are judged to be the direct physiological consequence of a medical condition. An example is found in symptoms of anxiety in a person with a parathyroid adenoma that resolve after surgery because the associated level of calcium in the blood returns to normal.

3. Substance-Related Disorders

In this section, disorders are described that result from the taking of any number of substances, defined as a drug of abuse, a medication, or a toxin. The substances are grouped into eleven classes that include alcohol and cocaine, a wide variety of prescribed and over-the-counter substances as well as carbon monoxide, inhalants, and other poisonous substances. The criteria for substance dependence, abuse, intoxication, and withdrawal for each class of substance, as well as the associated signs and symptoms, are all carefully delineated.

Because of the pervasive use of recreational drugs at all levels in our society, nonprofessional counselors will surely encounter persons with problems associated with this social reality. Their ability to respond is enriched by a grasp of the signs and symptoms of the most common types of drugs. These will also be discussed in more detailed fashion in a later chapter.

4. Schizophrenia and Other Psychotic Disorders

The term "psychotic," in its restrictive definition, refers to an individual having delusions or prominent hallucinations, with the hallucinations occurring in the absence of insight into their pathological nature. Here "psychotic" refers more broadly to a constellation of symptoms that vary to some extent across a variety of diagnoses. However, they characteristically include delusions, hallucinations, disorganized speech, or disorganized or catatonic behavior. The most common and familiar of these conditions is schizophrenia. Here the nonprofessional counselor will find the basic inclusion and exclusion criteria for these disorders.

Most counselors, even nonprofessional counselors, have some familiarity with the explicit symptoms of psychosis, such as delusions, hallucinations, and other signals of gross disturbances in thinking. Such seriously troubled individuals should always be referred as quickly as possible for psychiatric treatment.

5. Mood Disorders

The most prominent feature of such disorders is a disturbance in mood that is manifested by depression or elation and may include both depressive disorders and those now termed "bipolar disorders" because they exhibit mood changes in both directions.

Manic and hypomanic disorders are distinguished by the marked impairment in the person's social and occupational functioning and often require hospitalization. Depressive disorders also include a wide variety of mood disturbances and may require hospitalization, especially when suicidal thoughts are present.

Counselors will often be the first to interview individuals who manifest depressive symptoms. Knowledge of the various kinds of depression is, therefore, extremely helpful as we try to make judgments about the persons with whom we are working. These will also be reviewed in a later chapter.

6. Anxiety Disorders

Anxiety is the common denominator in all these disorders. In some, such as panic disorder, the anxiety is associated with symptoms that can be overwhelming and immobilizing. In others, such as obsessive-compulsive disorder, the obsessions may cause the individual to feel anxious and distressed while the compulsions help to control and neutralize their anxiety.

7. Somatoform Disorders

This group of problems involves physical symptoms suggesting a physical disorder for which no supporting evidence of an organic origin can be found. Nor is there any known pathophysiologic mechanism that could account for the disturbance. The symptoms must cause clinically significant distress or impairment in social, occupational, or other areas of functioning.

8. Sexual and Gender Identity Disorders

This group includes a wide variety of sexual dysfunctions that may involve disturbances in sexual desire or in psycho-physiological changes that characterize the sexual response cycle and that cause marked distress and interpersonal difficulty. Also included are the paraphilias (recurrent intense sexually arousing fantasies, urges, or behaviors, such as exhibitionism, pedophilia, sadism, and cross-dressing) and gender identity disorders, that is, strong and persistent cross-gender identification and persistent discomfort with one's own gender role.

9. Eating Disorders

Disturbances in eating behavior include *anorexia nervosa,* which is characterized by a refusal to maintain a minimally normal weight, and *bulimia nervosa,* which is manifested by repeated episodes of binge eating and self-induced vomiting. A disturbance in perception of body shape and weight is found in both conditions.

10. Adjustment Disorders

These disorders may be read as a psychological response to an identifiable stressor that results in the development of clinically significant emotional or behavioral symptoms. It must occur within three months after the onset of the stressor and may be associated with symptoms of depression, anxiety, physical complaints, withdrawal, or occupational disturbances. These are, in fact, the problems with which counselors may be most familiar and with which they may be able to intervene most effectively.

11. *Personality Disorders*

A personality disorder is an enduring pattern of inner experience and behavior that deviates from the expectations of the individual's culture, is pervasive and inflexible, has an onset in adolescence or early adulthood, is stable over time, and leads to distress or impairment.[2]

These disorders may go unnamed but they are familiar in everyday life. They flower out of pervasive patterns of disturbance in personality functioning and bloom in a variety of settings in the person's life. Of lifelong duration, the behaviors often cause problems for those who suffer from them in their social and work life. These latter problems are, so to speak, the effects of the problem and cause these individuals to experience subjective distress. The problem is so much a part of their nature that they often cannot observe it in themselves but they suffer from the reactions they trip off in others, such as employers or acquaintances. Counselors will be very familiar with this group of disorders and need to understand some of the more familiar patterns of behavior that constitute these disturbances.

Conclusion

It is important for counselors to understand that our knowledge of mental disorders and our classification thereof is in a state of constant development and refinement. Over the past two generations, for example, we have learned that many disorders that we considered due primarily to psychological factors have far more complex origins. Considerable research data suggest that disorders such as schizophrenia, mania, depression, panic attacks, post-traumatic stress, and impulse disorders are often associated with genetic, neurochemical, and neurophysiological abnormalities. As a result, approaches to the treatment of these disorders have been rethought and developed in fresh ways. To attempt to treat a serious depression without careful assessment and the consideration of medication may deprive individuals of the currently accepted and available treatment. Counselors, especially those who have limited training or experience, improve their chances of being truly helpful by acquainting themselves as thoroughly as they can with the ever developing insights of contemporary diagnosis.

– 15 –

LISTENING TO THE LIVES
OF OTHERS

COUNSELING IS A TALE about themselves told by people with help
from the universal languages of their eyes, their hands, and even
their shifting feet. They use all these accent marks as they try to tell us
the story that they want to hear and understand themselves. Much of
what persons tell counselors comes in anecdotal form, in a storytelling
mode as old as we are. We talk to each other all the time by telling stories, and even our tall tales tell something true about us. Telling stories
to communicate our experience is as human and natural as breathing.
Stories and illustrations are found in abundance in the garden variety
of common, personal problems with which counselors deal all the time.
How are we to understand them?

Telling our own story we bypass logic in order to reach the unconscious level of others in ways that defy superficial rational analysis.
That is why stories have always been a part of the civilized person's
resources. Myth and symbol remain potent means of communication,
and the art of the novelist consists in telling the truth about us while
telling a story at the same time. Counselors may understand this abstractly, but it is another matter to make ourselves into receiving sets
for the storytelling that constitutes so much of what people tell us.
Catching the dynamics of these stories — the living reasons they are
told, their "point," so to speak — is an essential art of counseling.

Novelist Graham Greene tells us how this processing of one's experience works in his autobiography, *A Sort of Life*. What he has forgotten,
he recalls, returns regularly in his novels.

> If one day [these forgotten details] find their way into a book, it
> should be without our connivance and so disguised that we don't
> recognize them when we see them again. All that we can easily rec-
> ognize as our experience in a novel is mere reporting.... Perhaps
> a novelist has a greater ability to forget than other men — he has

to forget or become sterile. What he forgets is the compost of the imagination."[1]

Individuals are not trying to entertain us through their stories; they are trying to explain themselves. They sift through their own experience, describing their relationships and the things that have gone wrong and the things that have gone right, pulling something loose, scraping it free of soil and holding it up for our inspection. Is this the root of my troubles? They attempt to trace down the source of their anxiety by describing the circumstances or events in which they face it in their lives. These narratives are, then, an invaluable source of raw material from which we can form an understanding of their authors. This, they say, is *my* life. Can you understand it?

This is particularly true with children, who almost always describe their life events in terms of simple stories. As psychiatrist Richard A. Gardner has suggested, adults sometimes fail to communicate with children because they respond to these stories with rational arguments or explanations. To reach the unconscious level from which the child's story proceeds, it is helpful for adults to respond in the same language of story. Stories bridge the gap between the unconscious levels of personalities more swiftly and surely than logic.[2] We are not suggesting that adult counselors should tell stories in response to the stories of others; we are pointing, rather, to the richness and subtlety of the material to which counselors should attune themselves if they wish to hear the inner resonations of the persons coming to them for assistance. These constitute a rich lode to be mined carefully by counselors who can gently "hear their way into" the meanings beneath the narratives that others are always telling us.

Hearing the Story / Missing the Point

Problems arise when counselors lose themselves in the details of the story, thereby missing both the person and the message in the process. True life stories are interesting and can easily arrest our attention. As helpers, we may get hooked on the story, wanting to know how it comes out rather than the reasons for its being told. Sometimes we may even wish to alter its ending.

It is not uncommon for novice counselors to discover that they are so intrigued by the details or the illustrations the individual uses that they mistake a journalist's understanding of the facts for a therapist's grasp of what lies beneath them. Finding ourselves stranded in illustra-

How to Miss the Point of the Story

- Get lost in the details
- Try to sort out the details
- Focus on the details and miss the message
- Indulge in countertransference distractions

tive material is both bewildering and stressful for, as with quicksand, any slight movement to escape gets us in deeper. We easily lose our perspective when we become so absorbed by or identified with the stories that we miss the person's motivation for using the illustration in the first place.

We may also get so caught up in trying to untangle or straighten out the details of a story that we smother at birth our own spontaneous reactions to those with whom we work. We end up with the pieces and no idea of how they fit. Without some sense of the whole, we can never fit the jigsaw puzzle of their scattered revelations together.

When the pieces all look the same to us, we may fashion responses to material that is presented only to illustrate the point that we are somehow missing. Caught up in colorful examples, we are hard pressed to respond simply and directly to others. Others reveal themselves in their narrative and the way they tell it. Our focus is on the person who is telling the story, not just on the meaty morsels of the story itself. We should try to make their long story short by responding to the question: Why is this person telling me this story at all?

Getting stalled at the level of the illustration means that we are preoccupied with the technique rather than the human essence of making a response. This may be a sincere counselor's most serious distraction. Taking this detour is ultimately stressful because it gets us out of the flow of the other's experience. We can get caught up in doing good and in doing well, the twin burdens of counselors who have become too earnest and, in a sense, too self-conscious about what they are trying to achieve. When we hear ourselves respond by tracing over every detail of the client's story we are almost surely trapped and bound by our own obsessiveness. It is one of the classic ways in which we helpers see so many trees we don't recognize the forest.

If we find ourselves so distracted by the incidentals of the story, we risk losing the person who is telling it. As we listen to others talk we not only hear something about them but, through our own reactions, something about ourselves. We may be paying attention only to those things that stir us or remind us of something in our own lives, that, in other words, set off countertransference feelings in us. If you wonder what that term means, you have just found out. We may avoid parts of the story that make us uneasy, episodes that cause us embarrassment or about which we would rather not think or speak.

Our profile stands out clearly in the way we hear and respond to the illustrative communication of others. Counselors who are aware of their own curiosity realize that, if they satisfy only this, it will lead them away from the individual and toward a projection of their own feelings onto the person. Such counselors may end up responding to themselves more than to the other person. We can unravel this and lessen our stress if we take the time to listen to our own reactions to the stories of others. That tells us a lot about ourselves and allows us to keep our reactions from interfering with the counseling process.

How to Hear the Story

Each anecdote trembles with echoes from less than conscious levels of personality. When we sense and pick up these signals, we begin to hear the real story others are trying to tell us, indeed, the one they are trying to tell themselves. Our response resembles the way a friend answers a friend who is in trouble, the manner in which a husband and wife respond to each other when one of them is in distress. These figures are not distracted by the details because they sense the pulsating core of the distressed person. That is what is important, and it is to this level, from which all the illustrations flow, that they respond. They understand that the illustration is just a way of getting this deeper message across. We must listen to others in the same natural and human way, responding to the underlying tones that give their stories color and meaning.

Clarify the Feeling Tone

No matter what the content of the story may be, the feeling tone will still be the most significant source of understanding for us. The person may be describing what sounds like a trivial or neutral incident — such as a minor disagreement between a married couple or an argument at work — and reveal much more in the tone than in the detail. Is the individual telling this in a *depressed* way? Is *anger* bubbling up

---

How to Hear the Story

- Clarify the feeling tone
- Appreciate the context
- Clarify the person's perspective
- Observe the person's role in the story
- Identify the story's theme
- Recognize when the story is repetitive
- Respond to the essential communication

---

beneath these words? Is there some *prizing of power* involved in what seems such a simple tale?

Appreciate the Context

This is not to say that the stories are completely unimportant in themselves. It is important, however, to put them into proper focus in relationship to the person who is telling them. These individuals, after all, offer us the context of their self-perceptions when they tell us the stories of their difficulties. They describe the significant figures in their lives, peopling the stage for us so that we can see their particular way of looking at themselves and their relationships with others. Stories are full of significant stage directions, entrances and exits, conflicts and expectations. The person stands at the center of this, and it is how that person emerges rather than how the story ends that is important. The question that is most helpful for counselors in getting this into perspective remains: To what am I responding, the person or the story?

Clarify the Person's Perspective

Are the individuals telling the story solely in terms of things that have happened *in the past?* Or is the narrative integrated with life's continuity so that it opens them *to the future?* Is something over and done with in their view? Or are there still possibilities for some growth and development? Are they mourning something? Or are they preparing to deal with a problem that is just emerging? Are they hopeful or despairing? Do they feel betrayed or deserted, or do they possess self-confidence on which they now draw in order to confront this difficulty?

Observe the Person's Role in the Story

How, in these stories, do the persons *cast* and *describe* themselves? Do they have *active* or *passive* roles? Do they assume responsibility or portray themselves as victims of circumstances? Do they accept some blame for what is wrong, or do they consistently locate the blame in sources outside themselves? The parts, so to speak, these persons see themselves playing reveal a great deal about them.

Identify the Story's Theme

Like the mood music in a film, the theme is central in any narrative as the connector that reveals the underlying meaning of the illustrations. The theme — is it courage, cowardice, fear, hope? — tells us how individuals experience themselves, the other people in their lives, and indeed their life in general. Often people are not aware of how clearly they describe themselves and their lives in the stories they tell. This is because the material may be coming from subconscious levels, making its entrance only in stories. That is why they may employ recurring themes, such as conflict or disappointment. In these scenarios the central questions become: What is the nature of the conflict? With whom is it experienced? What are the prospects for resolving it? The explanation of conflict through stories gives us clear signals about what persons perceive as their most important struggle. These are more than interesting stories; they are scenarios of the self, the open presentation of others to us.

Recognize When the Story Is Repetitive

Have we heard this story before? Perhaps it is not exactly the same story in its setting or details, but it is identical in theme and central conflict with one we have already been told. Persons repeat such stories over and over again for a simple reason: Because we don't catch on or fail to signal that we "got it" in the first place. When people repeat a story they are clearly saying, "This is important and I want some sign that you have heard it."

Respond to the Essential Communication

Understanding responses should be made as soon as we get a real feel for the essential communication of the client. This requires a professional sensitivity and a sense of timing that builds on what seems to be natural and appropriate. Ordinarily, it is not very helpful for us to interrupt people unexpectedly or before they finish telling the story in the terms and style that suit them. Nor can we wait too long to respond, or we will project ourselves as dull and passive in the relationship. Stories have a rhythm that makes it possible for us to intervene with a helpful response at some natural break or as the story reaches its conclusion. Individuals do not hold prompter's cards up for us but, as we listen, we discover that they intuitively provide these pauses in which we can make a response that shows we understand their story and, therefore, them as well.

As we become more sensitive to the undertones of the stories people constantly tell us, we are able to make rapid progress in getting at their real communication. While we do this we must monitor our own potential for interfering with the communication of the other, either because of our curiosity or some countertransference reaction. When we understand and control these reactions, we improve our capacity to receive even the subtlest signals that others send to us in counseling.

Counseling is not a tough job to get through, or a routine task to be accomplished but a relationship to be experienced. It is like and, indeed, *is* a part of life in which we are not solving a puzzle but trying to understand and respond to another person. As we become accustomed to hearing *into* the narrative, we respond more freely and with more of our genuine selves. Counseling becomes less a stressful test and more a satisfying real-life relationship for us and for those with whom we work.

– 16 –

TO WHOM SHALL WE GO?

T HE BIBLICAL QUESTION — "To whom shall we go?" — returns in the counselor's life with every potential referral, that is, whenever because of time, circumstances, or talents, we reach the limits of what we can do to help another person. Referring individuals on to other professionals is not uncommon, and a readiness to do so bespeaks a long view rather than a shortfall of ability. It is often the soundest clinical decision that we can make. Still, counselors may have varied and complex feelings about it, some of them about themselves, despite their theoretical recognition that making a good referral is in the best interests of the one they are seeing. Some also arise from the edgy implications of such a recommendation for the person being referred. Referral remains, however, constant and inevitable in our work and we must clarify our understanding of the process and our feelings about it.

The process of referral resembles a blank screen onto which we project many of our own inner experiences; we do, in fact, find out a good deal about ourselves when we face and deal with recommending that a person seek ongoing assistance from someone else. Our feelings and ideas about ourselves and our own counseling work come into sharp focus at such moments.

Referral often brings out countertransference feelings, the complex of emotions that we experience toward the other. It is difficult to proceed in counseling without an awareness of the many levels of our emotional reactions to those who come for help. One of the best preparations for the process of referral is to review our feelings for the individual, to name, face, and accept them as honestly as possible so that we can modify our own self-image and adjust the expectations we make on ourselves as counselors. Such feelings, if denied or distorted, only imprison us. The more accurately we counselors can symbolize these feelings to ourselves, the freer we become in all of our counseling work. Unrecognized countertransference feelings are a major source of stress for counselors. The moment of referral is also a moment of truth in which we face our need to monitor ourselves carefully so that we can control rather than be controlled by our inner experience.

Some counselors feel guilty about turning those they have worked with over to somebody else's care and feel that they are abandoning the person, especially if they have had ambiguous feelings about the individual at some point in the relationship. The decisive moment of actually making the referral may stir these up, especially in counselors who are very hard on themselves, in those of us who allow little margin for error and not much more for the garden variety mistakes that even seasoned professionals make from time to time with others. A good referral is hardly an abandonment when it is an honest recommendation in the other's best interest.

Some helpers regularly invest great energy into solving the problems that people cause by knocking on the office door in the first place. Referral can easily represent more of a solution for the counselor than for the one seeking help. This is the exception, however, and not the rule in the great majority of cases in which successful referrals are made.

Whatever we feel at the time of referral — good or bad, relief or anxiety — we necessarily communicate to the other at some level, often in nonverbal language. We cannot hide our genuine inner attitudes, and this underscores our need to become more sensitive to our own reactions and to their management during the process of referral.

Inside Stories

Whatever feelings we may experience about referral, we must clarify whether they are realistic feelings, feelings rooted in our own counter-transference, or whether they arise from the person's transferences. Like intertwined vines, it may be difficult to distinguish these, one from the other. It is as if there were two sides, or aspects, to each feeling that emerges, some from the counselor's dynamics, others from the person in counseling. Counselors who can sort these out, much like the skilled horticulturist, can identify them, address them properly, and see that no harm comes to either as they are parted by the process of referral.

If, for example, feelings of rejection arise in the referral, we need to distinguish those rooted in the counselor's *countertransference* (wanting to get rid of a troublesome person or seemingly insurmountable problem) from those coming from the individual's *transference* (the expectation that, after a lifetime of rejections, the counselor is just the next in line). Informed by our exploration of these seemingly snarled feelings, we can address and deal with our own feelings, if they are

> ## Countertransference Feelings Generated by Referral
>
> - Guilt about rejecting or abandoning the person
> - Relief at getting rid of a problem
> - Uncertainty about referral generated by person's transference
> - Fear of having others dislike us
> - Inability to tolerate others' negative feelings toward us
> - Hesitancy based on "You're the only one who really understands me."

present, and suggest to others that their feelings of rejection are familiar, that they may have a history of these and they should be an expected part of the separation whether they are warranted or not.

Unless we deal with our own inner experiences before we initiate the dynamics of referral we may easily give the impression of rejecting the individuals with whom we are working. This can become fairly complicated, especially if those coming for help have had a lifetime of being rejected by others. We may hesitate to add what appears to be another rejection to their record but, in the commonplace entanglements of counseling, the individuals may be testing us out to see if, in fact, we are going to be as rejecting of them as others have been. Obviously, we must be tuned in to several levels of interchange with those with whom we work if they are to make progress and we are to avoid being trapped or manipulated.

The possibility that individuals may be testing us, or even edging us toward rejecting them, may make some counselors hesitate to make a referral even when it is necessary. A referral, however, should never be put off merely because such possibilities of manipulation exist. Such possibilities need to be recognized and, in some cases at least, even talked about with the person. Sensible tactics are available to handle such situations without bogging ourselves down or needlessly hurting others. It takes listening, however, and an awareness of how many strands of the counseling relationship are drawn together when referral becomes a possibility.

We should not sound an uncertain note about the referral itself, as

> ## *Transference Feelings*
> ## *Generated by Referral*
>
> - Feelings of being rejected by the counselor
> - Hesitancy to accept referral because of counselor's ambivalence
> - Negative feelings toward the counselor
> - Feelings related to problems with finances

this only makes the other person react uncertainly as well. That may rob the process of some of its potential value, leaving our relationship with the other unsettled and ambivalent. Making a referral calls for a thorough cleaning of the emotional debris that may cling to the edges of the relationship. We always profit by attending to and clarifying to ourselves whatever we experience internally when making a referral.

The other person's feelings can also be very complicated. Just as the counselor's countertransference feelings come into play at the time of referral, so too do the transference feelings of the person with whom we are working. The other may openly like or dislike us, idealize or demonize us. Such reactions may be the fruit of transference feelings rather than of any direct emotional response to us. We should not be afraid of letting others express positive or negative feelings toward us, but we can accept them without attempting any in-depth exploration of them. The referral is being made to allow some expert decide if and when unconscious material should be explored. We should handle these feelings on the surface and, instead of taking them personally, we should view them as essential if lively elements of the human process of helping.

Counselors who are not aware of their countertransference feelings, or who do not know themselves well, may find that they cannot easily face the strong feelings others may express about them when referral comes up for discussion. They become victims of what might be described as excessive softheartedness and back away from this point of decision that is also a moment of truth, allowing themselves to be manipulated and missing the chance to help the other person in a significant manner. Certain professions — especially those attracting persons with a warm interest in and a need for close contact with others — are particularly vulnerable locations for this difficulty. These people avoid hard truths, fearing that these will cause them not to be liked, a notion unattractive to and unacceptable by them.

Such an experience is an enormous source of stress for such counselors and, while they recognize its negative impact on themselves, they may not know that they can deal with it more effectively by deepening their understanding of themselves and of these dynamics in the therapy process. They experience a real liberation when they understand that not all of the emotional reactions of their clients are directed at them, but that they have become the object of transferred feelings from other important individuals in these people's lives. Such counselors can prepare themselves by self-examination and by monitoring better the transference feelings of the clients.

It is not uncommon for persons to tell certain counselors, such as those working in schools or in church settings, that they cannot afford to get help other than that provided by the present counselor. This can be a major source of conflict for warmhearted counselors who do not understand the symbolic issue that may be involved and who may find this a very persuasive argument against making a needed referral. Any time feelings about money come up, they should be explored like any other attitudes that are verbalized during the counseling process. Counselors operate far more effectively when they do not take everything personally and as they attune themselves to the symbolic significance of many aspects of their relationships with others.

The Human Process of Referral

The process of referral should be integrated into the counseling relationship as closely as possible. It should not represent a sudden, dramatic, or distinct break but rather be the outcome of the growth we have shared with the other. Referral comes as a fulfillment of that growth so that we may, for their greater good, oversee the transfer of the person to someone else as an organic process. Working this out should not come as a total surprise to persons who have been prepared for this as a necessary step forward rather than back. We can easily and honestly make this outcome possible right from the start by being open and honest about this in the context of the counseling so that others understand that it may occur and why it may take place.

Fundamental to a successful process is telling the truth about the reasons for referral. Manufactured reasons never hold up, and a simple short statement of why the counselor believes that referral is necessary takes very little time and effects a great deal of good. We may feel that

---

Reasons for Referral

- Nature of the person's problem
- Limited competence of counselor
- Stagnant relationship
- Permanent or temporary change of location of either
  party

---

the other's needs are beyond our competence at the moment. That is
an admirable as well as a sensible reason to secure another therapist
for the person. We may feel that the individual needs help on a more
regular and long-term basis, something that, because of circumstances,
we cannot provide.

Referral may also be appropriate when the relationship does not
seem to be working out very effectively and, despite good will and efforts on the part of both, it does not seem possible to get it on the right
track. Some persons and counselors may not match up well because
of personality factors whose origins are beyond their easy recall. It is
not always possible to refer people in these circumstances, but it is an
important factor to acknowledge and to deal with on the conscious
level. Referrals are also appropriate if either the counselor or the other
is moving away. Reality factors necessitate such a change in many helping and other professional relationships. This may be experienced in a
minor key if either party is going to be away on an extended trip, a
vacation, or an assignment.

Knowing How to Go

It is important to anticipate these separations well in advance and to
arrange for an adequate referral to cover the period of absence. This
is obviously not something that should be brought up at the last moment. It is hard enough for some people to survive a counselor's being
away on vacation for a few weeks. Such separations should never be
presented as surprises but always carefully and thoughtfully anticipated
and discussed beforehand.

The point of reference, or general context for clinical judgment, is
always the greater good of the individual: What is the best thing for
this person at this time? We balance all the factors involved in such a

---

Elements of a Good Referral

- Unambivalence
- An appropriate resource
- A clear explanation
- Timeliness
- Personal contact with referral source
- Appropriate documentation
- Termination of counselor's responsibility

---

decision on this scale. We should also be ready and willing to answer questions about the referral and to explore the person's reactions so that our relationship is a carefully finished and full one even though it may shortly be brought to a close.

Part of our readily available counseling resources are the names, addresses, and various numbers of referral sources. Who is the best person? Where is the best agency? We do not want to look these up at the last minute. Building such a file takes some reflection as well as consultation with other professionals. It should contain the names of helpers who, because of professional training, personal characteristics, and location are well qualified to take ongoing responsibility for therapy for those we decide to refer.

It is also helpful if we develop relationships with a number of professionals in the community to whom we may make referrals. It is a common professional practice to send a brief note or make a phone call announcing our intention to refer an individual and to receive an acknowledgment when a contact is made. The referred persons, however, should ordinarily make the contact for themselves. We as counselors should send only the information that is asked for by the referral source and agreed to explicitly, generally in writing, by the person referred.

The process of referral is completed by our stepping out of the picture, making it clear that the individual is now the responsibility of another professional. The completed referral marks the end of our participation in the therapeutic process. This requires self-knowledge and self-discipline. Our feelings can betray us in these moments, especially if we find it hard to let go of a certain person or if our curiosity prompts us to find out how the person is getting along in the new treatment situation. Mature counselors recognize these possibilities in themselves and are neither surprised nor scandalized by them. They deal with them, as we must, without panicking or experiencing any lessening of their own professional competence or self-esteem.

Familiar Refrains

Sooner or later every counselor faces the following situation: The person referred to another person calls up to complain about the new therapist in phrases something like these, "I just can't talk to him the way I did to you," "She's not as understanding as you are," or "I just don't like him and I don't think I'm getting anywhere." The words vary but the music is familiar. We counselors may experience great stress when we feel that a referral has not worked out well. Sometimes we are tempted to intervene, to take back the responsibility of and for the person, or even, in some circumstances, to try to find yet another professional referral for the person.

All of these are moves in the wrong direction. Make any one of them and the persons we referred have us under their control. It is very difficult to escape once we have allowed ourselves to be manipulated back into managing or trying to rearrange a referral we have already made. Sometimes we do it because we are flattered by the one who complains about the new therapist, and sometimes we do it because we possess manipulable hearts. The healthy general principle to be followed in these circumstances demands that once a referral is made we stay out of the picture and that we resist any impulse to assist or otherwise interfere with the newly developed relationship.

It is appropriate to acknowledge the feelings of the person who calls; this can be done with understanding and without brusqueness. It should also be done to avoid getting ourselves reengaged and drawn any deeper into the new problems of the person. In a gentle and understanding way, we should advise such callers to discuss these problems in the only place in which it is appropriate to do so, the office of the person whom they are now seeing.

It is not the end of the world for individuals to encounter difficulties in relating to their therapists. It is often a good sign that something significant is happening. We counselors can verbalize this in a general way as we direct these persons back to the referral source for an in-depth exploration of their current feelings toward this new relationship. These people are now somebody else's responsibility, and we may damage them and the new relationship if we allow ourselves to become unnecessarily involved after the referral has been made.

Most helpers, whether counseling is full or part-time work for them, can easily contact the local medical and psychological societies to get lists of psychiatrists and psychologists for referral purposes. Other specialties, such as that of social work, can also be extremely helpful, especially in certain problems involving the families of those with whom we are working. Counselors should be aware of the hospitals with psychiatric facilities or clinics through which referrals may also be made. Every community has certain agencies, some run by the state and some privately, whose directors know well the local communities' referral capacities. A number of organizations — Alcoholics Anonymous, drug units, suicide prevention centers, and even Travelers' Aid — can be extremely useful in dealing with the varied problems that come up in the work of the counselor. A contact at one of these locations can relieve a great deal of stress and make it possible for us to be far more helpful to others. Knowing the right agency or professional to call at the moment of need equips us well for making helpful referrals.

Self-Help Groups

For a generation and more, there has been a bounteous harvest within most communities of resources that emphasize self-help. These groups focus on peer support and education and are available at low or no cost to vast segments of the population who need assistance in coping with developmental disabilities, chronic emotional and physical conditions, as well as specific life events such as divorce, the death of a child, or loss of employment. These groups do not provide treatment per se. Such resources ordinarily consist of people who share a common experience and who serve as helpers to assist others and participate in providing and disseminating information about the common issue and offering support based on their sharing the same experience.

Counselors should be familiar with some of the numerous self-help and mutual aid centers that have been established throughout the country. States such as Illinois and California have established detailed directories of self-help resources within those states as well as "800" numbers to expedite the process of referral.

The Internet is used as a resource for help about almost any illness, dysfunction, or conflict-laden situation. WEBMD, MEDEM, and a range of government agency Web sites provide people with accurate and useful information on subjects about which they are concerned.

Good Source.

The American Medical Association, the American Psychiatric Association, the American Psychological Association, and almost every other professional organization have information links that provide resources and directions about an extensive range of problems. Self-help books are available on almost every subject through bookstores and such Web sites as Amazon.com and Barnes&Noble.com. Some familiarity with these sites allows counselors to educate themselves and expand their ability to respond helpfully when individuals ask them for recommendations from such sources.

Helping Ourselves

Although many persons who do counseling say that they have neither the time nor the finances for it, some regular supervision or at least consultation about their work is indispensable to keep them fresh and alert in their helping activities. We counselors need continuing clinical education, not just intellectual stimulation, and the regular exploration with another professional of the various factors that may enter into one or the other of our helping relationships. Nothing is a more significant source of support and development for us as counselors than an opportunity to receive regular supervision or to avail ourselves of consultation.

It is a common practice in many areas for a group of persons who do counseling to gather together to discuss their work with some other professional person on a regular basis. When each member of the group contributes a small amount it makes it possible for a sensitive and affordable professional consultation to be obtained. Such forums provide a setting in which to discuss and make decisions about referrals as well as to learn about the resources of the community. These gatherings also offer a safe environment in which to deal with the accumulated stress of working on a day-to-day basis with persons with emotional difficulties. It is, in other words, a source of professional development and personal integration at the same time. This is the kind of professional assistance to which hard-working counselors can gladly refer themselves.

WHEN CAN I SAY WHAT I FEEL?

W HEN CAN I SAY what I feel? Although this question is often asked, it is not one to which a simple answer may be given. We begin to respond to this question with another one: Why do we ask this question in the first place?

Many therapists feel some need to involve themselves more actively and personally in their helping work. Sometimes this reflects their typical style of relating with others outside of counseling. Some individuals need to be personal with others; they are disappointed with relationships in which other persons do not "like" them. They are anxious until they see a flag of surrender to their charm raised by persons they help. The anxiety that results when they do not feel "liked" may cause some inexperienced therapists to do something about it, even as people do when they prompt responses of regard out of others. They find a way to do it, usually by inserting themselves and their own feelings into the therapy early in the relationship.

The expression of the counselor's feelings or the revelation of the counselor's problem may also reflect a current generalized notion about the democratic conditions of psychotherapy. This is part of the anti-expert point of view that demands that everybody stand on roughly the same ground at the beginning of therapy with neither party wiser than the other. Counselors who operate according to this democratic imperative feel that expressing their personal problems places them on the same plane with those they help.

Other counselors become anxious to express their own feelings in counseling because they are frustrated, at least on the unconscious level, in their obsessive efforts to follow what they presume to be the "professional" rules of carrying out therapy. They perceive these as a collection of "Don'ts." They are not to be personal; they are not to express their own feelings; they are not to interpret; they are not to answer any of the other person's questions. A need to break through this hedge of prohibitions may make self-expression more attractive to many counselors who have been overinstructed about their work.

Countertransference, Unrecognized

Some of the above experiences and others associated with the expression of the counselor's attitudes or emotions are often evidence of the counselor's countertransference feelings. In such yearnings we behold the face of operational countertransference. Many countertransference possibilities go unrecognized, unacknowledged, and unprocessed, especially for persons who do their counseling in connection with other professional responsibilities. Countertransference is, however, a common problem for all therapists, something with which we all must deal systematically if we are to be effective in helping others.

Countertransference, as discussed earlier, refers to the feelings — negative or positive — that arise in the helper toward the one being helped. As with transference, emotions really appropriate to other persons in the counselor's life history are projected onto the individuals opposite them. Counselors who have not dealt with their own emotional problems and conflicts are particularly vulnerable to the difficulties that the emergence of such feelings may cause. They tend to act out their own problems during the counseling process and use the expression of their own feelings as a way of resolving them.

The presence of countertransference feelings may be unsettling and stressful for counselors who do not have much experience or who lack opportunities for adequate reflection on, or proper supervisory consultation about, their own experience. These opportunities are the best help and hope for counselors in dealing with the many and varied emotional reactions that can arise in the course of working intensely and closely with others. It is hard for counselors who have had limited experience to separate themselves enough from their own feelings to examine their source and deal with them in a constructive way. Unresolved countertransference feelings, however, can be a prime reason for the premature expression of the therapist's own feelings in the counseling relationship.

Countertransference feelings may inspire a number of subtle efforts by us to involve ourselves more personally with those with whom we work. It is clear that some counselors live their own emotional lives in their offices, drawing down for themselves from the stores of affection they feel from those they help. Counselors who make themselves dependent on those with whom they work for emotional reinforcement may permit their own needs to dominate the counseling. This is a traditional hazard for inexperienced counselors. It can also plague overworked helpers who may have forsaken emotional satisfac-

---

Unrecognized Countertransference Feelings

- The need for affection from those we help
- The gratification of intimate sharing with those we help
- The desire to be liked and accepted
- Ambivalence about being an authority and professional

---

tions in other areas of their personal lives in order to meet their large case loads.

Dependence on the individual may develop easily, for example, in counselors who have always dealt with human problems in an intellectual fashion and who have not had much in-depth face-to-face experience with others. It can also develop easily in counselors who have had little experience with members of the opposite sex. The sudden, and often unprecedented, rewards of dealing for the first time on a fairly intimate level with a member of the opposite sex can be exhilarating, exciting, and satisfying, especially for counselors who do not know much about themselves and have not yet learned techniques of self-monitoring.

There are easily readable signs of this kind of countertransference stirring to life, however, and, taken seriously, motivate expanded self-exploration by counselors who find them pointing directly at themselves. Anything that smacks of "going well out of one's way" for the person is a prime indicator that this problem is present. Counselors who observe themselves needlessly rearranging and extending appointments, or offering help for situations quite separate from the counseling, have firsthand evidence of this classic emotional involvement.

Counselors should pay attention to their urges to overimpress those who come for help, to brag to them, for example, about other cases they have handled, about how hard they work, or about how little they are appreciated at home or by their colleagues. Such expressions of our own feelings are ordered to prompting appreciative responses from others. This is also reflected in the behavior of counselors who insist too much on controlling or supervising the lives and decisions of those with whom they work. Some of us seem afraid to let people take

> ## *Signs of Unrecognized Countertransferences*
>
> - Overinvolvement in the other's life
> - Overextending yourself for the other
> - Inflating your image with the other
> - Generating sympathy for yourself
> - Overidentification with the other
> - Acting out

responsibility for themselves because we fear that we may lose some influence over these people and therefore lose their affection as well.

If we want to avoid or deal intelligently with the complicating stress of these problems, we profit from deepening our understanding of the transference phenomenon itself. Reading is helpful in this regard, but in the long run some opportunity to discuss our cases with another person so that we can explore our reactions systematically is the best course for us to follow. Even if we feel that we are among the busiest of counselors we can find time to read and reflect on our own experience.

Counselors who take time for reflection can notice the clues to countertransference problems and begin to trace them down to their source. The chief clue, as MacKinnon and Michels note, is signaled "when the therapist is unable to recognize or refuses to acknowledge the real significance of his own attitudes and behavior."[1] This observation points to the disparity between what counselors do and what counselors *think* they are doing. The evidence for countertransference involvement may be clear and the refusal or reluctance to recognize or to interpret it accurately offers supportive evidence of the existence of the problem.

Examples include counselors who overidentify with the persons they help. The latter's struggle becomes their struggle, and the involvement escalates as it deepens into making decisions and plans that affect wide areas of the lives of others. A classic example of overidentification is found in the encouragement of behavior of which the counselor strongly approves. Standing up to one's parents, for example, may represent a victory less for the person being helped than for therapists over the authority figures in their own lives.

Another stressful area that may draw out our own feelings looms when those we work with learn more about us than can be learned during the hours of counseling. Counselors who discover that these individuals have picked up information about their families, their interests, or their own problems may find themselves actively on the defensive, or they may discover that it is difficult to get the focus back to the other's life. Should we find that we allow ourselves to be manipulated into discussing our own problems, we also learn that we may seriously compromise the therapeutic goals appropriate to counseling. This can also occur if we get involved with the other in some kind of business deal together. Getting involved this way is an example of "acting out" the transference and countertransference. It becomes an emotional *pas de deux* that symbolizes and signals the breakdown of counseling.

Counselors who, for example, buy things or make other financial arrangements or investments through those they help add elements to the relationship that can only harm it and increase their own experience of stress. Such trading with the other may become trading with the enemy and makes it virtually impossible to avoid inappropriate expressions of our own feelings.

The reciprocal transference-countertransference area must be surveyed with sensitivity and care. It is obvious that counselors who prematurely involve their own feelings without understanding what is happening may do more harm than good both to themselves and others. The occurrence of transference-countertransference feelings may also offer constructive occasions for the direct and fitting expression of the counselor's feelings. They can say no to business deals, they can refuse social meetings with those they help, they can use these occurrences to help others look better at themselves.

All counselors must reflect on the democratic and consciously antiprofessional notions that motivate many therapists to disclaim any special skills or training in helping other persons. An exploration of why counselors feel they must prove that they are human by confessing their own sins in a therapy session is therefore relevant. Such counselors may not have resolved their own feelings toward authority or professionalism, or they may not realize how important it is for them to be accepted and liked by those with whom they work.

Counselors who impose their own problems on the therapy situation out of due time may place themselves so much at the center of the relationship from the very beginning that they interfere with its ever making any progress. Counselors can profitably reflect on the image

---

Appropriate Self-Revelations

- When it helps our understanding
- When distractions intervene
- When expressions of positive regard enhance the relationship

---

they are trying to project. Sometimes they dress, speak, and even grow beards or affect other mannerisms that show their clear identification with some other therapist or teacher. There is some problem when a professional person borrows or excessively leans on somebody else's identity. Such counselors find it difficult to get themselves into the relationship in an honest and clean fashion because they are so preoccupied with acting the role of the master therapist. One is reminded of a once popular psychological lecturer who confessed without irony that, as he gazed at his shaving mirror in the morning, he reminded himself that he was not Freud. That is an extraordinary but classic reaction of those who are uncertain of their identity.

Following Our Healthy Instincts

Most of the "Don'ts" — those special rules that many therapists obsessively try always to keep in mind — do not exist in any absolute form. As we begin to trust our own instincts we do not feel bound by any of these commandments never to express our own feelings and our own opinions, or to answer questions that are proposed to us. We find a certain freedom to let ourselves show through in counseling, which is constructive and, in the long run, quite helpful to the counseling itself. It is perfectly safe, in other words, when we are aware of ourselves and can listen to ourselves while in relationship to others, we may express our feelings in a number of situations. These include such occasions as the following:

When we do not understand what the other person is trying to tell us or, for some reason that we cannot define, we feel that we are not in contact on a particular theme or point. When this occurs it is almost always more stressful to fake understanding than it is to admit that we are confused or that we have missed something. An honest expression of how we are experiencing the relationship at this point is perfectly appropriate. This can be done in a self-possessed and direct manner that expresses both our genuineness and our concern. Such a statement of our true feelings fits into the therapy; it is part of its truth and can only advance its purpose.

When we are distracted or cannot otherwise deal with some feeling that interferes with our capacity to respond to the other person. Such feelings operate on us whether we admit them or not. We begin, of course, by admitting them to ourselves. If this does not make them more manageable, it may be appropriate to mention these feelings in the course of the therapy. They are already present in the relationship because of their reality inside us. "I'm sorry but I cannot seem to hear you because I keep thinking about..." is a valid way of introducing this kind of annoyance. When expressing such feelings we must exercise care that the other not misinterpret what we are trying to say. For example, counselors who prematurely tell others of their attraction to them may find that this kind of expression — made ostensibly to clear the air — is interpreted by others in a way different from that intended. Counselors must use good judgment and not express feelings that are ambiguous, that may easily be misinterpreted, or that serve only to relieve them but do not help the relationship itself.

When a genuine expression of interest or caring fits the flow of the relationship. We know that counseling seems to improve if we like others. Counselors have been notoriously hesitant to express spontaneous concern for individuals out of fear that this would violate one of these famous "Don'ts." This may deny to the therapy an ingredient that is indispensable for its success. It is also very helpful for counselors to realize that it is not only acceptable but appropriate for them to express their own affection or concern for those they help at times. It is a liberating experience for others to realize that their counselors may like them but still do not try to take them over or possess them. This nonpossessive liking is a powerful component in successful therapy, just as it is in real life. It is the kind of response that mature persons are able to give because they no longer feel that they will necessarily become emotionally entangled or will be lost if they let these true feelings surface. The counselor who discovers the freedom to express genuine feelings of caring also achieves a new freedom of spontaneity that removes much of the stress of counseling work.

Reasonably self-aware counselors come to trust their own experience because it has been refined through their own sensitivity and reflection. Mature persons can always trust their own feelings because these feelings are integrated into their personalities. The best advice for mature counselors is to allow them to feel their own way as far as expressing their own feelings is concerned. They possess a reliable sense of when to do this because they can hear what is going on inside themselves as well as within their various helping relationships. They know when to listen and when to speak; they do not let artificial rules outside themselves predetermine their behavior.

– 18 –

SUPPORTIVE PSYCHOTHERAPY

N ONPROFESSIONAL COUNSELORS are very good at what is termed *supportive* therapy. This is a demanding approach because, while its goal is to keep persons focused on the conscious arena of their lives, its implementation demands, and depends on, an understanding of how their unconscious operates. Nonprofessionals, by their designation, provide services, otherwise unavailable, in the vast universe of everyday life to help people cope with their problems in an immediate, usually short-term fashion. Supportive counseling is the right thing to do when the time is limited, the problem is pressing, and the individual is sitting in distress across the room from us.

Supportive treatment is not as limited, although it draws from the same commonsense foundation, as keeping others from moving an accident victim before the medics arrive. It resembles more what the medics do, in accord with their training, in giving emergency treatment as they carefully transport the accident victim to another site for treatment. Supportive treatment is a more demanding art form because those who offer it are not just giving first aid or preparing the person for transit. They are treating the person in perhaps the only treatment setting the person may ever enter and, although referrals may at times be made, supportive counselors offer substantial, well-thought-out assistance that has clearly defined goals of helping others cope with their difficulties and function better in life.

The art demanded of supportive counselors is revealed in their ability to keep persons within the realm of their conscious awareness of their conflicts. To do this, they must be able to read the unconscious of the other, factor its influences into their strategy, and employ tactics in making responses that acknowledge but leave undisturbed the unconscious dynamics of those who come for help. They must work as a sculptor would on the softest of marble, measuring each stroke with great care so as to shape the surface without sending a crack through the whole. Supportive counseling demands an understanding of dynamics, or the material with which we are working, and highly disciplined skill in fashioning responses, or striking artful blows, that will give shape to the surface of the life of others without breaking them open completely.

This is not, then, second-rate assistance, but the sensible, possible approach for helpers who do not have the luxury of selecting the people who seek out their assistance or the available time for more intensive treatment. Supportive help does lead to what is best termed a limited but true insight. This insight is described as limited because it is restricted to explorations of the conscious and preconscious aspects of troubled persons' experience. The art is involved in focusing on those materials that can be recalled easily or with modest effort. This artfulness is also required to avoid tapping into unconscious aspects of experience, that is, that area demanding experience with unconscious dynamics and the time in which to carry it out effectively. The latter is the proper province of long-term, insight-oriented, or uncovering therapy, in short, the task of thoroughly trained professionals in psychiatry, psychology, and social work.

Important Distinctions

Counselors with some training sometimes feel that the recommended choice of supportive therapy is a somewhat unnecessary fettering of their helpers' wings. In truth, however, most of the treatment being carried out by professionals is, because of circumstances such as time, the aptitude of the persons being helped, reimbursement schedules, or mutual choice, that of the supportive variety. Some leading authorities, for example, the psychoanalyst Paul Dewald, have described long-term, insight-oriented treatment as on a par with elective surgery. Nonprofessional counselors will treat themselves and those who seek their assistance in a healthier and more constructive way if they proceed with some appreciation of the differences between these approaches.

Insight-Oriented Treatment

Insight-oriented treatment has as its goal the resolution of conflicts, that is, the deep exploration of the unconscious psychological roots of the problems whose twisted outer growth emerges in people's conscious lives in disguised and discomfiting ways. Therapists aim at unearthing these roots so that these individuals can, in a sense, break them open, examine, and, through understanding them, render their psychological power neutral. The objective of such treatment is the development of

Distinctions between Psychotherapies

	Supportive Treatment	Insight-Oriented Treatment
Goal:	limited goals and relief of symptoms	personality reorganization and resolution of underlying conflicts
Focus:	mainly conscious conflicts	unconscious and preconscious conflicts
Technique:	strategies to support defenses	increase scope of person's mental processes
Therapist:	freer to be themselves	generally neutral stance

fresh ways of adaptation and reintegration of the personality. This goal is very demanding because it calls for the maturation, from within, of the person, with all that this implies in the development of talents, better personal relationships with others, and greater freedom of choice about how this person will function.

Such treatment, which may take several years, also requires a major personal commitment of energy and time on the part of the person entering treatment. Not everyone can make such sacrifices because of their life, work, financial circumstances, and health plans. And, even if these factors are favorable, those seeking help may lack the psychological stamina to persevere in treatment. The decision to go ahead is made very carefully between therapist and the person and only after long and careful assessment of all significant internal and external factors.

It should also be observed that, if such serious treatment is undertaken without properly considering all the impinging elements, the process may fail, or result in stalemate, with the last state of those seeking help worse than the first. Their symptoms — the surface manifestations of their inner conflicts — may intensify and they may regress so that they become increasingly emotionally disabled.

In summary, the therapist undertaking this mode of treatment intends to enter the unconscious and must possess the extensive training and the finely honed skills to do this in a constructive and controlled way. The overall aim of reorganizing the personality is lofty, difficult, and extremely demanding. Nonprofessional counselors follow their common sense in not deliberately initiating such treatment plans. They sense that they should not naively employ techniques — especially those offered in short courses or workshops, such as dream analysis — that may accidentally dislodge unconscious material.

Supportive Treatment

Supportive treatment, informed by a dynamic understanding of personality, views the conscious, current life situation of the other as the proper field for constructive intervention. Those who employ it avoid any strategies that might, even indirectly or accidentally, pierce the membrane of repression that keeps the contents of the unconscious out of the person's active awareness.

The purpose of such treatment is to relieve the symptoms experienced by the person seeking help. This is done without any attempt to alter or rebuild the person's basic character structure. Counselors aim at bringing about external behavioral changes within the person's present, psychologically flawed adaptation.

Nonprofessional counselors, therefore, choose to *strengthen the healthiest defenses* of others, assisting them in a consciously insightful way to improve their functioning without descending to the depths of the unconscious or disturbing it in any way. We are not, as incidental if indispensable helpers, interested in rebuilding other persons but in assisting them to examine their conscious behavior and to alter it constructively. To this end, counselors may and should use any sensible and healthy device available to troubled persons to accomplish this goal. Some of these are discussed in chapter 1. These persons will, in the course of this help, achieve insights, but they will be into preconscious aspects of their motivation rather than into the remote unconscious sources of their behavior.

It is clear, in the course of daily life, that many people, through supportive treatment, learn to live much happier lives without changing their basic personalities. They may, as in physical illness, be forced to learn to live with chronic problems; that is, one of the outcomes of counseling may be that they accept and live more comfortably with themselves despite their psychological liabilities. Nonprofessional counselors must recognize that such persons, although functioning better within their limitations, may continue to have — and may need to have — various symptoms. Helpers must always be careful about demanding that people give up their symptoms and be equally circumspect by never promising them that they can help free them from their grip. The objective of supportive treatment for nonprofessional counselors is frequently that of helping others to weather a crisis successfully. Supportive techniques are the strategies of choice in dealing with people in crisis situations. Some nonprofessional counselors, thinking that they would do better by attempting more in-depth therapy, not only make a mistake in judgment but also fail to utilize the many resources they already have at their disposal to support the other successfully. Lawyers, for example, may provide enormously stabilizing responses by drawing on their technical expertise to help people understand and exercise their legal rights, or to straighten out their legal affairs, or to put their wills in order. Such responses strengthen people's sense of control and shore up their best defenses. Pastoral counselors possess a rich armamentarium of responses from the spiritual tradition of those they work with that can strengthen their defenses enormously. Prayer, ascetic self-denial, the avoidance of the occasion of sin, reassurances about God's love and forgiveness: these, among countless others, can be strong and positive reinforcers for helping people manage their troubled and troubling behavior.

How They Differ

Dewald emphasizes that, whatever the treatment mode, it is the relationship and the dynamic use of it by the therapist that forms the cornerstone of treatment, both supportive and insight-oriented.[1] Supportive and uncovering treatment are much more alike in utilizing the relationship than they are different in goals and techniques.

Yet they accent this relationship in ways consistent with their separate goals. The basic difference lies in the way the helpers use the instrumentality of themselves in the process. In insight-oriented treatment, for example, therapists strive to maintain a neutral stance, keeping themselves a vaguer presence in the relationship for the express purpose of exerting a pull on unconscious material. The more neutral and the less sharply defined therapists are in the relationship, the more the person will project transference reactions onto them, thus forwarding the essential work of getting at unconscious conflicts.

In supportive approaches, however, counselors should avoid engaging in behavior that will, in effect, act as a poultice to draw out this buried dynamic material. They can feel freer to educate, give measured advice, and, in other ways, remain concrete, well-defined personalities, thereby minimizing or dulling any magnetism for the iron filings of the unconscious. The less neutral we are, the less we challenge the main defenses and the more we keep the focus where it belongs — on the current conscious stage of the person's life and activities. This strengthens positive rapport and helps to avoid the complications of regressive transference distortions that can be so surprising and dismaying to nonprofessional counselors. The latter can, in a real sense, function as their best disciplined selves; they can *be themselves* as long as they respect the overall dynamic realities of the relationship. In general, supportive counselors want to use the relationship to promote identification and to strengthen specific defenses.

Thus counselors should recognize the defensive system employed by the other and adapt to it in the process of giving help. If, for example, persons use intellectualization as a main defense, we may realize that they are thereby avoiding emotional content, but that this is, in what is certainly not the best of all possible worlds, the best they can do to manage their way through life. We may choose actively to strengthen that defense, perhaps by recommending books for them to read, rather than challenging and weakening a defense they need in order to keep their psychological balance. So, too, we may allow persons to depend on us — literally, to lean on us — during a crisis period. While we might ordinarily view dependence on the counselor as less than ideal, we also recognize that this is indeed the most sensible way of managing this specific critical interval. Such techniques would not, of course, be employed in this way in insight-oriented treatment.

A Rule of Thumb Revisited

It may be helpful to restate here the rule of thumb for nonprofessional counselors in understanding their commitment to the supportive approach. If our main function is as pastor, doctor, funeral director, or teacher, and the person comes in relationship to us as our parishioner, our general medical patient, our bereaved mourner, or our pupil, we are on safe and solid ground with the supportive approach. If we are well-trained counselors or function fully as therapists and the person relates to us as one seeking therapy, we have shifted to a form of relationship in which we may evaluate, according to such variables as time, the character of our treatment plan. When we are nonprofessional counselors and sense that the needs of this person go far beyond what we can provide in a supportive relationship, we initiate referral to an appropriate professional resource.

PART THREE

– *19* –

READING THE SIGNS /
WORKING WITH FAMILIES

A S NONPROFESSIONAL COUNSELORS, we do not often see, much less try to treat, individuals suffering from the constellation of disorders characterized by cognitive defects or general medical conditions. Nonetheless, we should have some familiarity with such problems, especially with the cognitive defects of *delirium* and *dementia*. This general knowledge helps us in the counseling that is much more likely to come our way with the family members of those suffering from these serious and upsetting disorders. It is also possible that a person suffering from the early stages of dementia may come, or be brought, to us. Our knowing the basics about the signs and symptoms of these disorders allows us to discuss them with modest but comforting confidence. It allays the anxiety we might otherwise experience, strengthens us in supporting the relatives of the afflicted person, and enables us to know when and how to make an appropriate referral.

Delirium

Individuals with delirium experience a quickly developing change in consciousness and in cognition. Most affected individuals will already be in, or in the process of direct referral to, a hospital. The condition may be due to a complicating medical disorder or may be a result of exposure to a substance such as carbon monoxide, alcohol intoxication or withdrawal, or prescribed or nonprescribed medications. These individuals are inattentive, their minds wander, and they are easily distracted so that we must repeat our questions to them many times. Such persons are difficult to engage in conversation, appear disoriented, and are unable to remember what they are talking about. They may also be restless and show evidence of hallucinations or other perceptual disturbances. The condition tends to fluctuate during the day so that one

175

member of the family may visit the person and observe no evidence of the disturbance while another member, visiting later in the day, may find the person is incoherent, pulling at the bedsheets, and calling out to long lost relatives. The challenge to professionals, their physicians, is to identify the source of the problem and to draw up an appropriate treatment plan for the suffering person.

Our counseling is usually with members of the afflicted individual's family. If we are well informed about such illnesses we can help them understand the entity, its typical fluctuating course, and need for professional medical treatment. We should encourage family members to remain in close contact with the treating physicians so that they may cooperate intelligently on the overall care of the person. It is often helpful for the family to acquaint the physician with the patient's usual mode of functioning, response to stress, or any specific anxieties, such as that generated by unpaid bills or credit card debt, that may complicate the presenting illness.

We may reinforce requests that family members bring to the hospital some familiar and important objects, such as pictures or favorite souvenirs, that lessen the starkness of the hospital room environment by their comforting familiarity. Family members are often asked to provide reassurance by spending certain periods, or shifts, of time with the disturbed person. We may encourage them while gently fending off overanxious family members whose presence may be more disturbing than helpful.

For most individuals suffering delirium, the condition is temporary and reversible. We can educate and reassure family members about that. Otherwise, family members who misunderstand the nature of the patient's symptoms, imagining them to be permanent and irreversible, may express anxiety, panic, or even hopelessness that constitutes an added complication for the person and the treating professionals. If we are supporting from the side, or are the responsible physician, maintaining a calming demeanor is a critical contribution to the management of the stricken person and the concerned family.

After their symptoms of delirium are resolved, many persons will have no recollection of these frightening outward signs of disturbance. Others, however, may have very distressing recollections of their experience and will profit from ongoing support and counseling aimed at coping with these upsetting mementoes. If we are to be helpful in dampening the blaze of these anxieties, we should deepen our understanding of the disorder and of its lingering sparks of remembrance.

Dementia

Persons suffering dementia display a broad range of cognitive impairments, behavioral symptoms, and mood changes. There are many kinds of dementia, based on the nature of the underlying disorder, which professionals may or may not be able to identify. We are almost all familiar with the dementia of Alzheimer's disease, but dementia also can be a function of vascular problems, traumatic brain injuries, various metabolic illnesses, or infectious diseases such as HIV. The most prominent feature of the disturbance is memory impairment that may be accompanied by one or more of the following deficits: *aphasia* (disturbance in language); *apraxia* (an impaired ability to carry out normal motor activities even though motor function is intact); *agnosia* (a failure to recognize or identify familiar objects even though sensory function is intact); and a disturbance in *executive function* (the inability to plan, organize, sequence, or abstract).

Early symptoms may begin slowly but may gradually become perplexing to the affected individual and worrisome to their relatives. There may be memory loss for recent events often accompanied by apathy and subtle impairments in judgment, insight, and executive functions. Such persons may begin to lose valuables like keys or wallets, forget to turn off the oven or coffee machine, forget where they parked their car, lose their way home, or become lost in an unfamiliar neighborhood. As their illness progresses, such persons may pace repeatedly and wander, especially at night. These poignant changes create a problem of assuring their safety that is an onerous challenge for their families. We help families with our supportive counseling but even more if we can arrange a psychiatric consultation as early as possible. This allows better management of their symptoms and offers an opportunity to educate the family about the illness and its typical course.

We counselors are, in whatever our main role may be, often the first ones approached by the worried family. Most people have heard about but have had little experience with such problems so their first response, early in the course of the illness, is to normalize the deficiencies and behavior of the affected person. They do not want to do anything that may worry the relative over seemingly minor forgetfulness or lapses. They avoid challenges to the person's self esteem. As counselors, whether we are a social worker neighbor, the parish priest, or the family physician, we are, as the first ones consulted, in a position to help the family take an objective look at the changes they have noticed. Often our counseling aims at providing reassurance that an appropriate referral with a specialist is in the best interests not only of the potential patient but of the family itself.

A variety of supportive and behavioral treatments are available for patients with dementia, but these are usually offered in an institutional setting in collaboration with the person's medical treatment. Once the illness has been recognized and properly diagnosed and treatment interventions have begun, we may be called upon to work with the family members intimately involved in their relative's overall treatment. The long and difficult journey of a person with Alzheimer's disease is a passion play of countless frustrations and challenges for the members of their families. One of the earliest problems of emerging dementia centers on driving the car, a sensitive and universal symbol of our control of our own lives.

Mild dementia increases the risk of accidents and, early on, affected persons need to be encouraged to stop driving or to limit their driving to what may, at least for awhile, serve as designated safe environments. As dementia increases, the family will need to take a significant role in urging these individuals to stop driving altogether, an often emotional breakpoint. We counselors may be called upon to support family members in these delicate negotiations as well as in their maintaining good contact with the medical personnel involved in the patient's care. As counselors, we may also provide support to family members as they structure the person's living situation to guarantee safety. We also stand with them as they deal, as they inevitably will, with the frustrations that flower abundantly out of living with a loved one who has drifted out of range and can no longer respond in a logical and coherent manner to even the simplest of communications.

Basic principles of care for demented patients helpful for family members include: (1) keeping requests and demands relatively simple and avoiding tasks whose complexity may frustrate the suffering person; (2) avoiding confrontation and deferring requests if these anger the affected person; (3) remaining calm, firm, and supportive when the person becomes upset; (4) maintaining consistency and avoiding unnecessary change; (5) providing frequent reminders, explanations, and orientation cues to the affected individual; (6) recognizing any declines in capacity to function and adjusting expectations appropriately; and (7) bringing any sudden declines in function or the emergence of new symptoms to professional attention.[1]

In the early stages, one of the most difficult and emotionally laden challenges for family members is found in dealing with persons who manifest the signs of losing their independence, when they recognize, for example, that they can no longer keep their own checkbook or drive the car. Depressive symptoms may appear to complicate these already emotionally wrenching changes, and these also need to be brought to the attention of the professionals caring for the afflicted relative.

Counselors should be familiar with community resources for demented patients and their families. These include such organizations as the Alzheimer's Association (1-800-621-0379), support groups, various types of respite care, as well as nursing homes and long-term facilities. These are invaluable sources of help as we assist others. We should also have some mastery of available written resources on dementia. The Alzheimer's Association has a number of pamphlets, books, and videos that help family members learn about the care and treatment of loved ones stricken with dementia.

Mental Disorders Due to a General Medical Condition

This category is included to alert counselors to the possibility of mental symptoms emerging within the context of a physical illness. As counselors, for example, we should suspect some physical problem if the person exhibits unusual symptoms, such as a fifty-pound weight loss along with symptoms of a mild depression. This disproportion in the physical status and complaints of the person strongly suggest further evaluation. That symptoms of anxiety or depression arise about the same time that the person is diagnosed with a physical illness also suggests the need for further professional evaluation.

Some illnesses exist in which symptoms of depression are the first manifestation of an underlying physical illness such as carcinoma of the pancreas or systemic lupus erythematosis. Anxiety may be the first manifestation of hyperthyroidism. This is not to suggest that we counselors should play amateur physician or try to know the medical side of all of these conditions, or that we need to make clinical-like judgments about the root causation of the mental symptoms that people exhibit. We should rather suspect a physical illness if the symptoms are disproportionate to the condition, are not characteristic of the condition, or occur about the same time that some physical illness is diagnosed, or if individuals begin to manifest other signs, especially physical complaints, while they are seeing us. These real medical possibilities reinforce the importance of our establishing a relationship with a local referral source who can serve as a consultant in situations in which an accompanying medical condition is suspected.

– 20 –

DRUGS: USE AND ABUSE

T HE EXPLOSION OF DRUG USE, among people of all ages, and the
failure of many wars waged against it, is all too familiar to all of
us who engage in counseling, even in a nonprofessional or occasional
way. The difficulty, swollen by its own publicity, is a critical and almost
a defining element for large parts of our culture, and, despite massive
efforts at research and public education, it remains veiled in great confusion and uncertainty. Few educators or clergy work in their callings
very long without encountering the drug problem, either through those
with whom they directly work or through the concerns brought to them
by parents or others who want their opinion or their assistance in dealing with a problem that spreads across America from its ghettos to its
suburbs.

It is true that there is nothing new about drug dependence. The
problem of returning war veterans who acquired an addiction to drugs
during their tours of duty is hardly news. The hypodermic needle was
invented shortly before the Civil War, thus making widespread use of
morphine possible. The "soldiers' sickness" was the name given to the
problems of veterans of that war who became addicted to this drug.
At times, the use of morphine, opium, or other mind-altering drugs
was not unusual or punished in as staid a culture as Victorian England. Drug use has had a hundred masks in as many entrances into
history. Difficult as it has been to assess and monitor, we have made
some small advances in the ways we deal with what we call the drug
problem. Heroin, for example, was once employed as a substitute for
opium and morphine addiction and led only to a severe problem with
its own self-created dependence.

We have come to recognize that, for some persons with a prolonged
history of what is termed opioid disturbance caused by heroin use, a
useful treatment is the substitution of a longer-acting opioid, such as
methadone or LAAM (l-alpha acetylmethadol). Although these drugs
also create dependence, they have generally been shown to be effective
in improving the health status and social functioning of these per-

sons while also decreasing mortality and criminal activity. Aware of these risks and outcomes, the federal government has now issued strict guidelines that regulate the way this treatment is used.

Drugs and Youth

The cultural problems that flower out of drug addiction are many, various, well publicized, and yet often ignored. Sometimes these situations are overlooked because of our attitudes toward young people and what we judge to be their values and goals in life. We abound in documentation of the personal upheaval that follows when families are broken or when the intact family itself no longer constitutes the norm, denying stable emotional circumstances to individuals who need them to grow in a healthy manner. The day's headlines reveal the mix of social, psychological, and familial forces that shape the drug activity of young people.

It is important for all of us who counsel to have a knowledge and understanding of the nature of various drugs and the differences between them. We need such knowledge if we are going to be able to communicate credibly with younger people. Nothing betrays us more quickly than a lack of adequate information about an addictive substance. Quite frequently, adults, for whom the drug culture is often an alien and forbidding territory, have only general notions, and, in conversation, they tend to lump all drug substances together. This almost immediately invalidates them as trustworthy communicators in the eyes of younger people, who regard basic accurate information as the essential first move in any kind of dialogue. The familiar challenge thrown in every generation at older people — "Don't knock it if you haven't tried it" — builds on the revealing and, to youth, betraying ignorance displayed by people unfamiliar with drugs and the distinctions between them.

It is obviously essential to have some feeling for the passage of adolescence and the role that drug-taking plays both in shaping their experience and reflecting American culture at this time. Most drug use in any form by adolescents begins as experimentation, not very different from the curiosity-driven and perennial human experimentation with other unknown or forbidden activities. Most of us counselors can recall some experimentation, perhaps with alcohol, during our own adolescence.

Such exploratory or frankly experimental use of these substances cannot, however, be written off or taken lightly, especially in an environment that has suffered a blizzard of cocaine, ecstasy, and other designer drugs in recent decades. The use of the term "recreational drugs" offers a brutally deceptive rationalization for substances whose effects are far more destructive than recreative. The claims to heightened creativity under the influence of drugs, another familiar justification for their use, is given the lie in the shoddy, often almost incomprehensible products, including many movies, fashioned under their influence.

Survey data indicated that fully 90 percent of cocaine abusers used marijuana at the same age or an earlier age than cocaine.[1] This is important information because of the once widely accepted notion that marijuana use by teenagers and young adults was no real predictor of drug abuse in adulthood. Now it appears that this was falsely reassuring and that the effects may be quite the opposite, particularly in relationship to cocaine. Although all teenagers puffing on cigarettes may at first look alike, their habits and backgrounds offer counselors important information. Marijuana, along with nicotine and alcohol, are referred to as "gateway" drugs, and their use early in life along with "early evidence of aggressive behavior, intrafamilial disturbances, and associating with substance-using peers contribute to, and predict, continued substance abuse and the subsequent development of abuse and dependence."[2]

In this age group, "growing preoccupation with substance use, frequent episodes of intoxication, use of drugs with greater dependence liability (e.g., opioids, cocaine), and preference for routes of administration that result in quicker onset of drug effects (e.g., by injection or freebasing) and for rapidly acting preparations (e.g., methamphetamine) presage the development of substance abuse."[3] While such patterns of addiction are usually observed in late adolescent years, some individuals may not abuse substances until much later in life.

The Work of Adolescence

The work of adolescence, as Erik Erikson has pointed out, is the consolidation of our identity. We must come to terms with the various aspects of our personalities and our newly developed sense of ourselves as sexual, independent beings, so that we may move on to the stage of early adulthood with a good sense of our own personalities. Adolescence is difficult to define in a strictly chronological manner as there are late starters as well as those who develop prematurely. Some seem to achieve a sense of adult maturity without a great deal of struggle, while others, well beyond the last boundary line of late adolescence, are yet to resolve their developmental conflicts.

Central to the adolescent's development of an adequate identity is the challenge of separation and individuation. Adolescents must separate themselves from their own family setting in order to develop a true sense of who they are as individuals. This is routinely described as a struggle but it is not always marked by great tension or difficulty. It is, however, normal to observe this somewhat variable process under way during these years. It may be difficult to move toward independence when one is not yet on one's own financially or emotionally. Adolescence, as we know, can be a time of bafflement and strained relations between parents — even the most loving and understanding parents — and their children, who can seem suddenly remote from them. It is a life problem, however, that most sensible people are able to manage without their family's collapsing around them. Any notable lack of family stability complicates the work adolescents must carry out and may heighten their vulnerability to drug involvement.

Deferring Maturity

In addition, adolescents have been lavished with attention over the last generation, especially by marketing experts who have developed a world in which young people are courted for the very adolescent interests and tastes with which they must, sooner or later, come to terms. This contrived niche of pseudo-independence may explain why some find it difficult to do the work of solidifying their identities. Regarded as a highly desirable demographic class, they are treated as consumers and encouraged to satisfy themselves without delay a dozen times each day.

The task of bringing the elements of one's identity together is complicated for adolescents whose parents have never completed the work of adolescence themselves. Such parents seem to have extended their own adolescence. They have adult jobs, but they have incorporated drug use into their lives without examining its effects on them or their children. Because they have not resolved their feelings about authority, they often feel more comfortable trying to be friends with, rather than parents to, their children. Completing the work of adolescence demands adult models and, if these are lacking, the work may be done haphazardly or incompletely. The side effect is deferred maturity.

If we add the enormous impact of peer pressure, we can understand how adolescents, even though they are difficult to group under one heading, can bond in a separate cultural enclave in which drug use, which postpones dealing with reality while offering instant gratification, can be a tolerated but destructive problem. Simple solutions are not available for situations so compounded by interwoven cultural difficulties. We cannot, as adult counselors, merely point at younger people and challenge them to pull themselves together as we may feel that we once did.

Neither can we adults make the opposite mistake of trying to enter into and identify with the adolescent culture in some futile quest for rapport. There is nothing more awkward or ineffective than a middle-aged counselor trying to take on the dress or attitudes of younger people in the hope of reaching them. Adolescents recognize these older people as being extremely needy in their own right, and they do not find in them the kind of models they need in order to pass through their adolescence successfully. Adult attitudes, correct information, and participation in strengthening the community's values and institutions constitute the qualities nonprofessional counselors need in order to help adolescents mature and to deal with the epidemic problem of drugs in our culture.

Signs and Symptoms of Drug Abuse

Drug abusers are common in every calling and at every station in life but their drug taking is often not recognized or even suspected. In 1999, about 14.8 million Americans used illicit drugs. About 3.5 million were classified as dependent on alcohol.[4]

These individuals are not well understood. The drugs they use excessively often come from that grouping termed "psychoactive substances." These include any substances taken into the body that can alter a person's consciousness or state of mind. A great variety of drugs — sometimes in their natural form, sometimes prescribed, sometimes illegally manufactured and obtained — can produce the changes described as psychoactive. These include sedatives, hypnotics, anxiolytics, opioids, cocaine, amphetamines, phencyclidine, hallucinogens, and cannabis.

Although these drugs can produce an almost panoramic range of disturbances, ranging from mild euphoria to delirium, counselors can profit by understanding the common kinds of behaviors and symptoms that suggest drug use as their cause. Some basic concepts allow us to grasp the drug used as well as individuals in the context of their drug use, that is, what effects are sought, why, and at what risks.

The substance-related disorders range from those that relate to the taking of a drug of abuse (including alcohol) to the side effects of a medication or toxin exposure. All of these are referred to as substances, and their ingestion can cause a variety of symptoms. Alcohol will be discussed in a separate chapter, but the basic definitions regarding substances apply to it as well. The substance-related disorders are divided into two groups: the substance use disorders (substance dependence and substance abuse) and the substance-induced disorders (substance intoxication and substance withdrawal). The signs and symptoms of dependence, abuse, intoxication, and withdrawal associated with each of the eleven classes of substances are described in the *DSM-IV-TR*.

Counselors should have some familiarity with the various definitions related to substance use disorders. *Substance dependence,* for example, is defined as a cluster of three or more symptoms listed in the DSM-IV-TR. This includes *tolerance,* which relates to the need for greatly increased amounts of the substance to achieve intoxication or the desired effect or a markedly diminished effect with continued use of the same amount of the substance. *Withdrawal* is a maladaptive behavioral change, accompanied by physiological and cognitive changes, that occurs when the blood and tissue concentrations of the substance decline in a person who has used the substance for a long time. In response to tolerance, individuals may take increasing amounts of the substance to achieve their goal. In response to withdrawal, they may take more of the substance to quiet the onset of disturbing symptoms.

Such use of the substance becomes a *compulsive* activity. Persons taking the substances cannot seem to stop their use and their histories reveal previous efforts to cut down. They may commonly spend inordinate amounts of time obtaining or using the drug, thus interfering with their social, occupational, and recreational life. Although these individuals are aware that their life is in disarray, they may begin to withdraw from family activities, lose interest in their usual occupations, and evidence signs of depression while continuing to take the substance.

The term "substance abuse" is not the same as use, misuse, or hazardous use. It is rather *a maladaptive pattern of substance use that is associated with repeated adverse consequences flowing from the substance use.* As a result, the abusers may be repeatedly absent or late for work, truant from school, or negligent in carrying out family responsibilities. They may have repeated legal encounters due to furtive efforts to obtain money or drugs or they may have repeated citations for driving under the influence (DUI). They may continue the use of substances even when they have persistent and recurrent social or interpersonal problems such as intoxication-caused arguments and physical fights with their spouses. A diagnosis of either dependence or abuse demands that the individual demonstrate such behavior for at least twelve months.

Most people are familiar with the signs and symptoms of intoxication, although the specific manifestations may vary depending on the substance used. *Intoxication* is the development of a reversible substance-specific syndrome due to recent ingestion of a substance. It results in clinically significant changes traceable to the substance's effect on the nervous system that may include impaired judgment, impaired social or occupational functioning, and belligerence. Intoxication with amphetamines or cocaine, for example, may be accompanied by increases in blood pressure, respiratory rate, pulse and body temperature.

The essential feature of *substance withdrawal* is the development of a substance-specific maladaptive behavioral change, accompanied by physiological and cognitive changes that result from the cessation or reduction of substance after prolonged use. Amphetamine or cocaine withdrawal may be accompanied by symptoms opposite to those from intoxication. These may include depressed mood, fatigue, increased appetite, and agitation.

Cocaine

Cocaine is the snowy Everest that dominates the landscape of the drug culture today. The *DSM-IV-TR* tells us that "after a peak in the 1970s, the proportion of the population who have used cocaine in any of its forms gradually decreased until the early 1990s, after which the diminution continued but at a slower rate. A 1996 national survey of drug use reported that 10 percent of the population had used cocaine, with 2 percent reporting use in the last year. Crack use was much less prevalent, but the age group with the highest rate over the past year (5 percent for cocaine and 1 percent for crack) was 18 to 25 year olds."[5] Cocaine smoking is associated with more rapid progression from use to dependence or abuse than is intranasal use.[6]

Particularly serious about the current cocaine craze is the finding that in some forms it is highly addictive and its use puts the individual at high risk for medical complications. These latter may include those from arterial constriction and can lead to myocardial infarction, stroke, hypertensive episodes, and anoxia secondary to seizures. All of these can result in death.

When working with persons suspected of using or abusing cocaine, we should have some idea of the different forms in which the drug is used and their relative potential for producing dependence and toxicity.[7] These include the following:

Coca leaf chewing, an ancient method, common in South America, that involves toasting the leaves and chewing them or their ash along with an alkaline material. There is a somewhat slow absorption so that effects may not occur for five to ten minutes but may last for hours.

Oral use, in which cocaine is mixed with an elixir or some beverage and is absorbed slowly, with the peak level of the drug reached in about one hour. The possibility of becoming addicted to drug use is less when the substance is taken in this manner than when it is taken intranasally.

Intranasal administration, better known as "snorting," is one of the best known ways of using cocaine. It results in a relatively rapid onset of the "high," which comes on within two or three minutes and begins to fade in about forty-five minutes. Cocaine is often snorted at fifteen- or twenty-minute intervals to maintain the "high." Use by this method is complicated because of its potential for causing serious dependence as well as serious physical problems, such as nasal septum necrosis and perforation.

Intravenous cocaine use leads to a "rush" within thirty or forty seconds and its effect may last ten to twenty minutes. Because of its rapid onset and its short stimulation life, its potential for developing dependence is greater than the previous listed methods. A fearful complication of this method is found in the risk of becoming infected with the AIDS virus through the use of unclean needles. A further problem is caused by the inconsistent quality and character of street purchases for this intravenous usage. The user, therefore, cannot determine the effect of the drug so taken because the strength and purity of the dose cannot be determined accurately.

In *smoking cocaine,* coca paste is extracted from coca leaves with the aid of gasoline, kerosene, and sulfuric acid and is then mixed with tobacco and smoked in cigarette form or in a pipe. This results in a very rapid absorption of the drug (eight to ten seconds) with effects lasting five to ten minutes. Because the drug used this way acts so quickly — a "hit" as it is called — it is a highly addictive method. It also presents particular risks for developing lung complications. *Freebase* and *crack* are essentially coca paste prepared in specific manners to produce products that generate a more rapid "high." Crack is cocaine alkaloid mixed with sodium bicarbonate that dries into small "rocks." It is more easily vaporized and inhaled than other forms of cocaine, causing a rapid onset of its effect. According to Vereby and Gold, "The financial success of crack is attributed strictly to a marketing and packaging gimmick which made small amounts of high quality cocaine available at low prices, especially to people of low economic classes and adolescents."[8]

We counselors must recognize that the use of cocaine is extraordinarily risky. "Cocaine," according to Vereby and Gold, "may cause sudden death, regardless of dose, blood levels of cocaine, or route of administration."[9] In recent years, the Substance Abuse and Mental Health Service Administration (SAMHSA) has sponsored a Drug Abuse Warning Network (DAWN), which compiles the latest findings on the use of illegal drugs and the nonmedical use of legal drugs as reflected in Emergency Department data. In the twenty-one hospitals surveyed nationwide, there were 11,651 drug-related deaths, with cocaine the most frequently mentioned drug (4,864 mentions), followed by heroin/morphine (4,820 mentions), and alcohol in combination with other drugs (3,916 mentions).[10]

Because of its rapid action and its highly pleasurable and addictive qualities, interrupting or breaking the use of this drug is very difficult. As a result, the habit becomes the focus of the person's life, often resulting in loss of job, deterioration or destruction of interpersonal relationships, and even alienation from society, to that state of homelessness that is the final result of the addict's need to spend every available dollar to support the habit.

Other Drugs

Another form of drug abuse involves opioids such as morphine, methadone, codeine, and heroin, all of which are abused by persons who can obtain them illegally on the street. They are often used by the young, especially from the lower socioeconomic levels. The search for money to obtain these drugs accounts, in some communities, for the majority of their serious crimes. The most common symptoms of such drug abuse may be observed in scarred veins, the "tracks" that indicate intravenous drug use. Users also display frequent drowsiness, "nodding off," apathy, and difficulty in concentration. As a result, the use of these drugs contributes to a vicious if familiar circle — its effects deprive the user of generating any motivation to change things. These drugs are at times abused by health professionals, who have easy access to them. In addition opioid abuse is associated with a high death rate, 10 per 1000 per year of untreated persons.[11]

Sedative hypnotics such as Valium, Librium, and the barbiturates involve drug abuse whose most appealing aspect lies in their capacity, similar to that of alcohol, to deaden the pain or discomfort that many people experience in ordinary living. As a result, such persons are often housewives or other relatively well-functioning members of society who are able to maintain some semblance of a normal life. They may, on occasion, be obtaining these drugs by prescription from well-meaning physicians who may not realize how much these patients have come to depend on these medications. To help these patients, counselors must suspect and inquire about their use, while recognizing that many of these people, like alcoholics, deny that they are using them too often or in excessive doses. Careful evaluation, the development of an understanding relationship, and timely and strategic use of referral resources can help these individuals.

What Can the Counselor Do?

Counselors are not generally the primary agents of treatment for persons suffering from drug problems. We may, however, be part of the treatment team operating under the supervision of a mental health professional, or we may play some auxiliary role in working with such a team. We may, however, be called upon to identify affected individuals and to assist in steering them toward appropriate treatment. Our first challenge is to maintain a healthy vigilance about the possibility that someone may be using drugs excessively or be suffering from addiction.

We help ourselves and others by first making a survey of the symptoms of drug abuse. What surfaces when young people are on drugs? The general symptoms embrace changes in school attendance, in homework quality, in discipline, or in grades. This list also includes changes in physical appearance followed by a sudden or unusual emotional outbreaks or flare-ups. Further indications of drug abuse may be found in the furtive behavior of younger people about the subject of drugs or their possession. Adults should also note any sudden change of associations or social patterns in adolescents. A subtle but important indication emerges when young persons begin borrowing money from fellow students to buy drugs or when they begin to wear sunglasses at inappropriate times in order to hide the pupils of their eyes. Such activities as stealing small items from school or home may also suggest that a drug problem exists. When students are found in odd places during the school day — in closets or storage rooms — a legitimate suspicion of drug usage may arise. Obviously we must not be overzealous nor should we overinterpret these signs. We must be familiar with them and not naive about their possible meaning. These signals should alert us to make prudent investigations and careful judgments if we are going to be helpful in the many problematic situations that will come our way.

What can counselors do? Belkin suggests that there are three areas with which those who function in counseling roles must be active.[12] The first is *preventive*. This requires counselors to understand the drug problem and its manifestations as thoroughly as possible. It also requires counselors to participate in the development of drug education programs through which they can make adequate and up-to-date information available to younger people. Second, counselors may work *in a therapeutic way* with younger people. They may be the first ones to see those who have a serious problem with drugs, and they may need to refer them to other sources of ongoing help. Third, it may be the role of the nonprofessional counselor to maintain lines of communication between all the interested parties while arrangements for further help are being made.

We may add a fourth way in which counselors can keep themselves on what we might term a sensible therapeutic alert. That is by keeping current about the drug scene and related developments through consulting the Web site of the National Institute of Drug Abuse (NIDA — www.nida.nih.gov). The NIDA-sponsored Community Epidemiology Work Group (CEWG) tracks current and emerging trends in drug abuse for twenty-one major metropolitan areas. In early 2001, for example, this group identified a downward trend in cocaine use but identified several legal prescription drugs, such as clonazepan (a benzodiazepine) and prescription painkillers such as oxycodone (Percodan, Percocet) and hydrocodone (Vicadin) as emerging drugs of abuse.[13] Vicadin appears to be the most widely used of these substances.

Counselors should also be alert to the escalating use of MDMA (methylene-dioxymethamphetamine, or ecstasy), which is found especially in many normal recreational and social settings. Users often participate in dance parties known as "raves" and claim that energetic dancing and the drug use lead to increased energy, sexual receptivity, and feelings of warmth and openness that have led some to call it the "love drug."[14] Dr. Alan Lesher, director of the National Institute of Drug Abuse, warns that people have to

> understand that it's not a benign substance at all.... It's an incredibly potent stimulant; that's why people love it. It's both a stimulant and an hallucinogen. It causes tremendous increases in blood pressure, heart rate, etc. It has a dramatic hyperthermic effect; it increases body temperature tremendously. So it's dangerous

in raves and situations like that. . . . When people come in [with questions about using it] it has to be taken seriously. More and more people are losing control over their ecstasy use.[15]

Generally, nonprofessional counselors will not try to interact therapeutically on a long-range basis with persons suffering from major drug problems. Their skills, however, are well used if they can keep the avenues of communication open between younger people, their parents, and other responsible persons such as educational administrators. Counselors may also be involved on the administrative or legal level and with the larger community efforts to respond to drug problems. This may engage them in specific activities or more general educational activities with special groups such as fellow teachers, members of the clergy, or parents. This may also require their developing a relationship with law enforcement authorities, not as informers but as agents of communication and understanding.

The overall approach to those with suspected drug disorders includes a comprehensive psychiatric assessment. This is important because persons with drug problems often have other psychiatric diagnoses as well. Approximately one-third of hospitalized psychiatric patients, for example, also have a diagnosis of substance abuse disorders.[16] This reality requires counselors, after recognizing the problems of such persons, to refer them to an appropriate resource within the community. After assessment, such persons' conditions may require a range of pharmacological or psychosocial treatments. Depending on the character and intensity of the problem, such persons may be referred to a hospital, residential treatment facility, partial hospital care, or an outpatient program. Long-term treatment may also involve group therapy, family therapy, and a variety of self-help groups such as Narcotics Anonymous or Alcoholics Anonymous.

– 21 –

DRINK, DRANK, DRUNK

S o actress Carol Burnett entitled a program about growing up
in a family blighted by alcoholism. Almost everybody knows an
alcoholic or has one for a relative. We are not innocent about the scars
burned into the nation's heart and bounty by the misuse of alcohol. All
of us who counsel in any capacity will sooner or later become involved,
at least indirectly, in the problem, with alcoholics themselves or with
affected members of their families or colleagues at work. A pervasive
smog of stress arises from alcoholic problems. Difficulties with drinking
involve many persons besides the drinkers, multiplying stress manyfold.
The aura of alcoholism encompasses a cluster of people, invading each
with a different intensity of emotion. Although some counselors never
meet an alcoholic face-to-face, almost every day they get the whiff of
some alcoholic's breath in the life of at least one of the persons seeking
help from them. The person across from us may be a spouse or an
adult still unable to pull free of the shadow cast across their lives by an
alcoholic parent. The marks, the memories, and the stresses of problem
drinkers are found almost everywhere in American culture.

In recent years, the problem of alcohol use and abuse has become
more amenable to study. Against a background of increased cultural
concern and a better sense of the problem's dimensions and seque-
lae, research instruments have been fashioned to measure agreed-upon
criteria to diagnose the various levels of severity of what are now
termed "substance-related disorders." As a result, remarkable strides
have been made in assessing the international public health dimensions
of alcohol use.

As noted in the previous chapter, an important distinction exists
between dependence and abuse. Physiological dependence on alcohol
is characterized by evidence of tolerance or symptoms of withdrawal. If
it is associated with a history of withdrawal, physiological dependence
is understood as an indication of a more severe clinical problem and
prospect. Dependence is generally more problematic than abuse and
may contribute to major illnesses or death itself.

Alcohol abuse is diagnosed only in the absence of dependence, is characterized by fewer symptoms, and, therefore, suggests a less severe prospect. We identify it in the behavioral changes consequent to alcohol abuse that manifest themselves in impaired work or school functioning or in legal involvements.

Figures from the Epidemiological Catchment Area Study (ECA) — a catchment represents a defined locality served by a specific institution or group of resources — indicate that 13.8 percent of American adults have experienced either alcohol dependence or alcohol abuse at some time in their lives.[1] It was estimated that in the mid-1990s, the lifetime risk for alcohol dependence was 15 percent in the general population. The overall rate of current alcohol dependence is approximately 5 percent. It is also estimated that in some urban hospitals, as many as one in five intensive care unit admissions is related to alcohol.[2]

The Things We Carry with Us

For counselors, countertransference problems with alcoholics seeking help frequently arise as responses to transference reactions of theirs that crackle with rebelliousness, dishonesty, or aggression. These feelings may also emanate from our lack of knowledge about alcoholism and its treatment or our own experiences with alcohol as a problem in our own lives, families, or friendships.

As counselors we always profit from examining our own feelings about alcohol and alcoholic persons. Some trauma close to the bone can make it very difficult for us to be sympathetic to, or even interested in, persons with drinking problems. We may rule out working with them because we find them morally objectionable. None of us can be of much assistance to individuals with drinking problems if we have within us serious emotional blocks to the basic acceptance of these individuals as persons.

Many helpers function with a smattering of general impressions about alcoholism. They may not have read much or they may habitually respond out of instinct when they must deal with the problem. Such styles may be improvisations in reaction to the difficulties involved in getting a comprehensive and useful clinical picture of the alcoholic person. Nonetheless, we have a professional obligation to deepen our understanding through reading or by attending continuing education programs on the subject.

The basic principle in counseling is to keep the person, rather than just the person's problem with alcohol, in focus. Many counselors find it almost impossible to perceive such individuals as persons. The problem itself looms so large — and with such an unpleasant emotional aura — that compassion does not easily arise and establishing a helping relationship is difficult. It is easy to perceive a person with drinking difficulties as a *problem case* even when we intellectually agree that alcoholism is a disease rather than a personal fault. The effort to see drinkers as persons beneath all their disruptive and abhorrent behavior remains, however, fundamental if counseling is to succeed.

We may also share and need to examine the American ambivalence about drinking, the prime element in our national paradox about alcohol use. Some findings suggest, for example, that many Americans, as they are with other issues, are prepared to denounce alcoholism but are strongly against any measures or movements that threaten to interfere with their individual drinking habits.

This ambiguity about alcohol in our society has been transformed somewhat over the last generation, largely due to the organization MADD (Mothers Against Drunk Drivers) and changes in state laws. All states and the District of Columbia now have laws setting twenty-one as the minimum drinking age. The National Highway Transportation Safety Administration estimates that these laws have reduced traffic fatalities involving drivers in the eighteen-to-twenty-year age range by 13 percent and have, since 1975, saved an estimated 19,121 lives. The 15,786 alcohol-related fatalities in 1999 (38 percent of total traffic deaths for the year) represent a 30 percent reduction from the 22,404 alcohol-related fatalities, or 40 percent of the total, reported in 1989. In addition, an estimate 308,000 persons were injured during that period in crashes in which police reported that alcohol was present.[3]

The development of easily administered tests that measure blood alcohol level (BAL), with the legal limit in most states set at 0.10 grams per deciliter, have furthered legal efforts to control drinking by providing reliable indicators of intoxication levels. The use of such instrumentation has had a dramatic effect on this problem and has influenced the change in public attitudes toward alcohol abusers initially spurred by the consciousness-raising effects of organizations such as MADD.

Counselors may also have negative feelings about individuals with alcoholism because of the chronic relapsing nature of the illness. Alcohol use disorders have a variable course and are frequently characterized by periods of remission and relapse. The majority of those persons who are formally treated for alcoholism, for example, have at least one relapse episode during the first year following treatment, often within the first three months after completion of the program.[4] Professionals as well as nonprofessional counselors can easily become frustrated and irritated at the individual's inability to maintain sobriety and identify with family members who express some of the same feelings.

What We Know about Alcoholism

Genetic Vulnerability

Strong evidence suggests that, especially in findings on men, both alcohol abuse and dependence are related to a genetic vulnerability. The mechanism of genetic transmission, however, remains unknown. Whether such hereditary factors are also present in women is unclear. Nonetheless, some studies suggest that risk for alcoholism increases when one parent suffers from alcoholism (20 percent risk) and increases when both parents are alcoholic (20–50 percent). If the offspring are identical twins, the risk is even greater (54 percent).[5]

The Virginia Twin Registry Study demonstrates that environmental factors shared by family members have little influence on the development of alcoholism in males. The social use of alcohol, on the other hand, is primarily influenced by environmental factors such as peer pressure, cultural attitudes, price, and availability.[6]

Comorbid Disorders

With more refined criteria developed for the various mental disorders, it has been learned that the majority of alcoholic patients also suffer from an additional diagnosable mental condition, or "comorbid' disorder. Whether the alcohol or some other psychological condition is primary is not always immediately clear.

The most common comorbid disorder is second substance disorder. That is followed by antisocial personality, phobias and other anxiety disorders, major depressive disorder, and dysthymic disorder (chronic depressed mood). Anxiety and affective disorder occur together more often in women while other substance disorders and antisocial personality disorder occur together more often in men.[7]

In the majority of persons, the signs and symptoms of anxiety and depression are related to alcohol intoxication and withdrawal. They usually are resolved within the first few weeks of abstinence. Many psychiatrists observe the person for three to four weeks during a substance-free period before diagnosing the person with either an anxiety or mood disorder and before prescribing appropriate and specific medication. This caution is important because of the propensity of many of these individuals to misuse prescribed drugs. In those cases in which the person has a history of mood disorder that has been successfully treated, an earlier intervention and prescription of medication is indicated.

Vigilance for observing and diagnosing personality disorders is called for because these disorders often complicate efforts at detoxification and rehabilitation. Indeed, failure to diagnose and treat comorbid psychiatric disorders is the most common cause of failure in the treatment of alcoholism.[8]

More than 60 percent of individuals admitted for detoxification exhibit symptoms of clinical depression or dysthymia.[9] As noted above, it is not always clear whether this is a distinct mood disorder or whether it is indicative of symptoms that accompany intoxication and withdrawal. Because it is estimated that alcohol plays some role in 20 to 50 percent of suicides, counselors must take seriously any suggestion or threat of suicide in those who abuse alcohol.

This new understanding of the relationship between alcohol and other psychological illnesses, such as depression and anxiety disorders, should help counselors better understand and more sensitively read the symptomatology of the alcoholic persons seeking help from them.

The Children of Alcoholic Patients

It is estimated that one in five children live with an alcoholic person while growing up. Counselors are likely to have the adult children of alcoholics seek out help from them. These individuals, especially men, are vulnerable to developing alcoholism themselves. In addition, they often suffer the effects of growing up with a parent who was inconsistent and emotionally depriving. Some of these grown children of alcoholics watched as their nonalcoholic parent, often but not always the mother, experienced physical or sexual abuse at the hands of the alcoholic parent. In cases of childhood sexual and physical abuse, the author of such abuse is often found to be the alcoholic parent. A popular literature on the problems of the children of alcoholic parents has developed as well as programs and organized self-help support groups for them.

Resources for this group may be found easily on the Internet. Among these is the world service organization of Adult Children of Alcoholics (ACoA), which offers a twelve-step program (www.adultchildren.org).

The American Academy of Child and Adolescent Psychiatry also provides relevant publications on managing this problem (www.aacap.org).

Fetal Alcohol Syndrome

In recent years, increasing evidence has been developed that a specific fetal abnormality results from alcohol abuse during pregnancy. Fetal Alcohol Syndrome (FAL) results in a range of symptoms that includes facial abnormalities, such as a small head, along with heart defects, limb abnormalities, and delayed development with decreased mental functioning. It is unclear what level of alcohol intake is required to precipitate this syndrome, but the classic symptoms listed above are ordinarily associated with the heavy use of alcohol. Alcohol use during the first trimester is associated with greater risk than it is during the second, and the second gives rise to greater risk than the third trimester.

Because alcohol passes easily through the placental barrier and because of the unknowns cited above, women who are pregnant or who are trying to conceive are routinely advised to abstain from all alcohol. We should be aware of the effects of alcohol on the fetus as we may be consulted about this matter or may need to hand on sensible advice to others about these alcohol-related risks. We should refer women who have had serious alcohol problems before becoming pregnant to a support group whose focus is to help women avoid alcohol use while carrying a child.

Signs of Alcohol Abuse and Dependency

Since nonprofessional counselors may be the first helpers in touch with alcoholic persons, they must be able to recognize the clinical features of this problem. The timely identification and treatment of alcohol abuse and dependency are frustrated and made more complicated when denial is employed by the individual and, often enough, by the family and the general culture. Alcohol abusers are often reluctant to see doctors and avoid them because of feelings of embarrassment or their own conflicts with authority figures.

The early warning signals of alcohol abuse may include a failure to complete projects on schedule, chronic lateness, or not showing up for work, marital problems, mood changes, and increased aggressive outbursts. In such language do alcoholic persons reveal their problems.

Alcoholic Persons and Their Relationships

Evidence exists that suggests what many counselors will learn from experience: A person's relationships with family members and, as they are termed, "significant others," are critical influences in the post-treatment world of recovering alcoholics who are married or live with family members.[10] Problems within those families who have alcoholic members generate very defeating conditions that include poor communication, lack of coherent structure, and inconsistency in maintaining — or an outright inability to implement — commonsense standards of behavior within the family.

Studies also indicate that involving the spouse early in the treatment improves the marital relationship and the management of alcohol use during the post-treatment phase.[11] Counselors may also wish to refer family members to such Alcoholics Anonymous–related groups as Al-Anon (for spouses) or Alateen (for teenagers and children of alcoholic parents).

Treatment Strategies

The long-range goals of treatment for patients with substance use disorders include the reduction in the use and effects of abused substances, the achievement of abstinence, reduction in the frequency of relapses, and rehabilitation.[12] A variety of interventions is used to help achieve these goals. An intoxicated state may require medical treatment in a hospital setting. Or an individual's current problem may best be treated in a residential treatment program, by partial hospitalization, or on an outpatient basis. Specific drugs may be used to help achieve sobriety and stabilization, and a range of psychosocial treatments such as behavioral therapies, specific psychotherapies, and family therapy are often used. In addition, referral to self-help groups, such as Alcoholics Anonymous, are useful adjuncts to treatment.

Alcoholics Anonymous and Other Programs

As nonprofessional counselors, we should develop some relationship with local chapters of Alcoholics Anonymous and appreciate the organization's spirit and structure. The meetings offer members experiences of acceptance, understanding, forgiveness, and even confrontation. Central is the twelve-step program, which new members enter by admitting their problem, surrendering a sense of personal control over the illness, carrying out a personal assessment, making amends, and helping others. Spiritual resources are employed in this successful program, which aims at restoring sobriety largely through dealing with individuals in terms of their conscious perceptions of their problems. The emphasis, as in nonprofessional counseling, is on strengthening the person's defenses, the very function that nonprofessional counselors can handle very well.

As mentioned previously, most clinicians working in this field refer those with alcohol abuse and dependency to Alcoholics Anonymous as an adjunct to ongoing treatment. This reinforces the persons involved through group support and the repeated reminders of the disastrous consequences of excessive alcohol use. We should be familiar with the work of this group and with the twelve-step program required of those who enter. Although it is known that perhaps half of those who enroll will drop out, there is plenty of evidence of the real help that this program provides for many suffering individuals.

Nace found that 47 percent to 62 percent of active AA members reported at least one year of continuous sobriety. Outcomes are more favorable for those who attend more than one meeting a week, who have a sponsor or sponsor others, who lead meetings, and who work through steps six through twelve after completing a treatment program.[13]

Refusal to participate in Alcoholics Anonymous or other group-related treatments is not necessarily indicative of treatment resistance. At times, and for persons carefully evaluated and screened beforehand, individual psychotherapy, such as interpersonal therapy, or supportive-expressive therapy may be helpful alternatives.

A Core Difficulty

Despite advances in our recent understanding of alcoholism, many laypersons as well as professionals still perceive the alcoholic as an individual who makes a conscious decision to drink too much. They view alcoholics, in other words, as sinners, moral failures who choose their own uncomfortable fate. They judge them to be responsible for deciding to stop and to pull themselves free of the pit into which they threw themselves. Such people think themselves wise when they say, "Nothing can be done until they decide to do something for themselves."

At another level, it is recognized that an essential characteristic of alcoholism is that these persons can't control their choices about drinking. Much, however, can be done. Counselors should know that the most successful alcoholism programs are those that reach out to alcoholics rather than wait for alcoholics to come to them. Persons with drinking problems can respond to family interventions and to treatment when it is offered to them. Helpers should not construct an attitude that traps them into a role of waiting for alcoholics to prove that they are ready to get better. They should be ready to support families or friends in planning and carrying out interventions to get alcoholics into treatment.

What We Can Do by Ourselves or with Others

It is estimated that only about 10 percent of the 13 million persons suffering from alcoholism in the United States receive treatment. Despite this, because of the medical complexities and physical illnesses associated with alcoholism and withdrawal, psychiatric evaluation and treatment remain the preferred options. Because we counselors are frequently the first helpful contact for the alcoholic person we can be significant resources in assisting them and their families, offering the latter support after helping get the former into treatment.

Treatment for alcoholism is known to be successful with 70 percent of all those treated. This is manifested in a reduction, within six months, in the number of days they drink and in the improvement in their general health.[14] We can also play a significant supportive role in following up those who are working to keep sober after completing their treatment. Supportive responses are of great help to those who find the adjustment difficult and need encouragement to carry on or try again if they fail in some ways.

Counselors must also be able to recognize some of the complications associated with alcoholism. As observed, alcoholism is often the symptom of a deeper kind of difficulty and is often accompanied by a serious mental disorder. One may find, in certain alcoholic persons, evidence of harm to the body, such as cirrhosis of the liver, nutritional disorders, and damage to the central nervous system. A patient and careful evaluation by an appropriate professional of all the factors involved in an individual problem is obviously necessary. We can cooperate with other specialists, such as physicians and psychologists, who are capable of carrying out the necessary tests or getting the biographical information essential to helping the person involved. One may err dangerously by oversimplifying the alcoholic's condition.

Trying to understand alcoholics may test us severely because of the defenses they throw up against our helping them. Counselors who are prepared for alcoholics to act this way will not be surprised to find them using rationalization, denial, or dissociation in their presentation of themselves. It is interesting to note how easily our inquiries about drinking make the use of such defenses possible. Many forms ask whether we drink or not and then provide the classification "socially" for everyone to circle. Counselors must be aware of providing the same easy kind of rationalizations out of some ill-conceived pity or the wish not to embarrass or hurt their feelings. An overall concern for these individuals as persons is our best guarantee against hurting them.

There will be difficulties in establishing a therapeutic relationship with alcoholic persons. That is because alcoholics frequently suffer from low self-esteem. They need to be respected and they are very sensitive to any kind of judgmental or critical attitudes toward them. These only make them withdraw and become more defensive in the presence of the counselor.

Counselors must also be very gentle — but hardly softhearted — in their approach. It is very easy for counselors to be used by alcoholics who have been through similar situations before. They know just how to play on the sympathy of would-be helpers, how to keep them at a safe distance, and how to win them over to their side. Sensitive counselors, aware of this, will look beneath this behavior in order to respond to the true transaction.

Attentive counselors are careful not to probe too much because of the sensitivity of alcoholics. Neither should they press them into expressive forms of therapy for which they are psychologically ill-prepared. One cannot push these people too fast or too hard. Like packages stamped "fragile," they should be handled with care. They have an injured sense of themselves and reinjuring it in the name of helping them is a real danger for an overaggressive or moralizing counselor.

Counselors frequently function best if they are part of a treatment team. All the resources that are available should be employed in assisting persons with alcoholic difficulties. It is sensible for counselors in a certain area to set up a working relationship with colleagues who are physicians, mental health experts, or members of the clergy. They may also become acquainted with any programs in business or industry that attempt to identify and respond to alcoholic problems at an early stage.

Joining in efforts to reach out to the potential alcoholic is one of the most promising functions that a counselor can fulfill. This goes against the instincts of many counselors, however, because they may expect, because of some previous experience, to wait for, rather than seek out, persons who need help. Some participation in a team that recognizes the effectiveness of moving out toward the potential alcoholic at an important time should not be underestimated.

– 22 –

THE LANGUAGE OF
THE SERIOUSLY DISTURBED

M OST NONPROFESSIONAL COUNSELORS are keenly aware that they
have only the equivalent of a tourist's handbook of the languages
spoken by those persons suffering from major psychological difficulties.
Theirs is a land in which most of us have spent little if any time but
one that we may be compelled to enter even if we feel inhibited or
self-conscious because of our lack of fluency in language and unfamiliarity with the customs. We may have to function within the limitations
placed on anybody who has not had experience or training.

Ordinarily, we meet with seriously disturbed persons when we are
referring them on to other sources of assistance. As with travelers, we
must have enough knowledge to function without feeling, or being,
lost in such circumstances. We must know both how to recognize serious psychological disturbances and what, within our capability, we
can constructively do when we encounter people suffering from them.
We can reduce the stress associated with such experiences through anticipating some of the specific problems associated with working with
persons with these major difficulties.

The greatest stress for us as helpers lies in the difficulty intrinsic
to, and emblematic of, such problems — that of forming relationships
with individuals suffering from what has been termed psychosis. In the
DSM-IV-TR, we read the history of the classification of "psychotic":

> The narrowest definition of *psychotic* is restricted to delusions
> or prominent hallucinations, with the hallucinations occurring in
> the absence of insight into their pathological nature. A slightly less
> restrictive definition would also include prominent hallucinations
> that the individual realizes are hallucinatory experiences. Broader
> still is a definition that also includes other positive symptoms
> of schizophrenia (i.e., disorganized speech, grossly disorganized
> or catatonic behavior). . . . The definition used in earlier classifica-
> tions was probably far too inclusive and focused on the severity

202

of functional impairment. In that context, a mental disorder was termed "psychotic" if it resulted in "impairment that grossly interferes with the capacity to meet the ordinary demands of life." Finally, the term has previously been defined as a loss of ego boundaries or a gross impairment in reality testing. In this manual, the term *psychotic* refers to the presence of certain symptoms.[1]

Another source describes psychosis in this manner:

The term psychosis ... is roughly equivalent to the archaic term insanity. The general meaning refers to a patient's inability to appropriately assess reality. This assessment may be hampered by perceptual disturbances or marked dysfunctions in thinking. ... Psychotic symptoms may be quite obvious, or they may be hidden and elicited only by careful probing in a nonthreatening manner. Typically, the most dramatic psychotic symptoms are delusions and hallucinations. Delusions are beliefs that are fixed (unchangeable) and false. Beliefs that a patient has in common with his religious or subcultural group are not considered delusional. ... An hallucination is a perception experienced in the absence of an external stimulus.[2]

It is not surprising that helpers may find it difficult, or perhaps impossible, to generate much empathy for the experiences of the severely disturbed. Indeed, we may not feel comfortable being with them. We are struck by the fact that these people are so different from those with whom we usually work. They seem to represent not just an extension or exaggeration of ordinary conflict but a separate and more impenetrable psychological mystery. We may find ourselves reacting in a new way to psychotic persons. We may feel more distant from them and intimidated by what we perceive as their strangeness or "craziness." It is very difficult to find the human message in their confused communication and so the search for the person behind the symptoms can be intense and ridden with anxiety. At times, we may even feel "infected" by the feelings of the seriously disturbed and become frustrated and angry at our inability to break through to the other's personality. This may affect our self-confidence and challenge our sense of being helping and considerate persons. These side effects in ourselves are not the least of reasons for careful reflection upon the complexities of working with psychotic individuals.

Some of us may feel totally inadequate as counselors even with the idea of laying down the foundation for relationships with persons suffering from major psychological problems. Our uneasiness, unex-amined, may become a self-fulfilling prophecy so that we do not even attempt any of the many sensible and helpful things that are within the reach of most healthy and perceptive individuals. All counselors, full- or part-time, will eventually find ourselves dealing with seriously disturbed persons, sometimes without much warning. As the only re-sources available in certain circumstances, such as in a school or parish where everyone else looks to us, we may assume responsibility for de-cisions connected with responding to the needs of such persons. Even if we plan to refer these suffering persons for more intensive professional help than we can offer, much remains that we can do until a referral is achieved.

Shifts in Attitude

For many years, but especially after the development of antipsychotic drugs, it has been widely held that the sooner patients can be freed from mental hospitals and returned to their communities the better things would be for all concerned. It was felt that many patients stayed far too long in hospitals and that they sometimes remained there because society was uncomfortable with them and afraid of their return. They remained hospitalized, in other words, because they had no other place to go. A growing body of research came to suggest that deeply disturbed persons were not as dangerous as had been thought and that a return to more normal living circumstances would be positively helpful for almost all of them.

As a result, many persons who in previous times would have spent a considerable amount of their time in a hospital are now maintained in the community. Even counselors with limited experience can appreciate that individuals who formerly found sanctuary in institutions that pro-vided medical and psychiatric care as well as food, shelter, and some structure and social support for them along with breathing room for their families now receive a patchwork of services or no service at all, with results that we can see spread all about us in homelessness and interactions with the law.

With the changes in attitudes about the institutionalization of per-sons with chronic and persistent mental illness, bolstered by advances in the medication of these illnesses, in the mid-1950s America wit-nessed the beginning of a concerted effort to depopulate state hospitals (a phenomenon referred to as deinstitutionalization) and to develop community-based resources to support these persons. This movement was abetted by legal advocates of the "rights" of such patients to be free and, in some circumstances, to decide whether and what kind of treatment and medication to receive. This led to armies of such persons wandering certain sections of big cities, in which community-based treatment faltered, with minimal treatment or support.

The present approach for the psychiatric treatment of these and other seriously disturbed persons is expressed in this way: "Patients should be cared for in the least restrictive setting that is likely to be safe and to allow for effective treatment."[3] As a result, counselors will more frequently have contact with persons and their families who ordinarily, in another age, would have been institutionalized for long periods or, in some cases, for their entire lives. In addition, treatment resources for these people may not always be adequate and some, as it is said, will fall through the cracks and join themselves to the legions of the homeless, especially in the large cities. We counselors, therefore, need some understanding of (1) chronic mental illness, (2) the problem of securing treatment for this group of persons, and (3) some of the fallout, including homelessness, of deinstitutionalization and inadequate deployment of community resources.

Before we define some of the characteristic diagnostic categories associated with serious mental illness, we should note some relevant facts. First, we counselors should recognize that chronic mental illness is common in the United States, in which an estimated 22.1 percent of citizens aged eighteen and older (one in five adults) suffer from a major disorder at some time in their lives. Four of the ten leading causes of disability in the United States and other developed countries are mental disorders, specifically major depression, bipolar disorder, schizophrenia, and obsessive-compulsive disorder.[4] These illnesses bloom, as gardens do, in a rich variety of symptoms, follow, as rivers do, differing courses, and impose, as courts do, many disabling penalties.

Second, with the various treatments available, these individuals may experience periods in which they are relatively free of disabling symptoms. As a result, some individuals who receive adequate treatment may be able to reenter and function in society.

In the third place, we must appreciate that chronic mental illness is not necessarily an "all or none" phenomenon. Those with serious mental illness may have areas of functioning that are unaffected by their illness and, consequently, display some capacity for establishing relationships with others.

Because we counselors are often called upon to work with the families of individuals who suffer from schizophrenia, we should know that no single genetic factor has yet been identified with schizophrenia, although evidence from twin studies suggests some genetic vulnerability associated with the illness. For example, monozygotic twins (developed from the same egg cell), whether raised separately or by their biological parents, have a concordance rate, or are both likely to suffer schizophrenia, in 40 to 50 percent of cases.

Stress also seems to play a role in the onset and exacerbation of schizophrenic symptoms. It is has been observed, for example, that symptoms in vulnerable individuals often develop the first semester of college or, for military draftees, during the first months of basic training.[5]

One unforeseen consequence of deinstitutionalization is the increase in the homelessness of individuals with chronic mental illness. Current data suggest that approximately 12 percent of homeless individuals suffer from schizophrenia.[6] Such persons may be alienated from their families, lack the usual social supports, suffer additionally from drug and alcohol abuse, and be so disorganized that they are unable to follow through on treatment recommendations. Nonetheless, these persons not uncommonly enter the work of pastors, school principals, or lawyers. We should anticipate this contingency by identifying and establishing a prior relationship with available mental health resources whose counsel and assistance we may draw upon when we deal with these seriously troubled individuals who seem cut loose from other care.

Classifications of Serious Illness

Psychotic symptoms appear in the psychotic disorders but also in many different mental illnesses including dementia, depression, and bipolar illness. In the most common of the psychotic disorders, schizophrenia, psychotic symptoms are prominent and unmistakable outcroppings in those affected by them. Schizophrenia is a common illness that affects approximately 2.2 million American adults, usually surfacing in their lives between their late teens and their mid-thirties. This major problem interferes markedly with the capacity of persons to experience anything like a normal life. If there is any suggestion that this illness is present, the person should be referred for a complete psychiatric examination.

Schizophrenia's principal characteristics include such classic psychotic symptoms as delusions and hallucinations, along with a deterioration in their ability to function socially or to hold a job. In the *DSM-IV-TR* we find a list of symptoms that must be present to reach this diagnosis.

Diagnostic Criteria for Schizophrenia

A. Characteristic symptoms: Two (or more) of the following, each present for a significant portion of time during a one-month period (or less if successfully treated):

- delusions
- hallucinations
- disorganized speech (e.g., frequent derailment or incoherence)
- grossly disorganized or catatonic behavior
- negative symptoms, i.e., affective flattening, alogia, or avolition

Note: Only one Criterion A symptom is required if delusions are bizarre or hallucinations consist of a voice keeping up a running commentary on the person's behavior or thoughts, or two or more voices conversing with each other.

B. Social/occupational dysfunction: for a significant portion of time since the onset of the disturbance, one or more major areas of functioning such as work, interpersonal relations, or self-care are markedly below the level achieved prior to the onset....

C. Duration: Continuous signs of the disturbance persist for at least six months. This six-month period must include at least one month of symptoms (or less if successfully treated) that meet Criterion A and may include periods of prodromal or residual symptoms. During these prodromal or residual periods, the signs of the disturbance may be manifested by only negative symptoms or two or more symptoms listed in Criterion A present in an attenuated form (e.g., odd beliefs, unusual perceptual disturbances).

D. Schizoaffective and mood disorder have been ruled out.

E. The disturbance is not due to the direct physiological effects of a substance (e.g., a drug of abuse, a medication) or a general medical condition.

F. If there is a history of autistic disorder or another pervasive developmental disorder, the additional diagnosis of schizophrenia is made only if prominent delusions or hallucinations are also present for at least a month (or less if successfully treated).

Source: DSM-IV-TR, 2000.

Aside from these necessary symptoms, we should be alerted to the possibility that individuals may be suffering from schizophrenia when we observe a range of associated features. Persons with schizophrenia may, for example, display inappropriate emotions, affect, in the literature's language (smiling or laughing in response to a stimulus that normally elicits a different and more appropriate reaction); anhedonia (a lack of interest or inability to take pleasure in ordinarily pleasurable activities); abnormal movements (pacing, rocking, grimacing, posturing), or stereotyped behavior (uncontrollable repetitive mannerisms); and thought disturbances characterized by loose associations, tangential thinking, incoherence, and circumstantiality (talking all around a subject). These symptoms tell us that afflicted individuals experience difficulty in processing their relationship with the real world around them. We should seek a careful examination by a well-trained clinician if we want to reach an accurate diagnosis of the problem.

The first challenge for us as counselors is making a beachhead of emotional contact with such persons to lead to professional diagnosis and treatment. Counselors who are not well informed about serious mental illness or comfortable relating to such persons may, as we have noted, become angry, fearful, or even dismissive because of the individual's initial refusal to talk or communicate in any way effectively. In fact, many of these individuals are unaware that they are behaving in any abnormal way and lack any capacity to observe themselves or to have insight into the nature of their illness. They are often as afraid of us as they are of others, concerned that they will be misunderstood or harmed in some way. We need, therefore, to relate to them in a calm, reassuring, and understanding manner. In working with such persons, it is helpful to apply the well-tested interviewing guideline: The more disorganized the person, the more organizing the interviewer must be. We structure the interview carefully, avoiding the silences or the free-flowing interactions that are disconcerting for schizophrenics already burdened with disorganized and confusing thinking.

Obviously, we need to sharpen our understanding of the inner lives of schizophrenic persons if we are to be helpful to them and their families. This can, of course, be learned from firsthand experience and training, but it can also be gleaned from reading. The novel *I Never Promised You a Rose Garden*, for example, written by a young woman who spent years in psychiatric treatment and hospitals, is a revealing self-disclosure of the inner life of such a person.[7]

Simply Human

Schizophrenic persons have grave problems relating to other people. What healthy people seek, they avoid, and, seeming to distrust others, they have few, if any, friends. Sometimes they do strike up a relationship — more like an association — with others who also live on the far reaches of social approval. The best they can do is found in their marginal relationship with each other so they are often excluded from ordinary society. Fragility characterizes the best of their relationships.

Our fundamental challenge resembles a novelist's as we attempt to understand what it is like to view the world afraid of the experiences that most healthy persons prize and seek out for themselves. Schizophrenic patients fear closeness, and so they are ambivalent about the reactions of others toward them. At the same time, they may develop a dependency on others to guide and direct their lives.

For a long time it was thought that such seriously disturbed persons were not capable of forming "relationships," and that they were not, therefore, capable of having a transference experience with a therapist. The work of people such as Federn, Sullivan, and others indicated that this is not so, and that beneath all the strange surface behavior and withdrawal there lives a person capable of forming human relationships.

Indeed, these persons who seem so different are not quite as different as we sometimes suppose. Their problems generally arise from the same kind of situations that confront all of us in the human condition. Deep within them we find the capacity to react to the warmth, acceptance, and understanding that is little different from our own. If we remember this, we feel more comfortable with them and, less on guard and less anxious ourselves, can better understand their apparently indecipherable language. In our work with the seriously disturbed, it is critically important that we counselors present ourselves as willing and interested human beings rather than as slightly intimidated or uneasy evaluators. A little bit of humanity goes a long way in expanding our simple human effectiveness with these individuals. We will also experience one of the rewards of the hard work of counseling as we observe the real person begin to step forward, if only a few inches at a time, from psychological entombment.

Because of their emotional conviction that they are unable to care for themselves or to cope with life, such persons may present themselves in a very dependent manner. This feeling of helplessness partially explains why they sometimes regress to what seems a very primitive and dependent mode of adapting to the world, at times settling, it would seem, for almost total care of their needs by others. It is all the more painful for them to express their dependency because such self-revelation further erodes their self-esteem.

Projecting themselves passively — as receptive to being shaped and sheltered by others — is also very threatening for them. Healthy people realize that they are not totally independent and that letting themselves be dependent in some ways is an important part of living. Nobody can be close to others, or love them, without at times sharing a mutual dependence. However, this healthy adjustment is appalling to the seriously disturbed. If we understand their reactions — so different from those whose basic health allows them to tolerate the give-and-take of life — we will temper any urges we have to push too far, too fast, into the intimate areas of their lives.

The tendency of the chronically psychotic person to dependency is one of the most difficult challenges to any counselor, well-trained professional as well as nonprofessional, in working or relating to such persons. The goal of helping others is to enable them to become independent and full functioning. Such an ideal is beyond the capacity of the typical chronically ill schizophrenic person. If we remember that they are doing as well as they can, we will understand and adapt to their human limitations.

Strong Feelings

We are not unwise to expect hostility to bubble even beneath what seem to be bland exteriors. Persons with major problems are often very anxious lest their strong hostile feelings do come out. Their inner experience of these rumblings also explains why disturbed persons may seek to control us in our meetings with them. In this way, they make up for their own feelings of inadequacy. If we resent this behavior and become defensive, we may miss the message of such behavior. If we take their reactions personally, we quickly lose our footing in the relationship. When their effort to control us is viewed as part of their struggle to pull themselves together, we can accept and respond to it maturely and therapeutically. When we maintain perspective so that we can catch the sweep and pattern of the dynamics of the deeply disturbed, we can respond more effectively and also reduce the stress for the person we are seeing and for ourselves as well.

As counselors, we should never be surprised at the difficulties we experience in establishing emotional contact with schizophrenic persons.

It is not, as has been noted, because these persons are incapable of some measure of relationship but because they are so sensitive to human interactions that, to protect themselves, they draw back into their own private and isolated worlds. Our gestures and statements — routine fly balls to other persons we see — are as threatening as pitches aimed at their heads to schizophrenic persons. When we understand this, we will manage our responses with a greater respect for their vulnerability. We may learn that we must be more active in our counseling, more reassuring in what seems an almost naive way in dealing with these persons. Seriously disturbed individuals need these sincere, concrete signs that we recognize their needs and are trying to respond to them.

One of the greatest challenges in understanding these persons concerns the chaotic picture they paint of themselves and their worlds. Some observers suggest that this schizophrenic disorganization is, like jagged camouflage designs, their way of defending themselves against the threats of the world and other persons. This mechanism is at once both unconscious and effective. Such disorganization tests us counselors and keeps us at a safe distance at the same time. These people may be very difficult to follow but, if we can sense this disorganization as part of their defensive sparring, we may be able to catch the lonely and frightened persons beneath these maneuvers. It is to the persons rather than to their surface strategies that we must respond.

In these situations it is fatal to pretend to understand when we do not. Seriously disturbed persons are astute at picking up any hypocrisy, inconsistency, or failure to attend to them and what they are trying to say. We must constantly return to an old question: "What are these persons trying to tell me through the way they are treating me?" This enables us to keep the whole therapeutic situation in clearer perspective, to manage our own stress better, and to be more helpful to them.

Some Basics

There are certain basic kinds of information that we counselors may need to secure, especially if we are involved even for a brief time in working with such disturbed persons. It is important to find out — and as specifically as possible — why these individuals have come for help and whether and from whom they have previously received assistance. Inquiries about previous episodes may be very helpful in understanding the nature of and prognosis for the present difficulty. Some gentle questioning about their history, even about the kinds of symptoms they have experienced before, may provide extremely helpful information.

We may be called upon in an initial interview to help severely disturbed persons to define the problem that has brought them for assistance. Although they may be able to do this only in a very primitive and symbolic way, this communication is better than nothing and, if we are able to tease out the stress that precipitated their search for help, we may, in a few moments, make real progress in assisting these individuals. These persons may have sought us out, for example, as a response to their feeling of being overwhelmed, or having suffered some final humiliation, or some kindred "last straw" experience. Our ability to identify the occasion of their need for help may be an important key with which these persons may open to us their idiosyncratic vision of the world.

When we are sensitive to the meaning in the jumble of their communications we may well identify significant themes and topics amid their rambling accounts, their intellectualizing, and their obsession with circumstances rather than essences. It is helpful for us to realize that accuracy in making counseling responses is not the only quality that is important in working with severely disturbed persons. Catching the whole pattern or mood of others at the right moment is our most important response as counselors. It is also vital to communicate our commitment to understand rather than to judge these troubled persons. Nor should we ever underestimate the importance of this effort to understand, even when final and complete meanings may not be grasped for a long while. Imperfect understanding is better than no understanding at all.

We must respect the privacy that these deeply disturbed persons need. They are afraid of the world, and they need safe space because of their shaky feelings about their own identity. Again, sensitivity to how these persons write straight with crooked lines allows us to accept them and not to push them too hard to behave in ways that are beyond them.

We should avoid giving the idea that we can read the minds of these people. We may do this by overeager responses or overwrought interpretations, by any maneuver that puts us too far ahead of them in displaying insight about the situation. Advertising one's skills does not necessarily help others or us.

In the long run, if we can rid ourselves of our prejudices, proneness to intimidation, or fears about severely disturbed persons, we will perceive them much better as individuals and will also be present to them in a more genuine and helpful way. We should attempt no great tricks — any manipulation is ultimately destructive — in working with these persons. Our own humanity, sensitively shared, remains the strongest asset we have in any of our work.

What Every Counselor Should Know

The overall approach to individuals found to suffer from schizophrenia is well described in the recent *Practice Guideline for the Treatment of Schizophrenia* published by the American Psychiatric Association:

> Schizophrenia is a chronic condition that frequently has devastating effects on many aspects of the patient's life and carries a high risk of suicide and other life-threatening conditions. The care of most patients involves multiple efforts to reduce the frequency and severity of episodes and to reduce the overall morbidity and mortality of the disorder. Many patients require comprehensive and continuous care over the course of their lives with no limits as to duration of treatment. Goals and strategies of treatment vary according to the phase and severity of the illness.[8]

There is no cure for the illness, the origin of which is unknown, but treatment can alleviate many of the troublesome and disabling symptoms.

If there is any suspicion that an individual who comes for help is suffering from schizophrenia, we counselors must begin the process of referring the individual for an evaluation by a psychiatrist. It is not always a case of simply providing the person with the name of an appropriate referral source. In most cases, the counselor will have to obtain some kind of history to determine if there have been previous episodes, current stressful events, previous medications or hospitalizations, and past compliance with treatment recommendations. Because the person may not be able to relate in a direct and coherent manner, we may have to rely on a family member or friend as a source of such information. The family member is often an essential ally in the effort to get the proper treatment for the symptomatic person. The family member may be frightened by the symptoms and will need, through our good efforts, to acquire some understanding of them in order to achieve the desired referral.

The treatment of schizophrenia and any other psychosis is primarily pharmacological in the acute stages. The goal is to reduce the troubling symptoms that render the individuals unable to function adequately and care for themselves. Once they are stabilized and relatively asymptomatic and motivated, more supportive management and increasingly specific psychosocial interventions can be introduced. These may include training in basic living skills and social skills as well as cognitive and vocational rehabilitation and, in some instances, supportive individual or group psychotherapy. Most of us will have little to do directly with the actual treatment of such persons unless we work as part of a team in a specified treatment setting.

The concern of family members may also revolve around the fact that the affected family member exhibits suicidal thoughts. This development should be taken seriously since it is well known that approximately 10 percent of schizophrenic patients die by suicide.[9] A particularly serious concern arises when the suicidal thoughts are the result of a "command hallucination," a persistent voice urging the person to suicide. The use of drugs and alcohol also complicates this concern. When suicidal thoughts are present, psychiatric referral is indicated.

As noted earlier, due in part to the discovery of useful antipsychotic medications and a national consciousness about the nature of mental illness, many of the nation's mental hospitals have closed since the 1950s, and community mental health centers have been established throughout the country. The net result is that, for most individuals suffering from severe mental illness, hospitalization will be short term and treated individuals are returned to their community to live, most often, with members of their families. Having a member of the family who suffers from chronic mental illness is a stressful experience. Often these affected individuals are not motivated to get well, are unable to return to their pre-illness status, cannot work or contribute to family life, and remain fearful and dependent. Compliance with their taking the prescribed medication is also a source of concern for family members. These problems generate considerable frustration and anger among those who live with such persons. We counselors will often have to step in, at the request of family members, to help them understand these persons and to bring about more agreeable and less stressful ways of dealing with them.

Lastly, we should be familiar with resources available in the community, including both the professional and lay organizations that can provide pertinent information, referral sources, and written materials. These include the American Psychiatric Association, the American Psychological Association, the National Alliance for the Mentally Ill, and the National Mental Health Association, all of which can be contacted through their Web sites.

– 23 –

EVERYPERSON'S ILLNESS:
DEPRESSION

F ROM THE ORDINARY BLUES to the depths of a severe psychotic depression there runs a broad band of bad feeling. We have all crossed its borders at one time or another during our lives. Feeling "blue" or "down in the dumps" is personally familiar to everyone who does any counseling, indeed to any human being. Famous men like Churchill and Lincoln identified severe depressions during their lives; the British prime minister named his the "black dog." Writers like Evelyn Waugh and William Styron wrote books about theirs, and Mike Wallace of *60 Minutes* has acknowledged his long session of melancholy. We hardly need to be famous to have made an acquaintance of depressed feelings. We only need to be human.

Mood disorders span a wide spectrum of conditions, ranging from reactions to loss and other negative life experiences to severe, recurrent, debilitating illnesses. We generally work with the former, those persons who exhibit relatively normal states with some evidence of mood and cognitive disturbance.

Depression can mean something in general as well as something quite specific. In general, it refers to a symptom that can be present in many different psychological situations. Specifically, it can refer to a distinctive problem of which it is a dominant or important feature, as in a diagnosable mood disorder. As mentioned previously, persons experiencing depression are shot through with sadness, feelings of being helpless, discouraged, and hopeless. Individuals riding toward the far end of the continuum of depression cannot cope with life, yet they often resist help. They seem to dig a deep hole for themselves. They resist coming out of it, and they may not let you in even when you want to be of assistance to them. Having tasted the flavor of depression ourselves does not mean that we understand all its forms. Indeed, we save ourselves from serious errors by not generalizing from our own experience to the experience of those with whom we work.

215

How They Come, What They Say

As we move from the garden variety to the deeper, darker forests of depression, we observe certain systematic and predictable ways in which people react to them. At the outset, depressed persons try to make contact with other people, wanting to get help and making some effort to establish relationships with others. They are seeking, at some level of consciousness, some way to restore what has been taken from them in life. Sometimes this is through an unrealistic wish for a magical restoration of things as they once were. We may not notice this kind of thinking unless we can closely inspect the life of the depressed person.

As the problem becomes more intense, however, depressed individuals begin to give up. They appear more helpless, and it is difficult for them either to seek or to allow themselves help. Difficult as it may seem, even this is evidence of a psychological attempt to find a solution to their problems. Persons who are deep in the quicksand of depression not only feel bad but end up being bad for themselves. Depressed persons can be their own worst enemies, and it is common to observe self-destructive tendencies, either subtle or pronounced, in the depressed individual. Of all these tendencies, suicide is the ultimate self-destructive act. Suicidal thoughts do not usually come suddenly, however, and counselors should always take soundings in their relationships with depressed persons to pick up the signals of an increasing will to self-destruction.

Depressed persons can wear many disguises, and counselors must be able to identify these if we are going to establish effective relationships with them. Sometimes we catch the signals in our own reactions to persons who come with these problems. We may feel that there is something more beneath the surface, something dark and sad hidden beneath their exterior, something revealing itself in its concealment. If we are healthy, these signals lead us to a deeper level of understanding the person. In other words, we can discern on the radar screen of our own feelings the shapes of the depressions that others cannot consciously describe.

Some depressed persons at first meeting do not look at all depressed. They are able to deny their bad feelings and keep up a good front. They may acknowledge feeling "blah" or having no feelings or they may say that they feel anxious. As the interview progresses, however, depressed persons may begin to talk about events in their lives and how they reacted to them. As they do, their facial expressions and demeanor change. We may then suggest that such persons look sad, appear teary, or on the verge of crying and that such reactions usually signal depressed feelings. Our identification of their mood change as evidence of "depression" may come as a surprise to them but may also provide relief because what they have been feeling finally has a "name."

Some individuals complain of somatic problems, reporting an inventory of aches and pains instead of feelings of sadness. They complain about some bodily ill while denying any emotional upset at all. Such persons classically come to a general practitioner, clergy member, or other professional associates, elaborating on the physical concerns and, in the process, garnering a good deal of medical advice and prescriptions, vitamins, and other suggestions about nutrition, exercise, and holistic pursuits. We must be sensitive to catch the symbolic nature of the physical complaints as a substitute for the real problem about which such persons are unable to speak.

Given America's multicultural mix, it is also important to learn that in many cultures depression is expressed in somatic terms. Complaints of "nerves," headaches, and "liver problems" (in Latino and Mediterranean cultures), of weakness, tiredness, or "imbalance" (in Chinese and Asian cultures), of problems of the "heart" (in Middle Eastern cultures), and of being "heartbroken" (among Hopi) may all express the depressive experience.[1]

Symptoms of Depression

It is thought that, among Americans, only advanced coronary artery disease causes more days of disability than depression. It affects approximately 20 million Americans per year from every social class and age group and, although more frequent in women (20–25 percent prevalence), it is a significant illness among men as well (7–12 percent prevalence).

Although depression is eminently treatable, it is estimated that only about one-third to one-half of the persons who have the illness are properly diagnosed and only about 20 percent of depressed persons receive treatment from psychiatrists or mental health professionals. That depression is often overlooked or undiagnosed is the responsibility of all of us who counsel, irrespective of our principal calling. Ordinary people may hesitate out of embarrassment or lack of knowledge to share their feelings and depressive symptoms with full-time counselors or mental health professionals. Or they may feel that no one has the time to explore with them what is really wrong with them. They may go to their physician with complaints of fatigue, trouble sleeping, headaches, gastrointestinal symptoms, or other somatic disturbances (our more socially acceptable, less stigmatizing complaints) rather than confess what they might regard as "mental symptoms," their feelings of depression. Often physicians fail to "recognize" the symptoms of depression or "think about it" as a possible explanation for the person's complaints. A recent study found that although the majority of family practitioners feel comfortable counseling patients about smoking, alcohol use, and exercise, less than half are comfortable talking about diet, illicit drug use, depression, or stress.[2] Such findings encourage all of us who counsel to explore our comfort level with persons who express depressive feelings.

Most counselors see persons either in the early stages of a clinical depression or who have mild depressive symptoms. Our challenge as counselors is to monitor regularly such persons in the light of the established criteria for major depressive disorder and, if they fulfill these, to refer them for psychiatric consultation. In the last twenty years, major strides have been taken in the treatment of depression so that much suffering can be bypassed for both depressed persons, their families, and those providing the recommended treatment.

Reading the Signs

Counselors need to be familiar both with the following symptoms of depression and with the treatments available.

Change in Mood or Loss of Interest

Depressive disorders are distinct from the sad feelings and the low mood that occur in response to the normal and predictable stressors in everyone's life. Depressive disorder is a pervasive change from a person's ordinary mood and has strong biochemical influences involving disturbances in emotional, cognitive, behavioral, and somatic regulation. The primary sign of depression is depressed mood or a loss of interest and pleasure in nearly all activities.

When depressed, individuals become sad or gloomy or tend to feel hopeless about life and its possibilities. They may pull back from existence, seeming to lose zest for life, finding that interests they once had no longer stimulate them and saying that they just "don't care anymore." When people are initially suffering depression, they may be able to go through the motions of their regular activities, but they do not enjoy them. They will, however, perform them, especially at the urgings of others who think this activity will be "good for them." As the depression gets worse, however, they give up going along with such encouragement. It no longer works. Golfers no longer golf; bridge players cancel their scheduled games. They become indifferent to their surroundings and they withdraw into a quiet and somber outlook toward the people and events around them.

For the diagnosis of major depression, five or more distinct symptoms (including either the change in mood or loss of interest) characteristic of depression must be present nearly every day for at least two weeks.

Change in Appetite and Weight

Individuals who suffer from depression may lose interest not only in their usual activities but also in food, and they may seem to have no appetite. Others have an increased appetite and find themselves eating constantly. In both instances, these symptoms are likely to be accompanied by a measurable loss or gain in the depressed person's weight. Sometimes, the first obvious signal a person's family and friends pick up about their loved one's problem with depression is a shift in weight.

Change in Sleep Patterns

This is often the reason that individuals first seek help. Depressed persons may find themselves waking up in the middle of the night and having great difficulty returning to sleep or having difficulty getting to sleep when they first retire. Others may notice that, in contrast to their former pattern, they are beginning their day at about 4:00 or 5:00 A.M. simply because they cannot get back to sleep once they awaken. Less often, depressed persons may find it difficult to get out of bed in the morning and, in fact, spend most of their day in bed sleeping (hypersomnia in contrast to insomnia as previously described).

Psychomotor Changes

Some depressed individuals are very anxious, a state they telegraph to us the way a boxer does a punch. They pace the floor back and forth, wring their hands or scratch incessantly, and feel unable to settle down. Other depressed persons exhibit a reverse image of this behavior. They are slow in their speech and thought and may sit and make little movement at all. They may take a long time to respond to our questions and seem preoccupied and inattentive. After an interview, they may take four or five minutes for routine activities, such as buttoning their coats, finding their scarves, or adjusting their hats before starting their long, slow voyage home.

Fatigue or Loss of Energy

Depressed persons often feel completely lacking in energy and unable to carry out their ordinary daily chores. Getting up, getting dressed, and getting breakfast loom like impossible tasks and a full day's work is well beyond them. These symptoms often lead them to seek medical help. The physician may rule out any medical illness as a source of these complaints but may not be "tuned in" to these symptoms as signs of depression. Individuals may then return to us with the even more depressing message that "I've been told there's nothing wrong with me."

Feelings of Worthlessness or Inappropriate Guilt

Severely depressed persons may brood over long-past incidents, turning their guilt endlessly on the spit of their souls or discovering special messages or significance in their present experiences. Many of these incidents are, in reality, minor and insignificant events. Depressed people also tend to focus their feelings outward through the psychological mechanisms of projection and displacement, catching other people up in the net of their own depression and blaming them for their difficulties.

It is always useful to remember that depressed people have a knack for distorting their recollections of the past. They make it sound as if nothing but woe ever befell them. Their life stories are appalling in their lack of a good break or even random blessings. They do not remember happiness as normal people do not remember pain. It is important for us to grasp their distorted perception of their lives. Our understanding it is important in our helping them. As MacKinnon and Michels note:

> It is not unusual for the patient to portray his mood as long-standing and gradual in onset, whereas others describe the symptoms as relatively recent and abrupt. In a sense the patient is right; he has simply been concealing his depression from others, and perhaps from himself. As he improves, this process may reverse itself; in the early phases of recovery the depressed patient sometimes sounds much better than he really feels. This may lead to premature optimism on the part of the therapist, and is one of the factors that contributes to the increased risk of suicide as the patient starts to improve.[3]

Related to this exaggerated self-blame is a sense of worthlessness that permeates not only their verbalizations but their manner of relating to others. We may get a signal of this symptom when the person says something like, "You really shouldn't spend this time with me, I'm really not worth it. I won't get better anyway." If we do not understand this in the context of depression, we may be tempted to get angry or feel drawn into some kind of tug of war.

Diminished Ability to Concentrate or Indecisiveness

Depressed persons not only move and act slowly but are often also slow in their thinking. They are easily distracted, preoccupied, and unable to concentrate. They may complain of memory problems and of an inability to do their ordinary work. Often those who, prior to the depression, were able to make crisp, authoritative decisions find themselves now unable to do so. They may obsess over and over about possible outcomes, not trusting themselves to decide, or complain that many related decisions in the past have been in error.

Recurrent Thoughts of Death or Suicidal Ideation

These are common threads of concern among depressed persons. Up to 15 percent of individuals with severe major depressive disorder die by suicide.[4] Some feel that life is hopeless and that those around them would be better off without them. Others develop a rationale that death is the only way out for them. Counselors should not hesitate to question and explore such persons' feelings about "wanting to die" and other related issues. There is no need to think that if we bring up the idea of suicide it will provide depressed persons with some new idea as a way out of their pain. Talking about suicide may lessen rather than intensify its danger. Careful inquiry about ideas of suicide — how they might go about it, if they have the means to accomplish it — are all pertinent in the evaluation of depression.

We counselors should know that the interview is our chief tool for making an accurate diagnosis. No simple laboratory tests exist to determine if someone is depressed. When we identify an individual as having the range of symptoms associated with depression, we should make a referral for psychiatric consultation.

We should also be aware that there are mood changes that signal a number of other diagnostic conditions. We will probably meet individuals with dysthymic disorder, identified in persons with a chronically depressed mood nearly every day for at least two years. They do not exhibit the range or intensity of symptoms associated with major depressive illness. Many persons so afflicted never seek help of any kind because they have "always been this way." In the past, persons diagnosed with this condition were thought, in an outdated word, to be "neurotic," and the recommended treatment was psychodynamic psychotherapy. Currently, there is much debate as to whether dysthymia is a variant of the mood disorder spectrum or a characterological problem. Furthermore, some of these dysthymic individuals develop an episode of depression in the midst of their chronic depression and are then described as having "double depression." This ongoing controversy about the nature of dysthymia has led many psychiatrists to treat dysthymic individuals with antidepressant medications in addition to psychotherapy.

Depressed people sometimes exhibit behavior that is the opposite of deadened depression, a condition known as bipolar illness, formerly referred to as manic-depressive illness. The notion of "mania" suggests agitated and enthusiastic activity that appears to be 180 degrees away from that observed in the midst of depression. Manic individuals are constantly on the go, are difficult to contain, and in their conversations are easily distracted and quickly shift the gears of content. The media entrepreneur Ted Turner has been described in this fashion. Most of us counselors will have little, if any, contact with overtly manic persons. Their behavior is more likely to create a situation that requires an initial response from the law or emergency personnel. Referral for psychiatric treatment is imperative and, in the acute stages, treatment often involves hospitalization and medication such as lithium. The illness is chronic in nature, and these individuals are subject to periodic mood swings of depression and mania. Ongoing medication and psychotherapy are generally indicated. Although infrequently involved with the care of these individuals in the acute stages, we may be called upon to give educational and supportive care to either the treated bipolar person or family members at some time during the illness.

In addition to perceiving themselves and their difficulties differently, depressed persons also have a narrower range of thoughts than healthy persons. Their intellectual lethargy is matched by little drive or evidence of innovation. This slowness and restriction are also displayed in their outer behavior. As noted, they move more slowly, without the purposefulness of better adjusted people. Depressed people do not get into things on their own, or they move out of them quickly once they get into them. They tend to do things that do not demand much in the way of active participation or social involvement. They may, for example, sit and stare at TV, hardly noticing what is taking place before their eyes.

Listening to the Depressed Person

Depressed persons frequently talk about the symptoms of their depression rather than about the depression itself. As has been noted, they may express concern about their physical rather than their emotional health, reporting evidence of certain changes in their physical functioning. Although we know that their physical condition must be assessed by competent physicians, we must not dismiss the psychological signals in their complaints about difficulty in falling asleep or waking early, generalized fatigue, loss of appetite, or other seemingly bodily dysfunctions. Much of the over-the-counter medicine business activity depends on providing remedies keyed to these symptoms ("Have trouble falling asleep? Ask your druggist about . . . "). We watch this carousel turn endlessly because these individuals — never properly diagnosed or treated — keep trying nostrums that may address their symptoms but never touch their underlying depression. If we are wise, we do not dismiss these symptoms, or the medicines, as the destined meeting of crackpots with pill pots. The only way they may be able to describe their inner difficulties is through the pantomime of ineffectively self-medicating a complaint whose significance eludes them.

Some of us are sorely tempted to shake these persons loose with some commonsense confrontation. Such a response may make us feel better but it does little good, and may do some harm, to the symptomatic person. Far better for them, and us, is the restrained effort to listen carefully to them to identify, so that they may ultimately do the same, the roots of this wildflower of symptomatic protest.

Persons suffering from depression genuinely do want the attention and affection of other persons but, in the grip of their difficulty, they find that they are unable to respond in kind. Their human relationships fall gradually into disrepair because they simply cannot and do not give of themselves as they would have others give unto them. They drift away, like icebergs in the night, into chilly isolation. We may witness this near tragic process of their reaching toward others but turning them off because their only offering is their alienating clinginess and self-preoccupation. The reciprocating engine of their need sputters as they try to override the rejection they fear by intensifying their efforts to get other people to like them. Other people draw back from their initiatives, scrambling away from being captured by their needs instead of being prized as themselves.

As noted earlier, depressed individuals characteristically seek out social relationships in the beginning phases of their difficulty. Their needy moves to foreclose rejection, however, earn them rejection, a condition they unconsciously inflict on themselves. Their defense makes them offensive to those whose attention they want to capture and their last state — suffering in silence, mad at themselves and at others for their troubles — is worse than the first. Those around them pick up their hostility although they remain unaware of it themselves. Others have rejected them, they tell us, thus confirming their feeling of being disliked and making them feel worse about themselves.

Naming the Problem

Our task as nonprofessional counselors is to determine the true meaning of the evidence of depression offered to us by those seeking our help. Is it a sign of a very serious episode, a chronic life difficulty, or an aspect of a normal grief reaction? Because it is not always easy to sort out such a situation, we should maintain enough distance so that we can view a total picture of such persons' lives. Seeing them whole is seeing them true. We keep our balance by examining and integrating information offered by or gathered from family members and friends of depressed individuals.

As we deepen our experience, we will hone more keenly our sensitivity to differences in the deeply disturbed from those suffering milder difficulties. We grow in trusting the indicators of our own reactions to these people. For example, when we meet with psychotically depressed persons, we sense a greater distance from them than from less troubled persons. Inside us a seismograph-like line departs from normal limits as it registers how hard it is to reach and identify with them and how challenging it is to experience empathy for their situation. We feel their alienation in our own alienation from seriously disturbed persons.

We are less discomfited, the seismograph wavers little within us, as we establish relationships with persons suffering from milder forms of depression. We do not sense a gulf opening between us and feel closer to them. Other evidence, such as their ability to function socially and at work, confirms our reactions. We need to read all these indicators as carefully as pilots read their dials if we are to make judgments that will be timely, appropriate, and constructive for depressed persons.

Depression raises its hand in its symptoms to announce its presence as mild, moderate, or severe. Mildly depressed persons manifest few symptoms and suffer only minor impairment in their ordinary lives. The moderately depressed advertise their problem by their number of identifying symptoms and encounter real problems in carrying out their ordinary responsibilities. The severely depressed reveal their diagnosis in their unmistakable symptomatology and in functional impairment and distress in which they may be seriously suicidal or unable to take basic care of themselves.

Treating Depression

Depression, when untreated in any way, is estimated to last approximately six months. These months, however, are marked for the depressed by torments from negative thoughts, decreased social activity, negative relationships with others, and the everyday burden of very unhappy lives. Treatment, by its nature, interrupts this vicious circle and can diminish the intensity and duration of these torturing symptoms.

Mildly depressed individuals may choose supportive therapy alone without medication. For many people, especially when the onset of their symptoms is linked to a significant, identifiable life event, such as the death of a spouse, this approach may be quite successful. If the symptoms do not begin to resolve, however, after a reasonable period of time (usually four to eight weeks), we should reevaluate and consider other interventions.

The treatment of moderate or severe depression typically includes a combination of antidepressant medication and psychotherapy. Persons experiencing an acute episode should be referred to a psychiatrist to ascertain their ability to care for themselves and whether suicidal thoughts are present. In such an acute stage, these persons may require full or partial hospitalization. Antidepressant therapy is almost always recommended for them and is successful in resolving the symptoms in at least 70–80 percent of persons so treated.

Although it is generally recommended that the psychiatrist provide both the pharmacological and psychotherapeutic treatment to these persons, "split treatment" is increasingly utilized in some settings. In these circumstances, the depressed person receives psychiatric management that includes antidepressant medication from the psychiatrist and psychotherapy from such other trained professionals as social workers.

Although this approach has been justified as more economic than regular psychiatric treatment, little supporting data exists.[5] When "split treatment" is used, it is essential that the treating psychiatrist meet regularly with the depressed person and maintain regular communication with the professional or nonprofessional counselors involved.

What We Should Know about Depression

We are often the first ones to interview persons suffering from depression. More often than not, such persons make their first step toward help by consulting their pastor, personal physician, teacher, or other counselor to speak about their changed mood and the life events to which it may be related. The onset of symptoms is often insidious, developing over a two- to four-week period. These persons may have experienced minor symptoms for months and tried, in the great John Wayne American tradition, to "handle" them "on their own."

We should not presume that we understand but quickly determine if any traumatic life event was correlated with their change in mood. Such events, especially those involving great loss, are often the flames that ignite these slow-burning feelings, especially if this is their first episode of depression. Ironically, gain may be as depressing as loss, for people who cannot cope effectively with some success. In either instance, we may help these persons with supportive therapy as they gather the materials with which to rebuild their lives and the strength to adapt to the changes that have occurred.

If such an individual fails to respond constructively and symptoms intensify, it is time for us to refer the person for psychiatric consultation. Current thinking supports initiating psychiatric treatment early rather than late, that is, before persons evince severe symptoms that either disable or grossly interfere with their lives.

We should also appreciate that although mild depression may be resolved and never occur again, depression is characteristically episodic and recurrent. It is estimated that approximately 75 percent of persons who experience depression will suffer another episode at some time in their lives.[6] This periodicity alerts those of us who work with depressed persons to find out if they have had previous episodes and, if so, what, if any, treatment they have had.

If persons have had previous treatment for a depressive episode, psychiatric referral is indicated. We are faced with a reality with little comfort in it: Many people have blurred or hazy memories about previous significant mood changes. Often a relative or close friend who accompanies these persons can better provide this crucial information about previous episodes. For example, a man in his early thirties, the traditional time when first episodes of depression are anticipated, may come for help after experiencing a failed romance. He may have little memory, however, for major mood problems in his teenage years that may, in fact, have been true episodes and may not have been treated.

Eliciting such essential information is one of the tasks that we can take on, confident that what we find will be helpful in responding to the person.

There is no specific genetic pattern of transmission associated with major depressive disorder. A familial pattern, however, does exist in which major depression is one and a half to three times more common among first-degree relatives (siblings and parents) as compared to the general population.[7] Among persons suffering bipolar disorder, a much higher rate (1 to 24 percent) of bipolar illness is identified in their first-degree relatives. A higher rate of major depressive illness (4 to 24 percent) is found in their first-degree relatives.[8] Twin and adoption studies also provide strong evidence of a genetic influence in the occurrence of the disorder.

Don't Be Surprised If . . .

Navigating our way through the stressful work with depressed persons is modulated if we can read, as sailors would the stars, the psychological patterns that tell us where we are and in what direction we are going. Many persons, as we have observed, who suffer a loss employ the psychological mechanism of identification as a way of getting the lost person or object back. They absorb the lost person in some way into their own personalities, introjecting them in such a way that they possess the lost friend or relative in a new way. We may easily see that depressed persons have taken on the characteristics, interests, hobbies, or even the symptoms of the person who has been lost. They may carry on the work or cause of the lost person as an effective way of symbolically recapturing and holding on to what has been denied them.

Depressed persons, as we have also noted, can be very angry, angry with the person who died for abandoning them, but find it difficult to express this directly or outwardly. Do not be surprised if you are one of those onto whom the anger gets displaced. When persons suffer a loss and come to us for help, they really want more than help, more than being told that we will help them to help themselves. In truth, they may want us to become a substitute supplier of affection and support as replacements for the lost person. They may press us to solve their problems and may be very disappointed when we resist this. Depressed persons want more than healing. They want everything back, and this largely unconscious need can become an important dynamic in the counseling process. Counselors who do not realize this can easily be lost in the ensuing confusion.

Stress builds up exponentially when these persons besiege us with strong expectations for help that we cannot provide. This can intimidate us, especially if counseling is not our main occupation, and we may feel guilty and uneasy because we cannot give what life itself does not yield to these genuinely suffering people. The risk is that our guilt may then be woven into the counseling dynamic. This can happen quite easily and quickly, and we must be very attentive to our own reactions and be in command of ourselves in the face of what can be heartrending situations. Failing this we may find ourselves boxed into a position we cannot really fill and making any effort to do so may seriously harm our providing any help at all.

The edge of paranoia, fine as a razor blade, is the adjustment style of depressed persons who may alternate their depressed outlook with an intensely suspicious one. By employing the mechanism of projection, depressed people shift the blame for their difficulties onto others. For paranoid persons, projection is a highly functional defense and serves their purposes well. Paranoid styles do not come cheaply, however, and the amount of distortion that this adjustment introduces into their lives is not small or unnoticeable. They pay for their projection in an impaired ability to make accurate discriminations about the world around them and in deteriorating social relationships. Healthy people can only take so much of the paranoid style and pull away intuitively from their manipulative grasp. High-riding paranoid persons will then slump back into depression. We may well observe these emotional shifts within the same interview with persons suffering from this difficulty.

Hurting Themselves to Heal Themselves

A principal but not well-understood trait found in depressed persons is their talent for hurting themselves. Some people, as we know, seem accident prone, while others suffer an endless string of misfortune in which bad luck is the only kind of luck they have. In depressed persons, these are often holes that they unconsciously dig and stumble into by themselves. Some seem to be magnets for misplays in life. We must be alert to discern such a pattern in their problems. Many interpretations exist for the meaning of such masochism. Some observers feel that their self-punishment allows them to maintain control over events. If they take the blow before someone can inflict it on them, they keep control of the environment in their own hands. Some analysts suggest that this dynamic explains why some people always volunteer for the most dangerous jobs.

Self-punishing behavior can be easily misinterpreted by others and can, in fact, be the source of the specious healing called "secondary gain." Their investment in woe reaps dividends of sympathy, concern, or being exempt from the rules. We may, in fact, sense this dynamic occurring in therapy sessions with such depressed persons. Mindful of the principle that these individuals always re-create for us their typical behavior with others, our picking up their masochistic behavior can be highly significant in our counseling with them.

Some persons manifest this masochism to us, for example, by taking each new awareness or insight, not to go deeper in understanding themselves but to deploy as further evidence of their own badness or general wretchedness. Obviously, such persons are not ready to use insight therapeutically. We should proceed very slowly with them, not pushing too hard but understanding that what we must help them grasp is not the apparent content of surface problems but their dynamic of using them against themselves.

Shifting Our Style

We have earned our fatigue after a day of working with depressed persons. Not only do we need to attune ourselves steadily to the dynamics beneath the surface that give depression its true meaning, but we may need to take a counseling stance that differs from the one we are accustomed to, and comfortable with, using. We may, for example, have to be more active with these persons than we typically are with other persons who come for help.

In the initial phases of counseling, we may have to introduce more structure into the relationship than it is customary for us to do. Such departures are necessary when persons are incapable of saying or doing much about, or for, themselves at the beginning of therapy. To wait for them may impose on them a psychological burden that they are incapable of carrying as they begin counseling.

As noted, depressed persons may want far more than we can ultimately give them. If so, they start trying to get this right from the start of therapy. Such persons approach counseling with a dulling mixture of pessimism and passivity and little willingness to commit themselves with much determination to dealing with their problems. Understanding this style, we will need more than the usual patience and may need to accept additional responsibility for initiating the counseling itself. This is not a betrayal of principle but a practical extension of what it means to understand people in trouble. It is speaking back in the same language with which they address us.

When very seriously disturbed people come for help, somebody else often comes with them. They may have had great difficulty in convincing the depressed person to get help. Counselors may find the booklet *Helping the Depressed Person Get Treatment* published by the National Institute of Mental Health a useful tool in helping those working to achieve this goal.[9] Sometimes depressed persons are so withdrawn or so passive that they can hardly speak for themselves. They need others with them to describe their problems. It is a good idea to get as much information as possible from their companions. Although counselors must always avoid the impression of talking behind a person's back, they can, with permission and without subterfuge, question a companion thoroughly. Individuals suffering depression of this magnitude will necessarily be referred for psychiatric evaluation. Our involvement is usually in the early meetings — this may take more than one session — that are focused on getting sufficient information to facilitate a referral.

In an attempt to respond directly to depressed persons, we deal first with their difficulty in speaking, or even in seeming interested in speaking, about themselves. This is clearly a symbolic message to us and may indeed be the first one to which we may offer an effective response. Such depressed persons are actually communicating clearly to us, presenting themselves in this special and significant silence. It hurts too much to talk. We can respond directly to this.

They're Dancing as Fast as They Can

As we grow comfortable with the understanding that depressed persons relate to us as they relate to others, we will not hurry them. Nor will we become impatient with the slow pace, hesitations, and repetitions that may characterize such depressed persons' presentation of themselves. Through this fractured and delayed modality, depressed persons reveal what it is like to experience their dark difficulties. They are constricted, emotionally and logically, and pushing them hard may make us feel better, but it won't help them at all. This is not the time or place to challenge them. Depressed people need receptivity, patience, and a great willingness on our part to discern and understand their tortured patterns of life.

If our only response is reassurance, we will not really be helpful. When people are mildly depressed they are critical of themselves. They need to express these negative feelings, and we counselors should not abridge their right to do this. We should allow them to get these feelings out and allow them to deal with them at their own pace.

We deal very gently as seriously withdrawn depressed patients fumble with the locks that must be opened on their ability to tell us their story. As noted, we may have to be more active than we usually are in early interviews with people. Therapists who are too passive, who play the waiting game too exclusively, may make already depressed people feel greater frustration and incompetence about themselves. As a result, they will feel more depressed. We must be flexible enough to change the way we do things in responding to these people. This may slow down the counseling, but that is what is called for if we are to help these persons and manage our own stress well.

– 24 –

STRESSED OUT
AND ANXIOUS

I F NORMAN MAILER accurately chose "ego" as the word of the twentieth century, it crossed the border of the twenty-first arm in arm with its first cousin "stress." People bear a wearying consciousness of both themselves and their stresses into our offices every day. If they are not spontaneously concerned about their lives and their pressures, a thousand voices remind them every day of their troubles and how to treat them. Television and print commercials take up the chant across the flat depressed plains of the Prozac Nation: we are tense, run-down, and live in various post-traumatic syndrome states. Fear and anxiety, worry and uneasiness — these are psychological complaints that, like the biblical jar of oil, are consumed but never diminished. What, me worry? You bet.

Many remedies sell themselves by tapping in to the national blues and worries, telling people that their contents — take this pill, take that, the usual side effects are these, ask your doctor or pharmacist — help them cope with stress and anxiety. Medication and meditation have boomed in the bazaar of human difficulties. Still, we must understand the basic *psychological* character of both fear and anxiety if, as wise counselors, we are to be of help.

Sigmund Freud made a clear distinction between what he termed "normal" and "neurotic" anxiety. While the term "neurotic" has disappeared from the clinical vocabulary, most people understand and accept this distinction. Fear was caused by "real danger...which threatens from some external object." "Neurotic anxiety," on the other hand, is present if a person's reaction is "disproportionately...greater than in our judgment it ought to be. It is by this excess that the neurotic element stands revealed."[1] While we are chiefly concerned with this latter anxiety, especially in its free and undifferentiated form, there are facts about fear with which we should also be familiar.

232

The Management of Fear

The classic definition of fear associates it with some definite object — a person, a thing, or an event in the environment. A logical connection can be made between this phenomenon and the subjective experience of fear. This feeling is an appropriate and helpful response in many situations in life. It is suitable in many of our interactions with persons and our life circumstances. Healthy fear alerts us to and protects us from danger. We would be totally vulnerable to our surroundings were it not for the information that fear gives us.

We frequently work with persons who have quite legitimate and understandable fears. These may be connected with some forthcoming event, such as a major examination, a surgical operation, or a dangerous and potentially harmful relationship. Psychological research confirms our sense that these fears should not be ignored. We should rather assist people to understand the meaning of the experience that prompts the feeling. Often when people are not helped to understand the source of their fear, they use ineffective mechanisms to preserve their psychological integrity. They may look away from the fear, for example, placing themselves in greater peril. There are sensible things we can do to help people manage their realistic fears constructively.

First, we must avoid telling people they really don't have anything about which to be afraid. Since their fear is telling them exactly the opposite, a sensible and measured effort to understand the circumstances in which they find themselves is in order. Research by psychologist Irving Janis illustrates this situation for us.[2] Recognizing that major surgery involves pain as well as a serious threat to bodily integrity and a variety of other frustrations, Janis investigated the experience of fear in the surgical wards of a general hospital. He found three patterns of emotional response. There were those patients who worried excessively in advance of their surgery. They openly admitted their extreme feelings of vulnerability, attempted to postpone the operation, were unable to sleep without sedation, and constantly sought reassurances from the hospital staff. After the operation these subjects were much more likely than the others to be anxiety ridden.

Another group of patients experienced a moderate kind of fear in anticipation of their surgery. They were sometimes worried and tense about certain aspects of the operation, such as the nature and mode of the anesthetic. They did, however, ask for and receive realistic information about what was going to happen to them. Although they felt somewhat vulnerable, their concerns were focused on realistic rather than imaginary threats. These people were much less likely than the others to display any emotional disturbance after the operation. They evinced high morale, cooperated well with the hospital staff, and were not as disturbed as others with the many nursing procedures that they had to undergo.

A third group of patients had very little fear in anticipation of their surgery. They were always cheerful and optimistic about what would happen. They denied any experience of feeling worried, and they slept well and seemed to operate in a fairly normal way. Janis suggests that they "appeared to have unrealistic expectations of almost complete invulnerability." After the operation their vulnerability surfaced and they were much more likely than the other patients to display anger and resentment toward the staff. They complained and were uncooperative.

Janis concludes that a moderate amount of fear in anticipation of the realistic dimensions of some forthcoming event is helpful because it prepares people to deal with actual dangers and the experience of deprivation they will undergo. The first two groups were able to rehearse in advance some of the unpleasant things they were going to go through. They could listen to and take account of the realistic information that was given to them. As a result they were not caught by surprise and they felt fairly secure as the events unfolded around them.

The key variable here seems to be *the amount of information provided in advance*. The third group of patients, who displayed practically no fear beforehand, had no idea what was really going to happen to them. Those who experienced a moderate amount of fear were much better informed. What can we conclude from this research? It makes sense not to cajole people out of a valid experience of fear. It is not constructive to hide from them information that, if delivered in a mature and not overwhelming way, they can use to prepare themselves for a difficult event. The constructive side of fear allows people to prepare themselves sensibly for the realities that lie before them. The old, but still not retired, idea of helping people to keep a stiff upper lip, with the coda that what you don't know won't hurt you, is not humanly sensible. As counselors, we can frequently serve as significant mediators for the kind of information — whether it has to do with going to a hospital, a courtroom, or a strange distant place — that helps people manage their fear constructively. We may also wisely apply it in our own lives.

Anxiety as a Signal

Freud first drew our attention to the signals anxiety hoists like a ship's flags to inform us of the breaking weather. Anxiety runs up the ego's warning about some internal conflict within us. Classically, this clash pits some unacceptable impulses against the psychological forces trying to suppress them. This anxiety mobilizes defense mechanisms to protect the integrity of the ego itself. The experience of anxiety sends a message in the clear even when this cannot be associated consciously with any distinct event or object. We may often work with people experiencing raw and undifferentiated anxiety. What may be described without sophistication as a case of jangled "nerves" is actually a symbolic manifestation of an internal psychological reality.

We examine anxiety here as constant a visitor to the psyche as tremors to the earth, a condition difficult to describe even though its effects are deeply felt. Just feeling on edge or jumpy does not indicate that a person is experiencing a state of pathological anxiety.

Persons experiencing a true psychological disturbance feel some kind of uncontrollable dread and apprehension. They feel that something bad is going to happen, but they are not sure when, where, or why this will be. A dark cloud shadows their steps and they cannot overcome their tensions and restlessness by acts of the will or in response to the reassurances of their friends. Their physical reactions — rapid pulse, elevated blood pressure, difficulties in breathing — are the signals of the emergency measures the body is taking to prepare itself for the nameless threat. When this condition seriously interferes with their ongoing lives or when someone suggests that they should see a counselor and try to get to the bottom of their worries, they knock on our door for help.

Reading Lessons for Counselors

Anxiety symptoms are the Rosetta stone of the suffering human person, bearing a language that, above all others, we counselors must be able to understand. We should never be surprised at the indirect and disguised way in which human conflicts reveal themselves to us. Indirection is a profoundly human style of expressing ourselves. I don't know where to begin, we will say. If healthy people employ it, we should anticipate that troubled persons will as well, if in a more exaggerated form.

Victims of acute anxiety cannot explain much about their difficulty in a conscious or orderly way. When this experience is episodic — when it is not steady but comes in intense and unpredictable bursts — they cannot tell why it has happened or when it will end. They frequently feel that they are about to die. It is a haunting and disturbing experience. These people are not faking nor are they merely trying to get sympathy from those around them. It is very wearing on them, and occasionally it is equally taxing on counselors or others who are supposed to help them.

Sensitivity is needed in the diagnosis of anxiety states, especially because of possible complications from associated physical complaints. We wisely remember that many physical conditions cause the same symptoms that are found in anxiety states. These include hyperthyroidism, cardiac disorders, disturbances of the cerebellum and the semicircular canals, some toxic conditions and disorders, as well as many other physical illnesses. These symptoms should be attended to carefully and in many cases these persons should be referred for professional medical evaluation.

Whenever a country's economy stutters, many persons react anxiously to the possibilities that suddenly present themselves. Will they have a job next year? What about that credit card debt? Will my pension survive? Will we lose the house? When such fundamentals are threatened, people are subject to this experience of free-floating anxiety. When threats fill the air like raindrops, you are bound to get wet. Anything — strikes, layoffs, foreclosures on home and dreams — can leave persons feeling suddenly lost in a culture they thought they understood. Although not the direct causes, these landslides expose conflicts previously covered up within people. As counselors, we cannot control the economic status of the world nor much else about the environment. We are aided considerably, however, when we can appreciate the stress these factors introduce into the lives of those with whom they work. In such circumstances, the various languages of anxiety are spread open before us.

Stress rises like fine and irritating smog off our work with anxious individuals because it is difficult for them to explain what their problem is. They lay it on our desk, wrapped in vagueness, challenging us to understand it. The better part of wisdom tells us that knowing what to avoid is as important as knowing how to proceed sensibly.

Sometimes well-meaning friends complicate the difficulties of people suffering from extreme anxiety by blandly and blindly urging them to overcome it with a muscular old-fashioned determination. When persons are already experiencing something close to panic, such advice can tear their adjustment apart. They may then try to escape and, in fact, it is under just such pressure that some people leave counseling altogether. Counselors who respect the unconscious variables in play here never push people too hard about their conscious behaviors or decisions. Harried persons need less advice and more simple acceptance and understanding.

Seeking help is already complicated for them because their anxieties have made them cautious about committing themselves to others. Hurrying people who can only take one small step at a time makes them stumble and become more uncertain of their direction. Being patient tries our own patience when we already find the symptoms bewildering and, out of a desire to establish some core understanding of the problem, we may push people too hard toward a definite conclusion, almost certainly making things worse.

Another temptation under the pressure of stress is to intellectualize about the tensions and difficulties under which we all live. Philosophical and theological ruminations about the star-crossed conditions of modern life and a guiding Providence may sound soothing, but they do not touch the heart of serious difficulty. It may be goodwilled but it is almost always a mistake to associate the cultural awareness of existential anxiety with the experience of anxiety that comes from within persons themselves.

Being Anxious Ourselves

We counselors must also read accurately our own experiences of anxiety to understand what they tell us about ourselves and about the conflicts other persons are experiencing. If we listen sensitively we can pick up many messages in how we resonate to those sitting across from us. We may realize, for example, that we too are vulnerable to the same kind of difficulties, that whatever the person is dealing with makes us react in telling fashion, telling about us, that is. We want to avoid, for example, the unnecessary defensiveness this might set up in us. Catching the signals sent by the other or set off in ourselves allows us to make our way sensibly and surefootedly through the process.

It is also true that the specific kind of anxiety that others touch off in us does tell us more of their story, too. Persons with free-floating anxiety may make us generally uneasy and restive, while persons who are paranoid will upset us in a very different way, making us feel that we are the object of attacks made by them to diminish our authority. Counselors sometimes undervalue the information they are constantly receiving. They are their own best consultants when they pay attention to what the other does to them. Far from being static or a source of stress, our own reactions help us in our understanding and assisting others.

When Anxiety Becomes a Disorder

Although all of us are anxious now and then, only a small percentage of us evince, in number or intensity, the symptoms that lead to *anxiety disorders*. As counselors, we may be the first ones approached about these almost ubiquitous feelings, so we must be ready to identify those that flow from the more serious and pervasive problems that require referral for professional evaluation and treatment. The ability to make these early sightings is a skill of the highest order through which we give a well-timed recommendation that makes a great difference in their lives.

Generalized Anxiety Disorder

Until 1980, patients with chronic generalized anxiety and panic attacks were diagnosed with *anxiety neurosis*. Treatment was generally psychological therapy possibly coupled with some mild antianxiety medication, often prescribed by the person's general practitioner. The 1980 *Diagnostic and Statistical Manual, DSM-III,* carved panic disorder out as a distinct syndrome. General anxiety symptoms were designated *generalized anxiety disorder*, defined currently as "excessive anxiety and worry" about a number of events or activities that occurred more days than not for a period of at least six months.[3] These individuals have excessive concern about such issues as being late, the whereabouts of their adult children, and the health of just about everyone they know. They often complain of such symptoms as muscle tension, sweating, and nausea. We may see these persons for an array of complaints that may or may not respond to a supportive psychotherapy.

When these symptoms lead to social and occupational impairment, these persons are likely to turn first to their primary care physicians. The physicians generally review such persons' medical status, use of caffeine, which in excess can cause anxiety, and their use of other substances, such as alcohol. If their medical condition is stable, a referral for psychiatric evaluation may yield a diagnosis of generalized anxiety disorder. Treatment often consists in a combination of psychotherapy and medication such as the benzodiazepines (such as Valium and Xanax) or other antianxiety medications. If resources are available, relaxation therapy, biofeedback, cognitive behavioral therapy, and anxiety management techniques may also be used.

Panic Disorder

Persons experiencing panic disorder have recurrent unexpected panic attacks followed by at least a month of persistent worry about having additional ones. A panic attack is a discrete episode of intense fear or discomfort in the absence of real danger and is accompanied by a specified number of symptoms such as palpitations, sweating, chest pain, nausea, or fear of dying or becoming mentally ill. The attacks may be totally unexpected or may be associated with certain situations or cues. These are so frightening to people that they often go to the emergency room convinced they are dying or, if they are reassured that they are not, they remain unconvinced and repeatedly seek medical consultation and testing.

Fears about having subsequent attacks can lead to agoraphobia, a fear of being in a situation from which escape is impossible. They also fear that help will be unavailable if another panic attack occurs. Rather than risk that possibility, many of these individuals stay at home. Their work and social relationships, as well as their general functioning, are markedly affected. Demoralization and depression are commonly associated with this disorder.

Cognitive behavioral therapy and an appropriate medication are both treatments of choice for panic disorder. Neither treatment has yet been found superior to the other. The behavioral therapy aims to correct misinterpretations of the meaning of the somatic symptoms and to eliminate the person's avoidance behavior that complicates the attacks. In addition, although many psychiatrists use both modalities or a combination of medication and some other kind of psychotherapy, long-term outcomes have not been well studied. Because the best studies have focused on the treatment of specific symptoms, the treating psychiatrist may employ a variety of strategies in devising a treatment plan for a particular person. This may involve group or family therapy as well as individual treatment. It is generally accepted that panic disorder is a chronic, relapsing illness and that long-term studies are needed to clarify the best ways to treat it.

Panic disorder is a serious illness with a potential for complicating features. For example, as many as 50–60 percent of panic disorder patients experience an episode of major depressive disorder at some time.[4] In addition, in a large epidemiological study, 20 percent of persons with this problem and 12 percent of those with a history of panic attacks had attempted suicide.[5]

In our relationships with chronically anxious individuals, the onset of panic symptoms sounds a general alert so that we may promptly but carefully inquire about them and, if indicated, make a timely professional referral. We must also recognize that, because of their anxiety, they may well refuse further evaluation or referral. Their concern may be, as noted, that, as they put it, they are "going crazy" and that nothing can be done for them. Because of their worries about their physical status, they may be hesitant about and resistant to, taking any prescribed medication. One of our most important roles is to work with the physician and family members to help the person understand and accept the recommended treatment. Because many of these individuals are afraid to leave the house even though they accept their need for help, we may need to follow up with family members to help the afflicted person obtain the available help.

Obsessive-Compulsive Disorder

The essential features of this disorder are recurrent *obsessions*, that is, persistent ideas, thoughts, impulses, or images experienced as intrusive and inappropriate and causing marked anxiety and distress, or *compulsions*, expressed in repetitive behaviors such as hand washing or checking the house locks, or repetitive mental acts such as praying or counting. These behaviors prevent or reduce anxiety or distress rather than deliver any pleasure or gratification. These symptoms can be severe and time-consuming and can give rise to intense distress or significant impairment in ordinary functioning in life. These persons recognize intellectually that these ideas or behaviors are unreasonable, but that does not overcome their emotional need to carry them out anyway.

Until the mid-1980s, obsessive-compulsive disorder was perceived as ordinarily rare and poorly responsive to treatment. With the advent of large-scale epidemiological studies and more precise diagnostic criteria, more people have been identified as suffering from this disorder, reaching a prevalence of perhaps 2 percent. The disorder's onset is usually insidious and, although it sometimes begins in childhood, it typically appears in adolescence or early adulthood. Some evidence identifies a familial pattern in the presence of the disorder, suggesting a genetic predisposition. Many people do not recognize obsessive-compulsive disorder as an illness and do not seek treatment. Instead, they tend to isolate themselves and carry out their rituals in secret because they recognize that their behavior is irrational and will appear "strange" to those around them.

"Scruples"

Persons often come for help, especially to a religious counselor, because of concerns or "scruples," as they are called in certain religious traditions. These are obsessions about beliefs they may or may not profess, or about sins that they may or may not have committed. They fear they will go to hell, and they may engage in complicated rituals, again within the context of their respective religion, in order to diminish the anxiety engendered by their ideas. Religious counselors may readily recognize that these are not spiritual problems and these symptoms are of such a nature that referral for psychiatric treatment is indicated.

These persons often carry a burden of religious scruples but a sackful of other obsessions as well, such as *contamination fears* in which they worry about catching an illness from touching some object, such as a restroom doorknob. Scrupulous persons often reject the notion that they are suffering from a psychiatric disturbance, insisting that theirs is a crisis of faith that only a religious counselor can help. If the religious counselor has a good working relationship with a psychiatrist, they can often work together to deliver proper psychiatric treatment while assuaging the religious concerns of these people at the same time.

When psychiatric evaluation confirms the diagnosis, treatment consists primarily of medication (antidepressant medications are currently the treatment of choice) and cognitive therapies aimed at extinguishing the repetitive thoughts and intrusive behaviors. The outcome of treatment with this group of patients, as compared with treatment for other anxiety disorders, is modest. Perhaps 50–65 percent of treated persons have a moderately good response to medication. For this reason, especially with that subset of persons with religious scruples, pastoral counselors and others may be enlisted to work together with psychiatrists and psychologists to help relieve their plaguing anxieties. Even when individuals experience considerable improvement in both the intensity of their symptoms and the degree of their impairment, the course of the illness is chronic and fluctuating, with improved outcome dependent on continuing treatment.

Acute Stress Disorder and Post-Traumatic Stress Disorder

Some anxiety disturbances emerge only after exposure to an extreme traumatic stressor. These similar diagnoses are differentiated in this manner: an *acute stress disorder* emerges within the four weeks following the exposure while symptoms of the *post-traumatic stress disorder* usually begin within three months of the trauma, although their emergence may be delayed for months or even years. The stressor, the source of the trauma, must be extreme and directly experienced by such persons as threatening death or serious injury to them or harm to another person's physical integrity. It may also be touched off by witnessing such an event or of learning of such a trauma affecting a close family member or associate. In response to the trauma, symptomatic persons may experience fear, helplessness or horror, and persistent episodes or "flashbacks" and "reexperiencing" the trauma along with feelings of emotional "numbness." They also avoid any stimuli associated with the trauma and evince symptoms that include wakefulness, angry outbursts, difficulty concentrating, and nightmares.

The treatment of diagnosed *post-traumatic stress disorder* combines medication for the control of symptoms with psychotherapy. Herman has suggested three phases in the treatment of these individuals. In the first stage, the person needs to feel safe and protected from further traumatization. The therapy is aimed at helping persons experience some sense of control in their own environment. The second stage involves reintegrating the memories related to the trauma so that these persons may objectively "look at" the event in the context of their lives. The last stage involves facing and overcoming the feelings of withdrawal and avoidance that are associated with this syndrome.[6]

A high likelihood exists that we nonprofessional counselors will encounter persons subject to these stress disorders. Although this diagnosis first emerged in popular consciousness in the wake of the Vietnam War, subsequent research demonstrates the disorder's frequency in the general nonmilitary population. In one study, for example, 9.2 percent of members of an HMO (Health Maintenance Organization) in a metropolitan area qualified for the diagnosis.[7]

Frontline Work

Often the first person on the scene of a tragedy, especially a disaster, is the police officer, firefighter, local pastor, or well-meaning neighbor. Counselors, often nonprofessionals called "peer counselors," may also be in the front ranks of those who first hear their story from youngsters sexually abused, elderly people who have been assaulted, spouses who have been physically abused, or anybody affected by a sudden disaster. The general psychological approach to dealing with disaster and traumatic events is to help affected persons "talk about it." That is why, after major disasters, such as tornadoes or school shootings, psychological resources are set up, in which both professionals and nonprofessional counselors are available to those who choose to utilize their services. Clinical studies show that one of the crucial coping strategies is the degree to which the affected persons use, or abuse, their social network. Often social support is available immediately after an event but diminishes as time goes on. Sometimes affected persons reject support or in some way demean those who would provide help. The manner in which persons avail themselves of such resources is related to their overall ability to cope with the experience.[8]

Talking does not simply *release* pent-up emotion but also helps individuals gain better *control* over their emotional responses. Persons are debriefed to themselves by sorting out fragmented memories of the event and achieving real understanding of what, at first, seems an overwhelming and unintelligible experience. This counseling also allows these persons to be *heard* by another empathic human being.[9]

Caution is not misplaced in this matter. A major misunderstanding floats in the consciousness of the public about the usefulness of "getting it all out" about some traumatic event. Although it is useful for people to talk about their experiences — and most people want and need to do so — this may not be the best option for everyone. The impulse to "do good" needs to be restrained because, for some individuals, talking about the traumatic event may traumatize them all over again. Forced talking may increase their sensitivity to the event, rendering them less, rather than more, able to cope with it.

As counselors sensitive to these possibilities, we must listen carefully to pick up even faint signals that persons are less spontaneous, more withholding, and possibly emotionally unable to talk about what happened to them. All of us bring our own pace and our own capacity to cope with us into the vale of trauma. We key our responses to that potential rather than demanding that they react in some ideal manner. Support them to get out what they can as they can.

A debate continues in the psychiatric and psychological literature about the usefulness of "debriefing" after a traumatic event. Some studies suggest that the intervention of teams of well-trained professionals can diminish the development of post-traumatic symptoms. Other studies suggest that such interventions can actually worsen the outcome.

Those who work with individuals immediately after a major trauma can provide assistance by (1) encouragement and direction to help persons regain a sense of mastery and control; (2) encouragement of the use of existing support systems; (3) practical assistance in obtaining food, shelter, information, and directions for restoring losses; (4) assessment of their need for more formal support, such as specialized psychological services; (5) gentle encouragement to review the events they have just experienced, mindful that some individuals remain overwhelmed and need to remain temporarily in "denial" about the event; (6) education for affected people about the common reactions others have had and that they can expect, such as insomnia, nightmares, irritability, and intrusive thoughts.[10] These responses may be sensibly and safely orchestrated to assist traumatized persons who face external and internal chaos.

Phobias

A *specific phobia* is a marked and persistent fear of clearly discernible, circumscribed objects or situations. This may, for example, be fear of flying in an airplane, standing on heights, or seeing blood. Exposure to the object or situation provokes an immediate anxiety response that affected persons recognize as unreasonable. As a result, these persons consciously avoid the fearful object or situation or, if unable to do so, endure exposure with intense anxiety. This diagnosis should be given only if this pattern of avoidance interferes with the person's daily routine, occupational functioning, or social life.

Social phobia occurs when the same general symptoms rise to a stimulus that is social or involves a performance that may lead to embarrassment. The socially phobic may fear speaking in public, for example, because others may notice their anxiety, their quivering voice, or their trembling hands. These symptoms may seriously compromise their social lives and prevent them, for example, from accepting advancements in their occupation if public speaking is a component of the new position.

The Epidemiological Catchment Area study found that phobias are the most common psychiatric disorder in the community, "more common than major depression or alcohol abuse or dependence." The estimated one-month prevalence in the United States is 6.2 percent.[11]

Persons suffering from such a phobia experience pathological fear. Psychoanalytic theory suggests that such fear is originally and unconsciously associated with a situation that touched off an inner psychological conflict. The phobic mechanism works by displacing this anxiety onto some other situation or object. Affected persons then fear this latter situation as a substitute for facing what would be so anxiety producing in the original difficulty. Thus people can fear riding in certain conveyances, being in certain kinds of rooms, or having certain kinds of pets. These specific phobias represent the distillation of another very strong fear whose origins are found in an unresolved and unattended inner conflict.

Whatever the object of the phobia may be, it symbolizes the original stimulus for conflict or anxiety. Here again a familiar emotional compromise is struck within the individual. People suffering from phobias actually substitute the experience of fear for the experience of anxiety. They would rather be afraid of a specific, identifiable object or situation than be hounded by a nameless and vague kind of anxiety. They are uncomfortable but in a way that is different and more acceptable. They know, at least on the intellectual level, that what they now fear cannot really hurt them because they can do something to avoid it. They thus make their anxiety manageable by displacing it onto some place or object that they are able to avoid, thereby using control of the situation to control their own experience of anxiety.

This is heady stuff for some counselors who long to interpret people's conflict by reading the symbolic significance of their phobia. Most people are familiar with the long list of phobias to which Greek prefixes were once added — such as claustrophobia (fear of closed places) or agoraphobia (fear of open places) — because this symbolic linkage is often quite striking. This is the same kind of temptation to which moviemaker Alfred Hitchcock regularly succumbed, using heights, birds, trains, and tunnels for superficial sexual analogies. That may go in entertainment, but not in art or good counseling.

It is very tricky to try to interpret the symbolic meaning of phobias and commonsense counselors do not attempt it, even if they are confident that they are correct. The problem is that the same phobia may, in different persons, represent very different kinds of conflicts. It is very easy to be wrong because so much depends on the individual life history of the person coming for help.

There is no specific pharmacological treatment for phobic disorders but, in severe cases, psychiatrists may prescribe mild antianxiety drugs, including such benzodiazepines as Xanax or Valium on an as-needed basis. Behavioral therapy, which requires the expertise of a highly trained professional, has been useful for the treatment of specific phobias. Social phobia has been treated with social skills training and cognitive behavioral techniques (CBT). In the latter, the phobic person learns to identify and challenge performance-related thoughts that generate anxiety. They learn to rehearse the feared behavior with specific cognitive and behavior techniques. In a specific CBT approach of Heimberg's group, patients are provided with a cognitive-behavioral rationale for the etiology and treatment of social phobia, followed by real-life practice situations and the identification of maladaptive responses. Weekly homework assignments are also utilized. This approach has reported a 75 percent success rate that remains superior at a five-year follow-up.[12]

Counselors may be called upon to offer a good deal of reassurance at certain times to these individuals. This can be done through reviewing with them that other people have had these experiences and that it is not unusual for them to have such concerns. We can comprehend and express, without censure or disdain, an appreciation of what they are experiencing. Sometimes these people are asking something like, "Can you help me?" or "Am I going crazy?" Such questions have no direct answers. They symbolize the enormous concern these persons feel about their lives. We respond, therefore, not to the content of their question but to the level of their concern. This is always appropriate and will, in itself, offer the kind of reassurance that such persons need to be able to move forward.

– 25 –

THE PROBLEMS
OF HEALTHY PEOPLE

S TRESS HAS BECOME a familiar, indeed, a pervasive notion in our consciousness. Although it is generally considered a negative by-product of modern times, stress is not wholly, and perhaps not even mainly, an oppressor. It is true that excessive stress can overwhelm and even immobilize us, but stress is absolutely necessary for our healthy growth and achievement. Optimal stress results in optimal functioning. Too little stress or too few challenges lead to boredom and still waters unruffled by even the backwash of progress.

We can judge stress in its effects and look to research to understand something about its causes. "Stress," however, is used to describe both our inner and outer experience concerning reactions that are both physical and psychological. The notion of stress fits the human person, catching the varying qualities of tension that necessarily surround any kind of active living. Stress can be a hurricane or a headwind in sailing and our way of heading into it may determine whether it moves us forward or beaches us.

We counselors must deal with our own stresses while we manage the stresses of other persons. The nature of the main work of some counselors is powerfully stressful. Chaplains, doctors, medics, and workers in correctional institutions or high-pressure environments experience stress as an occupational hazard. Stress sizzles in them and in the persons with whom they work because of the urgency of the demands for decision and response that are made on them.

One of our mechanisms of choice in scaling the jagged mountains of life is *denial,* the common denominator of all psychological defenses. This does not necessarily make denial a bad thing. Were we not able to deny certain aspects of our experience, it would be almost impossible to carry on in any kind of serious emergency situation. Denial protects us from overwhelming psychological pain and confusion. We employ denial less usefully when we protect ourselves against examining the

247

stress that we need to examine to be well adjusted in our life and work. We can end up wearing psychological blinders so dark and stiff that we may not see the things too important to miss in helping other people. Our way of handling our stresses offers a Christmas tree of clues about ourselves and how we work with others.

Imperfect but Healthy

Only a basically healthy person can live an average life well. All too often, we associate strength of personality with the heroic dimensions of adventure and challenge. Some persons, however, court great challenges for pathological reasons. It is quite another thing to lead an undramatic, quiet, and, so to say, average sort of life. Living this way does not attract publicity, headlines, or perhaps any great financial reward, but it does demand a sound sense of oneself and a capacity to withstand stress in its constant, everyday forms.

Stress, we remember, is a side effect of the well-lived life. Lives, like objects in motion, cause friction. There is plenty of stress associated with every profession and as much or more with being a spouse or a parent. These stresses flow from being healthy. When persons are in a close relationship with each other — such as that of husband and wife — they necessarily experience the stresses that go along with the love that is prized as one of the greatest of life's blessings. People who are close to each other can also easily hurt each other. They miss each other intensely when they are apart and, because their relationship tunes them better to everything, they experience all of life more keenly than they would if they remained at a safe distance from human intimacy.

So, too, stress is a necessary by-product in the lives of persons with great integrity who are dedicated to their work. The kind of performance they offer in their callings, the sincerity of the commitments under which they work, their "losing" themselves in their labors, define them but also generate a special stress that is absent for persons who approach their work more casually or with less responsibility. That is why it takes a healthy person to live a challenging life, and that includes an average life, well.

Adjustment Disorders

Nonetheless, healthy people may be subjected to stressors that are more than they can effectively manage. An *adjustment disorder* is a psychological response to an identifiable stressor or stressors that results in the development of clinically significant emotional or behavioral symptoms. To meet the definition, these symptoms must develop within three months of the event and be resolved within six months of the termination of the stressor. The symptoms must be greater than would be expected in view of the precipitant stressor or must result in significant impairment in social or occupational functioning.[1] When, for example, the stressor is the loss by death of a loved one and gives rise to symptoms, *bereavement*, not adjustment disorder, is the appropriate diagnosis.

The stress may be due to a job loss, marital separation, examination failure — any of the significant changes or losses that may occur in life. These problems are to the emotions what the common cold is to the physical body of the individual. They arise in situations that, sooner or later and at some stage of their lives, people must face and to which they must adjust.

It is not the nature of the stress in itself that generates the symptoms. These garden-variety stressors would upset most people. The problem is that persons, for whatever reason at this particular time, are unable to cope with such stresses in their usual fashion. Their failure to cope effectively results in symptoms that interfere with their lives. It is this departure from normal that alerts us to the person's need for some help.

Scoring the Stressors

For almost two generations, there has been an increasing public awareness of the relationship between stressful life events and the development of symptoms. In 1967, Holmes and Rahe published the "Social Readjustment Rating Scale," which ranked numerically the stressful impact of forty-three life change events on persons. The death of a spouse, for example, was assigned a value of 100; pregnancy, a value of 40. It was originally suggested that an accumulation of 200 or more life change units in a single year would constitute more stress than the average individual could withstand.[2] These ratings were widely publicized, often with the simplification characteristic of popularizing scientific findings.

In the following decade, many researchers challenged the notion of relating an absolute degree of stress with the onset of illness, suggesting that how people cope, even with massive amounts of stress, is dependent on a wide variety of factors. For example, different groups of people, such as the elderly and college students, were subjected to a different range of stressors and perceived their meaning in very different ways. In 1978, Dr. Holmes himself, based on his continuing research, offered cautions about relating life changes to the onset of illness, reporting that age, marital status, sex, socioeconomic status, ethnicity, level of education, and culture all contributed to how the stressfulness of a given event was perceived and experienced.[3] If we regularly work with individuals subjected to such major stressors, we should be familiar with this literature and apply it, not cookbook style, but with a subtlety of judgment that serves us and those we see well.

Symptoms

Variety characterizes the psychological symptoms that individuals experience in the midst of an adjustment disorder.

Anxiety is a leading psychological reaction in adjustment disorders. It wears many hats, from generalized tension to an obsessive preoccupation with a detail or obligation of life. Persons may experience restlessness and irritability or find it difficult to concentrate on their ordinary work. They may begin to behave in ways that reflect anxiety but that are not characteristic of their usual reactions. Anxiety has a hundred homely faces.

Sometimes persons will report a depressed mood, marked by tearfulness or feelings of hopelessness. They may also complain about depressive symptoms such as disturbances in their routines of sleeping and eating. Somatic complaints are often cloaked in vagueness, such as generalized fatigue, abdominal pains, or the other poorly differentiated physiological symptoms. People talk to themselves and to us through these complaints.

Occasionally persons with an adjustment disorder are surprised by the new and unexpected behaviors in their lives. They may begin to drink excessively, have suicidal thoughts, or arrive chronically late at work. All of these, in ordinary circumstances, would be both unacceptable to and uncharacteristic of the affected person. These efforts are usually described psychologically as *maladaptive*. These stressed persons are attempting to solve their problems through strategies that often make them worse.

Howsoever ineffectively, they are trying to reduce their anxiety by behaviors that cause them other difficulties. They may, for example, seek other satisfactions to make up for the loss they have experienced. Thus the individual, never before belligerent, who begins to get into fights in order to settle difficulties at work is exhibiting *maladaptive* behavior. Persons who find that they are taking time off from work for some frivolous and expensive pursuit of relaxation cause problems through roundabout efforts to solve problems. So, too, individuals may try to make up for what they feel they have been deprived of by drinking or promiscuous sexual behavior. Such fated campaigns to make themselves whole sometimes suddenly appear in the lives of persons who have experienced a recent major loss, for example, an upsetting medical diagnosis or the death of a spouse.

Maladaptive behaviors are like fireworks, distracting people in their work and relationships while giving unmistakable signals that something has happened to them. Some stresses are related to an event that is itself limited by time, such as the length of a court trial. Other stresses are not so limited and, as they continue, we may observe an increase in the symptomatic signs of an adjustment reaction. We must be able to read these unhurriedly, carefully, and always in the context of the affected person's life.

Under the impact of an acute stressor, such symptoms usually flare up rapidly and burn down to ash quickly as well. If the stressor is chronic, however, the symptoms may ignite more slowly and flicker for a longer period. When the symptoms last longer than six months after the end of the initial stressor, we should ask whether some other problem, such as a major depression, is also present and requires referral.

Often we observe the salvo of symptoms from these transient episodes without understanding their possible relationship with other things occurring in these persons' lives. These exploding signals of distress often meet with reassurance — the "buck up, carry on, be a man" code — that may relieve the counselor but denies persons the chance to explore the reasons that make this crisis so difficult for them. Indeed, they are trying to tell themselves and us what they cannot directly or easily describe about what is wrong with them. They know that they are not themselves, that they are doing things that they ordinarily do not do. Bluff reassurance often undercuts these persons just as, at the opposite end of the continuum, overdiagnosis delivers a graver interpretation of the person's condition than it merits. Neither approach helps these troubled individuals.

It is better for them, and better for us, to listen carefully so that we may identify the kinds of events usually associated with adjustment disorders and see if similar occurrences can be identified in the life stories these people are trying to tell us. This underscores the importance of understanding of the context of these people's complaints. We will find helpful clues in the often fully detailed background information they share with us.

Threats to Self-Image

The problems people try to describe for us, often repeatedly and with great patience, may not be related simply to the "usual suspect" losses of position, financial security, or marital stability. At stake and under threat from such losses is their whole idea of themselves, their self-image.

We all make our way through life as the person we advertise ourselves to be, the image of ourselves we develop over the years. We identify ourselves according to the strengths and weaknesses we allow ourselves to recognize in our personalities. That picture is our passport, and we cling to it through every port of entry and departure in our journeys. We experience severe stress if this picture of ourselves is challenged or shaken by some life event. Any threat to our self-confidence or our self-esteem can be expressed through depressed symptoms. When we can no longer preserve intact the image we have of ourselves, we become vulnerable to the variety of situational disturbances previously discussed. The depressive symptoms that follow a challenge or a destruction of a person's self-esteem may be traced to some sudden onslaught of stress. Thus famed director David Lean was unable to make another movie for over a decade after the unexpected assault on his self-image as a creative artist that accompanied the savage critical reception of his 1970 film, *Ryan's Daughter*.

Self-confidence and self-esteem may be attacked in many ways, of course, and we counselors can only allow individuals to tell the story of their own lives as simply and truthfully as possible. Speaking of their self-esteem, they offer a very particular and significant view of themselves. We must let them reveal themselves to us, allowing them to cut through the underbrush of detail and example at their own pace but missing none of the trees on which they make a significant mark. We already know that if we listen they will come to us with the truth. To do that well requires us to restrain our own impulses to get to the point or to offer support or reassurance. Give healthy people time and space and they will resolve their problems in front of us.

Treating Adjustment Disorders

To treat adjustment disorders, we may draw on a range of strategies rooted in good common sense. Three-pronged and essentially pragmatic in approaching an acute problem, this response focuses on reducing the stressor if possible, strengthening the person's coping skills and defenses, and maximizing the person's support system.

We may make it easier for these persons to explore the recent past by general questions about the events that have taken place lately that seem to be related to their coming for help. We let them focus on the particular situation that precipitated the problem. Was it abrupt, unprepared for, unsoftened by support or understanding that was expected? Variations in these elements can significantly alter the impact of loss. Their personality structure is critical here and, as the normal range of personality is very wide, so too is the range of abilities by which people may respond to their losses. Their past experience is also important. Individuals who have weathered many difficulties, who have literally learned the hard way about life's power to alter or take away the things we prize most, are generally better prepared to deal with a new but not novel experience.

The lack of available solutions forecloses quick resolution and increases the intensity of some problems. We all cope better with problems when there are alternative doors we may open to find a way out. If these are all securely closed and our choices removed, the impact of the stress may be multiplied.

Our general and understanding statements invite people to review recent occurrences and make it possible for them to lead us to the relevant experience of loss, the core of the problem with which they are attempting to deal. Our empathic responses should help them to refine their concerns, their available resources, and the differing paths they may follow. We may be able to educate them about the elements of the problem ("People often find it helpful to . . . ") or the resources they may contact for further information. Such interventions often help these stressed individuals to develop a more realistic perception of the event as well as some plan of action by which they can get better control of themselves and their besetting problem.

The Human Condition

That people carry on under what seem insupportable burdens remains one of the continuing mysteries of the human condition and one of the constants observed through psychology. Some individuals can sustain very severe blows and yet seem to right themselves and handle life with continuing self-confidence. Others find that the struggle is never less than difficult and that any single stress may throw them off balance, making it difficult to carry on their ordinary activities.

We need to reflect on the soundings we take of the deep events in other persons' lives. Ordinary people are very helpful in assisting us to understand them because they are anxious to talk to someone who will be understanding about the experience that has cost them so much. They will reveal and identify their strengths and weaknesses. From soundings taken of these we understand their capacity to resolve their problems and support them as they move toward doing this.

How many other stresses are these people balancing on their shoulders at the same time? An accumulation of stressful experiences may be far more injurious to them than a single stressor in an otherwise well-balanced life. Helpers need a feeling for the total picture in order to gauge the kind and amount of assistance that may be most significant for these persons. We may conclude, for example, that medication may alleviate some of their symptoms, such as sleep disturbance, and make a referral for this to their primary care physician. If their symptoms fail to be resolved within a reasonable period of time, we should review their overall status and consider referral to the appropriate mental health professional.

– 26 –

INTRODUCTORY NOTES
ON PERSONALITY DISORDERS

IT IS NOT UNUSUAL to discover — although it is difficult to admit — that despite our best efforts there are persons we cannot seem to help. We fail to reach them or they do not seem able to respond. For whatever reason, we fall short of what the textbooks urge us to achieve: a healthy and helping relationship. This is a particular source of stress for many counselors, especially those who do their counseling work in connection with other professional responsibilities. The reasons for this are clear.

Most counselors like people, and for this reason they get into this special work of helping other persons. When they meet people who do not like them or with whom they cannot establish a successful relationship, they are frustrated and disappointed. Such clients represent a challenge to many counselors' basic stance toward people and life in general. Failures can intimidate and upset them.

These people also frustrate other typical ideals of counselors, namely, the optimistic American and democratic notions that, with a little effort, we can stand on common ground with almost anybody; that things can be worked out; and that no matter what the difficulty, some kind of a solution is always possible. It is extremely stressful when non-cooperative individuals challenge such basic personal and professional beliefs.

It is typical of many conscientious counselors to blame themselves too much in these circumstances. They feel guilty that things are not working out when, in fact, the problem may not be entirely their fault. It may be helpful to recognize certain clinically defined groups with whom counseling is characteristically difficult. Without a sensitive appreciation of their personality structure, it may be bewildering to attempt to understand or work with them.

Moreover, it is difficult to manage the feelings these people can generate in us. These two dimensions are closely linked with the immediate and long-range possibilities of helping them even in a modest way. Some feeling for their lifestyle and their way of relating to others makes us more positively helpful and assists us in dealing with our own counter-transference feelings. When we see these persons in perspective, we can keep these issues clear and also make more sensible and appropriate referrals to other sources when this seems the right thing to do.

Personality Disorders

Some of those with whom it is difficult to work in counseling can be best understood under the descriptive category of *personality disorders*, a classification taken from the *Diagnostic and Statistical Manual of Mental Disorders-IV-TR*. Some object to any kind of labeling of the behavior of other people, but the descriptions of this manual — with which all counselors should be familiar, as has been suggested before — can have practical positive benefits for both counselors and those with whom they work.

A personality disorder is an enduring pattern of inner experience and behavior that deviates markedly from the expectations of the individual's culture, is pervasive and inflexible, has an onset in adolescence or early adulthood, is stable over time, and leads to distress and impairment. Currently, the diagnostic manual defines ten personality disorders that are divided into three categories based on descriptive similarities. The first, Cluster A, includes the paranoid personality, the schizoid personality, and the schizotypal personality disorder. Individuals with these disorders often appear odd or eccentric. Cluster B includes persons with antisocial, borderline, histrionic, and narcissistic personality disorders who often appear dramatic, emotional, or erratic. Lastly, Cluster C includes persons with avoidant, obsessive-compulsive, and dependent disorders. These individuals often appear anxious or fearful.[1] Counselors know from experience that many persons have features of one or more of these disorders. Some individuals, therefore, may carry two personality diagnoses or, when no precise diagnosis can be offered, are assigned the diagnosis of "personality disorder, not otherwise specified."

These persons do not manifest symptoms; rather, they display a distorted way of living and of managing their affairs and their relationships with other persons. Personality disorders, like many other things difficult to define, may suffer from the use of analogies; they do, however, resemble the proverbial tree that grows the way the twig is bent. Many individuals with personality disorders do not come for help in an anxious state unless their underlying problem has precipitated some other difficulty in their lives, such as the loss of a job or the breakup of a marriage. Ordinarily, they arrive in counselors' offices because of collisions on the behavioral level. Such persons do not have subjective complaints about the state of their souls as much as they have problems in living and working in reasonable harmony with others. Because they do not have much subjective anxiety, they do not ordinarily seek counseling help on their own.

The notion of the enduring nature of personality disorders and the fact they manifest themselves early in life is particularly relevant when the onset of a personality disorder is linked to advancing age. In this instance, the counselor should suspect some other process at work such as an unrecognized substance use disorder or the development of a medical illness.

A Common Problem

Personality disorders are common, estimated to occur in approximately 10–18 percent of the general population.[2] It is also well established that, in outpatient and inpatient psychiatric populations, approximately 50 percent of the patients have personality disorders in addition to their primary psychiatric or substance use disorder. This reality often poses a complication to the treatment of the primary disorder. Take, for example, a young depressed woman who is prescribed anti-depressant medications to alleviate her depressive symptomatology. She may also have borderline personality characteristics that contribute to her shifting perception of her physician, a function of the defense called "splitting" that is characteristic of borderline patients. She sometimes perceives him as "all good" and caring for her interests and at other times "all bad," "cold," and "uncaring." The result may be erratic compliance with the medication regime that is central to the treatment of her major depression.

Lawyers, members of the clergy, personnel managers, and other such persons meet a great number of people suffering personality disorders without ever recognizing the nature of the disturbance. These truly affected persons may recognize that things are going wrong in their occupations or in their domestic lives but still be unable to know why. They know that things are just not working out, but they have little insight into their own involvement in the situation. Frequently they are referred by other persons, such as supervisors or family members, who know that they are in trouble but feel incapable of being much positive assistance to them. Very often this is because the disordered persons have had a long record of losing jobs or of marital difficulties and are finally pushed to seek assistance by those around them.

They do not see themselves as the major contributing cause to their own difficulties. It is much easier to blame others for the problems that arise with the boss, or to make their spouse the responsible party in any difficulties at home. They cannot perceive the flaws in their own approach to life, and they are therefore not discomforted by the way they do things. They may be puzzled by the consequences, but these can be projected out as the responsibility of others. The twist in their personality seems so much a part of their self-enclosed system that they may not realize it is there.

In a strange but true way these persons are frequently never told the real reasons when they get into conflict at school or in their work. Supervisors and educators choose to rationalize rather than to tell the truth when they fire an employee or dismiss a student — a common problem for many people in authority. Individuals suffering from personality disorders are not helped to understand that the patterns of their behavior get them into trouble; they are usually told that the reason lies in poor academic or occupational performance, or that extraneous considerations have dictated the move. These efforts to avoid the hard truth leave such persons in the dark, which they already find difficult to pierce or comprehend. Because they are seldom confronted about their behavior and its inadequacies, they are denied even an elementary option about doing something about themselves. The work histories of such individuals often contain a record of similar incidents of dismissal after conflict with co-workers or with authority. Despite this, these people fail to observe their pattern and their own responsibility for it. There is a kind of psychological naiveté about them that permits them to seem innocent or oppressed when they explain themselves to counselors.

There is no established etiology or final judgment on the development of personality disorders. Although they can be recognized, it is difficult to sort out their antecedent causes. Some theorists believe that there is a genetic component, a constitutional predisposition for this difficulty; others emphasize early life experiences.

The person who grows up in a family in which the other members have suffered from personality disorders — such as being fearful and suspicious of all strangers and remaining in isolation from them — may identify strongly with these defective adjustments because no other model has been provided. The experience of a childhood in which few discriminations between good and bad are made by elders, or in which there is great inconsistency in the application of discipline, may give rise to confusion or misunderstanding about what is appropriate human behavior. Children who develop personality disorders may have learned early and in a confused way the patterns of reaction in which they persevere throughout their lives largely because of the inadequacy of their early uncorrected experiences. The child who is gratified and reinforced in deviant behavior or who is allowed to get away with misbehavior without ever being corrected may emerge into adult life with the very problem we have been discussing.

Psychoanalytic theory has contributed to our understanding of these disorders and provides a basis for widely accepted therapeutic responses to these individuals. Central to this is the identification of the usual pattern of defenses available to the persons in their relationship to the world around them. Healthy persons possess a wide range of defenses that they are able to use in their everyday functions. For the personality-disordered person, however, their storehouse of defenses is limited, and they are constricted and lacking in flexibility. They have only one pattern of response that over time is predictable and maladaptive. For many of these persons treatment is unsuccessful largely because they are not aware of their disordered functioning, nor do they perceive themselves as part of the problem. In those individuals who are motivated to change, however, psychodynamic therapies are often utilized. This therapy aims to assist these persons in identifying the ways their behavior is maladaptive, often by learning to recognize when their defensiveness is activated. When this occurs, individuals can, under the guidance of the therapist, learn new ways of responding that lead to more adaptive and acceptable behavior.

In recent years, psychiatric treatment has explored additional strategies to help persons with personality disorders. A range of psychopharmacological aids have been used in these disorders. For example, antidepressant medications have been used to modify the aggression or impulsivity associated with some disorders. In addition, cognitive behavioral therapies that aim to change focused disordered cognitions or behaviors have been used.

As counselors listen carefully, they may get a feel for the lifelong quality of the personality disorder pattern. Such a judgment is made, not to trap the person in this category of diagnosis but to define the terms of the relationship and to allow counselors to develop their own role in an intelligent and informed manner. Counselors can thereby avoid errors both in responses and in the expectations that they place on the person's behavior and their own capacity to be of help. Some understanding of the diagnosis of a personality disorder frees counselors from experiencing unnecessary frustration and inappropriate guilt when they find such persons are difficult to work with or to help very much.

PERSONALITY DISORDERS: CLUSTER A

P ARANOIA STANDS JUST OFFSTAGE, ready to enter the play when anything goes wrong. It recites no lines but rather projects a mood
that sets theatergoers on edge and sends them, suspicious and suspected, into the night. Paranoia infiltrates postmodern times with a
widespread sense of vulnerability to malign forces — random violence,
untrustworthy institutions ranging from church to state, the loss of
safe places and secure relationships, the pressures of special distortions
that overpower reality. It is the amateur's favorite diagnosis as it is the
pundit's favorite charge. The vaguer it is, the better it works, whether
about the Trilateral Commission, the New World Order, the Kennedy
assassination, the cache of alien creatures in Roswell, New Mexico, or
the suspicion that your churchgoing neighbor is a Kremlin-loving spy.

A little paranoia goes a long way and we counselors must cleanse
ourselves of it and inoculate ourselves against it if we are going to help
people effectively. What does paranoia mean and how are we likely to
encounter it?

The Paranoid Personality Disorder

The *paranoid personality disorder,* first of the Cluster A group of personality disorders, carries as its essential feature a pattern of pervasive
distrust and suspiciousness of others whose motives are interpreted as
malevolent. Its onset in early adulthood may be variously expressed.
This is not a grab-bag designation, however, and good diagnosis depends on careful and precise observation. In addition to the above
requisite characteristics, individuals must exhibit four or more of the
following features: (1) they suspect, without sufficient basis, that others
are exploiting, harming, or deceiving them; (2) they are preoccupied
with unjustified doubts about the loyalty or trustworthiness of friends
or associates; (3) they are reluctant to confide in others because of un-

warranted fear that the information will be used maliciously against them; (4) they read hidden demeaning or threatening meanings into benign remarks or events; (5) they persistently bear grudges and are chronically unforgiving of insults, injuries, or slights; (6) they perceive attacks on their character or reputation that are not apparent to others and are quick to react angrily or to counterattack; and (7) they have recurrent suspicions, without justification, regarding the fidelity of spouses or sexual partners.[1]

Persons burdened with this problem — who bristle with chronic distrust and suspicion — often enter the lives of every counselor. It is far less likely that we will encounter persons suffering from related paranoid psychotic conditions as schizophrenia, paranoid type, and delusional disorder. The latter disorders are characterized by persistent psychotic symptoms such as delusions and hallucinations.

Most of us will identify such individuals when their usual pattern of distortion crosses the fine line of reality and their ideas become delusional. The informing signal for us is found in their rigidly adhering to and beginning to act on their distorted ideas as if they were real. In a delusional disorder, for example, individuals who feel (unjustifiably) deceived by their spouses may consult a lawyer to file for divorce despite the protestations of the spouse and clear evidence that the suspicions are unfounded. In these people, the suspiciousness and distortions have become so fixed and remain so uncorrected by reality that they may be said to be delusional.

What Are They Like?

Few people suffering from major psychological problems are exactly the way ordinary people imagine that they will be. Madness may have one terrifying and bizarre stereotyped face for many people, but in reality serious problems have many faces. Persons with a paranoid personality disorder may appear a little distant, but they can be quite impressive, especially as we first become associated with them. This aura quickly dissipates, however, and, as some authors have noted of the paranoid person, as people know him better, they like him less.

We may identify these persons in their capacity to make us uneasy. Our feeling reactions to others, as in many similar situations, are a fundamental source of data we may confidently draw on to recognize these people and their problems. They make us uneasy through the hostility brewing just beneath the surface of their self-presentation. Just by entering, they can curdle the atmosphere in a room. Typhoid Marys of suspicion, they infect others who become argumentative and resentful.

At times, they seem totally preoccupied with fairness and its application in various ways or causes to life. Although there is no one close to them, they can be acutely sensitive to the inner states of others, and the suspiciousness they exude puts and keeps other people on guard.

In a society in which people may not know very much about their next-door neighbors, such persons can keep their suspiciousness on high without very many other people knowing about them. Their suspiciousness protects them because they keep clear of intimacy and do not confide readily in others. Their high-alert readiness to be distrustful proclaims, as a flashing warning signal might, the centrality of their serious paranoid problem. Their deep suspiciousness is expressed through the attitudes, tastes, and causes of the social culture with which they identify.

Their Stance at the Plate

If they were baseball players, we would learn as much as a veteran scout from the way they stand in the batter's box. Their habitual stance and their swing at the pitches is revealed in their styles of human relationships and in their way of communicating with other people. We will note quickly how they distort things, perverting or twisting the meaning of other people's words or behavior. This mode represents confusion in their sense of identity about what is part of their personality and what is separate from it. This fundamental set toward reality explains their pulling back from communicating except to themselves. This also explains their hypochondriacal complaints, products of their intense focus on themselves and their inability to reach out and make true investments of themselves in others.

Their way of communicating has an odd flavor and leaves a strange taste. They may be fascinated with unusual means of communicating — or being communicated to — including such modes as extrasensory perception, mysticism, and similar phenomena. These strange means of communication advertise their impoverished efforts to make human contact, to move away from self-concern and to reach other persons.

Their receiving and sending system is overgrown and distorted by their paranoid difficulty. If, however, we can see that these sometimes bizarre and sometimes estranging signals represent the efforts of lonely, isolated, and frightened persons, we have a better understanding of them. This perspective also enables us to keep ourselves free of becoming tangled in the specifics of their distortions. We should never enter the distortion of the other. The specifics may fascinate but it is their mechanism of constructing and using them to which we should give our attention.

Food for Distortions

We understand that the context of the distortions reported by paranoid persons is so strongly determined by cultural events that they may change with the generations, if not the seasons. Persons who once focused their suspicions on Russians may now switch to the Chinese or some agency of the United States government. Real world problems offer them the grains of sand from which they construct elaborate castles of distortion.

Recent years have seen the development of what we might informally term the paranoid distortion in public life. This describes an event that is fictional in nature, a construction based on some paranoid motivation — such as, for example, the Tawana Brawley case in New York in the late 1980s or distortions built into political campaigns. In the former case, in order to avoid punishment by her stepfather, a young girl invented a tale of being abused and raped by white police officers. This distortion, seized upon by politicians and given daily media exposure, took on a life of its own that endured, to harm race relations, even after the girl admitted her falsification of events. Similar distortions occurred in the 2000 presidential election, charges of stolen elections and uncounted ballots being treated as real long after impartial recounts had revealed their politically motivated, distorted character. Such paranoid distortions, while not classifiable in the literature, may be the phenomena with which nonprofessional counselors may well have to deal. They must be prepared to take their measure, identify their dynamics, maintain their own balanced view of matters, and interpret their meaning and power to others.

Culture supplies the paranoid individual with different "pseudo-communities," as psychiatrist Norman Cameron calls them, at different times. Such affiliations in paranoia partially explain the intense hatred and persecution of certain religious and racial groups at different periods in history. It also explains why we are never free of "conspiracy theories" about major historical events. There are many vague groups, from the media to the Mafia, in which paranoid persons may currently invest their pathology. The specific qualities of the distortion may also be affected by individuals' family background as well as by other features of their own personality structure. It is not the story, colorful as that may be, that is the prime concern of the counselor. It is the reason for using such stories, the motivation for this style of communication that we must tease out for understanding.

An exacerbation of paranoid suspicions may be touched off by some event that threatens these persons' self-esteem or forces them to taste failure in one way or another. The loss of a job or a lover, or the anticipated or fantasied loss, all work the same way. Sometimes competitive experiences may occasion paranoid behavior. Confinement, as in an intensive care unit or in a jail — in any closed institution or subset of an institution — for a sustained period of time may also precipitate paranoid reactions. These feelings are sometimes the result of these persons' being forced to submit passively to an actual or an imagined attack on themselves. There is almost always some morsel, however small, of truth to nourish their reaction. They use this bite of reality as evidence of a gourmet dinner of paranoid plotting.

Paranoid persons may also become strongly jealous of and harbor deep suspicions about their spouses, centered on some presumed betrayal of trust in their marriage. Marriage, alas, with its demands for intimacy, is a garden for healthy people but dark and fertile ground from which paranoids harvest their distortions. A chance meeting at a downtown coffee shop with a high school beau can be escalated by the paranoid spouse into an affair that has been going on since graduation.

Ready to Fight

Persons suffering from paranoid personality disorder seem always ready for a fight or a court suit. This impulsive pugnacity attests to the hostility always at a boil inside them. They may be suspicious, feeling themselves to be loners, but they are experts at collecting injustices and good to go for any quarrel, forever attributing bad will to those around them. Everybody, as they see it through their distorted lenses, is "out to get them."

This explains why these persons are sometimes intensely preoccupied with law and order and the rules governing them. They may even take up some training in self-defense or gather guns or other weapons for their protection. Paranoid mistrust leads them to insist on the letter that kills the spirit of every law. Such individuals can act in no other way. These behaviors betray their profound psychological need and difficulty rather than positions freely chosen by them. They cannot appreciate the spirit of a law because it is so difficult for them to appreciate the meaning of any other person's experiences. They just cannot make room in themselves for others. Laws, therefore, serve the function of controlling their own inner emotions, of keeping them in check. Bracing themselves with the law, they may project an impression of great capability, giving the impression that they can get along without anybody else's help.

Persons with paranoid personality disorder sometimes believe and act on the principle that the end justifies the means and so they invoke a missionary-like zeal in pursuit of their rigid and distorted opinions. They may associate themselves with militant crusading groups. Their special pathology, wrongly channeled, would make them great consumer advocates, licensing them, in a sense, to distrust others and to accuse them in public. After associating themselves with an extremist group, however, they become uncomfortable because, of course, they cannot trust their fellow members. If the group is composed of relatively sane persons, these healthy people will soon feel that there is something wrong with this new member. Their dynamic betrays them, playing itself out repeatedly as their pathology leads them back to isolation. Although they want to be close, they have a strong fear that they will be betrayed. That is one of the reasons that they are so suspicious.

Counselors may pick up a feeling for these people through noting the deadness in their sense of humor. They are not alive, spontaneous, or capable of reacting with the kind of easy laughter characteristic of healthy people. There is a lacing of sarcasm in these individuals' efforts at humor; they use it in the service of their own emotional needs but their style of humor is controlling, humiliating, and hurting. The jokes they make leave others feeling uncomfortable. Paranoid people are not easy to win over by some innocent endearment. They cannot appreciate it, will read other meanings into it, and will be put off by such attempts at rapport on the part of counselors.

The Age of Rages

We may encounter paranoid personalities if we are consulted about episodes of aggressive or destructive behavior such as those termed "road rage," mother concept to an extended family of media-dubbed "rages," ranging from playing fields to parking spaces. While outbursts of unmodulated aggression attributed to frustrated drivers have been the subjects of widespread news media coverage and even congressional hearings, the evidence suggests that it may not be as widespread or well-defined as it appears in our media-driven beliefs about it.[2]

While "rage" has been attached to a hierarchy of incidents, from airborne attacks on flight attendants to earthbound fights between Little League parents, the notion of an "epidemic" seems a function of the intensified reporting of the kinds of incidents that we have always had with us.

We may, then, perform a useful service, if consulted on outbursts given the misleading shorthand name of rage attacks, to maintain a professional-like demeanor, resist adding to a potentially distorting mood of hysteria, and to intervene as we would in any situation in which we may be able to identify a paranoid personality disorder among the participants. We may be constructive educators by helping people to see these incidents in calmer perspective, to respond in accord with the principles previously discussed, and to make sensible referrals for further evaluation or treatment if we deem this necessary.

Working with the Targets

Special mention should be made about the targets for the distortions of paranoid persons. They, rather than the offending person with a paranoid personality, often come to us for help. It is not uncommon, for example, for paranoid persons to threaten or accuse others of shameful deeds or threaten to circulate the news of these to damage their reputations. Often people shrug their shoulders and say that such persons are merely "crazies" who will do no harm. Others, however, see them as potentially dangerous and become quite disturbed at finding themselves the objects of their suspicions. In such circumstances, we need to assess as best we can whether the involved individuals are serious about these accusations and have, in fact, become delusional. Such paranoid persons need psychiatric consultation and the objects of their suspicions need reassurance and instructions to keep their distance and not to enter the paranoid distortion by responding to it.

It is true that most persons whose thinking is distorted are harmless. Counselors are well advised, however, when consulted about or by persons with histories of distorted thinking, to evaluate the evidence of their previous aggressive behavior. A careful and prudent judgment about their potential for real aggression is critical and is fundamental in making a sensible evaluation of such situations. In such instances, we may be counseling a person who has become part of another's paranoid delusional system. Ordinarily, such counseling should be done by a psychiatrist who is better prepared to respond both to the accused and the delusional person.

Remember! You're Not the Disturbed One

What to do: If the person before us is indeed the object of serious accusations or even letters that suggest such accusations, what can we do? Usually, the threatening persons are responding to psychotic delusions and are seriously ill and need appropriate assistance. Persons who are objects of their distortions may need legal as well as psychological advice and we should, of course, limit our suggestions to areas about which we know something. We should refer them to lawyers for legal advice and psychiatrists for psychiatric advice. In general, these people should be urged to be courteous but distant in their dealings with such bothersome individuals. There are a number of things, however, that it is wise for people *not* to do.

What not to do: Do not ignore the situation. This can be especially dangerous if the accusations continue and if there is really no hard information about the nature of the accusers and their potential aggression. When a number of unknowns exist, it is dangerous to counsel persons to "forget" such a problem. Rather, they should be referred to a psychiatric resource that can help them address the situation.

Persons should not be urged to try to win such people over by being nice to them. This is sometimes the spontaneous reaction of accused people. Being nice to persons who are made more defensive by friendly gestures makes things worse. Nor is it wise for persons, or us in their name, to try to frighten accusers or to try to fend them off by some show of force. This involvement at close range almost always worsens the situation and leads to bad outcomes for everybody.

Cautions and Expectations

It is difficult but necessary to view paranoid persons in perspective with as much sensitivity as possible. Paranoid persons generally present themselves to us negatively and uncooperatively, saying, in effect, "We do not need help." They deny paranoid ideas and complain instead of tension and concerns that arise in their relationships at work or at home. Usually these problems are attributed to other people. This primitive form of denial can be observed in almost all paranoid persons. Reaction-formation and, of course, projection are other defenses they regularly employ.

As noted in the psychoanalytical literature, persons with paranoid personality traits project onto others their own hostile feelings in order to diminish the anxiety and stress that arise within them from their own unacceptable feelings and impulses. They use projection to protect themselves against their own consciousness of aggressive impulses, their need for dependency, and any warm or affectionate feelings. They also protect themselves from being betrayed or put off by other persons. This unsubtle use of denial also allows paranoid persons to blot out certain parts of the human situation too painful for them to admit into consciousness.

We can expect with a high degree of confidence that paranoid persons will reject the role of the one in need of help. We will sense the anger in these people even when it is expressed silently. The air brims with the feeling, and only the most insensitive person could fail to pick it up. When paranoid persons are referred for help against their own judgment, they frequently express their hostility by refusing to speak. This does not mean that they are withdrawn from awareness of the environment. They sense quite clearly everything that is going on and their silence is an overt hostile act, one that both conceals and expresses their anger at the same time.

We must hone our skills to understand how the meaning of a paranoid person is compressed, like data on a diskette, into the self they put on display. This is not a time to try to win them over by gestures of friendship or efforts to establish rapport that might not be fully sincere. Persons with paranoid thinking are charm-resistant and are not easily tricked into talking. They are already saying something through their silence that is loud enough for us to hear. We should catch the point of what they are so unmistakably doing. There is plenty to hear in such hostile silence. If we do hear it we make entrance into a world in which they feel oppressed and offended by other persons. Contact is thereby made, not on the surface level but with the lonely and frightened individuals hiding behind this hostile behavior.

Sometimes paranoid patients fix their gaze intently at those who attempt to help them. This can make us very uneasy because we feel we are being thoroughly scrutinized. Despite this, we can maintain our calm and express our interest while also demonstrating that we will not be intimidated or be made to turn away by such glances. This is a way of meeting them, eyeball to eyeball, not to stare them down but in an effort to see behind this defensive style of presenting themselves.

Not Being Trusted

We should, of course, be prepared to experience the mistrust that they so characteristically exhibit toward others. The management of this mistrust and hostility constitutes the crucial issue for us in relating to these persons. The perspective that allows us to see beneath the hostility and enables us to pick up their deep longing for and fears of a close, trusting relationship is essential. As a result, we maintain a somewhat distant and impersonal, albeit professional, stance since the notion of intimacy is so threatening to these paranoid persons. If we can listen in a nonjudgmental manner and communicate interest and consistency, persons with paranoid distortions may eventually feel more comfortable and able to begin to address their problems.

In maintaining this consistent distance, we remain aware that paranoid persons will repeatedly reach out in attempts to defeat us. As noted, they want to beat us to it by rejecting us in order to defend themselves against being rejected by us. Seeing this clearly helps us to be self-possessed and to refrain from becoming defensive in explaining ourselves or in trying to win them over. We may have to be more restrained and slightly more distant than we usually are in expressing our interest and concern. We need not be cold to avoid trying to reach these individuals by overwhelming them with attention. We push gently and at a slow pace as we enter the intimate territory that is so uncomfortable for paranoid persons.

We should also expect paranoid persons to test us and our trustworthiness constantly in a wide variety of ways. They may, for example, accuse us of arranging our desk in some way designed to get a reaction out of them. They may even verbalize this or accuse us of trying to trick them in some fashion or other. Counselors who have survived such experiences can tell tales of how trying and stressful they can be. Paranoid persons sometimes behave like hurt animals, evoking a natural response of reaching out to them, but, as our helping hand gets closer, we should not be surprised by a further hurt-animal response of self-protective biting. They find themselves in a very painful situation, desperately wanting and yet fearful of someone coming close to them.

One way these persons test us is through trying to get us to agree to certain conditions. They may ask us to promise that we will not refer them to someone else or to a psychiatrist for medication. Those counselors who agree to these deals may find themselves embarrassed later when they cannot or should not fulfill them. The outcome may be a broken promise, just what paranoid persons need to prove that the counselor is, in fact, untrustworthy.

In general, we should avoid agreeing or disagreeing with the points or statements made by paranoid persons. It is very easy, in an effort to make things run smoothly, to appear to go along with them. We think that faking them out a little will not hurt, but it almost always does, because these people are knife-edge sensitive to any signs of untrustworthiness or inconsistency.

Nor is there wisdom in debating these individuals. This is not the meaning of counseling in the first place, and, in the second place, it is a grievous therapeutic error. Some counselors, however, caught up in the surface of what they hear, involve themselves in this before they know what is happening to them. It is hard to retreat when one has already crossed the border.

The Challenge of Referral

Many counselors feel that they should refer a person with a paranoid personality disorder to a more skilled therapist who will be able to take them on as a long-term patient. We should anticipate difficulties in trying to do this because just the idea of referral may disturb some of these individuals greatly. They are very sensitive to any restrictions on their freedom or to any manipulation of them into a forced passivity. We must be open and consistent if we are to reach what is healthy and build our relationship on it. This is difficult to do because they can be so hostile, and, at times, may even intrude into our private lives. Counselors must preserve limits, shielding our own personal lives and not allowing such persons to undermine what we know to be our obligation to them.

The treatment of these persons is very difficult because of their tendency to mistrust the therapist. Skilled therapists, who are consistent and persevere, may be able to help these individuals test out their paranoid ideas within the treatment sessions and eventually introduce some cognitive and behavioral techniques that enable them to function in a manner that is more realistic and less stressful. The judicious use of medication is also recommended in certain individuals when paranoid thoughts become more severe. People with paranoid personalities often do poorly in group psychotherapies.[3]

What do we feel? This significant question is important because some counselors do experience a real dislike, occasionally even a fear, of paranoid persons. If this is our experience, and if we have not previously dealt with it in some way, we should not try to help such persons. We will only make things worse for ourselves and for them. It is wise to remember that paranoid persons do to us what they do to everybody else. All persons who try to establish a relationship with them find their efforts frustrated, the result of the paranoid persons' reaction to the threat of any incipient intimacy. They know how to disrupt relationships. They are good at it because they have been doing it all through their lives.

They are also expert at making other people feel anxious. When they get others to experience anxiety, they then perceive this reaction as some form of rejection by the other persons. Paranoid persons are very good at accomplishing this, and they can trip up and ensnare inexperienced counselors very easily. They may humiliate them, for example, by wheedling some bland reassurance from them, making good-intentioned helpers feel foolish.

We therefore need self-possession and an ability to accept our own deficiencies so that we will not become defensive when we are challenged by paranoid persons. We also need a capacity to handle people who are suspicious and mistrustful. Such individuals repel relationships, straining us enormously in our efforts to understand them. Counselors who cannot accept these conditions should seek help from some other counselor or resource to deal with the situation presented by the paranoid person. This is a much better option than getting involved in a situation beyond one's capacity and experience.

The Schizoid Personality Disorder

The person suffering from the *schizoid personality disorder* reveals, from early adulthood, a pervasive pattern of detachment from social relationships and, in relationships with others, a restricted range of emotional expression. The diagnosis is made if such individuals possess four or more of seven characteristics: (1) neither desires nor enjoys close relationships, including being part of a family; (2) almost always chooses solitary activities; (3) has little, if any, interest in having sexual experiences with another person; (4) takes pleasure in few, if any, activities; (5) lacks close friends or confidants other than first-degree relatives; (6) appears indifferent to the praise and criticism of others; and (7) shows emotional coldness, detachment, or flattened affectivity.[4]

They may be referred to as "loners" by those around them. They may be able to maintain themselves successfully in an occupation that does not require social interaction and they may develop a way of relating to their families that is nonthreatening or nondemanding. Unless a crisis arises, we will not often see these individuals in any kind of therapeutic situation. In such circumstances, they may require referral for medication to control acute symptoms and, on occasion, referral for long-term psychotherapy. Group therapy and social skills training are also sometimes useful.

We are more likely to be consulted by family members or work associates who question the schizoid person's adjustment to life. Often well-meaning associates would like these persons to be better socialized, when, in fact, they are functioning as well as they can. Education about the nature of the disorder can be useful in these instances, especially if we offer some explanation about the limited ability of those suffering from it to tolerate or enter and participate in ordinary social discourse.

The Schizotypal Personality Disorder

Persons burdened with the *schizotypal personality disorder* often appear and are regarded as odd and different. This pervasive pattern of functioning is present as the grain is in wood. It may be perceived in the sapling growth of childhood and is usually unmistakable in the leafed-out development of early adulthood. It is a pattern of social deficits characterized by acute discomfort with, and a reduced capacity for, close relationships with other persons. They exhibit eccentric behavior along with distortions in their thinking and their way of seeing the world. For a diagnosis of schizotypal personality disorder, individuals should manifest five or more of the following characteristics: (1) ideas but not delusions of reference, that is, perceiving the words or deeds of others as having a special meaning for them; (2) odd beliefs or magical thinking that influences behavior, such as telepathy or having a "sixth sense," and is inconsistent with the beliefs and expectations of their cultural context; (3) unusual perceptual experiences, including bodily illusions; (4) odd thinking or speech that is vague, circumstantial, or stereotyped; (5) suspiciousness or paranoid thoughts; (6) inappropriate or constricted emotion; (7) behavior or appearance that is odd, eccentric, or peculiar; (8) lack of close friends or confidants other than first-degree relatives; and (9) excessive social anxiety that tends to be associated with paranoid fears rather than negative judgments about themselves.[5]

These individuals never seem to "fit in." They may wear clothes that are stained with food or do not match; they are mildly unkempt and exhibit odd mannerisms. They may be preoccupied with paranormal phenomena and talk about their special powers to read people's minds. They may use words and phrases that are indirect or stereotyped that can only be described as "odd." They do not relate well in social situations, and most people tend to avoid them because of their inability to understand or empathize with them.

Few nonprofessional counselors will have much contact with such individuals, although they may be contacted by family members seeking help for them because of concerns about their adjustment. Persons with a schizotypal personality disorder may, under stress, exhibit transient psychotic symptoms and, because of this, require consultation.

In addition, these individuals frequently suffer from major depressive disorder.[6]

If the counselor is consulted by such a person or by others because of problems in the workplace, the counselor should know that there has long been interest in the relationship between the schizotypal personality disorder and schizophrenia. There appears to be a genetic link between the two with the disorder more prevalent among first-degree relatives of individuals with schizophrenia than among the general population.[7] Some of these individuals do go on to develop full-blown schizophrenic illness.[8] As a result, psychiatric consultation is indicated so that the appropriate diagnosis can be made. Most difficult to distinguish, but necessary for accurate diagnosis, are some of the thinking patterns evidenced by schizotypal individuals. These persons may express an idea of reference which is an incorrect interpretation of an event as having some personal meaning for them alone. This same idea, however, may be evidence of a rigidly held belief that belies a delusion.

In relating to these individuals, the counselor should maintain the same general approach as to other individuals with Cluster A personality disorders. These people do not feel comfortable with other people, are protective and suspicious, and are threatened by intimacy. The counselor who evokes a calm, sensitive interest in the person while allowing for a healthy distance and consistent emotional neutrality is most helpful. These individuals, despite their needs and distress, are vulnerable to flight when they feel misunderstood or threatened.

A limited number of these individuals may gain from long-term psychotherapy and a variety of cognitive behavioral measures and skills training. Given the recent research on the link between schizophrenia and this personality disorder there is increasing use of antipsychotic medications to attenuate some of the more troublesome symptoms.

– 28 –

PERSONALITY DISORDERS: CLUSTER B

CLUSTER B of the personality disorders describes individuals we have all met, or sat next to, at some time or other in our lives. We remember them because they often appear dramatic, emotional, or erratic. This grouping includes the *antisocial, borderline, histrionic, and narcissistic* personality disorders. *DSM-IV-TR* makes clear that this clustering system, although useful in educational and research situations, is bound by many limitations and has not been well validated.[1] As a result, some of these personality traits are not readily or easily determined. We may meet many times with individuals encumbered by these disorders before we can confidently read and establish their overall pattern of relationships.

Individuals may also present with characteristics of more than one personality disorder so that, on occasion, two personality disorder diagnoses are eventually assigned. Our goal as counselors is to assess, as best we can, the dominant, indeed, signature motif, of their inflexible and maladaptive pattern of behavior. Important in all personality disorders, a good feel for the Cluster B disorders is critical because this diagnosis, as ruly as the carpenter's measure, will determine the structure of treatment and the expectations of outcome.

The Antisocial Personality Disorder

The *antisocial personality* has lived long, if carelessly, in popular consciousness and in scientific psychiatry. Those suffering this disorder, like well-masked guests at the midnight ball, are very difficult to identify and to meet truly or to engage in treatment. This condition has been pondered and described for centuries, and individuals suffering this personality disorder have been variously described as "moral imbeciles," "psychopaths," or "sociopaths." Like those suffering from the rest of the extended family of personality disorders, persons with

275

antisocial personality disorder suffer from a lifelong ingrained difficulty that reveals itself not in symptoms but in disordered behavior.

Antisocial persons seem, in major ways, to be unsocialized, that is, they have never integrated the manners or morals that most people learn as they grow up in a family and a community. They live instead to meet their instinctual needs without making the needle jump on the seismograph of conscience, indeed, without concern for its judgments or those levied by community standards. They persistently violate the laws, codes, and common sense of interpersonal behavior, and they keep on doing so even after they are caught, judged, and severely punished.

The person with an antisocial personality disorder exhibits a pervasive pattern of disregard for, and violation of, the rights of others that begins in childhood or early adolescence and continues into adulthood. For this diagnosis to be made, the concerned individuals must be at least eighteen years of age and have engaged in such behavior at least since the age of fifteen. There may well be evidence of this behavior before the age of fifteen. The diagnosis of *Conduct Disorder* is given when, as pre–fifteen-year-olds, they engage in deceit, stealing, destroying property, persistently violating rules, or behaving aggressively toward other persons or animals. Because persons with antisocial personality disorder repeatedly engage in deceit and manipulative behaviors, we ordinarily rely on other sources to gather the information we need to entertain or make this diagnosis. To assign it to these persons, they must engage in at least three or more of the following behaviors: (1) failure to conform to social norms expressed in lawful behaviors by repeatedly performing acts that are grounds for arrest; (2) deceitfulness, through repeated lying, the use of aliases, or by conning others for personal profit or pleasure; (3) impulsivity, that is, acting on the spur of a sudden feeling without any planning ahead; (4) irritability and aggressiveness, acted out in repeated physical fights or assaults; (5) reckless disregard for their own safety or that of others; (6) consistent irresponsibility, evidenced in their repeated failure to sustain consistent work behavior or to honor financial obligations; and (7) lack of remorse, obvious in their being indifferent to, or rationalizing away, their hurting, mistreating, or stealing from others.[2]

The Charmer

Those persons exhibiting antisocial personality disorder are superficially engaging and often charming and have sometimes been romanticized as such in popular entertainments. The brutal and unromantic truth is that they indulge in behaviors dangerous for themselves and for others. These include abusing spouses and children and defaulting on bills and other financial obligations. They are not good at sustaining monogamous relationships, and, seemingly unconcerned for the truth, frequently use a con man's tactics to wheedle or swindle things out of others, such as an old person's life savings, with no concern for the impact of what they are doing. Their attractive qualities are not even skin deep and, without regret or remorse, they leave a wake of loss, pain, and unhappiness behind them.

The surface glitter may get in our eyes, blinding us, at least temporarily, so that, unless we have had previous experience, we may not identify them immediately. Like consummate actors, they know how to draw down their stores of seeming charm and goodwill to flatter, with Academy Award style, those who may be able to help them. Experience that and you have experienced them, their lifestyle and modus operandi in one package. Many helpers are made vulnerable by their sincerity and eagerness to their manipulative style. Those who are innocent, both in themselves and of the dynamics of this personality disorder, can be used, harmed, and disillusioned by being manipulated by them.

The Slaughter of the Innocents

The commendable widespread interest in the plight and rehabilitation of convicts has summoned many volunteers, including members of the clergy, to enter, at least part-time, into this field of work. Religious persons are characterized by a strong motivation to help other people. Their desire to fulfill this ideal, especially with a population in great need, sometimes leads them into naive and entrapping relationships with antisocial personalities. Unsophisticated but honorable helpers may have bad experiences in doing good with these persons, finding that they have been used and that their efforts to help have been considered neither significant nor important by the persons involved.

We cannot, as counselors, afford cynicism in reflecting on these realities. The lack of familiarity with the careless wiles of persons with antisocial personalities may lead clergy members — as well as lawyers, judges, and countless other helpers-in-general — into bad judgments about people who are ready to go on swindling, robbing, dealing in drugs, and even murdering their fellow citizens without any qualms about it.

All counselors can learn a good deal about the antisocial personality by reading such books as Norman Mailer's nonfiction novel *The Executioner's Song*.[3] It is the story of the murderer Gary Gilmore, who became an international celebrity in the mid-1970s while his lawyers fought an extended battle to win commutation of his death sentence. So skillfully does the artist capture the flavor of Gilmore's pathology that the reader will feel something very close to the emotions generated by antisocial individuals in person. It is a classic evocation of this syndrome and its manipulative and disruptive role in American culture.

Many such persons survive without being detected or properly understood. Readers of Hervey Cleckley's *The Mask of Sanity* will be familiar with this.[4] Counselors may reflect for themselves on how an emphasis on impulse gratification — do what you like when you feel like it — is widespread and is only gradually disillusioning for those who commit themselves to this code of life. In other circumstances, actions are made to seem reasonable because "no one else will know what happened" or because "everybody is doing it." A tinge of the antisocial attitude attaches like grime to many of these widely publicized and often celebrated cultural slogans. Counselors may often meet persons harmed by trying to live this way. We will see less often, if at all, the people who talk them into it.

Where Do They Come From?

The prevalence for *antisocial personality disorder* is 3 percent for men and 1 percent for women. Although many theories attribute their lack of inner controls to the inability of these persons to make adequate attachments to their parents or to their lack of discipline and training early in life, the exact cause, or etiology, is really unknown. There is evidence that it is more common in biological first-degree relatives than in the general population. It is also associated more often with those in the lower socioeconomic class and in urban settings.[5] It is a common diagnosis among prisoners, with approximately 75 percent of inmates so diagnosed.[6] Persons who are dishonorably discharged from the military, are chronic substance abusers, fail to pay child support, or live chronically in homeless shelters are frequently found to suffer from antisocial personality disorder. Their lives often end suddenly and tragically in murder, accidents, or suicide.

Major Signs

Persons with antisocial personality disorder lack close interpersonal relationships. Friendship requires exactly what the antisocial personality cannot give. None of us can be a friend for very long without having to give up something of our own concerns or without postponing some gratification. Friends are considerate, a sentiment beyond the ken or reach of the person with antisocial personality disorder. They can take but cannot give, and this is almost always reflected in their stormy and disrupted marital histories. Their inability to form relationships that are close and meaningful also makes it difficult for them to profit from counseling and psychotherapy.

Characteristic of antisocial persons is their apparent lack of anxiety, guilt feelings, or any other subjective discomfort in the wake of their behavior. They may sound sincere in expressing regret, but this may be discounted as it is a chord they cannot strike. We can also read their problem in their defective sense of judgment. Thus, in psychological testing, they give socially inappropriate answers to simple questions, such as what they would do if they found a stamped addressed letter on the street. Sensitive psychologists recognize the test behavior of these persons who, even when they strive to make a good impression through answering the questions the way most people would, frequently "spoil" the response by laughter or a condescending attitude.

These people usually have a poor school and occupational history. They are indeed con artists who depend on their superficial charm to get them through the obligations that other people face more straight-forwardly. They are bound to reveal themselves somewhere along the line, at least to the subtle observer. They do not do well in the military, although they may be found in the ranks of soldiers of fortune, mercenaries, and guerrilla warriors.

Coleman, in his *Abnormal Psychology and Modern Life*, also mentions the way in which persons with antisocial personality signal their problem by rejecting all constituted authority and discipline wherever they are.[7] They also possess a quick ability to rationalize and to project the blame for their socially disapproved behavior onto others. Another characteristic that counselors profitably observe is that, in the long run, these people are irritating, disappointing, and distressing to others. Read them from the end back to the beginning and find how they eventually harm other people after a beginning sprinkled with seeming charm or attractiveness. Coleman cites Ferdinand Demara Jr., "The Great Imposter," as an example.[8] This man, who became something of an American legend, continually falsified physician's credentials, claimed to have carried out surgical operations, and engaged himself in a wide variety of assumed professions. His actions differ greatly from those of murderers or major lawbreakers, but the essential dynamics of his behavior remain the same. We may find these persons entertaining in the first act and only really see them as they are in the third-act revelation of their hurting and disappointing other persons. We can be confident that antisocial personalities will do to us what they do to everyone else.

They show very little evidence of guilt but may experience some of the relatively undeveloped foreshadowings of guilt in such reactions as *shame* or in *fear of public disapproval*. They do not want to get into the discomfort of tight spots, but that does not indicate that they have any true guilt about the behavior that may get them there.

In other words, persons with antisocial personality disorder do not feel much at all, and such emotions as they have seem to be shallow. Not much seems to be going on in them, and counselors, aware that they are not making contact with these people, may blame themselves. This is only one area of counselors' feelings that is informative as we pick up signals from these persons. We should not blame ourselves too quickly, but rather profitably examine this lack of emotional contact for its dynamic information. It may be our first clue that we are working with a person with antisocial personality disorder.

It is not surprising to find them *impatient* and *oriented to immediate pleasure*. This does not mean that they enjoy things the way other persons do. They cannot have the same kind of deep appreciation of things, and it would be dangerous to read our own capacity for feeling into their reactions. The pleasures they seek are more related to psychological needs than to the rewards of genuine interpersonal relationships. Their relationships may look the same as those of healthy people, but they are not the same.

For this reason these individuals may respond to frustration by impulsive outbursts of aggression. They do not react as healthy people do, indeed, they cannot because they have no well of empathy to tap. That explains why their actions can be marked by what others identify as cruelty or sadism. Another feature of their emotional reactivity is the *episodic* quality of their outbursts. They boil up like sudden and violent storms that leave little aftermath. Ordinary persons have a difficult time calming down after getting upset. This is not true of these individuals, who may wonder at the unsettled reactions that other people have to their outbursts. They may seem genuinely surprised that what they have done has generated waves of concern around them.

Sometimes persons with antisocial personality disorder, for their own reasons, go through the motions of living like law-abiding citizens. Many criminals crave the respectability that goes with achieving the American dream. They attend church and even participate in its activities. This behavior does not arise from any internal conviction but rather from a desire for the glow of the appearance of gentility. The lives of antisocial persons are often entangled in secondary complications. They may organize their socially acceptable veneer as a surface for a hidden life of bizarre and socially unacceptable behaviors. Persons who need a powerful drug care little about how or what is involved in getting it, and their actions provide a good example of the antisocial personality in action in certain segments of society today.

Why Do They Come and What Can We Do?

Persons with antisocial personality disorder seldom come for help on their own. They are sent by others who have had to deal with their disordered behavior either at work, in school, or in some other setting. They come but, as is so characteristic of them, they may not even admit that they have been sent by authorities.

It is important for us to deal clearly with their reason for coming. This cannot be kept a secret, nor made to seem other than it is in reality. Deception is so much a part of everything they do that these persons are highly sensitized to such behavior and pick it up if we try to employ it. We cannot dissemble, then, but must be open and honest, especially if we already have information from another source about why they are coming to see us.

It is important to realize that these persons *do not trust counselors*, or for that matter, anyone in authority. We should expect this and, as in other circumstances, read our own feelings as vital sources of information about the relationship. Our emotional reactions are enormously helpful both in understanding them and in working out the challenges of trying to help them.

Persons with antisocial personality disorder unconsciously *attempt to get us into the kind of relationship* that will lead to disappointment for us. We counselors are, in their argot, "marks," that is, targets of choice for their con-man instincts. Despite their charming patter and their ingratiating manner, they are sizing us up, taking our measure for how they can, for their own benefit, take advantage of us.

We will, in fact, *feel this register inside ourselves* as our being manipulated and the health in us will react with a certain appropriate defensiveness, a being on guard within ourselves. This is a healthy reaction to the swift movements of these individuals to set up counseling relationships in the image of all their other relationships.

At this stage inexperienced counselors, who may be unaware of or yet to learn how to read their own feelings, may snap at the tempting bait dangled with a shining lure before them. They thereby add themselves to the long list of those who have been set up, charmed, and rendered harmless by these persons. We may, if we are just starting to do counseling work, be enlisted in their cause by an overeagerness to help, that sureness that, although such persons may have had bad breaks before, they are on the road to rehabilitation now. Wanting too much to do good, we may involve ourselves in a classic destructive relationship. After we commit ourselves wholeheartedly to the person with an antisocial personality disorder, our hopes for helping them may soar. At some level these persons grasp that and, as we grow more enthusiastic, they prepare ways to hurt, to disappoint, to make a "mark" of us.

This damaging bind is our destiny when we let our good hearts outrun our good therapeutic sense. Once hurt by these easy betrayers we may shrink back, letting our skills go saw-toothed and rusty instead of honing them for our use as older and wiser counselors. We must remember that, as Jimmy Breslin once put it to one of the authors, "These guys'll heist you just to have something to do." Admitting this possibility from the start and listening carefully to the tumblers fall as such persons seek for the combination to unlock us protects us from being conned and deepens our capacity to be effective in this difficult situation. As counselors sensitive to the dynamics playing in plain sight, we avoid the worst stresses of our work, the unnecessary ones for which, without reflection, we volunteer.

Variations of the Stockholm Syndrome

It is said that all society has some liking for the outlaw. The Stockholm Syndrome describes the way that captives come to identify with their captors. There is some truth in this. We may find ourselves rooting for the criminal even though we may not wish to admit this publicly. Such feelings can be present in our helping relationships as well. We may, for example, experience a certain envy for the seemingly carefree lifestyle of the antisocial personality. This is particularly true if we feel a great can't-put-it-down burden in our own personal and professional commitments.

Such subtle admiration may lead us to relate in a nontherapeutic way with these persons. We may allow persons with an antisocial personality disorder to become our surrogates at the edges of society, an adventurous delegation of ourselves that can lead to many compromises in the counseling process itself. Enjoying the deviousness of such individuals may lead us into waters beyond our depth.

We are more likely to become involved with persons with this disorder unwittingly rather than directly. We may, for example, be working with a person who to all appearances is well-motivated and agreeable. In a short time, however, it is apparent that the person is working *against* rather than *with* us. The person may begin drinking, begin an affair, or display flagrant irresponsibility in work or family obligations. Our good-faith efforts are thereby undermined. Such persons seem totally unaware that they have failed in any way and consider our feelings of being betrayed and disappointed unrealistic. Should such a scenario develop, we should examine the behavior as a sign that a deeper personality disorder is present.

This is an important discovery because a fairly general consensus tells us that most therapies are unsuccessful in changing antisocial behavior.[9] Some targeted behaviors, such as aggression and impulsivity, may be reduced with medication. It is generally felt that the most effective form of treatment occurs within confined settings, such as prisons, where external constraints can substitute for internal, moral discipline.

Few of us nonprofessional counselors are called upon to work in any therapeutic way with these individuals. Armed with knowledge about the nature of and treatment outcomes associated with this disorder, our challenge is to recognize persons with *antisocial personality disorder* and acknowledge our inability to change them. When we are confronted with persons suffering this disorder, referral to some resource that can provide the necessary environment and constraints will, in the long run, be most beneficial to these persons and to society.

The Borderline Personality Disorder

James Joyce's H.C.E., "Here Comes Everybody," comes to mind in examining the borderline classification. Persons with *borderline personality disorder* exhibit a pervasive pattern of instability in their interpersonal relationships, self-image, and emotions. They also give evidence of marked impulsivity that begins in early adulthood and manifests itself in a variety of contexts. The heterogeneity and overlapping nature of this diagnosis have been noted by many researchers.

It is important for us to acquire some in-depth knowledge of this disorder so that we may take proper soundings of, as well as sensible responses to, the special difficulties we may experience with persons suffering from this disorder. The manipulative pressures exerted by borderline persons, for example, can seem as heavy and stifling as the weight of the sea. Personnel directors or marriage counselors may be the first ones to observe and be confused and perhaps feel swept up in and misunderstood by the intense feelings that are so characteristic of these persons. It is difficult to exaggerate the stress that can be associated with working with those with borderline disorders. Urgent, then, is a good working understanding of their way of relating to others. Their style can also be read in the impact that they have on us, as we will explore later.

What Is Borderline Personality Disorder?

Persons are diagnosed as suffering from borderline personality disorder if they display five or more of the following characteristics: (1) frantic efforts to avoid real or imagined abandonment; (2) a pattern of unstable and intense personal relationships characterized by alternating currents of extreme idealization and devaluation; (3) identity disturbance manifested in a persistently unstable self-image or sense of self; (4) impulsivity, acting impetuously in at least two potentially self-damaging areas, as, for example, in spending, sexual activity, or substance abuse; (5) recurrent suicidal gestures, threats, or behavior, and self-mutilating behavior; (6) affective, or emotional, instability generated by marked mood reactivity, as, for example, intense episodic euphoria, irritability, or anxiety; (7) chronic feelings of emptiness; (8) inappropriate, intense anger or difficulty controlling anger as, for example, in frequent displays of temper, constant anger, or recurrent physical fights; and (9) transient, stress-related paranoid thoughts or severe dissociative symptoms, such as transient depersonalization.[10]

We may not initially understand the source of distress when persons empty out on our desks a sackful of the problems and symptoms characteristic of the borderline personality disorder. A mixed bag of symptoms and behavior tumble out. Some of these persons are very impulsive while others display prominent emotional instability, and still others engage in behaviors that resemble those associated with the antisocial personality disorder.

Borderline personality disorder is not uncommon and is estimated to occur in approximately 2 percent of the population. It is, however, frequently misdiagnosed or underdiagnosed.[11] Because these persons often make suicidal attempts and engage in disruptive behavior, they generally require psychiatric care. In addition, they often suffer from other Axis I psychiatric diagnoses, such as major depressive disorder or substance use disorder. It is estimated, for example, that as many as 24 to 75 percent of these individuals experience *major depressive disorder* at some time in their lives.[12] Their personality disorder is often a complicating factor in the treatment of their primary illness because of their inability to form stable relationships with the psychiatrist and their vulnerability to "acting out" in destructive ways.

The origin of borderline personality disorder is unknown, but there is a clear familial clustering with first-degree biological relatives who, compared with the general population, are five times more likely to have the disorder.[13] Women, by a three-to-one-ratio, are diagnosed more frequently than men. There is some thought, however, that many men with the disorder are misdiagnosed as having either antisocial or narcissistic personality disorders.

What Are They Like?

A common feature of persons with borderline personality disorder is their difficulty with human relationships. They seem unable to attach to persons as other people naturally do. They appear to withdraw from relationships out of fear of losing them. They are acutely sensitive to the scenario that the person with whom they form a relationship will surely abandon them at some time, leaving them feeling alone and empty. Under threat of separation or a shift of the other's attention away from them, they readily become frantic and impulsive. Such reactions may be observed when their therapist goes on vacation. They will, in fact, often describe their basic feeling of one of emptiness and, to make up for it, seek out activities whose stimulation assuages their feeling.

Persons with borderline personality disorder are intensely demanding and cannot share another person easily. They often become intensely angry if "their friend" has other friends or their therapist has other patients. Observers describe the rage and spate of activity that follows any threat to their need to control their environment as a "storm" because of its sudden and enormous output of psychological feeling and energy. To fend off feelings set off by real or imagined separations, they may also engage in activities such as suicidal gestures or other potentially destructive activities. Why? To manipulate others into feeling guilty and regretful about taking their vacation or seeing other patients.

One of the unmistakable signals that alerts nonprofessional counselors to this condition is the person's capacity to switch from overidealization to devaluation in interpersonal relationships. As counselors we are the subjects of these classically mercurial, unpredictable, and, for the unprepared, highly bewildering emotional shifts. "Splitting" is typical of the borderline personality disorder and is one of the principal clinical indications of the presence of this complex disorder. The split may, as mentioned, occur with one person, such as the helper, or it may divide the staff or other groupings as part all good and part all bad. This splitting can wreak havoc in certain settings, such as an office, and its disruptive effects may be traced back, like a trail of gun-powder, to the person with borderline personality symptoms holding the match.

Persons with borderline personality disorder indulge in impulsive behaviors that may bring injury to them, in, for example, sexual activities, eating binges, shoplifting, or substance abuse. Such behaviors are distinguished from their not infrequent fashioning of suicidal threats or gestures and their engaging in self-mutilating behaviors. One feels the borderline pathology in their sudden shifts from what seems to be normal into depressive, anxious, or irritable moods. As noted, they often complain of feelings of emptiness or boredom and experience persistent uncertainties about who they are, how they want to be, and with whom they want to relate. Their real impact on helpers, however, is through their anger, samples of which predictably occur in counseling. We feel this anger as strong, poorly controlled, and intimidating.

The suicidal threats, gestures, and attempts commonly authored by these individuals should be taken seriously. Approximately 8 to 10 percent actually complete suicide, a rate fifty times higher than that of the general population. Managing the suicide risk is a major challenge to anyone who works with them, especially among those who are described as "chronically" suicidal. The highest risk of suicide appears to occur when they are in their twenties and when they also suffer a concomitant mood disorder or engage in substance abuse.[14]

What Can Nonprofessional Counselors Do?

Many of these individuals have been subjected to physical or sexual abuse as children. As a result, they often expect therapists and others who allegedly have their interest at heart to be untrustworthy and potentially hurtful to them. Because of their difficulty with interpersonal relationships, they often have a history of job loss, divorce, and other disruptive life experiences. We helpers help ourselves greatly by cutting our observing selves free of the entanglements that sprout thickly in relationships with persons with borderline personality disorder so we may view them with some clinical objectivity. One of the main problems caused by these suffering individuals emerges in their countertransference reactions to those who work, live with, or try to assist them. They are easy to dislike and therefore to reject or to punish, reactions that join us to the long line of persons who have succumbed to their involving pathology. Enough distance to maintain perspective is therefore essential for keeping the sense of balance we need to help them.

Psychiatric management that consists of a broad array of ongoing activities and interventions that should be instituted by the psychiatrist is the model for treatment of persons with the borderline personality disorder. We may be the first ones to see and identify these persons and may need to see them more than once as we arrange for a referral to the psychiatrist. In the interim, we may seek consultation from professional resources. Usually they suggest that we take some sensible steps, such as not seeing them more than once a week, monitoring the intensity of these meetings, and effecting the referral as rapidly as possible.

Although psychiatrists may suggest a broad range of specific therapies, they are the ones responsible for responding to such persons' crises and monitoring their safety. They also work to establish and maintain a working alliance and provide education about the disorder. A frequent problem in the therapy of borderline persons arises from their tendency alternately to devalue and idealize other persons and to engage in what we have described as "splitting." When there are multiple clinicians or collaborators in the treatment, the psychiatrist may suddenly be perceived as "all bad" whereas the others may be perceived as "all good."

At other times, the treatment situation may be so conflictual for these persons that they take refuge in the referring counselor, now perceived as "all good" in contrast to the psychiatrist and other clinicians who are now "all bad." In these circumstances, we should not be manipulated into seeing the person "just this once" to straighten things out. Upon closer examination, we will find that countertransference feelings of "rescue" are engaged and are not useful in these circumstances. We must urge these persons to return to their psychiatrist and be forthcoming about their dissatisfaction with treatment.

Specific treatment strategies involve psychotherapy, particularly psychoanalytic or psychodynamic psychotherapies and dialectical behavioral therapy.[15] Medication is used to treat specific symptoms, such as poorly regulated affect, impulsivity, and cognitive perceptual symptoms. Couples therapy may also be useful as an adjunct to the main treatment. Family therapy, used alone, is not recommended as treatment for borderline personality disorder.

Some researchers observe that, although the lives of borderline persons may be chaotic, especially in early adulthood, some of them, particularly those who also suffer from affective problems, seem to settle down as they enter middle age. Our main challenge is found in coping with the engulfing self-presentation of these people no matter what their age may be. We need our intelligence and good sense, as well as the assistance of others, to identify the heavy load of transferential material that is piled on us when we try to relate to these individuals.

The Histrionic Personality Disorder

Beginning counselors, as MacKinnon and Michels note, find "the hysterical patient one of the easiest to interview; the experienced psychiatrist finds him one of the most difficult."[16] On the surface, people with histrionic personalities seem extremely attractive and interesting. A new counselor, meeting them for the first time, may be impressed with their vivacious qualities, their attractive looks and way of speaking, their seeming warmth, and their apparently serious intentions about pursuing therapy.

Therapists who have earned their battle ribbons have worked with these people long enough to realize that things are not what they seem and that the superficial qualities mask an emotional impoverishment and uncertainty that make working with these people extremely difficult. Inexperienced counselors may also find themselves flattered by the kind of attention they seem to get from these people who, as we will observe later, use seductive maneuvers as a matter of course. The inexperienced counselor, in other words, often feels good about meeting an attractive patient. The bad comes later.

It is true that we never get bored working with these self-dramatizing persons, but we soon discover that the seemingly pleasant terrain is shaped by complex and intertwined subterranean forces. We can spare ourselves a great deal of stress by carefully studying our own reactions when we are suddenly enthusiastic about someone like this seeking our help. We should wait to hear what is going on beneath the surface and spare ourselves the disappointment of discovering that these persons are not nearly so emotionally rich or able as we had supposed.

Histrionic Characteristics

The essential feature of the *histrionic personality disorder* is pervasive and excessive emotionality and attention-seeking behavior. These individuals often have characteristics of other personality disorders, especially the borderline and antisocial personality disorders, but there is a distinctive flavor to the histrionic person. The diagnosis requires five or more of the following personality characteristics: (1) these persons are uncomfortable in situations in which they are not the center of attention; (2) their interaction with others is often characterized by inappropriate sexually seductive or provocative behavior; (3) they display a rapidly shifting and shallow expression of emotions; (4) they consistently use physical appearance to draw attention to themselves; (5) they have a style of speech that is excessively impressionistic and lacking in detail; (6) they evidence self-dramatization, theatricality, and exaggerated expression of emotion; (7) they are suggestible, i.e., easily influenced by others or circumstances; and (8) they consider relationships more intimate than they actually are.[17]

It is estimated that perhaps 2 to 3 percent of the general population suffer from this disorder. Although women have most often been diagnosed with the histrionic personality disorder, many researchers believe that just as many men have the same disorder but express it differently. Men, for example, may persistently draw attention to themselves by their dress or their bragging about their athletic or sexual prowess, and they may be unable to relate intimately to another human being because of their persistent focus on themselves.

These people seem unaware of the impact of their behavior on others. They may also seem a rather mixed configuration, somewhat prudish in one moment and then quite the opposite in the next. Hence our difficulty in being sure that we have an accurate understanding of them. They may exhibit characteristics, such as attention-seeking, manipulativeness, and shifting emotions, that remind us of the borderline personality disorder, but borderline personalities are also self-destructive and experience chronic feelings of emptiness and a fear of being alone not shared by persons with histrionic personality disorder. This person and the person with antisocial personality both tend to be impulsive, superficial, and manipulative, but their reasons for behaving in these ways are quite different.

We are struck, however, by the energy these persons invest into looking attractive. This is something that registers in our own feelings. We can trust our own feedback as a valid if provisional indication of the kind of person with whom we are working. They want attention, and they employ self-dramatization in their colorful self-presentation. They find ways to make themselves the center of attention. This is but one of the features that make them interesting and place them in such sharp contrast with other persons who struggle to speak about their difficulties and themselves. They put on a show for us.

These persons entertain us in speech, appearance, and general style. They may flirt and bring gifts. They emphasize just what learning therapists are waiting to hear, feelings and their inner experiences. They do not, like the phobic patient, talk concretely only about their external behavior. To no other group can the old saying be better applied: it's not what they say but the way they say it that reveals the truth about them. They do not, of course, hide themselves consciously. They present themselves in the way they have learned in the course of their development.

These people can season long afternoons of counseling with an erotic flavor, especially if the counselor is a member of the opposite sex. This offers us a clear sample of how they relate to everybody else and is not a response, as we might naively suppose, to something attractive about us. Some counselors who have never experienced seductive behavior from an attractive person at close quarters may mistakenly find the experience exciting and flattering. If they respond as if this were a real exchange by, for example, accepting the invitations of the seductive person, they set themselves up for the fall that classically completes the maneuver. These histrionic persons may seem to promise a lot, as the old saying goes, but they are not at all ready to deliver.

If we evince any sexual interest in response to what seems like an open invitation, the histrionic personality will pull back, indicating that is certainly not what was in mind. They seem genuinely unaware of the effect of their demeanor, and when they close the trap they leave others feeling frustrated, defeated, and puzzled. This, in fact, is one of the ways in which histrionic persons make their way through life. They flirt, lead people on, hardly realizing the way these maneuvers affect those around them. For them, this is a major problem in living because it does not deliver any satisfying relationship to them and it tends to leave them more alienated and lonely as people recognize and protect themselves against this behavior.

Histrionic persons have been depicted often in the movies and on the stage. They can be observed in certain professions where their flamboyance and style is accepted and where their lack of follow-through in relationships is not considered such a surprise. They have a way of speaking like Bette Davis playing an edgy fashion editor or a movie queen, using gestures and delivering superlatives such as "fabulous" and "sensational" about even the most ordinary events. They have a way of advertising their emotions in public that is often embarrassing to and is judged inappropriate by others. They may embrace a casual acquaintance with excessive emotion and sob uncontrollably at the wedding anniversary of a distant cousin.

Where's the Love?

We are not then surprised to learn that histrionic personalities have enormous difficulty experiencing and expressing their emotions. They do not understand nor do they experience love and intimacy as the living core of sharing life deeply with another person. They only *seem* to relate warmly, and, if we are sensitive, we will catch the pathetic bluff of this superficial presentation of themselves. We will note that the intimacy they seem to offer so generously in the beginning of counseling never goes anywhere. It is a flat and echoing vestibule to their personality, the doors to which never open fully on a gracious and roomy place. There is no place to go after entering the vestibule because these people can offer no better hospitality than that.

The general seductiveness is their mode of making themselves known to us. They seem to use their bodies intuitively, trying to signal a concern for love and tenderness. They are not looking for this, however, but they do seek more shallow words of approval, applause, and protection. They do not really want to be close to another person; they would not know what to do with real intimacy, so physical proximity becomes a substitute for genuine emotional closeness. Anyone with much life experience realizes how unsatisfactory such an effort at relationship can be.

They are always looking for love, using their seductiveness to achieve what they understand to be love, only to find that their approach cannot build or sustain any mature relationship. Most of these remarks concern the way hysterical persons relate to people of the opposite sex. With members of their own sex they are far more antagonistic and competitive, seeming to deal with them as though they were threats to the possibility of their achieving the adulation or attention they seem to crave so ardently.

Male histrionics may, in fact, present more of a facade of self-confidence, a studied capacity to run their own lives with serenity and self-assuredness. They may seem very "macho," but this kind of behavior is almost always a sign of the weakness that they feel inside themselves. They experience fear and anger that they cover up with a more superficial kind of behavior. The man who feels that dressing the right way, having well-developed abdominal muscles, wearing the correct fashions, as well as possessing an extensive knowledge of what wine to order, may attempt to make up in these ways for the lack of confidence he experiences within.

The Problems

It is clear that these individuals present serious countertransference problems. They invite, indeed promote, countertransference through their seductive attention seeking. If we fail to recognize this, we may find our own position compromised, our own feelings confused, and our own ability to help seriously impaired. We need to draw on our own resources and powers of self-observation to keep the relationship in balance. Needless to say, histrionic persons can be a source of enormous stress. That is why it is so important for us to reflect periodically on our feelings as honestly as possible. We soon appreciate the seasoned therapist's measured approach to such clients.

They are basically self-indulgent and want to be cared for. We can feel the self-concern histrionic persons generate in much the same way that ordinary, healthy people can feel the psychic emanations that come from self-centered persons. The vanity and narcissistic qualities of these people are quite obvious. They need attention and they want it now. They live outside ordinary people's time, in a zone of their own. They cannot put things off, nor plan very well for tomorrow. Some observers note that, for clear psychological reasons, histrionic persons are sometimes attracted to individuals with an obsessive personality disorder. They marry and supply each other's lacks. The one keeps things in order, while the other provides a kind of vivacity and sense of freedom unavailable to the partner. That, of course, does not necessarily make a good match. Often it is when such a couple seeks help for marital difficulties that we can identify the partner with the histrionic personality.

Persons with a histrionic personality disorder are known to profit from individual psychodynamically oriented psychotherapy. The focus is on their use of emotionality, the defenses that such persons use to avoid intimacy, and the transference issues. Generally, these individuals do not do well in a group setting and a skilled therapist is necessary for work with them in couples therapy.

The Narcissistic Personality Disorder

As a sign of their overall cultural struggles, Americans have been preoccupied about narcissism for over a generation. The widespread self-reference and self-absorption of the late twentieth century — being both engrossed with and imprisoned in the ego — have provided an attentive audience for psychiatry's debates about this personality disorder. Elements of narcissism are found in every personality, of course, and the maintenance of adequate self-esteem is not always easy even for the most psychologically robust among us. If we all understand the devastation that can follow from a blow to our self-image we are not, for that reason, all suffering from the kind of disorder that experts have in mind when they discuss this entity.

Characteristics

Individuals suffering from pathological narcissism, or the *narcissistic personality disorder*, exhibit a pervasive pattern of grandiosity in fantasy or behavior, a need for admiration, and a lack of empathy that begin in early adulthood. As is well observed, narcissistic traits are common in adolescence and it is generally recommended that the diagnosis not be applied until an individual reaches adulthood. It is a fairly common condition, estimated to affect about 1 percent of the general population but 2 to 16 percent of those seen in medical or mental health clinics. It is approximately three times more common in men than in women. Certain rock stars, politicians, and "celebrities" are sometimes cited as contemporary examples of this personality disorder.

For the diagnosis to be applied, individuals should have five or more of the following characteristics: (1) they have a grandiose sense of self-importance, expressed in exaggerating their achievements and talents, and their expectation that they will be recognized as superior without commensurate achievements; (2) they are preoccupied with fantasies of unlimited success, power, brilliance, beauty, or ideal love; (3) they believe that they are "special" and unique and can be understood by, or should associate with, only other special or high-status people or institutions; (4) they require excessive admiration; (5) they have a sense of entitlement, that is, unreasonable expectations of especially favorable treatment from others; (6) they are interpersonally exploitive, that is, they take advantage of others to achieve their own ends; (7) they lack empathy, that is, they are unwilling to recognize or identify with the feelings and needs of others; (8) they are often envious of others or believe that others are envious of them; and (9) they manifest arrogant, haughty behaviors or attitudes.[18]

What Counselors Must Understand

It is important for us to understand that persons with narcissistic personality disorder do not take kindly to any kind of evaluation. Because of their perceived superiority and their feeling that only the "best" expert in the field can know enough to be of help to them, they tend to be disparaging and haughty to lesser authorities. Here again, nonprofessionals will profit both as persons and as helpers from their careful appraisal of those who suffer from this problem. As with persons with borderline disorders, we will experience the pathology that flows from these clients in a firsthand and often confusing and upsetting manner. The need, therefore, to identify transference material, as well as to recognize countertransference reactions, is paramount if we are going to survive and be helpful. Narcissistic persons exert intense pressures on any potential helper, viewing the counseling as a competition, for example, and seeing the helper in a disdainful way.

The treatment for these individuals is generally a psychodynamic or psychoanalytic psychotherapy. Different theories have informed the treatment so that different strategies are implemented by different schools of thought. Groopman and Cooper summed up the divergence: "Where Kohut sees structural defects of the self, Kernberg discovers pathological defensive organization; where Kohut finds hidden elements of positive transference, Kernberg perceives latent negative transference; and where Kohut advises the unimpeded efflorescence and empathic encouragement of narcissistic idealization, Kernberg insists upon its early interpretation."[19]

While experts still debate the best method of treating narcissistic personality disorders, the first concern for nonprofessionals is to avoid being incorporated into their psychological maneuvering. These individuals have a fragile sense of self-esteem and are so hypersensitive to the least criticism that they are easily stimulated to angry reactions. We should recognize the potential gravity of narcissists' reactions to loss or the threat of loss. Their rage can be literally murderous in nature and effect, and it may well be the pathology beneath the killing or other physical harming of spouses at the time of marital breakup.

Persons with narcissistic personality problems may, therefore, be especially disruptive to the already challenging nature of marriage counseling. Their sense of grandiosity and entitlement, coupled with their seeming inability to feel empathy for others, make them difficult to work with and, in certain circumstances, dangerous to others. We should consult professionals if we have any questions about such persons and refer them promptly if we conclude that they need evaluation and treatment by more highly trained therapists.

– 29 –

PERSONALITY DISORDERS: CLUSTER C

The Avoidant Personality Disorder

Within Cluster C of personality disorders, in which, as noted, individuals appear anxious or fearful, we first examine the *avoidant personality disorder*. By early adulthood, those suffering from this disorder reveal a pervasive pattern of social inhibition, marked by feelings of inadequacy and hypersensitivity to any negative assessment or evaluation. They appear frightened and tense in personal relationships with their "antennae" constantly sweeping the environment to pick even the smallest evidence that they are incurring the displeasure of others.

Persons with an avoidant personality disorder should manifest at least four of the following characteristics: (1) they avoid occupational activities that involve significant contact with other persons out of fear of criticism, disapproval, or rejection; (2) they are unwilling to get involved with people unless they are certain of being liked; (3) they show restraint within intimate relationships because of fear of being shamed or ridiculed; (4) they are preoccupied with being criticized or rejected in social situations; (5) they are inhibited in new interpersonal situations because of feelings of inadequacy; (6) they view themselves as socially inept, personally unappealing, or inferior to others; and (7) they are usually reluctant to take personal risks or to engage in any new activities because they may prove embarrassing.[1]

Perhaps less than 1 percent of individuals suffer from this disorder. Often described as shy or timid, they do anything they can to avoid feeling humiliated or rejected. We are all familiar with children who are "shy." Ordinarily such children grow up and grow out of it. The children who later manifest this avoidant personality characteristically become more isolated and hypersensitive as they approach adolescence and early adulthood, that interlude whose challenge is to forge relationships as the foundation stones of a healthy life. These persons back away from or avoid social situations, such as teenage dances or sporting events, because they are not assured that they will be asked to dance or participate as a team member.

Acquaintances often respond to their fine-edged fear of criticism by reassuring them that, despite their concerns, they will be accepted by others. As one drink is never enough for the alcoholic, one reassurance is never enough for them. They may have to be asked or urged repeatedly to attend some function. Only when they are certain that there will be nothing to fear will they attend. These fears seriously impair their social and occupational functioning.

The recent college graduate with avoidant personality disorder may have excellent credentials and be well prepared for work in a specific type of research. This person may, however, fail to show up at the job interview, not because of lacks in the college record, but because of fear of being rejected. Such graduates rationalize their behavior by saying that the interviewers would not approve of their clothes, their hair, or something else, anything else they can think of. If they do show up, they may compromise their chances for employment by crying, blushing, or showing signs of marked anxiety in the interview itself. Such an outcome, a fulfillment of the prophecy of their early problem, reinforces their avoidant behavior for the future. They may subsequently settle for a much lower paying and less intellectually stimulating job because it does not entail a series of interviews with senior scientists and administrators. They may be able to marry eventually, choosing someone who is a protective, indulgent spouse who "runs interference" for them in social situations.

Some observe the similarity between social phobias and the avoidant personality disorder and believe that these two disorders are actually one viewed from two different perspectives or that they differ in focus although they are similar and related. Social phobia, for example, is related specifically to performance in social situations, while the avoidant personality reacts in multiple dimensions of life. Many individuals with other personality disorders also share characteristics of the avoidant personality disorder, but certain notes distinguish them. The social isolation of the schizoid person, for example, delivers a certain comfort but the fears of the avoidant disorder bring only discomfort, preventing individuals from establishing relationships they would like to enter. The diagnosis is applied only when such individuals' personality characteristics fulfill the criteria and are judged to be inflexible, maladaptive, and the cause of significant anxiety as well as functional impairment.

Treatment

Treatment for this problem follows the clinical assessment of its manifestations as well as the identification of its underpinnings. The history and primary symptoms influence the choice of a specific psychotherapy. Some individuals, for example, may respond well to interventions developed for the treatment of social phobias. These include skills training, cognitive therapy, or desensitization therapy. Others, who have developed avoidant fears and behaviors as a result of early childhood trauma, may benefit from a range of therapies similar to those used for the treatment of post-traumatic stress disorder. In addition, some medications are extremely useful in diminishing symptoms of blushing, stage fright, and other manifestations of the disorder, allowing these persons to engage in a more normal life.

The Obsessive-Compulsive Personality Disorder

Common and tough, obsessive difficulties are the source of great stress for those of us who counsel. Obsessive persons both need assistance and make it difficult to deliver. They are not very happy and don't quite know how to help themselves achieve happiness. Reaching them with effective therapeutic help challenges the most skilled of therapists. Because these difficulties occur so frequently, we need an understanding of people suffering from them and of our own reactions to their frustrating style. If we are not full-time counselors we can at least learn to avoid mistakes in working with them and how to manage our own reactions to them.

Not everything described with the words "obsessive" or "compulsive" necessarily belongs to the same family of emotional difficulty. Many people may have obsessive traits and function within the range of normal behavior without meriting the diagnosis of an "obsessive-compulsive disorder" or an "obsessive-compulsive personality disorder." Being obsessive may, in moderation, serve people well and contribute to their achievement and high performance.

People may also have experiences that resemble those of the obsessive-compulsive disorder but not really suffer from it. Obsessions or compulsions may surface in all of us as, for example, when a favorite song plays itself over relentlessly in our mind, a momentary urge to do something bizarre passes fleetingly through our consciousness, or, after driving a mile away from a vacation house, we double back to check that the windows are closed and the doors are locked.

Persons with true obsessive-compulsive disorder are relatively easily diagnosed because of the disturbing and anxiety-provoking character of their obsessions and compulsions. Persons with *obsessive-compulsive personality disorder,* in contrast, begin early in adulthood to be pre-occupied with orderliness, perfectionism, and mental and interpersonal control, paying for this through a loss of flexibility, openness, and efficiency. Whether one's preoccupations and inflexibility have so spun out of control as to result in obsessions and compulsions is a matter for careful clinical judgment. We must also remember that many persons with obsessive-compulsive disorder also suffer from an obsessive-compulsive personality disorder.

Approximately 1 percent of the population suffers from this disorder, which occurs more in men than in women. Many men, who protest to love their work and constantly overwork, harming their family and social life in the process, could not do otherwise. They are caught in the vise of a personality structure that is unbending in its unrelenting demands. Only when something "gives" — the spouse threatens divorce or the job is eliminated — does the seriousness of their disorder reveal itself.

For the diagnosis of obsessive-compulsive personality disorder to be made, persons should exhibit four of more of the following behaviors: (1) they are so preoccupied with details, rules, lists, order, organization, or schedules that the major point of the activity involving them is lost; (2) they exhibit perfectionism that interferes with task completion, that is, that they are unable to complete a project because they cannot meet their own overly strict standards; (3) they are excessively devoted to work and productivity to the exclusion of leisure activities and friendships in ways not accounted for by obvious economic necessity; (4) they are overconscientious, scrupulous, and inflexible about matters of morality, ethics, or values in a manner not accounted for by cultural or religious identification; (5) they are unable to discard worn-out or worthless objects even when they have no sentimental value; (6) they are reluctant to delegate tasks or to work with others unless they submit exactly to their way of doing things; (7) they adopt a miserly spending style toward both self and others, viewing money as something to be hoarded for future catastrophes; (8) they manifest rigidity and stubbornness.[2]

Understanding the Personality Structure

Much of what we understand about the obsessive-compulsive personality disorder, which forms the basis for psychotherapeutic interventions with these individuals, derives from the original notions of Sigmund Freud. These people use the defense mechanisms of displacement, condensation, and symbolization as well as isolation, reaction-formation, and the mechanism of undoing. In other words, they speak a very special language, a dry and containing tongue that encases their emotions and enables them to live outside them. Researchers feel that these manifestations are frequently related to underlying conflicts about authority and external control and that the threatening impulses the person strives to keep under check are frequently hostile or sadistic ones. It has been suggested that the root conflict — which such persons cannot consciously acknowledge — is between being *obedient* and being *defiant*, between wanting to please and wanting to act out against authority. It is an experience that rubs the psyche raw. Such persons try to get life down perfectly, to cover all moves on the board, so that nothing can go wrong and no hurt can take place.

As Salzman has observed, the typical persons with this disorder have a need to

> gain control over one's self and one's environment in order to avoid or overcome distressful feelings of helplessness. The concern about the possibility of losing control by being incompetent, insufficiently informed, or unable to reduce the risks of living produces the greatest amounts of anxiety. The realization of one's humaneness — with its inherent limitations — is often the basis for considerable anxiety and obsessive attempts of greater control over one's living.[3]

Many churchgoers are familiar with obsessive-compulsive persons whose behavior is sometimes generated in highly controlling ecclesiastical environments, the observance of whose perfectionistic codes allows them to overcome the threat of damnation. Whole lifestyles have been spun out of this psychological conflict, and many individuals who come to us suffering from either obsessive-compulsive personality disorder or obsessive-compulsive disorder can trace their condition back to unfortunate experiences with organized religion.

Salzman also cites such persons' seeming need for omniscience, noting that "the obsessional can be comfortable only when he feels he knows everything or is engaged in the process of trying to know everything." Those afflicted with this problem use such experiences as doubting, putting things off, or not deciding as a way of avoiding situations that would reveal their deficiencies and so prop up their illusion of perfection. Obsessive-compulsive persons may exaggerate their own self-importance less as a function of reality than of the high standards and impossible demands they make on themselves. The ritualization of behavior becomes important because it provides a focus for the person's attention, "thereby," according to Salzman, "distracting interest away from other matters."

Persons afflicted with obsessive-compulsive problems taste little of life's joys. They tend to be conforming because they allow themselves short rations of freedom that they do not enjoy. It is too frightening for them at some level of their awareness so they are more comfortable being dependent on those who will tell them how to live their lives. They really prefer security to satisfaction. Yet they often resent the person in "authority" telling them what to do. This combination compromises their capacity to enjoy things even when they have the money and leisure to do so. Frequently they turn hobbies that are suggested to them by well-intentioned friends into new forms of compulsive work. In short, it suits them — by keeping their conflicts at bay — to hold tightly to their style of living, and no argument will persuade them to change their minds.

The Challenge

It is not enough, of course, just to know about the characteristics of the obsessive-compulsive person. We must learn how, in our own heavily scheduled lives, to establish working relationships with them when they ask for our help. The same challenge faces individuals who must relate to such people as family members or as associates at work. An understanding of their dynamics and the highly symbolic ways in which they express themselves is, therefore, indispensable for even a common-sense kind of relating to them. Work closely with such individuals and we learn how easily we can be absorbed into their defensive system. That system resembles the protective inky fluid shot out by the squid to obscure its movements when it is in danger. Obsessive-compulsive persons blur our perception, making it more difficult for us to see them, in order to keep at a safe distance from us.

The first thing we can do to help ourselves is to reflect on this style, built on stores of hidden and misunderstood anger, that seeks to confuse and keep us off balance, to keep us away from significant emotions by enveloping us in the massive intellectualizations so characteristic of this syndrome.

We learn quickly that working with these individuals is different from working with most other troubled people. Once they get into the session, obsessive individuals give very little of themselves away, reminding us of old pros at a press conference who expertly fend off reporters by saying nothing in several different ways. Obsessive persons are not, however, charming about it. They are not open and eager to talk about their emotional problems. They reveal the outline of their conflicts in the contours of the blanket they throw over themselves.

Counseling sessions with them, as Saul Bellow said of certain phases of life, can seem "a series of long afternoons." Not only long, but dry and boring because that is their defense against emotional contact. They keep the insulation on their inner wiring and, even though we can read this as an unconscious evasive maneuver, it works when it keeps us and the interview under their own control.

Reflective counselors who have learned to be participant-observers in their work learn to mark the undulations within each counseling session. If we manage to get inside, they duck away to control the fear and anger that wells up when we seem to get close to them. This trying rhythm of approaching meaningful material only to find the lid quickly snapped into place will become familiar to us.

We need to distance ourselves from this interaction so that we may discern the emergent pattern. As we grasp the way these individuals avoid emotional material, we begin to understand their classic, painful, but useful style. We may use the pattern itself in furthering the counseling as long as we can keep free of its abrasive impact and avoid being neutralized by it.

Good Beginnings, Good Endings

Some researchers observe that, because of their passion for categorization, these individuals cut the body of a counseling session free from its beginning or its conclusion. What happens before a session actually starts or after it is concluded is ruled out as being of no importance. That, of course, explains why the beginnings and the endings of appointments with them can be instructive for us. Persons with this disorder often reveal more about themselves at these times than they do in the course of the counseling interview.

If we are perceptive, we pick up the melody of their overture and exit music. They are telling us about themselves in everything — their style, their clothes, their seemingly innocuous introductory remarks, and their closing statements and behavior. We can mine this rich ore for clues about their underlying conflicts. They also provide relevant subject matter to which we can direct their attention during the session. These first and last statements may be the closest to emotional expressions that these people make.

The obsessive-compulsive person may, for example, mention a key subject at the very close of a session by saying something like, "I'm surprised you didn't ask me about my job today." Miss this and miss a critical self-revelation about their difficulties.

These individuals are expert at using offense as their best defense. Some counselors, especially those not bloodied by much experience, may not read what is happening and may be bewildered by the way these people seize control of the counseling itself. For example, such persons may throw us off guard by getting us to explain something we have said or to defend some other aspect of our professional behavior. When this occurs, we may be irritated and respond to our distress rather than to the psychological reality that lies beneath this defensive maneuver. We must recall how hard it is for these people to seek the help they badly need. They fend off the threat that such help symbolizes to them and, as we appreciate this, we will look beneath these strategies with more understanding for them and less stress for ourselves.

What Can We Counselors Do?

Since a principal objective of counseling is to establish some genuine human contact with the other, and since this is precisely what these persons try to avoid, what can we do about it? It is helpful, first of all, to check our own reactions, those precious messages inside us in which we read some truth about the nature and development of this counseling relationship. For example, if we listen to ourselves and find that we are bored, we can be fairly sure that we have not established any real contact with the other person. If we find that we are irritated, we know that we have made contact but that such individuals have responded through their defensive systems rather than with their inner personalities.

If, however, we find ourselves interested and humanly responsive to such persons, we have established a relationship with the healthy parts of such persons. This feeling feedback is reliable when we are disciplined in listening to ourselves. This reading our own psychological thermostat guides us through the dry thickets to the green patches of genuine relationship with these heavily burdened persons.

The particular genius of the thwarting obsessive style is the use of communication to destroy the goal of communication. Many obsessive persons are present physically but absent psychologically during the counseling. They may look away from us, avoid eye contact, speak inaudibly, and, as a final touch, refuse to listen very carefully to us even when they appear to be doing so. They are good at not being there, and it is hardly surprising that this can be very frustrating to us. Think of how uncomfortable they must be to employ such a defense.

Sometimes obsessive persons become tutorial, delivering little lectures or suggestions to us about how the counseling is proceeding or about some technical point of psychotherapy about which they may have consulted the authors themselves. We must resist this frontal assault on our counseling ability by seeing this behavior as an end product of their internal disharmonies. They are trying to save themselves much more than they are trying to hurt us. We can view this with some good-natured compassion and respond with acceptance as well as some recognition of what these persons are trying to do. We may point out to them how we perceive this kind of maneuver. "You feel more comfortable when you can keep me under control, don't you?" is a realistic response that is not punishing but appropriate to what is taking place.

MacKinnon and Michels offer a number of practical strategies for this situation.[4] They suggest, for example, that when the counselor senses that the obsessive person is not paying attention and is not, therefore, hearing what the counselor says, it would be better to stop and draw some attention to what is taking place. This gives us a chance to tap into what these persons are really thinking but not directly communicating when we are speaking to them. It provides, in other words, a way into the interior landscape of these persons. When this can be done gently, for example, by asking them what they are musing about and then pursuing its theme, the situation is far more realistic than pretending that counseling is going on when it really isn't.

The theme behind these reflections, of course, is that counselors must not focus so much on the incidental elements of the counseling that they miss the overall maneuvers that constitute the basic style of others. There are many clues to this in the resistance that such persons manifest and, if we want to understand, we will not hesitate to follow these leads in a concrete but nondefensive manner. These flags, tiny though they be, indicate where their concerns really are. Easy to miss or shrug off, they remain, when carefully interpreted, very helpful symbols.

Countertransference Concerns

As we pick up the signs of the emotions beneath the systematic defenses of others, we look for early opportunities to point them out in our responses. We try, as always, to keep our responses as close to the experiences of others as possible, but we also remember that not far beneath the surface they are angry and that any response that gets close to the truth may make them overtly angry. We simply must learn to live with this if we hope to be effective.

Don't try to patch things up with them. This is a natural inclination for most of us when others seem to be offended by something that takes place in the counseling. This is particularly true for us if our counseling is done in the context of another professional identification. It is much better to let them be angry, to let them experience what they have been hiding from and through this find a way, for the first time, to react less defensively about this emotion.

We do not strike back at them when they get angry. That is a response to our own needs rather than to the real meaning of this occurrence in the obsessive-compulsive relationship.

Nor should we let them patch up the situation. That sounds cruel, but once emotions are expressed in a relationship, it is not therapeutically sound to try to hide them or pretend that they did not occur.

Don't argue with them. Obsessive defenses are basically intellectual in nature, and these individuals resort to them in order to gain superiority over us. Arguing is a doomed activity. There is nothing they like better than an argument that simultaneously enables them to rebuild their intellectual defenses, waste time, and frustrate us. Because these individuals are good at getting into unreasonable arguments with us, it is important to remember that the arguments *are* unreasonable and that logical responses are clearly doomed from the start.

Our best effort is to relate the anger to its causes even when this must be done inch by inch by pursuing this emotion into the interior of the persons in order to find some bit of the truth beneath their symptomatic behavior and style of relating with others. After we do this, the counseling may really begin. To accomplish this requires us to be tuned in to ourselves and to these persons, to keep our own feelings under control, and to know and stick to our objectives.

Treatment

Because their personality features are frequently the source of difficulties at work and in family and social life, individuals with obsessive-compulsive personality disorders are more likely to seek treatment than are persons with other personality disorders. Although outcome studies are few in number, psychotherapy is most often recommended as the treatment of choice. This may include a number of approaches — psychodynamic psychotherapy, cognitive behavioral therapy, or other focused or problem-solving psychotherapeutic techniques.

Therapy is usually a lengthy process, marked by the pitfalls we have described. Many of these individuals, however — in part, because of their personality features — are able to persist and work diligently at the tasks involved in therapy and eventually achieve successful changes in their overall adjustment. In recent years, a variety of antidepressant medications has been found to be effective with some individuals.

The Dependent Personality Disorder

We have all known people who are well described as dependent personalities. An accurate diagnosis of dependent personality disorder is made difficult because its characteristics are so common in other conditions. Nonetheless, persons with a *dependent personality disorder* advertise clearly their pervasive and excessive need to be taken care of. They exhibit a pattern of submissive and clinging behavior that begins by early adulthood, designed to elicit care giving and arising from a feeling that they are unable to function adequately without the help of others.

The diagnosis requires the presence of five or more of the following personality characteristics: (1) they have difficulty making everyday decisions without an excessive amount of advice and reassurance from others; (2) they need others to assume responsibility for most major areas of their lives; (3) they have difficulty expressing disagreement with others because of fear of loss of support or approval; (4) they have difficulty initiating projects or doing things on their own because of their lack of confidence in their judgment or abilities rather than a lack of motivation or energy; (5) they go to such excessive lengths to obtain nurturance and support from others that they may even volunteer to do things that are unpleasant; (6) they feel uncomfortable or helpless when alone because of exaggerated fears of being unable to care for themselves; (7) they urgently seek another relationship as a source of care and support when a close relationship ends; (8) they are unrealistically preoccupied with fears of being left to take care of themselves.[5]

The possibility of overlap governs our care in making a proper diagnosis. Persons with borderline personality disorder, for example, are often afraid to be alone and feel the need to be with others. When threatened with abandonment, however, they become angry, rageful, demanding, and often resort to "splitting," perceiving one object as good and another object of their attention as "all bad." Dependent persons are more likely to try even harder to appease, submit, *do anything* to keep others from leaving them. Although they share a vulnerability to being alone, these two conditions are worlds apart. Persons with a histrionic personality disorder also have strong needs for reassurance but, instead of trying to attract the other by docility and compliance as dependent personalities do, they try to attract others by making themselves the center of attention. Treatment strategies and countertransference issues are quite different in these situations.

What Are They Like?

Dependent traits are common to all human beings and are, especially at certain stages, essential components of life. It is obviously appropriate for children and adolescents to exhibit dependent behavior. It is not unexpected periodically in the adult years, as during stressful interludes, times of illness, or with the losses that go with increasing age. It is expected, indeed, a desirable condition in the appropriate circumstances, and the gracious acceptance of help is part of healthy adaptation. Many human beings, once independent, refuse any expression of dependency. All of us, for example, have experienced aging persons who refuse to acknowledge any trace of dependency, to their detriment as well as that of others close to them. The diagnosis of dependent personality disorder, however, should only be considered when the person's behavior is clearly in excess of the cultural norms or reflects exaggerated and unrealistic concerns.

At first meeting, such persons may seem very attractive, agreeable, and congenial. They appear somewhat compliant but are easy to get along with and never cause any difficulties. If we have leadership roles in a group — as teachers, pastors, or other authority figures — we may gradually become aware of their increasing dependence on us. They always seem to wait to see what we will do or say before they act. They may begin to ask our advice about what to wear, what to study, with whom to associate, and where to buy groceries. We gradually sense that such persons cannot make a move without checking with us first. We feel trapped, as Gulliver did, bound by a thousand tiny threads. Even if we ask them to do some unpleasant task, to volunteer for a job no one else wants, they seem to respond gladly and with no complaint. There is little suspense in this revelation of their true natures by those suffering dependent personality disorder.

We sometimes wish such persons would challenge us, confront us, or at least disagree with our advice. But dependent persons would not dare "cross" the person whom they feel so dependent upon and without whose counsel they feel that they cannot function. The potential for drift on a forbidding sea is overwhelming when they are threatened by the loss of their anchor.

In social life — and often in family life — these relationships can become very conflicted. The demanding and clinging behavior of dependent persons produces the very opposite of what they want. It repels those they admire or need, driving them away from them rather than closer. Persons burdened with dependent personality disorder tend to stifle and engulf the desired others, provoking the abandonment they fear. Dependent adolescents whose congenial presence and compliant behavior seem a blessing become a great problem when, as young adults, they stay on, failing to pursue career goals, content just to be around the home, socializing with the family, willing to take on errands and tasks around the house, but never "getting on" with their own lives.

Treatment

Often family members or associates recommend that these persons get treatment. Treatment is primarily psychotherapy and adjunctive therapies such as psychoanalysis and a variety of psychodynamic, cognitive, and behavioral therapies. Supportive therapy and group therapy are also used with some individuals.

The countertransference issues that arise in response to these persons' dependent traits need to be carefully monitored. Most therapists are initially pleased if others carry out all that is suggested without disagreement. This plasticity may, however, be a sign that nothing is happening in the therapy, that all is at a stalemate, and, in fact, the therapist has become the new object of their dependency. This can generate feelings of annoyance and a wish to be "rid" of such persons, thus igniting a flare-up of their original fear of being abandoned and rejected. Persons with a dependent personality disorder can make great strides in changing their behavior and achieving a more mature adaptation to life when they have an understanding and skilled counselor.

PART FOUR

– 30 –

MARRIAGE COUNSELING

PARADOXICALLY, although marriage counseling is a perennially sensitive and difficult challenge, many people, counselors among them, feel great self-confidence, warranted or not, in giving advice about the married state. Despite our rates of divorce and remarriage and the extension of this category to accommodate unmarried or same-sex couples living together, everybody knows how to stabilize or improve other people's relationships. This may be a response to the poignancy of relationships in conflict, a distraction from our own troubles, or the feeling that what we have learned the hard way is worth sharing.

The effectiveness of our counseling married couples varies inversely with the degree of our unexamined self-confidence. We should approach counseling couples humbly, ready to learn rather than to teach and with modest expectations of what we think we can achieve. Many couples look for help, but that does not mean that they, or their problems, are really alike. As we enter the world of couples, we find that it is a zone filled with psychological traps, surprises, and complications for which there are no easy escapes or solutions.

How Did This Couple Ever Get Together?

We may find ourselves asking a question about this couple sitting before us. They look at everything so differently, there seems to be so much more conflict than comfort, and yet, here they are, trying to work out their relationship. How, we wonder, did this couple ever get together in the first place? Both folk wisdom and research offer answers to this puzzlement. Yet the question persists, reminding us of the caution with which we must step onto this stress-fractured bridge that connects the persons before us.

That the question of what attracted them to each other occurs to us illustrates the emotional complexities that are in play, like fiber optic cables crowded with thousands of messages, many of them at the unconscious level. We move prudently and with restraint because we understand how easy it is to trip off transference and counter-transference problems that may confound the already bewildering problems at hand. The intimacy that is intrinsic to the marriage relationship, the complications caused by the couple's conscious and unconscious attitudes and experiences as well as our own, along with prevailing cultural expectations beyond our control, meet and intermingle in ways that need subtle monitoring in this counseling.

The Culture around Us

Counseling is never done in a vacuum, and everybody is influenced by the environment in which people enter marriage at this time. Along with other institutions and symbols of authority, marriage has been a city under siege with no relief column to raise it in sight. It is not surprising that some young people hesitate, or find themselves ambivalent for reasons they cannot name, about entering the married state.

Successful marriage is good for human beings. People, therefore, still seek to be married, even after leaving a failed union behind them. Married people, especially men, are healthier on a number of physical and emotional measures than single persons and function much better than those who were once married. The institution of marriage is not being rejected, although it is obviously under pressure. The problem lies, as counselors learn, with those entering it.

Nine out of ten Americans do get married even though half of first-time brides and grooms eventually get divorced.[1] About three-quarters of men and two-thirds of women remarry; of these, about 60 percent of the men and a little over half the women get divorced again. Single-parent families are now the most numerous in America, and in many cases these persons are working toward remarriage with the challenge of building a family "blended" of the children from the previous marriages of the new couple. These may be multiple as well.

Of the adults who seek mental health services, about 40 percent complain of some problem in their intimate relationship with their spouse or partner. The coexistence of marital distress and depression in one or both partners is reported in about half the cases. Domestic violence is not uncommon in America, and, after a generation and more of presuming otherwise, it is now reported that children of divorce carry the scars of persistent exposure to marital disharmony and violence into adulthood. They do not function as well as their friends raised in the happy homes of stable marriages.

Divorce is a field of fire for those who pass through it. As a source of stress, it is thought to be second only to the loss of a spouse or other close family member, and during the year or two of the intense phase of this process the parties may suffer serious physical or emotional problems. These are the realities of the storm-filled world out of which distressed couples, bearing sorrow and anger in their baggage, emerge to ask us, of all people, for help.

Scrubbing Up

To minimize the stress and distorting effects of such factors on marriage counseling, we may begin doing something that we can control. We increase our sensitivity to our own inner experience, calibrating it so that we do not overload and overwhelm ourselves in the process. We help ourselves and the counseling as we become aware of the wide range of emotions we, along with everyone else, have about marriage and friendship. We also have a store of personal peeves and hurts, rewards and triumphs related to these. We profit by examining any strong pulse of feeling we detect in this area, not only to sense its presence but also to read and modulate its influence on our counseling relationship.

As marriage counselors who want to manage this mass of potential stress sensibly, we may model ourselves on surgeons preparing for an operation. We "scrub up" beforehand to cleanse ourselves of the emotional infections that may interfere with counseling. We carry this self-purification out by scanning an inventory of our past and current feelings about our own experiences in human relationships. We must lower our own defenses against identifying these in order to understand and deal with them.

One of the subtle feelings to which we counselors need give attention before involving ourselves in marriage or couples counseling centers on our potential readiness to choose sides early in the process with either the husband or the wife. We may not consciously set out to support one party against the other but, unless we are aware of how smoothly and swiftly we can be emotionally enlisted by one or the other, we may be easily enrolled on this or that side. This may be the major source of stress for many of us who, deciding that one spouse is right and the other wrong, invest our energies with unchecked partiality on the side we feel, often for unconscious reasons, to be in the right. We are then no longer mediators of communication as much as seconds shouting advice to our "fighter" and providing refreshment and moral support between rounds.

If, for example, we see one spouse before the other we may be vulnerable to being persuaded by this first version of events so that our choice of sides is immediately determined. This risk is intensified if we counsel only part-time as one dimension of some other professional activities. If we are not accustomed to listening to and understanding ourselves, we help fulfill the prophecy that the first persons seen have a terrific opportunity to get their viewpoint across with a maximum amount of illustration and conviction so that this story becomes the permanent subtext of the relationship. Unless we helpers go on alert to our potential in this regard, we may be trapped by it so that the subsequent counseling may be permanently distorted in favor of the first person we see and the first story we hear.

This can happen, for example, when a tearful and attractive woman speaks to an inexperienced counselor about the difficulties she is having with her husband. We could be that counselor who, not clearly aware of the dynamics of transference and countertransference that can so quickly be activated, may sympathize strongly with the woman and become her advocate without noticing that or how it happened. An examination of the feelings of such counselors, that is, a look at *our* feelings, might reveal that we not only feel sympathy for the wife but that we are actually angry at the husband. Were we to examine ourselves, we would learn how this enlistment syndrome takes place. This pledge of self may reflect our own experience or that of our parents or other members of our family. Such quick enrollments on one side or the other place a mortgage that must be paid off immediately to free our understanding and counseling effectiveness.

Only balanced counselors — and we all feel that this describes us — can accept and deal with the fact that one of the partners may, even unconsciously, actively attempt to get their support from the first moment of contact. We counselors cannot ignore or react defensively to these preliminary issues without running the risk of blowing the fuses that bring the light to our counseling work.

Alone or Together?

Closely related to this fundamental idea is the easily developed conviction that, viewed from the outside, a marriage in which one of the partners is receiving psychological help and the other is not can be defined as a "healthy one–sick one" relationship. It is an easy temptation in these circumstances to blame most of the difficulties on the partner who is receiving professional assistance. This does, after all, provide a handy explanation for what conflicts might be present. It is never so simple, however, and counselors must be wary of feeling that the only true perceptions are given to them by the spouse who is not in therapy.

Such spouses are in a relationship, and no relationship is a one-way street. Only if we remain open-minded can we appreciate the complexities of communication and experience that bring a man and wife to the point of seeking help. Committing ourselves quickly to one spouse or the other, either out of sympathy or by concluding that the partner receiving psychological treatment is necessarily the one at fault, generates twin dangers for all counselors but especially for those whose counseling is only one part of other responsibilities.

There are many theoretical arguments about the advisability of seeing married couples individually or together in counseling. This is the subject on which every counselor must reflect in order to be able to anticipate the counseling arrangements well in advance and to avoid having them arise haphazardly or by chance. Such a decision is based on the counselor's experience, the degree of comfort with which the counselor can operate with more than one person, and the nature of the presenting difficulty. Arguments for seeing couples together are highly persuasive as they are based on this situation's natural re-creation of their ordinary interpersonal style, but good reasons also exist for seeing couples separately, at least for a time at the beginning of counseling.

It may be important, for example, for us to evaluate carefully the factors that contribute to a full and sensitive understanding of these two married persons. Sometimes it is only as we develop a full appreciation of each individual that we can make a prudent decision about how the partners should be seen. We may conclude that in a particular case husband and wife must work together from the start on some maladaptive pattern of behavior they have fashioned in their life together.

On the other hand, we may also decide that the partners have special and separate psychological problems that need individual treatment before they can come together to work on the specifics of their relationship with each other. This judgment is obviously important and can be made only if we are acquainted with the relevant elements of psychological diagnosis. How they will be seen is a significant issue that should be discussed jointly with the couple early in the counseling. Giving the man and woman a voice in this basic decision strengthens the possibilities of their making continuing therapeutic progress. Such sensitive decisions require a prudential judgment that can be made only if we are aware of and properly demagnetize the emotional iron filings that cling to all parties involved.

What Are We Trying to Do?

What are our goals and how clearly have we defined them before the therapy begins? This is a relevant question for those professionals principally involved in fields other than psychology and counseling. We may be committed by our profession or by our particular work within our profession to viewing marriage in a certain way. For example, the clergy may want to save the marriage at all costs for reasons of religious belief and family integrity. If we are lawyers we may evaluate the relationship in terms of a legal consequences, the specifics of a divorce settlement, or other related issues with which we work everyday.

Aside from the possible philosophers among them, physicians may handle only the medical aspects of a couple's difficulties, giving general advice about marriage from the viewpoint of this specialty. In a number of jurisdictions, couples seeking a divorce must first see a counselor for a prescribed number of visits. Such counselors may find that they are motivated in one way or another either to maintain the relationship or bring it to an end. Certain religious denominations require premarital counseling or instruction, especially for very young people, sometimes with a view toward delaying their decision to marry.

Counseling that is done under such pressures and with such goals in mind—even when these are not consciously verbalized—introduce elements that may well pull the counseling out of its place on neutral ground. A heavy investment one way or the other on our part before we begin working with husband and wife can obviously predetermine the outcome. We need not abandon our values or convictions about marriage—indeed we must be well aware of them—to monitor them so that they do not prejudice the counseling.

Many such areas need examination in relationship to our goals. Some counselors have very strong feelings about the moral, ethical, or legal issues connected with marriage and divorce. Everybody has certain convictions about these emotionally laden questions. The challenge is not to sacrifice their convictions but to be able to take them into account so that they do not interfere markedly with the counseling. Enough difficulties are involved in marriage counseling without complicating them with factors that we can identify and isolate beforehand. In some situations, we may have to exclude ourselves from cases in which our feelings are too involved.

Currently, the notion of the therapist as a scientist operating from a value-free position is being questioned and put aside. As mature adults, we carry within us commitments to values, but in the particular work of marriage counseling, a prime value lies in concern about the integrity of the therapeutic process itself. In other words, a true directing value of counselors calls for us to discharge our obligations to our clients in a moral and responsible way. We must be sensitive to the values possessed by others, recognizing, for example, how their values play a part in their lives, allowing them to explore and express them in the counseling relationship.

It is also quite dangerous to force our own values on others, especially if these are foreign to their tradition and belief. That is not the role of the counselor. In the long run, we have a moral and ethical obligation to allow people to make decisions according to their own personal values. We are not preachers or proselytizers, and we would be false to the profound values that are the foundation of counseling were we to assume these roles.

Kinds of Problems

What kinds of problems do married people have? The list is inscribed on the tablets of the human condition and includes all the simple sad staples of life: arguments about money, in-laws, abrasive personal habits, the discipline of the children, and sexual problems. These are the intersections where the accidents occur, leaving broken things and bleeding people. There are, in fact, many manuals packed with recommendations on how to handle these problem areas more constructively in marriage. Some marriage therapists follow some very simple guidelines that signal a happy marriage. They include such admonitions as "live a simple life," "spend less than you earn," "learn to yield," and "manage your moods." These are, in fact, simply common sense. Where these obvious suggestions are applied they can, in fact, do great good. It is sometimes surprising to discover how poorly acquainted some people are with the commonsense steps — such as the use of a budget — that can reduce friction in their married lives.

While all these suggestions may in fact be helpful, they can easily lead us to become enamored of the *fallacy of the reasonable solution*. It is tempting to use practical solutions because they are aimed at specific problems and they offer positive activities or attitudes that often prove to be very helpful. The difficulty, however, is that reasonable solutions often fail even in the lives of fairly reasonable people. They don't work *because the problem is not a reasonable one;* it is an emotional one and it defies the laws of logic or rational analysis.

Most people encountering difficulties with each other do recognize what would be a reasonable thing to do but they find it very difficult to implement such notions. They fail at the reasonable thing; they act unreasonably precisely because of the emotional factors that block their capacity for rational solutions and tempered dialogue. There would be no need for any counseling if reasonable solutions could be easily applied. Sometimes it is very stressful for us as counselors to see reasonable solutions spurned. Such a course seems, in itself, unreasonable, impractical, and frustrating. The essence of counseling, however, lies in our helping people to reintegrate reason into personality through exploring the emotions that cloud and inhibit it. We should expect people to be unreasonable; that is why they are sitting across the office from us.

In working with married people, we must listen to them rather than just to the problems they describe. Most of their problems are given only as illustrations of something they find difficult to define about their lives together. They are trying to sort out their feelings and get to the bottom of themselves. It is a great relief for us to realize that we need not have rational solutions to all the concrete problems presented in the course of marriage counseling. For that matter, we don't have to have solutions at all.

Now is the time to recall the counseling basics that require that we understand and respond to the persons having problems rather than to the problems themselves. We need not know how to solve the problem, but we must be able both to understand and to express our understanding of the individuals involved. The more that, as counselors, we drift away from responding to the persons with whom we are working, the more surely we move toward quagmires and dead ends. We get involved with these if we read too many lists of marital problems as well as too many rational "how-to-do-it" solutions to them. It all seems so reasonable that we are surprised endlessly to rediscover that these "solutions" do not automatically work.

We reduce our own stress when we get back just to understanding the persons involved in the counseling; as understanding helps husband and wife to appreciate their emotional entanglements, they become reasonable on their own.

Counseling Is Not Cooking

Nothing tempts us, in any enterprise, as much as a shortcut. It is practically a character trait for Americans. That explains the *Reader's Digest,* speed reading, frozen food, and fifty snippets of great music, specify CD or Cassette, sorry, no CODs. It also explains how our own stress gives us a reading, much as a thermometer provides one of heat, of the pain experienced by people who bring their tattered marriages in for repair. Their suffering may be so great and so urgent that we may be attracted by formulations that promise a better focus and a way out of their conflicts that is briefer by far than the months and years it took them to get into them in the first place.

One of John Cheever's characters discovers the beginning of wisdom by learning that "there is no cure for autumn, no medicine for the north wind." We need wisdom of the same kind if we are going to help men and women move at human speed toward resolution of their problems in living with each other. Perhaps we begin by realizing that men are not from Mars any more than women are from Venus, that they are both of the earth, "the right place for love," as Robert Frost writes, but no place for shortcuts when it runs into difficulties.

If we are rightfully skeptical of popular how-to books, we should also be cautious in trying to apply the insights from the clinical literature on brief treatment techniques. Manuals of shorter procedures are increasing in response to the shrinking number of hours for which insurers will provide reimbursement. Highly trained professionals may be able to incorporate some of these approaches into their marital counseling without running the risk that we nonprofessionals run, of implementing them as we would the recipes from a cookbook.

Thus, for example, in what is known as behavioral couple therapy, endorsed by the Clinical Psychology Division of the American Psychological Association, therapists are encouraged to use "as a framework for assessment and treatment," the "7 Cs" of character, cultural and ethnic factors, contract, commitment, caring, communication, and conflict resolution.[2] Trying to remember and apply these factors may unbalance the tray of straightforward counseling we are already trying to carry without dropping anything. Professionals may integrate these considerations gracefully, but, if our counseling is incidental to our main identification, we are wise to restrict ourselves to the approach through which we can combine support and help as simply and directly as possible.

The Mediator

Mediators are found in such bristling environments as hostage and labor negotiations. Nobody said that this would be easy. As mediators in marriage counseling, we may find ourselves between gladiators highly practiced with swords and nets. Our role is to help them lower their shields and sheathe their weapons long enough to be able to hear each other again. One C at a time is enough as we concentrate on communication between estranged married couples.

We are called upon to hear the deep and sometimes confused messages being conveyed by couples who no longer listen to or cannot hear each other, and to translate these so that husband and wife can again begin to communicate directly. Holding our own here requires extreme sensitivity and a practiced skill for which textbooks, "reasonableness," or quick solutions are no substitute. In marriage counseling, communication is dead center, the bull's-eye we cannot afford to miss. Such skills as we have are here put to the test. The central ingredient remains our awareness of ourselves and of the messages rising within us or raining down on us from the partners with whom we are working. Managing these various levels of communication taxes our abilities, and we need to keep them well honed to function well. More important than knowing the 7 Cs is making sure that we do not become stale, distracted, or otherwise take our attention away from helping others to hear each other.

These demands explain why marriage counseling places so much stress on us as we engage in it. It requires constant attention to the emotional nuances of the partners' statements as well as the ability, without being enlisted by either side, to convey to each exactly what the other is saying. Only such careful mediation, comparable at times to tile setting, can reopen a long shut-down relationship. If we miss in the process of communication, we miss in everything.

Attention Must Be Paid

There is no more fundamental question than: "How can we miss doing the thing we realize to be one of the most important aspects of counseling?" We may "miss" if, for whatever reason, we stop hearing, when we become as dulled to the couple we are trying to help as they are to each other. We may become a third party to, rather than a mediator of, their relationship. We might as well be part of their family, a witness rather than a counselor. We may be drawn into this unless we maintain a good perspective on our role. It is then easy to be carried along in the governing current of their relationship much as they are after they stop paying enough attention to each other. We increase the hazard if we are overworked or are neutralized by our familiarity with similar cases or our preoccupation with our own problems.

Like athletes, we need to be in shape for our work; maintaining our psychological edge, essential to all counseling, is indispensable in working with couples. The image of the counselor as a harried, battle-scarred, overburdened practitioner who has already seen and heard everything has no place in the demanding work of marriage counseling. Being fit for the arduous work of paying close attention ensures our readiness to hear accurately and humanely. This requires that we get enough rest, maintain a reasonable counseling load, realize that we cannot save everybody, and keep in touch with our own inner lives. Oddly enough, these corollaries of counseling fitness are the ones most frequently violated, especially by those who, as professionals in other fields, let themselves get so busy that their workday becomes a blur.

Be Ready to Be Surprised

No counseling houses more unexpected twists and turns than that involving married people. The unexpected in the everyday illustrates how our unpredictability is one of the most challenging as well as charming aspects of human nature. We may have made a check mark only to find that people do not do what we would bet that they would do, especially when they are married to each other. Such peculiar discoveries teach us not to be overconfident in making predictions about what may or should happen. Some married people are willing to settle for less, or for only a bit more than we think they should get or deserve from life.

People define happiness in many different ways. We must let them stick together, if they so decide, or separate, even if we would wish for another outcome. We may interpret a decision to separate as a failure on their part but, in many instances, a difficult choice may represent, for the couple, a true success. Couples who have never really been in touch with themselves or with each other may achieve this through counseling and realize, perhaps for the first time in their lives, who they are and what their relationship really means. While no one may wish for this kind of outcome and while it may challenge the religious and philosophical ideals of many, it is nonetheless the homely truth about how real life is loved. Happy endings are not always the order of the day, and to be disappointed or to feel we have failed because of an outcome that goes against our grain is never appropriate. Hard and good decisions are not necessarily happy ones.

Be prepared not to understand fully what is going on. The distinctive and sometimes idiosyncratic manner in which people satisfy each other's unconscious needs shapes their relationship and the course of counseling. This may give rise to a great deal of behavior that is un-

> ## *Tips for Marriage Counselors*
> Be prepared:
>
> - For the unexpected
> - Not to understand fully what is going on
> - For the partners to grow at different rates

predictable precisely because we cannot accurately trace it down to its unconscious source. We must remain alert to these subtle shifts that change the whole balance of the relationship and thus give it a new face. But the couple may not always be able to interpret or appreciate the reasons for their choices. They only sense the shifts and see their effects.

Be prepared for the partners to grow at different rates. For example, if one begins to respond and improves in self-understanding and in behavior, this may have strong repercussions on the other partner. Such partners are accustomed to relating to others who have remained fairly static for a long period of time. When a change occurs, the mode of relationship learned in other circumstances no longer works very well. Something has happened, but it is difficult to chart it accurately. Yet we can see these partners shifting in what is bewildering for them and may be so for us as well. This kind of dynamic occurs in many combinations, and husbands and wives, long accustomed to their former ways of behaving, may be thrown for a loss. We counselors may need time to sort this out as well.

Another example may clarify this. A woman who has exhibited somatic symptoms for years, begins, in the course of marriage counseling, to improve. She has fewer physical complaints but, as she becomes less demanding, her husband responds by emerging from the passive and quiet role he had assumed previously to avoid upsetting her. He now becomes more active. This reciprocal change happens too quickly for the wife, even though her initial improvement has triggered it. Because she is not prepared for a change in her husband as a result of the change in herself, she can only revert to her former style and evince somatic symptoms again. Such sequences of behavior can occur very easily in marriage counseling. They may be hard to follow and we need a measure of patience and an adequate perspective if we are to grasp what is going on.

Currents in the Air

Another influence on the course of marriage counseling arises from the philosophy and opinions about marriage that, as noted previously, receive widespread publicity through the multiplied twenty-first century media and quickly become conversational topics in the varied environments, business and social, of the married couple. Magazines at checkout counters advertise articles on the latest styles of living together, adjusting to marriage, or finding or bestowing sexual satisfaction according to trendy patterns. The cultural fallout is comparable to the Perseid meteorite showers that rain down every August; they are bright, thrilling, but represent something that is quite distant from us. They also often burn out quickly.

While there is little that is historically new in any of such heavily advertised developments, they may represent startling and novel ideas about marriage and relationships for a great many persons. Counselors must be aware of these influences; they must hear not only the couple but the background music, all the harsh and sweet melodies of the world, of the drama of their marriage. The almost constant daily airings of material once held back by social restraints creates pressures because they reveal the already existing marital stress fractures that may have been better defended under previously unquestioned outlooks on man, woman, and marriage. People may say, "Yes, that's us," or "That's how I feel too," to a wide variety of contemporary descriptions of married or marriage-like experience.

This is a difficult area because so many shifts in these popular discussions take place, and also because these discussions can be used as a shield against other interpersonal problems. There is always a danger to human relationships when highly emotional issues can be compressed into slogans that can be emblazoned on the flags of the never quite fully adjourned battle of the sexes. These powerful slogans may provide forceful symbols and points of reference for many hitherto unexpressed feelings. Activists use slogans to stir such reactions from a public that is thereby enlisted in some cause. A similar phenomenon can occur in marriage in which slogans detonate landslides of feelings of which the partners were previously only minimally, if at all, aware.

It is clearly common sense for us to remain neutral about these issues and to be sensitive to the fact that arguments about such questions and causes may mask other unnamed internal difficulties. It is also common sense to avoid the role of a crusader on any of these questions. The most that counselors may be able to do is to help others to understand and take greater responsibility for themselves and their relationships with each other. The high-voltage quality of many current discussions makes it all the more important for counselors to be aware of the many levels of significance that are present. Counselors only increase their own stress if they lose control and allow marital or any other kind of counseling to become a forum for the intellectual discussion of such issues. This takes counseling far afield and allows people an escape from their fundamental counseling work of exploring themselves.

When we hear excessive discussion of contemporary issues, we can be fairly certain that we are observing a defense mechanism operating. Its defensive character is evident when the dialogue goes round and round without moving the counseling forward.

A further signal of a defense in play is found in the vehemence of the feelings in these discussions. Complaining partners seem suddenly to discover, and give expression to, a trove of deep and as yet unexpressed feelings, some of whose origins antedate the experience of marriage itself. For example, a twenty-five-year-old woman suddenly expresses almost violent feelings of anger at finding herself a wife and the mother of three children. It is not that she does not love her husband and her children; rather, it is the long pent-up and perhaps denied emotion of being cheated out of a better chance at life by her overdemanding father. She has always had these feelings but has only now become aware of them because of the public discussions about other women who feel "trapped" in similar lives.

This woman has carried these unresolved conflicts with her into her marriage. They had probably caused friction of one kind or another before, although their true nature and roots had never been recognized. They doze rather than sleep deeply in her psyche until a contemporary discussion provides the symbols through which she becomes aware of them. The resolution of these conflicting feelings — rather than an intellectual discussion of the women's movement — becomes the first order of business. Until she can understand these long-repressed emotions she cannot explore her relationship with her husband.

It is clear from this example that although her discontent manifested itself in her married life, it could be traced back to a much earlier period. Working through the long-denied emotions of being robbed of her best chance at life enables her to separate her own experience from that symbolized in general by the women's movement. It does not help to argue with her or to encourage her to be "reasonable." She is, in fact, far more realistic once she can express her frustration. Such situations, in which counselors offer supportive help as people deal with material easily recalled to consciousness, are not uncommon.

While it may be difficult for counselors to keep abreast of everything that is going on in their culture, they should make some systematic effort to be informed about the major issues connected with areas of human development, marriage, and the family. An acquaintance with the contemporary world is essential for counselors who wish to understand those who come for help.

Most people who do counseling are familiar with professional publications that offer dependable information and perspectives. They should also try to take advantage of seminars and workshops for updating on the background material relative to their marriage counseling work.

Less often cited but nonetheless important are the other ways in which our culture speaks to us. We have to listen to films, serious books, novels, and other shapers of our impressions about married life and related values. Less deep but still informative are popular magazines and even television talk shows. The latter are often staged or display the ruin of culture but they still tell us something about the world in which we and those who come to us live. As trained listeners, we must also hear what is being said — and catch what lies beneath what is said — in all these cultural manifestations.

It Suits Them

After we have worked hard at understanding, patiently taken life histories, done a reasonably good job at facilitating communication, perhaps even made a first-class referral, couples may still surprise us by what they decide to do. As we listen to the couple and perhaps witness many examples of their incompatibility, we may conclude that this is a misalliance, that this relationship is knit together by barbed wire strung across territory filled with land mines. The relationship appears, by sensible measure, to be a painful disaster. And yet they stick together.

For such situations — and, indeed, for many other entanglements — we need a diagnosis that is not found in textbooks of any kind. We can only conclude that, for some people, the relationships in which they find themselves are the best they can do and all they can do. Indeed, they can do nothing other and survive.

In short, *it suits them*.

We may never understand why or how this can be true, but we will reduce our own stress and be more helpful to others if, in certain

circumstances governed by unconscious entities that it is not our business to disturb, we let people be as they are, linked by need at depths
that defy our taking soundings of them. Everybody knows couples like
this. They cannot get along together and they cannot get along apart.
Whatever may finally explain it — and that is a job beyond us as nonprofessionals and perhaps beyond most professionals — it suits them to
live this way. It is as much philosophical as it is psychological wisdom
to recognize and accept this reality. If we know when to hold them,
we must know when to fold them. When a relationship somehow suits
nobody but the couple, it is time to let them continue, perhaps with
occasional support but without any false expectation that major, or
much minor, change will occur.

– 31 –

COUNSELING PERSONS
WITH SEXUAL PROBLEMS

O UR BEDROCK PRINCIPLE is as simple as common sense and good clinical judgment. We do not treat sexual problems; we try to understand men and women who have sexual problems. Our focus is consistent with what we strive to achieve in all our counseling work. We understand persons rather than problems. We do not sink shafts into the depths of others to mine the glittering veins of unconscious material, but support them on the conscious level as they explore themselves and their lives. As it is healthy for us to focus on persons rather than problems, so in this work it is also healthy to view ourselves not as crusaders but counselors.

Sexuality has been heavily politicized by various causes and campaigns, some of them honorable and some of them manipulative. Unfortunately, nothing has been more common than the use by ideologues on the left as well as the right of other persons' sexuality for their own purposes. Healthy common sense tells us that we are not to be enlistment officers for one sexually associated cause or another. Being apolitical does not mean that we are amoral. We fulfill our ethical and moral obligations by responding as skillfully as we can when dealing with persons anxious or troubled by some sexual conflict or attitude. Our morality is expressed in our being as effective as possible as nonprofessional counselors who hold themselves to professional standards.

As counselors, we are enlisted in no crusade, and the very best gift we give to people troubled by some sexually related problem is an accurate understanding of them and their world. People turn to us because they feel that they can do so confidently and freely, that we, of all those arrayed in their universe, seem approachable, that they can tell us their story without fear of interruption or indictment. They turn first to their pastor, their doctor, their teacher, their coach, or someone in a like relationship of easy trust with them.

The objective of those seeking help is not complex. They want to tell us the story of their lives, perhaps never narrated before to anyone, not even to themselves, and of the anxieties or agonies they suffer in understanding or expressing their sexuality. As in all the situations we have discussed, they want to tell us — as we, of ourselves, may wish to tell others — of the problems that they have in just being human. The trust they invest in us is a bridge built by them that arches half way over the swift dark waters toward us. Can we complete the span with our own trustworthiness so that it will bear our weight as we meet on it?

Why Are They Telling This Story?

How does this happen? The essential element in raising this link is their readiness to try to talk to us about something that is difficult for them to talk about to themselves. They lack the language to describe their sexual distress except in half sentences or in symbolic ways. Ordinary men and women want to tell the truth about their sexual problems even in seemingly confusing and contradictory ways. It may be helpful to recall the origin of the word "problem" in the Greek: *pro* (forward, toward) and *ballein* (to throw). They throw their concerns at us and our task is to catch and label them correctly.

In working with persons troubled by some aspect of their sexual experience, we ask ourselves, *Why is this person telling us this story in this way?* We respond to the best answer we can give to that question rather than to the surface content or to some intriguing example. The latter are given to us only to illuminate what they are driving at, not as subjects to be pursued in themselves. People only use illustrations to help us understand them, not to distract us.

We attempt to catch what their story is about and incorporate the sexual uncertainty or conflict into the overall pattern of their narrative. Even when we carefully avoid offering a cure for a specific problem, our accurate and humane understanding provides something else of great value — the experience of being heard and understood, perhaps for the first time in their lives, in a way that relieves and strengthens them to continue their work in counseling.

Our lack of technical knowledge or clinical sophistication may, in fact, assist us in responding to persons with sexual problems. As non-professionals, we may be free of the need to make the absolutely perfect and polished response that some persons attempt when they are in training to be professional therapists. That is why the person seated next to a troubled individual on an airplane may, simply by uncomplicated human understanding, have a profoundly therapeutic and lasting effect on the latter, even though they disappear into the crowds at the terminal and never see each other again.

A Healthy Alliance with Unhealthy Possibilities

Building the bridge with troubled persons is really the construction of what is termed a "therapeutic alliance" with them. From the healthy part of ourselves, we reach the healthy part of the other's personality. That is the medium of effective counseling. This is the platform on which we stand together to survey, name, and understand the conscious elements of the person's problems. This vantage point may afford us a view of dynamics within others that are hidden from them even though they influence their behavior. We do not, in our supportive counseling, choose to enter this domain. We avoid this, or blundering into it, as a sea captain does, on nights with no gift of moon, a shield of rocks at a harbor's mouth. We mark its outline in our imagination, acknowledge its existence, and trim our course to enter the calm port waters undamaged and undamaging. Our understanding of the personality dynamics of others allows us to keep clear of the deeply submerged materials without denying them, to appreciate their significance, and to use our knowledge to make good referrals for more specific treatments.

Our grasp of the powerful underground currents in counseling also allows us to monitor the transference and countertransference feelings that are as natural to counseling as heat shimmering above the desert plain. In the context of a sexual problem, these feelings may intensify and become eroticized, adding to their potential to confuse, engulf, or damage us and those we want to help. When we are sensitive to the transference feelings that may arise and be played out in the counseling, we are also sensitive to the person we are trying to help. Even as part-time counselors we must pick up the messages that these other persons may experience feelings toward us that are not directed toward us at all but are transferred from their feelings toward some other significant person in their lives. People regularly reproduce with us the style of relating they have learned in growing up, offering us a sample that allows us to understand them rather than to use it as a basis of relationship to them.

That transference feelings may be tinged with eroticism, especially when the persons in whom they arise are discussing sexually related or sexually expressed problems, should not surprise, embarrass, or entice us to misread them as if we were their stimulus and their object. It is only human that countertransference feelings, common in therapeutic relationships, may arise in us as well. Mature counselors do not immediately interpret this interplay of feelings as the dawn of either a romance, a sexual adventure, or flattering evidence of their sex appeal. These dynamic reactions are not to be acted upon but to be observed by the mature part of ourselves, even as we must evaluate dozens of other experiences each day from the healthy promontory in our personality.

We deal with transference issues in sexual counseling as we would in any other counseling activity. Since our objective is to keep the unconscious material sealed, so to speak, to prevent it from breaking through in our counseling relationships, and to deal with persons on the conscious level, we naturally avoid behaving or inquiring in any way that might set these feelings off in other persons. As we have noted, we do this by sticking to their concrete life situation and fashioning our responses so that they keep the concentration on the present, on current particulars, on what others are immediately aware of or can easily recall. We make no interpretations or probes that may pierce the covering of their unconscious.

We remain, as it is said, *abstinent,* doing nothing to stir transference to life and, should it intrude, nothing to explore its depths. We may contain it on the conscious level, when it bids to interfere with the relationship, by saying something like, "It is not unusual for people to have feelings about their counselors that are really from other important relationships," and to turn the focus back to the immediate circumstances of their conscious functioning. Should the feelings persist or seem beyond containment by such skills as we possess, we may review the case with a mentor or supervisor so that we do not distort our perception of it, so that we may monitor our own countertransference reactions, and come to a judgment about whether it is time to refer this person for assistance to a professional who can provide long-term assistance. As a rule of thumb, we are on track if we are in a therapeutic alliance, that is, if we are relating to the other from the healthy part of ourselves to the healthy part of others. That is not a hard judgment for healthy people to make.

It is also possible that, without breaching the unconscious, we may refer persons to accredited professional sex therapists who may be able, through behavioral and cognitive treatments, to assist these persons in dealing with the symptoms of their sexual problems without delving into the deeper personality issues to which they are tethered. While charlatans abound in any realm of helping, many highly ethical, well-trained sexual therapists are available to deal with the overt conscious aspects of people's sexual conflicts or complaints. Whatever our main calling, we should be acquainted with such professional resources in our communities and perhaps even establish a relationship with them so that we understand and can easily follow the protocols involved in making referrals to them.

The Languages and Dialects of Sexuality

Nothing associated with human beings lacks complexity, and sexual activity bears the weight of all that is unresolved and uncertain, as well as everything that is rich and sure about us. We are wise not to give simple answers when even straightforward questions may flower from intricately rooted plants. That we will not, in a lifetime, master an understanding of the many and various meanings of human sexual expression and exchange does not inhibit us from constantly working at grasping their subtleties and nuances.

People who come to us may have only the slightest glimpse of what may lie beneath the problems about which they want to talk. What we may hear, codified in the symptom, is the deeper significance of what they describe. Sometimes all that they sense about their sexual symptom is its surprisingly driven quality or that the sexual expression does something for them — expresses something — in a way that no other language can.

There is no Berlitz crash course for this language and its many dialects. How do people express themselves in their sexual communication? Some persons are frustrated because sex in real life is never as it is in books or in the movies. Its romance may be marred, and it may not make them happy or lead them into greener pastures of intimacy with others. Their story may be told in the symptom language of dissatisfaction that sexuality is not integrated into their lives. We need to stick to the language they are speaking and not introduce a new one of our own, such as that of moral evaluation. Although there may be moments of necessary education if their sexual activity threatens their own life or the lives of others, our task is not to stop people from behaving in certain ways — they must and will do that for themselves — but to understand the psychological factors that lead them to this activity in the first place. An informed moral outlook bids us to hear the story beneath the behavior, such as their own puzzlement that they keep on doing things that bring them unhappiness rather than sexual fulfillment.

Other people try to speak a sophisticated sexual language in order to bolster their self-esteem or to establish a socially approved identity. The mechanics of the sexual difficulty — of performance, for example — is not the problem that needs to be understood by us or by them. These persons are not sinners or perverts but humans struggling for something essential that can only be achieved through a healthier relationship with themselves and with other persons. It is not enough, of course, to treat this as an intellectual puzzle. Many of them have worn themselves out reading, thinking, and talking about their dilemmas. They cannot understand the sexual language in which they are symbolizing their conflicts and in which they are talking to themselves.

Thus, sexuality may be used to ward off rejection, to reassure themselves that they are loved by someone else, to get some feel of successful intimacy. Most counselors are familiar with persons, especially teenagers, whose sexual lives are searches for the solid affection, the being wanted for themselves, that sexual activity cannot in itself produce. The problem is not just the short-term one of stopping them from being promiscuous but the long-term one of understanding themselves and why and how they are using sexuality in a deceivingly pragmatic and self-defeating manner to achieve goals that cannot be attained in this way.

While counselors may be clergy members or educators who normally preach and teach moral ideals and practices, they lay aside their didactic roles to try to understand, and so to help others to understand, how people may use sex for self-esteem, to ward off loneliness, to reassure themselves about their human identity, or overcome feelings of inferiority, only to find themselves distraught and transformed into restless searchers for these goals to which sex does not lead them. The positive task of moral education rests on helping people to hear and understand the nonsexual uses of human sexuality. To assist others we must improve our ability to hear, understand, and translate simply the languages and dialects of human sexuality.

We should also be aware that some persons will come to us anxious about the possibility of acquiring a physical illness through sexual contact. They may be either well or ill informed about the specifics of such infections such as HIV/AIDS and other sexually related infections. HIV/AIDS will be discussed in the next chapter, but sexually active persons should be aware of the rampant spread of such infections as genital herpes, an infection spread by sexual contact and that can be medically controlled but is subject to recurrence. It ordinarily manifests itself in painful genital lesions. Before concern over it was overshadowed by the AIDS epidemic, it was a major public health concern. As the new century dawned, renewed concern has been expressed as the Centers for Disease Control and Prevention reported that the prevalence of herpes simplex virus type 2, the cause of most cases, had increased 30 percent since the late 1970s, with more than one in five American adolescents and adults now infected. Of the estimated 45 million who carry this disease, 80 to 90 percent do not realize it because many never experience the symptoms associated with it.[1] While we may respond to the emotional distress people express to us, we cannot directly treat the problem except through wise and prompt referral for medical care. We must also understand and be able to educate people about the nature and treatment of this somewhat silent but serious problem.

Basic Notions for Nonprofessional Counselors

We must have faith, if we are reasonably healthy ourselves, in our ability — possessed by the healthy community as well — to recognize, even in a blunted and blurred environment of nondiscrimination of these issues, to tell the difference between what is healthy and unhealthy in human sexuality. When sexuality is part of a relationship that expresses genuine liking and responsible love between persons, then it potently reinforces, by its own depth, an already deep reality. When sex is used to express interpersonal guilt, hate, or some other form of hostility, when it expresses boiling emotions in one person that are not related to the good of the other, the transaction is marred by its unhealthy components. It is not hard to tell that the sexual abuse of children is unhealthy as well as illegal. Nor is it difficult to grasp that sadistic, manipulative, or exploitative sex practices are unhealthy even in an age when people may shrug them off or rationalize them away as a matter of personal choice or preference.

We need not be rigid, authoritarian, or insensitive to respect the reference points that are vital to our understanding of human sexuality and its expression of something deep in our personalities. As nonprofessional counselors we contribute to the health of culture in general and people in particular through helping men and women to achieve a better understanding of their sexuality.

Because we are active in other callings, we can also reinforce and support the healthy instincts of the community and those movements and organizations that contribute to the overall health of that community. Many of these solidify the institution of the family and so promote the source of the healthy growth that includes healthy sexual development. Recent surveys strongly undergird the positive effects of healthy religious values on achieving and maintaining the growth of persons whose health is reflected in the way they fashion relationships and express their sexuality in successful intimacy with others.

By being understanding alone, we reassure people who are anxious about themselves and make it possible for them to tap into their own health in order to see in better perspective and to deal more effectively with their relationships and their lives.

Sexual Dysfunctions

Human beings have suffered greatly from society's difficulty in what we have described as speaking and understanding the language of human sexuality. Sexual dysfunctions, as they are termed in the scientific literature, admit of no facile solution and, despite the flood tide of informational literature on, and medications for, sexual dysfunctions at present, people do not easily profit from theoretical or intellectual discussion. Nor do they find medication a substitute for relationship. The totality of this book is meant to be a resource for our reflection by our observing selves of ourselves in action. That is the central and indispensable review and reinforcement of the healthy and mature self needed for counseling work. Responsible counselors should be reasonably aware of and comfortable with their own sexual feelings and should also be well acquainted with the current literature on human sexuality.[2]

Knowing Enough to Make Referrals

Aware of our limitations, we cannot and should not attempt to solve all sexual problems. We are not less as counselors for spending much of our time referring people for more specialized help with their sexual difficulties. Understanding persons who have sexual problems so that we can make timely and well-informed referrals is a significant and indispensable contribution to their welfare.

As noted already, we should acquaint ourselves with the professional sex therapists in our area, learning their credentials, licenses, or board certification, their ethics, and their sense of integrity in dealing with persons seeking their help. Checking with local medical or other professional societies is the best way to verify the qualifications of such therapists.

We travel best through this territory with a good map that we study carefully beforehand and follow without succumbing to the distractions of the many tempting side roads. Our destination is what is best for those we are helping, and we cannot be blind guides without suffering their biblical fate of dragging them down into the pit with us. Most of us find it very helpful to follow an inclusive protocol in our interviews with persons suffering sexual complaints so that we will have enough information to make the most helpful referral for them. Unless the person merely needs reassurance about some common worry, such as about occasionally bizarre fantasies, our objective is almost always to make a good referral for specialized treatment for these persons. It is helpful to elicit as complete a case history as possible, including their age, general physical health, and current life stresses in order to clarify their possible relationship to the onset of the complaint. Alert to sexual dysfunction that seems chronic, long-standing, and resistant to psychological intervention, we follow up with referral for professional evaluation and treatment.

Everyperson's Complaint: What We Should Know

Because our main calling may be in medicine, law, education, or pastoral service, we are not sexual therapists. Nonetheless, people with sexual problems may first speak of them, as we have observed about many problems, with us. There is pain enough for everyone in the findings that 43 percent of women and 31 percent of men, along with 50 percent of couples, experience some form of *sexual dysfunction*.[3] It is a very human problem and our principal response is that of human understanding rather than judgment or quick advice.

Sexual disorders are divided into three groups by *DSM-IV-TR*.[4] The first, *sexual dysfunctions,* are understood as impairments of sexual desire and/or of the sexual response cycle whose origins may be physical or psychological. The second, *paraphilias,* are recurrent intense sexual urges or behaviors that involve unusual objects, as in fetishes, or activities, such as bondage, and that cause severe distress. The third, *gender identity disorders,* are characterized by strong and persistent cross-gender identification accompanied by persistent discomfort with one's assigned sex.

We need not seek or evaluate more details than troubled persons may offer about their problems as we prepare to assist them with a professional referral. We do need, however, to be well acquainted with the normal sexual response in both men and women.[5] It is helpful, as well, to gather some general life history and, if we are physicians, to take a good medical history of those seeking our help. Sexual problems are often the result of physical problems, such as postoperative conditions, hypertension, malignancies, or infection. Substance abuse and the use of certain medications such as antidepressant, antihypertensive, and anticonvulsant medications can all cause sexual dysfunction. Aging may contribute to erectile dysfunctions in men, especially over the age of sixty, and the decrease of estrogen in aging women may cause narrowing of the vagina and a decrease in vaginal lubrication that can cause discomfort.[6] Sexual dysfunction may also be caused by psychological difficulties and, while these are usually complex, they may range from fear of inability to perform and recent childbirth to a history of sexual trauma or clinical depression complicated by family or financial stresses.

Our understanding response to their feelings about talking about themselves and their sexual difficulties is one that can do no harm. If these persons feel that they are being heard, they will hear themselves better and be able to tell their stories more fully. Our principal response, therefore, flows from understanding the feelings of these persons about revealing their sexually related difficulties. We may well need to deal with our own discomfort at hearing or discussing such matters before we can convey true understanding to these persons.

We may ease the way for them by such general statements as: "I know it is hard sometimes for people to talk about such things, and perhaps you feel that way but still may want to discuss something in this area." Our questions may be gentle but more focused: "Is there something about your sexual life you would like to discuss?" "Have you experienced any changes in your sex life or anything you would like to change?" "Are you satisfied with your sex life?"

It may be important to find out, in the age of AIDS, if these persons are sexually active and if they understand what AIDS is all about. Many persons have only a general idea about AIDS and dangerous or naive ideas about how it is spread or how they can protect themselves from becoming infected. Many persons mistakenly believe, for example, that new drug regimes for HIV infection will protect them from contacting AIDS even from infected individuals. We will discuss this further later on, but it is important that any persons who do counseling work have up-to-date and accurate information about this and other sexually transmitted diseases.

If people identify an area of concern, we should get enough information through gentle questioning to help make the best referral possible. It is better not to frame questions with a *why* that expects an explanation but rather to propose them with a *what,* as "What do you think caused this to occur?" We may wish to find out if they have sought other counsel, or if and what they have read or heard about the difficulty they are experiencing. In the same tone of understanding, we should help them clarify what their goals are in coming to see us. We can gauge their motivation through these inquiries and perhaps help them clear up misgivings or misapprehensions that would make them less well disposed to accepting a referral.

A broad array of treatments is available for the wide range of sexual dysfunctions. Our task is to deal with the feelings about the problem, to help others clarify the problem and their attitudes toward further help, and to make a prompt referral to a professional who will ultimately decide on the best kind and course of future treatment. We may gain great knowledge about sexual problems from our experience and from reading or workshops. All of this should be used in the service of providing ongoing assistance to the distressed persons who seek us out.

The Most Likely Problem Situations

Many of us whose counseling is associated with other work will find that we are the first ones consulted by an *institution,* such as a school or a church, by *relatives* of those in some way concerned, or perhaps directly by *persons* involved in some problematic sexual activity. We are consulted because of our principal job, knowledge that we offer counseling, or a reputation for good sense and understanding. Often, the sexual problem will be one of what are termed by *DSM-IV-TR* as *paraphilias.*

Paraphilia (para = alongside, beside, unfavorably + *philia* = tendency toward, abnormal attraction to) is the term now used to describe behaviors once termed *perversions* or *sexual deviations.* As noted, these are revealed in "recurrent, intense sexually arousing fantasies, sexual urges, or behaviors, involving nonhuman objects, or the suffering or humiliation of oneself or one's partner, children or other nonconsenting persons that occur over a period of at least 6 months."[7] In this context, whose sensational elements give rise to varied emotions in those who may consult with us, the ultimate diagnosis should be left to a professional. That diagnosis is ordinarily made only if the person has acted on the urges or is very distressed by them. It is helpful, however, to understand that paraphilias occur almost always in males, that those suffering them may always need related fantasies to achieve sexual arousal, and that some persons experience these only during times of stress.

Pedophilia is the most common of the *paraphilias* and is the most likely of these behavior constellations to be brought to our attention. The *DSM-IV-TR* defines it as sexual activity with a prepubescent child.[8] The person who carries this out must be at least sixteen and the victim must be at least five years younger than the perpetrator. Most of the victims are girls, and they are often relatives of the one acting out the paraphilia. While it is true that most pedophiles are heterosexual, there are instances, as in pedophilia of Catholic priests, in which the victims are almost all male and homosexuality or ill-developed sexuality seems to be an issue.

Whether the occurrence is pedophilia, however, or one of the other paraphilias, we should be generally familiar with other disturbances within the classification. These include *exhibitionism,* the exposure of the genitals to unsuspecting strangers in public; *fetishism*, achieving sexual satisfaction with nonliving objects, such as ladies' lingerie; *frotteurism,* sexual arousal by touching or rubbing against a nonconsenting person, often in a crowded place; *sexual masochism,* sexual pleasure from physical or mental abuse or humiliation that, in a very dangerous form, *hypoxyphilia,* involves oxygen deprivation, as in staged hanging, often resulting in accidental death; *sexual sadism,* in which sexual arousal comes from causing mental or physical suffering to another; *transvestic fetishism,* in which heterosexual males cross dress for sexual arousal; and *voyeurism,* in which sexual arousal comes from watching an unsuspecting person who is naked, disrobing, or involved in sexual activity.

Typically, our involvement occurs when an interested third party, such as a relative or school principal, or other institutional authority, contacts us for assistance after they discover such behaviors or receive such reports themselves. While individuals with these problems may ask, or, sometimes, be told, to see us, they are not generally self-referred. An incident occurs, it is reported, and we are consulted. We must think about what and to whom we are responding.

What We Can Do / What We Should Not Do

Our best service may be to respond first to the discomfort, anxiety, and puzzlement of the relative or authority figure. We can bring calm to a situation that may be quite agitated and confusing and help people make intelligent and well-informed decisions about their obligations in these circumstances. Legal obligations may demand, if a felony has been committed, reporting the behavior to the proper authorities. If we interview the persons involved in the paraphiliac behavior, we focus on their reactions to their problem's coming to the attention of others, get a general history of their psychological functioning, and arrange for the appropriate referral. We do not, as nonprofessional counselors, accept these persons in counseling relationships.

We may have opportunities to educate the various persons or institutional representatives involved about the nature of these problems and their potential treatment. As mentioned earlier, individuals with paraphilias do not often seek out treatment on their own. They are usually discovered in the act by some family member or are arrested for the behavior. The rewards of intense pleasure that individuals receive from these behaviors reinforce themselves and make them so difficult to give up that some liken it to a compulsion or an addiction.

When these persons are in treatment, they often try to convince their therapists that they have given up the behavior when, in fact, they have not. Because of this, effective treatment may require some monitoring of their activities and behavior. Even with this, and what sounds and seems like goodwill, the prognosis for paraphilias is not good and people often fall back into it after giving it up during treatment or while under supervision. While psychotherapy has not proven very effective with these people, some behavior therapy, using techniques of desensitization, aversive techniques, and conditioning processes, has helped modify the way many of them function. Some medications, such as antidepressants, may decrease the compulsive and impulsive pull of the problem and so lessen their urges toward these behaviors.

We can bring good judgment and restraint to situations that often set off anxiety and anger in those affected by such incidents. Only in recent years have organizations, such as Roman Catholic dioceses and religious orders, developed policy manuals to follow when, for example, charges of pedophilia are made against church personnel. Networks of concerned persons and of victims and their families have also identified themselves and become active in movements designed to avoid such incidents or to seek compensation for victims. It is by no means a subject that is covered up, as it once was, and the once routine behaviors of reassigning personnel to other parishes or schools after periods of treatment have largely been abandoned.

Paraphilias remain highly charged behaviors, however, and our role, in helping the circle of people affected by each incident, can be significant without being intrusive or judgmental. Helping people to understand and to deal sensibly in these situations requires all the understanding, knowledge, and skill that we possess.

– 32 –

COUNSELING THE HIV/AIDS
PATIENT

NONPROFESSIONAL COUNSELORS, like almost all Americans, will inevitably enter relationships with persons stricken by HIV (human immunodeficiency virus) and its late manifestation, AIDS (acquired immunodeficiency syndrome). We may be consulted by individuals suffering directly from it, or, more likely, by those in their family or circle of friends affected indirectly by it. While as nonprofessional counselors we prudently work toward referring those touched by this illness to experts, especially to the remarkable teams of professionals found in most large hospitals, we still need an understanding of this haunting killer that, like a tornado, slashes a wide path of physical and emotional devastation across the human landscape.

Our best preparation to offer sensitive and compassionate help is an accurate understanding of the rumor- and superstition-shadowed illness itself. HIV is a human retrovirus first discovered in 1984 (although the illness had been diagnosed in the early 1980s) that can produce profound immune deficiency. Early in the disease's onset, this virus selectively invades certain human cells, especially "T-helper" lymphocytes and the central nervous system. Once the infection has occurred, however, the virus multiplies rapidly within the body, generating a significant response from the immune system as it attempts to rid the body of the virus. Within three to six weeks after the initial HIV infection, most individuals experience a flu-like syndrome. Many people interpret these symptoms as variants of the flu rather than as evidence of HIV infection. Others do not suffer the flu-like syndrome, remaining nonsymptomatic and, therefore, unaware of the virus's presence in their body.

Current knowledge suggests that eventually a *viral set-point* is reached that varies among individuals and represents a balance between viral reproduction and the immune response.[1] This set-point is also a flash point for, as it is reached, individuals enter a phase, perhaps

340

of many years, during which the body maintains a delicate balance between viral replication and the immune response. In the same interval, however, the HIV infection invades almost every organ system of the body. A change in the balance between the spread of the virus and the body's immune response is registered in the number of "T" lymphocyte cells. As they decrease in number, the more compromised the immune response becomes and the more advanced clinical diseases emerge. To forestall this development, the current treatments for HIV aim at reducing the viral load in the service of maintaining an effective immune response.

In most cases, sometimes only after many years, clinical diseases begin to emerge, signaling the failure of the immune system to stave off the invader illness. These states are often manifested by opportunistic infections such as pneumocystis carinii pneumonia, herpes simplex, fungal infections, tuberculosis, or such other devastating conditions as dementia or carcinoma. The diagnosis of AIDS is then assigned, indicating advanced immunosuppression (the failure of the immune response) and foreshadowing eventual death.

The Extent of the Problem

The Centers for Disease Control and Prevention (CDC) monitors the incidence, prevalence, morbidity, and mortality from HIV/AIDS in the United States (www.cdc.gov/nchstp/hiv_aids/dhap.htm). Approximately 650,000–900,000 persons in the United States are infected with HIV, about 0.3 percent of the population, or 1 in 300 Americans. Approximately 33 million people in the world are estimated to be living with HIV. In recent years, the number of those who die from AIDS in the United States has dropped dramatically, mostly as a result of the efficacy of treatments that slow the replication of the virus. The rate of new infections, however, remains approximately the same, 40,000 cases per year. To put the problem in perspective, the CDC reports that, as of 1999, 113,167 Americans were living with HIV infection, 299,944 were living with AIDS, while 430,441 deaths have been reported since the onset of the epidemic.[2]

The Counselor and HIV/AIDS

We need to understand the distinction between HIV and AIDS, not only because of the different challenges involved in responding to persons in these distinct categories, but also because of the serious social and legal complications associated with having the illness. When we are counseling these afflicted individuals, we should also develop a close working relationship with those treating them medically so that we may integrate our responses as best we can into the overall treatment protocol.

Our first challenge often arises through our relationships with individuals who are not known to be suffering from the illness but who engage in behaviors that put them at high risk for developing HIV. HIV is transmitted through body fluids. Those most likely to be the source of HIV are blood, semen, vaginal secretions, and breast milk. Although tears, saliva, and urine can conceivably be the source of HIV, such modes of transmission are highly unlikely. The behaviors that can promote HIV infection include unprotected sexual intercourse with an HIV-infected man or woman or the sharing of unsterilized injection equipment used in either medical or illegal circumstances.

In addition, HIV can be transmitted from an infected mother to her fetus during pregnancy, at the time of birth, or through breast feeding. We should, however, understand that men who have sex with men constitute the group most vulnerable to HIV infection. Although we know this, modifying human behavior is never easy, and, should we identify people in these high-risk circumstances, we should refer them to appropriate resources. Success is not automatically assured by making a referral; but many of the resource personnel who work with HIV patients are well equipped to respond to the diversity of their needs and to monitor their clinical status.

A harsh sidebar to the story of this illness is revealed when we find ourselves as counselors to marital partners or potential partners, one of whom is either infected with HIV or at high risk for the illness. This reality generates a range of feelings within us as well as within those who come for help. The many questions that arise may require consultation with a number of professional and community resources.

Another face of the problem is uncovered in the estimated 90 percent of persons infected with HIV who are unaware of it until AIDS develops.[3] In such circumstances, individuals with HIV may unknowingly live a normal life, in the course of which they may unwittingly infect their partner. This is obviously problematic for those persons who engage in high-risk sex behaviors. Either they or their partners may have serious but largely unexpressed fears, concerns, and ambivalence about their relationship, which is daily shadowed by the possibility of potential harm to one or both members of the relationship. As counselors, we may be totally unaware that such issues lie, partially submerged, at the deepest level of the couple's concerns. We must be objective and yet keenly attuned to them if we are to help them to give voice to their unsettling concerns.

We counselors may, in fact, be unaware of our own lack of ease in coming even within hailing distance of the subject of HIV in our work with people. We may well harbor countertransference feelings about the illness and how it is contracted and what we think it represents and so be ready to place blame on one party or another. We may be angry that the infected person may express an interest in engaging in sexual activity, for we may judge that its deprivation is not an unreasonable punishment for engaging in such risky behavior, as it seems clear to us that their lack of control or care is directly traced to the onset of the illness. But we are not judges, prosecuting attorneys, or agents of the avenging angels and must recall that, beneath all the troubles and seemingly self-defeating behaviors, we are dealing with human beings who have come for help.

We may know that some individuals engage in promiscuous behavior and fail to warn their partners of their HIV status. The possibilities for such complex and disturbing problems are endless, and we need to monitor our responses so that we do not go beyond our sphere of competence and sensibly and humanely refer such persons to the resource that may be able to help them more than we can.

Problems may also arise because many persons with known HIV live without overt symptoms for an average of ten years before AIDS develops.[4] They may feel well and want to live a "normal" life that includes sexual activity with their partner. Or they may wrongly assume that because they are faithful to their medication regimen that sexual activity no longer poses a risk for infection to the other party. Such issues may arise in what we think is everyday and otherwise quite ordinary counseling. We must be prepared to hear correctly, respond sensitively, and refer sensibly to medical personnel when this is appropriate.

To Test or Not to Test

HIV status can be clarified by antibody testing. We may encounter individuals who are concerned about their HIV status but who avoid testing either because they are afraid to know the results or because they do not want to deal with the reality of a positive test result. Other persons may worry incessantly about their status even though they continue sexual behaviors that may put them at high risk for the illness.

Learning of a positive HIV test may touch off a range of reactions for which these persons often feel unprepared. They are unexpectedly faced with moral decisions that must be made about the impact of their current behavior on others as well as about revealing to family, friends, and other associates previously private knowledge about their sexual identity, practices, or substance use. Nonetheless, their reactions to a diagnosis of HIV, much as with the diagnosis of any terminal condition, include human experiences of fear and anxiety to which we can respond directly and effectively. These afflicted persons immediately understand that the path suddenly lighted up before them leads into a dense forest of complex, demanding, expensive, and lengthy treatment. Still, it can stave off for a long period the development of full-blown AIDS. They may also grasp what may come with physical illnesses, such as racking fevers, an escalation of deadening fatigue, and the possibility of increasing social rejection and isolation as they grow weaker and their appearance changes. Many also face the stressful prospect of disclosing the nature of their illness to their parents or loved ones.

It is not unusual, therefore, for these individuals to express themselves in angry, desperate ways, as the massive weight of the sickness settles on them. We can, even as nonprofessional counselors, support them in these trials by our understanding and by identifying and buttressing their healthiest defenses. We can also offer them education on the subject in the rumor-filled universe of their suffering, referral to sources experienced in dealing with the problem, and provide the commonsense psychological benefits of just being with them when there is not much else that can be done.

As is apparent, HIV/AIDS is not an illness in which we can automatically employ the kind of responses that work in situations in which the basic problem is, for example, the identification and exploration of feelings. There is more to it than that and, while we can be helpfully supportive, we cannot supply the medical insight or assistance they may require. The potential for medical complications is real in these individuals and, as we have noted, can result not only in opportunistic infections, such as pneumonia, but also in central nervous system disturbances, such as dementia. Although offering emotional understanding may help, these suffering human beings cannot be managed as whole persons only by responses to the way they feel about themselves or their situation.

The Law and HIV

There are important legal issues related to HIV testing with which we should familiarize ourselves. Complicating the problem further is the reality of home collection tests that bypass contact with the usual publicly funded testing centers and medical resources. These pose particular problems because they are not usually associated with the pre- and post-testing counseling that many professionals cite as an important component of the overall care of the HIV-positive person.

There is a significant public health interest in the prevention and spread of HIV that has led to legislation in most states aimed to protect the confidentiality of HIV-positive individuals while simultaneously protecting the public's health. The APA Guideline summarizes the legal climate of HIV:

> Most U.S. states have legal requirements surrounding HIV testing that require written informed consent and a minimum amount of pre- and post-test counseling — both to those who test positive and those who test negative. Furthermore, many states are required to report positive HIV test results to public health agencies. Some states mandate that the report include the name of the individual who tested HIV positive. All states have mandatory name reporting when a patient is diagnosed with an AIDS-defining condition.[5]

The technical diagnosis and the responsibility to report this illness belong to medical professionals. The other counselors, in whose company we stand, such as members of the clergy, teachers, and concerned friends and colleagues, will, however, find themselves dealing with the emotional aura that throbs brightly and painfully around such issues. We need to be well informed about the issues of confidentiality in order to protect the HIV-affected individual as well as about the public's interest in preserving the health of the community. Confidentiality is often an issue because HIV individuals may feel well physically for many years, and they are gravely concerned that any revelation of their condition may aversely affect their contracting for insurance coverage or health benefits, or their job security.

It is generally accepted, however, that there are limitations to confidentiality, especially when others may be harmed by the actions of the HIV-positive person. It is also generally accepted that persons with HIV, especially those recently diagnosed, should inform their recent sexual partners and those with whom they have shared injection equipment about their HIV status and, therefore, about the risk of infection to which they have been exposed.

Back to Basics

As nonprofessional counselors, we must nevertheless deal with counter-transference feelings in these relationships. A study of health care professionals dealing with AIDS patients done in the late 1980s revealed patterns of unresolved reactions that may arise for nonprofessionals as well. Sixty-three percent of the professionals "were skeptical or did not believe assurances by experts that health care workers who observe safety guidelines are at minimal risk of contacting AIDS from patients.... Twenty-six percent of all respondents feared that they would become victims of AIDS if they continued their present work."[6] Yet the remarkably human correlate of these fears is that "97 percent expressed a firm commitment to caring for AIDS patients throughout their illness and the dying process." Although there is greater understanding of the illness than at the time of the survey, the emotional burden of dealing with individuals who harbor a fatal, infectious illness remains. These are often young persons who appear well and who engage in a variety of behaviors not consonant with good health. That we may harbor the same misgivings along with the desire to help them should not be surprising. We must acknowledge and monitor these feelings, as we would in any relationship, so that they do not interfere with the counseling process.

The importance of a team approach to the treatment of HIV patients cannot be underestimated, and sensible counselors continue to refrain from taking on the roles of trained professionals. The commonsense rule tells us to remain within the limits of our own background and training when dealing with HIV or any other major illness. Following home-field rules restricts us but allows us to stay in the game, offering the great help that comes from our just being human, just being ourselves.

Desperately sick people do want to talk, when they have the energy to do so, and they need listeners. The surrounding cluster of family and friends often want to talk as well, especially during the long, uniquely enervating hours of waiting in hallways and parlors that go with hospital visiting. This is obviously one of the principal areas in which we and other nonprofessional counselors can work effectively. Even here, however, we draw on our simple human capacity to understand the woes of others without making any attempt to explore their origins or, in any sense, to "treat" them by psychological means.

As we have strongly emphasized, we should work with other persons on their *conscious* level of functioning, avoiding unconscious material and disowning strategies that may, even without our advertence, break through the surface of the ill person's psyche. We are doing the best thing we can for others when we remain consistent in using this approach with those stricken by any manifestation of HIV and with the surrounding company of their relatives or friends. Commonsense helpers are never called upon to do *uncovering* or *reconstructive* therapy. There is hardly time for the well-trained to do this in a terminal illness, and in any case it would work against the reasonable goals of really helping individuals to manage their way through an illness that is already overwhelming.

On the conscious level, the main objective is, as has been noted, to champion those resources of personality, imagination, and spirituality that are found, to some degree, even in the most gravely ill of us. Pastoral counselors are well aware of the usefulness of a supportive exploration of the HIV person's core beliefs and meaning of life. This is especially true given the often negative attitude expressed even by some clergy ostensibly representing their religious affiliation. Even when such resources can be evoked only in a muted and minor key, they can be the decisive strengths by which human beings not only manage but transcend the ravages of mortal illness.

Wise nonprofessional counselors do not tamper with the defenses of the HIV patient. Whatever they may be — even if they include elements of rationalization or distortion at times — they ordinarily represent the best these individuals can do at the moment. We do not use confronting techniques with people who, battered by chronic disease, have enormous difficulty in just inhabiting their own personalities in any vital or resonant manner. Supporting conscious defenses of the HIV/AIDS patient, even when these do not seem ideal to us, is enormously beneficial. Most of us have a healthy sense of our own limitations, allowing us to draw on our own healthy reserves in responding to persons in distress. This wholesome using of our best selves, and not trying to do the work of the psychiatrist or clinical psychologist, is the hallmark of common sense that shows through in us at our best.

The intermingling of physical and emotional reaction and causation is highly complex, and we must take our cues from the specialists who have a more subtle and informed understanding of how these operate in each individual case. This is of particular importance in an illness in which, as noted, the infection of the central nervous system may give rise to symptoms that may seem totally emotional in nature but, in fact, are expressions of an extension of the illness.

Common Psychological Reactions to HIV

Perhaps one of the most challenging groups with whom we work is composed of individuals who have tested positively for HIV but who are currently symptom-free. These persons are faced with a painful and anxiety-provoking reality. They carry the HIV, but in their minds they do not know when or if they will be stricken with AIDS itself. The disease has been tracked only since 1981 and, every year, more of these persons do come down with the illness. Still, the medical evidence, while seeming to suggest a certain inevitability about AIDS following HIV-positive testing, has not proved this. It is clear, however, that the longer one is HIV positive, the more likely one is to develop AIDS.

The recent antiviral therapies have introduced new hope as well as new anxieties for these individuals. Most HIV-positive individuals have access to such therapy, but the treatment regimen is vigorous and demanding. If medication doses are missed, treatment effectiveness is reduced dramatically. Failure rates increase sharply with less than 95 percent adherence to the regimen, meaning that if more than one day's dose out of ten is missed, treatment is dramatically compromised.[7] New problems are also emerging as individuals who have been well controlled by medication for some time begin to experience resistance and a "breakthrough" of viral replication with evidence of escalating immune dysfunction. The always lurking specter of AIDS becomes a reality and a source of massive disappointment and considerable stress.

Such persons live, therefore, under a shadow and need the kind of understanding support that we nonprofessional counselors can provide successfully. Often, such individuals confide their anxiety about their condition first to a member of the clergy, a general practitioner, or a respected teacher or coach. These first-line counselors are in an excellent position to assist them psychologically and spiritually and to refer them for professional help when, in their judgment, the time has come for it.

Aware of the above cautions, we helpers will still recognize in HIV patients psychological reactions also observed in other patients with terminal illnesses. Perhaps the most common — and, it might be said the most human — is *denial*. When we are suddenly faced with a crushing piece of news, even the healthiest among us employs the mechanism of denial — it can't be, we say — if only to gain time and space in which to begin to regroup ourselves psychologically and admit the truth of the event. Just as we can expect and accept such a reaction in ourselves, so we should expect and accept it in patients who have been given a diagnosis of an HIV-related illness.

We cannot survive without denial, so the helpful counselor will allow individuals the use of this necessary and essential defense so they can look away from the cold shadow of threat long enough to ward off panic. Denial also allows individuals to express an insurrectionary reaction, a rejection, often bitter, of the medical verdict that so suddenly deprives them of their independence and their future. The ability to differentiate this reaction from a dangerous variant of it is indispensable to us as counselors. At times, some individuals employ denial not to reorganize interiorly and to adjust to the illness but to mask its reality and their own hostile and destructive impulses. Such massive denial is always primitive and dangerous.

These persons may, for example, recklessly engage in sexual activity with many partners without regard to the consequences for themselves, others, or, eventually, the public in general. They seem bent on revenge, on infecting the world that has deprived them of their own health and is soon to take their lives. Such patients reject any therapeutic assistance. Their rebuffs to those who wish to help them are not difficult to identify even by nonprofessionals.

Such reckless sexual activity is not limited to the recently infected person. In many areas of the country, especially in gay communities, it is not uncommon for individuals to lose their lover and many close friends, while still young, to AIDS. These survivors go through a bereavement process that may be complicated by the fact they themselves are HIV positive. There are reports as well that the partners of those who have died of AIDS may engage in high-risk sexual behavior and suicidal thoughts as a feature of their bereavement.[8] In addition, in recent years, in some communities, a behavior called "bug chasing" has emerged. This occurs when HIV-negative persons actively seek to become infected with the AIDS virus. Some advertise on the Internet to obtain infected sexual partners, sometimes offering lethal specifications. Some observers suggest that this seemingly romantic pursuit of the illness is a manifestation of bereavement.

When such potentially destructive impacted embitteredness is encountered, we should not try to temper the anger or to cajole such persons into more rational behavior. We should, however, encourage these persons to seek consultation with the appropriate HIV/AIDS and psychiatric resources. One well-known expert in the HIV/AIDS field, for example, in commenting on the denial that leads to such behaviors, described taking his patients with him on his rounds in the AIDS ward

of his hospital so that they may see the seriousness and the outcome of
this fatal illness.

We must also be alert to the occurrence of suicidal thoughts among
this group of individuals. Early studies of HIV-positive male patients reported a high rate of completed suicides, 66 percent greater than among
the general population.[9] In more recent years, with the introduction
of antiviral therapies, a better understanding of the course of the illness, and the greater number of organized resources for responding to
the psychosocial aspects of the illness, suicide rates are only modestly
elevated and comparable to those in other medically ill populations.[10]

Lastly, we must be aware of the frequency of other mental disorders
that may be present in this population. Substance abuse disorders,
major depressive disorder, and adjustment disorders are common
among HIV-positive individuals. Exacerbations of previously diagnosed
psychiatric illnesses may also be anticipated among certain individuals at some time during their chronic illness. These developments, of
course, prompt us to make appropriate referrals.

Additional Reactions

As counselors to persons with HIV, we may be the first ones to notice the small signals of profound neurological changes under way in
them. For example, when individuals, most strikingly among the young,
describe periods of forgetfulness or report or give evidence of difficulties in concentrating or a slowing of their thinking processes, these
signs are often discounted as understandable incidental psychological
reactions to the massive burden of the illness. These mild symptoms,
however, should alert us to the possibility that these reactions fore-
shadow deeper central nervous system disorders such as *HIV associated
dementia* (HAD). Delirium, with features such as insomnia and restlessness, is more frequently encountered in hospitalized HIV patients.
Nonetheless, if we pick up signs of these problems, we should refer the
persons for a thorough medical examination.

While we remain alert to these possibilities, we usually encounter the
truly psychological complications of this illness group. These include
demoralization and *despondency*, desolating feelings that lay waste to
the psyche. In turn, the damaged spirit of the HIV-infected person, evidenced by a negative self-image, affects the entire world of the afflicted
individual, straining social and work relationships until they are no
longer manageable. This further isolates such persons, compounding
their already severely compromised level of psychological functioning.

Initially, these persons may react with denial, anxiety, anger, and sadness, which may be marked by efforts to strike some bargain in regard to health and sickness. Later, they may express a mixture of other emotions, including guilt, anger, and self-pity. This period, marked by a sharp decrease in self-worth, may find these persons estranged from family and friends. A return to drug use and dangerous sex practices may occur at this time.

These persons may also gradually begin to accept themselves as persons compromised by the nature of the illness. They may begin to appreciate the unique character and quality of each passing day. As the complications of AIDS emerge, anticipation of and preparation for death may take a prominent place in their consciousness. This may be marked by a fear of complete dependency on friends or strangers. If we want to be of real assistance to AIDS patients at this time, we must respect their unique journey and understand that they will die, not as any textbook or expert suggests, but as best they can. This pilgrimage through a final illness is made, like the rest of life, humanly, imperfectly, and not without nobility.

Chronically afflicted HIV patients experience an illness that, bad enough in itself, also carries the seeds of social disapproval and ostracism. We nonprofessional counselors can respond in this very area, for what we can bring, in place of medical expertise, is our gift of compassionate understanding. Nothing deepens the isolation of the chronically ill more than the pressure, sometimes generated even by well-meaning friends and relatives, for them to be "normal" again. This distinctive void can be entered, if not filled, by us if we can grasp at least some of the feelings of such demoralized patients.

– 33 –

SUICIDE: WEIGHING THE RISK

WHETHER WE ARE CONSULTANTS or counselors working directly with suicidal patients, the question of making a judgment on the possibility of an actual suicide is central in any helper's concerns. This razor's-edge condition, in which the stroke may be smooth or savage, in the next moment or not at all, exacts a high price of stress from everybody working with such persons.

Can we inform ourselves more fully and come to better judgments about the likelihood of suicide by those seeking our help? We remember, of course, that these persons are not operating in a vacuum but are cooperating with us, or someone else, in seeking help for themselves. Those at risk generally give clear signs not only of their distress but also of their suicidal intentions. Do guidelines exist to assist us in making better judgments and, therefore, better therapeutic responses to those prone to suicide?

Most experts believe that *determination* to commit suicide is the clearest signal that we can receive and that three facets may be identified in every suicide: *specificity of the means, lethality of the means*, and *availability of the means*. When these conditions are realized we may conclude that the likelihood of suicide is very high.

Some years ago the Los Angeles Suicide Prevention Center developed a *lethality scale* to assess suicide potential. The lethality scale provides a checklist of factors that sharpen our perception and our capacity for prudential judgment by recapitulating much of what is known about persons who actually complete suicide. It includes the following:

1. *Age and sex:* The potential is greater for men than women and for persons over sixty-five.
2. *Symptoms:* The potential is greater if the person is depressed, cannot sleep, feels hopeless, or is alcoholic.
3. *Stress:* The potential is greater if the person is under severe stress.
4. *Acute versus chronic aspects:* The potential is greater if there is a sudden onset of specific symptoms.

352

5. *Suicidal plan:* The potential is greater in proportion to the plan's lethality, organization, and detail.

6. *Resources:* The potential is greater if the person has no family or friends.

7. *Prior suicidal behavior:* The potential is quicker if the person has a history of suicidal attempts.

8. *Medical status:* The potential is greater when there is chronic, debilitating illness.

9. *Communication:* The potential is greater if persons lack outlets or have been socially rejected.

10. *Reaction of significant others:* The potential is greater if others punish or reject the person.

Additional information regarding the evaluation of suicide risk is noted in Table I on the following page. In addition, the Public Health Service's Centers for Disease Control and Prevention has developed a Web site to help individuals, family, and friends, as well as communities recognize the signs of potential suicidal behavior and to take an active role in the prevention of suicide (www.cdc.gov/safeusa/suicide.htm). The site includes a list of readily available resources as well as the telephone number of the national suicide hotline (800-784-2433).

A Richer Context

More recent work focused on children and adolescents enriches the context of our understanding. "The overwhelming proportion of adolescents who commit suicide (over 90 percent) suffered from an associated psychiatric disorder at the time of their death. Over half had suffered from a psychiatric disorder for at least two years."[1]

This exacting study and review of the literature further notes that adolescents who try suicide differ from those who only think about it in having "more severe or enduring hopelessness, isolation, suicidal ideation, and reluctance to discuss suicidal thoughts."[2] It is thought that about 2 million adolescents attempt to kill themselves every year and about 700,000 of them receive some treatment afterward. While the teens who attempt suicide are more likely than those who only think about it to experience associated psychopathology, such as a mood disorder, they often make the attempts during a relatively brief adjustment reaction. It has also been found that gay, lesbian, and bisexual youth "are at increased risk for suicide attempts, often having multiple risk

Table I
The Evaluation of Suicide Risk

	Low Risk	High Risk
Sex	Female	Male
Age	Midyears	Adolescence; old age
Marital Status	Married	Single, divorced, alone
Psychiatric conditions	Character disorders; situational disturbances	Depression; alcoholism; schizophrenia
Setting	Rural areas	Urban areas
Level of religious activity	Churchgoer	Nonchurchgoer
Geographic location		
United States	Mid-Atlantic region	Mountainous Western
Other countries	Italy, Netherlands, Spain	Romania, Austria, Switzerland, Scandinavia, Japan, German-speaking

Source: J. M. Stevenson, in *The American Psychiatric Press Textbook of Psychiatry,* ed. J. A. Talbott, R. E. Hales, S. C. Yudofsky (Washington, D.C.: American Psychiatric Press, 1988), 1023.

factors (i.e., depression, prior suicide attempts, substance abuse, sexual victimization, family conflict, and ostracism at school)."[3]

One of the recommendations of the American Academy of Child and Adolescent Psychiatry is especially relevant to those of us who counsel as part of another calling: "Even the skilled clinician can find it difficult to differentiate between benign and ominous suicidal behavior." While many will never make a repeat attempt, others "who make only a mild 'gesture' may eventually commit suicide." We pay close attention to the next observation: "The term 'gesture'...to denote a nonlethal, self-destructive action that is deemed a cry for help or a manipulation without serious intent, is therefore misleading, because it minimizes the potential risk for future suicidal behavior."[4]

The American Foundation for Suicide Prevention provides a checklist for assessing child or adolescent suicide attempts in an emergency room or crisis center (Table II). This might well be used in our own settings in certain circumstances.

Nothing substitutes for prudence on our part in estimating the relative probability of a suicide attempt. We may assemble all the information and fail to integrate it properly because of some factor, perhaps

Table II
Child and Adolescent Attempters
at Greatest Risk for Suicide

Suicidal History
- still thinking of suicide
- have made a prior suicide attempt

Demographics
- male
- living alone

Mental State
- depressed, manic, hypomanic, severely anxious, or have a mixture of these states
- substance abuse alone or in association with a mood disorder
- irritable, agitated, threatening violence to others, delusional, or hallucinating

Do not discharge such a patient without a psychiatric evaluation.

Source: American Foundation for Suicide Prevention (1999).

within ourselves, that we have not weighed sufficiently. It is also possible that, on the basis of only some of this information, we could make an inappropriate judgment about the danger of suicide and the way to handle it. As counselors, we cannot allow the dramatic aspects of suicide potential to hurry us or to force us into misinterpreting information that is central to making a decision and planning a response to suicidal persons. The process of making a recommendation in this area is intrinsically stressful and we must respect and be patient with ourselves as we formulate our decision. As nonprofessionals, we should always make every effort to have an evaluation made by a person with expert training and experience.

Things to Avoid

Our first challenge as we deal with the difficult and delicate question of potential suicides is *overreacting*. To monitor ourselves in this regard makes common and clinical good sense as part of our role is to be a stabilizing influence as well as a mediator during a time of confusion. Avoiding panic, we gain greater freedom to sort out the situation and to establish priorities about what actions are to be taken as calmly as possible.

In a popular culture that worships "coolness" in its heroes, we must not overplay our seemingly casual mastery of the situation by *under-reacting*. We stand apart from the culture's preference for the studied indifference of "No problem," as this outlook cannot belong to alert and sensitive counselors. We may, however, observe it in others who are dealing with suicidal persons, and we may be called on to help people develop a realistic sense of the danger rather than allow them to repress it under a false mantle of calm. The difficulty is compounded because suicidal persons who are met with the reaction of overcontrol on our part may feel that they have simply not gotten through and that their only resort is to take more drastic measures. A sense of coolness, in other words, may push suicidal persons close to the brink of self-destruction precisely because it projects the kind of emotional unresponsiveness that is most painful to them.

It is also important for all those working with potential suicides to avoid doing things that we know won't help. For reasons difficult to understand, doing exactly the wrong thing is precisely what some people, even when they know better, do in the face of a crisis. Whether they do these inappropriate things in order to avoid the challenge, or whether they simply do not understand its true dimensions, the effects are the same. It does little good, for example, to try to cajole deeply depressed persons out of suicide. Neither is it sensible to try to distract them by talking about other things. It is equally vain to try to get them interested in some other activity. The threat of suicide must be dealt with, the message must be taken seriously, and inappropriately trying to be "cheerful" can be very harmful.

Closely related to the overcheerful attitude is that emphasizing the negative aspect of the suicidal person's characteristically ambivalent feelings. Arguing against suicide on the basis of its undesirable consequences ("This won't make things better," "Don't you know your church says that this is a serious sin?") may only reinforce the glum outlook of these persons and convince them that nobody truly understands their situation. A costly but easily made mistake is to hear and respond to only one part of a two-pronged statement, saying, for example, "You feel pretty desperate" when a person is saying, "Sometimes I feel I can make it and at other times I feel I can't."

Things to Do

Obviously we should be keyed to the total communication of suicide-prone persons and not hesitate to place the positive aspect of their statements in contrast with the negative: "You say you also have lots of things you like about life"; "There are reasons for, as well as against, staying alive; can you tell me something more about these?" This gives suicidal persons an opportunity to investigate their positive resources at a time when these are vitally important to them.

We need not hesitate to verbalize the possibility of suicide when we are dealing with depressed persons we consider to be suicide risks — even before they mention suicide themselves. This does not put a new idea into their minds but may, in fact, diminish the symbolic power of actual suicide by showing that the thought can be accepted and understood by others. Even if these persons deny thoughts of suicide, the inquiry, if made sensitively, can be helpful in challenging them to see themselves in sharper focus. Fear of mentioning suicide only interferes with counseling effectiveness with those clients who otherwise manifest the qualities associated with this problem. It is what they want to talk about but many cannot find the right words to express themselves without our help.

Because suicide can give rise to many difficult and uneasy feelings in us, we may well and wisely explore our own feelings before we commit ourselves to suicide work. Some of us may judge that we have neither the temperament nor the patience to work closely with someone who is contemplating suicide. It is always better to recognize our limitations with various kinds of persons needing help and to be prepared to refer them for assistance from others. We can never hide what we are really feeling, and we should never soldier on under the transparent cover of repression or denial. A good therapeutic relationship depends on its containing no false notes and may be the strongest bond that depressed or hopeless persons can forge through us with life itself.

Most of us understand and attempt to relate to suicidal clients as persons, balancing our concerns about their behavior with a genuine understanding and acceptance of them as individuals. This builds a relationship that may sustain such persons through the more critical phases of contemplated suicide. The kind of relationship we have is of critical importance not only for supplying strength to others but as the foundation for making timely and sensible referrals to others more experienced and skilled in dealing with suicide risks. Referring people to other professionals is not a "failure" on our part but usually a mature decision to assist others as much as we can while remaining within the bounds of supportive helping. Suicide risks profit from both the referral and from the sense of strong support we give them through our relationship with them.

The question of sensible referral arises regularly in our work as nonprofessionals. In no other situation is it more important for us to avoid panic while we draw on the resources of the community on behalf of these troubled persons. Again, being able to make a good referral at the right time is greatly enhanced by our already having developed good relationships with local physicians, psychiatrists, psychologists, social workers, and others who work every day with such emergencies.

Attempted Suicide

Sometimes our only contact with individuals comes after they have made a suicidal attempt. The general principles regarding sensitivity and understanding apply here, of course, as do the criteria cited earlier. It may also be helpful, however, to review what could be expected in counseling after there has been an actual effort at self-destruction. Some clinicians suggest that many patients experience a reactivation of the suicidal drive after an unsuccessful attempt. Successful management of this recurrence of the urges to self-destruction becomes, then, the most crucial aspect of continuing counseling. Schneidman and Farberow's well-known book on suicide suggests the following three phases of therapy in this situation: the *acute*, the *convalescent*, and the *recovery*.[5]

During the *acute* phase counseling may be directed toward adequate protection for the individuals coupled with relief from their experience of anxiety and hopelessness, as well as some effort to improve their relationships with family and friends. Hospitalization is often necessary because its environment lessens tension as well as the possibility of solitary isolation. We must be aware of the feelings these persons have about having attempted suicide. It is not appropriate to probe for these but it is essential to listen carefully as, even in bits and pieces, they come out. Their talking about what is important to them in the wake of their attempt provides an opportunity to catch the pattern that is discernible even in seemingly rambling and disordered reflections. It may look like debris but the truth of the matter will be there.

The *convalescent* phase for those who attempted suicide begins when they are ready to return to their former environment. During this period, as well as that of recovery, persons are, of course, vulnerable to the reactivation of the suicidal urge. They are back in the situation that originally precipitated the difficulty. During this time we remain carefully attuned to them and, perhaps more importantly, to the members of their families who may also need counseling. Family and friends are particularly helpful as those who made suicide attempts return to old scenes and familiar circumstances. Successful counseling with the persons close to those who have tried to kill themselves may help to restructure their attitudes in such a way as to relieve much of the stress that precipitated the original incident.

This may be an ideal time for family members to make important decisions about shifts in lifestyle, jobs, and other circumstances whose modification will help suicidal persons. Such discussions should be carried out, however, in the presence of those who made attempts rather than behind their backs. The convalescent period is also a rich opportunity to acquaint family members with the kinds of psychological responses and the types of resources that are available should an acute crisis arise again.

The convalescent phase allows us to help family members read the messages that they may have missed before. For example, it has been found that agitated persons who finally make a firm decision about suicide may then experience a period of tranquility before carrying out this decision. This calm is frequently misinterpreted, however, as a sign of their improvement rather than the consequence of a firm decision for self-destruction. During this calm before the final storm, family members may react with relief and look away with less concern, thus rendering the environment more vulnerable for them as well as the suicidal persons. They are least prepared just as the tide of determination crests in those intending to end their lives.

Prevention

We step back during the *recovery* stage to allow the persons, stronger now at the broken places as Hemingway put it, to return to normal life. They may limp a little, but they no longer need crutches. They must make this reentry on their own, gaining confidence with each successful day. While family, friends, and counselors may be on *stand-by,* they do not do the work of reentry for these people.

It is hard for some of us to accept that we are not God and that, although we do our best, we may neither prevent nor postpone suicide or any other unhappiness in life. There is brutal wisdom in the psychological axiom that persons who want to commit suicide will eventually be able to do so no matter how we may try to prevent it. We, therefore, need a healthy approach to our own imperfections and limitations or we will never help anybody. We cannot make impossible demands on ourselves or take responsibility for all the things that other persons do. We say yes to life for those with whom we work, but we must be prepared for the fact that some of them will still say no. It is being human, rather than superhuman, with them that allows us to help them at all. This capacity to be realistic in the dangerously unpredictable circumstances connected with suicide frees up our humanity — our sensitivity and responsiveness to troubled individuals and their families when they are most in need of them.

A great deal of information is now readily available from a number of resources.[6] We who are on the frontlines without extensive specialized training must hone our sensitivity to the risk factors for both suicide and suicidal behavior and be prepared to make the timely referrals previously discussed. Little discussed but highly relevant is our role in advising members of the media to restrain coverage of individual suicides. We may be in an ideal position to limit the publicity that, at times, may inflame the imagination of others who have been thinking about suicide.

It has been learned that school programs for teenagers that stress the role of mental illness and that encourage self-disclosure to their friends or others do not reduce either suicidal behavior or increase seeking help for it. The idea, often presented, that suicide is a normal response to stress is not helpful and may, in fact, be harmful. So, too, talks and lectures about suicide to young people should be discouraged because they may set off ideas of suicide in disturbed adolescents who have never entertained them before. The American Academy of Child and Adolescent Psychiatry suggests, instead, systematic screening programs for adolescents between the ages of fifteen and nineteen and referral for evaluation of those teens who exhibit a high risk profile for suicide.[7]

– 34 –

DEATH IN OUR CULTURE

W ORKING WITH DYING PERSONS is well recognized as a significant source of stress whether we do this only occasionally or as a regular part of our work. It involves us in relationships, each with a slightly different tone, with those who are dying, their families, their physicians, and a wide range of friends and others who, like lawyers and funeral directors, play a part, some as supporting characters, others in bit parts, as death takes over the stage.

Over the last generation and more, death has been spoken of and examined, for various reasons, by social scientists, economists, and even marketing specialists who, as the millennium passed, detected an interest by members of the Boomer Generation in managing their own deaths as they have, as they believe, so many other aspects of their lives. Classes on death, its course and its rituals, have been introduced into educational systems, and symposia and workshops are devoted to it regularly. Death and violence as a steady diet in our entertainment also focuses on mysteries and conflicts in the depths of the human personality that we have hardly begun to investigate.

Americans try to solve with characteristically pragmatic verve many of the problems associated with death that have been described in the growing body of literature about the subject. In the same way that Americans have approached sex, they now approach death, with a determined effort to understand it and, in a way, master it through everything from meditation to improved techniques and therapies, as well as New Age and traditional spiritual approaches. The record, in both cases, is mixed.

Death, for example, has been considered by some of its students as a problem of management, something that causes difficulties on a social as well as a personal level and is therefore amenable to improved methods of dealing with it. Thus a "trajectory of death" can be plotted on a graph and marked, as a business curve is, at its most significant or crucial points. But death, much like sex, still eludes those experts who think that measurement, organization, and economic analysis are effective or even efficient ways to deal with it.

A complex mystery attends both death and sex that we may sense and not trap with such pragmatic approaches. The person is at the center of both death and sex, and neither experience can be understood unless the person is kept in very close focus. The more death or sex is treated as something that can be abstracted from human personality, the more estranging is the effect of such investigations. Death and sex, if they are anything, are profound human experiences.

Death and sex are interwoven subjects worthy of meditation more than measurement. We are just beginning to deal with both of them, and there is far more we do not know than what we do know about them. There is, for example, a strong erotic component associated with death. Although it is seldom discussed, it is nonetheless part of our cultural pull toward death and is thus a psychological vector with which we should have some acquaintance. We realize, of course, that sex and death have been around a long time, longer even than taxes. Indeed, what we see as a recent interest in death is not in itself anything new. It is rather a revival of an interest that was very strong centuries ago when persons were quite concerned about dying, and many books and reflections were published on the subject of how to die well. The famous *Ars Morendi*, or *Art of Dying*, was first circulated in ancient Rome. The realization that not everything about either sex or death is absolutely new helps us to keep our own perspective steady and to trust the wisdom of our best and healthiest human instincts in dealing with both subjects. Human sensitivity and common sense are still our best equipment in dealing with people whose lives are touched or put into conflict by these subjects.

The first relevant counseling principle, therefore, is based on the most fundamental perceptions of effective counseling: just as we respond and relate to sexual persons and not to sexual problems, so we also relate to dying persons and not to the problems associated with dying.

The Too Easy Management of Death

We need to season ourselves with wisdom in order to evaluate all the whispers, rumors, and speculation about death that resonate throughout our culture. Death can be treated as superficially as sex by those who, never having thought deeply about it themselves, depend totally on the writings or observations of others — on the politically correct position of the moment, for example — to form their opinions.

Good things can always be done badly and it is common sense to recognize that not everybody has the sensitivity or depth that is required to deal with the human issues associated with dying. Not so many years ago, shallow courses on death in some schools featured the students' planning the teachers' funerals — teachers as substitute deceased, that is. Now that death itself has intruded on school life these *faux* death courses seem cruel and immature prophecies. The Angel of Death slays the narcissism, the fascination with self at the center of such courses. Film director Martin Scorsese was responding to something deeper, grimmer, more human in his film *Bringing Out the Dead* about the emergency workers who do just that in New York City.

Such serious attempts to meditate on the attraction and repulsion of death mock the faddish elements of working with the dying. Death has become a temporary but intense interest for some. This has also happened to many otherwise serious activities, such as prayer and prison reform. One must be alert for the self-centered people who deal with death as an "in" subject; they add to the stress for everybody else who is seriously concerned. As critic Benjamin DeMott expressed it several years ago.

> The most dismal trend is death mongering. Elisabeth Kübler-Ross's *On Death and Dying* was an exceptional work but bad apples are strewn among its offspring. Writers who use — quite seriously — phrases like "low level grief" ... books that nag the reader ceaselessly with the question, "Have you done your death work?" ... chapters describing hospital conversations between a dying man and a base form of life called "Death Researcher." Friend, "the death researcher" seems ever on the point of saying, friend, are you aware you're dying? Lady, don't you see you're through?[1]

We may reduce some stress by keeping such people as far away from patients, family, and health care workers as possible. No area demands unadorned humility more than that of working with the dying. Such work can be very stressful but it is also very deepening. The anxiety of uneasiness associated with working with dying patients is not all that there is to the experience.

Through entering into a person's efforts to come to terms with death, we can purchase life ourselves. We are changed for the better by such experiences rather than just depressed by them. That is why fundamental counseling attitudes, stripped of pretense or a need to impress, are essential. Only what is real works, and what is unreal always makes the stress surrounding death more intense.

A Fundamental Question

We need to trust in the best in ourselves, drawing on our insights and a level of sensitivity in us that is present even though seldom tapped to respond to the symbolic and displaced expressions of feeling that are common during the process of bereavement. There is a numinous quality to some practical questions that have significant implications for the healthy resolution of the grieving process itself. We are involved in these by being involved with the dying and their families.

Should the dying person be told of the situation? This has been argued for years but most evidence suggests that there are good reasons to be truthful with dying patients. They have a remarkable capacity for sensing their own condition, and they also demonstrate a great willingness to talk about their illness and the prospect of death with those who listen to them without giving them bland reassurances of one kind or another. Human persons possess enormous potential for facing difficult situations. We underestimate people and what they can achieve spiritually and psychologically — humanly, if you will — if we tiptoe around this brimming reservoir, leaving it untapped.

It is important for us to work this decision through with the spouses of sick persons. This is, after all, a part of their life experience, an aspect of their relationship a couple should be able to deal with together. Several years ago, playwright Robert Anderson wrote of his own sadness that he had not told his wife of her imminent death. Looking back, he felt that he missed sharing something with her that was very important. He had not been truthful with her and, in his quest to save her from pain, he now realized that he had ruled out something richer and more important — their facing together the challenge of death.

If this can be done — and we are often the key mediators in this area — these people not only share something profound, but they may be able to anticipate some of the problems of grief and even deal constructively with some of the practical questions that will arise at the time of death. We cannot and should not force people to discuss these things, but if we are understanding and accepting, we may be able to journey with people into feelings they need to explore about themselves and each other in view of the prospect of death.

Obviously, we must avoid being morbid or dragging in such subjects unnecessarily. The key that they may pick up glints of its presence in our listening, in that sensitive readiness to hear what the others are ready to talk about, and helping them to put this into words. This is at the heart of all counseling. Done gently and correctly, it not only diminishes everybody's stress but deepens the experience for everybody, including us.

Children Wiser Than We

As nonprofessional counselors we quickly learn in working with children that they can hear the unfiltered unconscious speaking directly. This is true in children suffering life-threatening illnesses who may ask, or speak very directly, about death. From the age of ten, the concerns of children can be strikingly adult. They understand death's universality and irreversibility and often ask questions that go right to the heart of their concerns.

These are questions, in a sense, for all of us, and it is not unwise to allow the children to give their own answers. We are better as witnesses than as guides to their remarkable capacity to identify their own fears and wonders and to deal with them. Helping them give a name to their chief fear is a service of enormous benefit. Sometimes, giving them simple information, such as the reason in some treatments for hair loss, enables the children to deal effectively with this otherwise extremely upsetting development.

Doing the human thing spontaneously — as with hugging and touching — is what is called for in these circumstances. Our best support may be given to the parents whose best instincts should be encouraged. It is also sensible, for the sake of other siblings, to keep family life as normal as possible. This is the one of the unique contributions of the Ronald McDonald homes that provide a "home away from home" for families of seriously ill children who are receiving treatment at nearby hospitals. In 2001, there are 206 such homes in 19 countries that are supported largely by local businesses and volunteers. It is better for these children to have days that are lived in an average healthy way, neither ignoring, spoiling, or making them intensely conscious of how different they are.

In the same way, counselors, although not often the ones to make such decisions, should realize that most persons want to find out the truth about their own condition. Many of them sense it on a less than conscious level anyway. We should not conspire to disguise or dissemble when sensitive honesty, which differs greatly from blunt and crude bad-news breaking, can be helpful to the gravely ill individual.

Palliative Care

It has been asked of palliative care whether it is end-of-life care or a

> broad and integrated physical, psychological, social, and spiritual
> care for patients with serious diseases that may be life threaten-
> ing. Most of the authors ... believe they should care for patients
> with advanced, incurable illnesses when aggressive treatment of
> pain and other symptoms may be needed. Several believe that
> palliation and care are not mutually exclusive and that palliative
> care should be practiced during all stages of serious illness, even
> while aggressive curative treatment continues. The exact point at
> which a patient's palliative care should begin remains a subject of
> discussion.[2]

We should be acquainted with and have some contact with the palliative care procedures and with one of its pioneer providers. The Hospice
Movement, founded by Dame Cicely Saunders in 1967, and the programs of this widely expanded initiative aim at allowing people and
their families to receive care that addresses not only physical illness but
also the other major areas of suffering associated with the end of life —
the physical, social, emotional, and spiritual needs of people. Care is
administered at home or in special environments usually by teams of
professionals skilled in providing such care. This is in contrast to the
isolating death experience that occurred in hospitals and nursing homes
in former times. This approach to death may be more important than
ever in a culture in which publicity about the easy termination of life has
mounted in recent years. Perhaps we are dangerously ignoring the fact
that for many sick people life remains desirable and that they should
be given every assistance to live it fully to the end.

Some Fundamental Attitudes

Among the human principles that we should remember are these:

Dying people want to talk rather than be talked to. We are not
experts on what dying people should hear. However, in struggling to
share with us those things they want to express while the light still
lasts, they are experts on revealing to us what is important to them.
And dying people will tell us what is significant to them if we give
them a chance. We must restrain ourselves, then, especially from using
the cliches with which we sometimes fill the uneasy space of a death
room. Before dealing with dying persons, we must come to terms with

---

Fundamental Attitudes for Counselors of the Dying

- Dying people want to talk rather than be talked to.
- Presence plus the vulnerability that goes with it is essential.
- Dying persons speak symbolically.
- Dying persons are subjects, not objects.
- Counselors deal with more than the dying process.

---

whether we actually trust that common people do have some sense of what is important for them to deal with as they approach life's end. We should be ready to listen to them.

Presence plus the vulnerability that goes with it are essential. There is no way of donning an antiseptic disguise in a relationship with a dying person. We have to be in the relationship, not on the side of it nor at the kind of safe psychological distance we can be so skilled at introducing. The best thing we have is who we are, just as we are. Who we are may not be perfect but is eminently suitable for such work. Our flawed humanity is what enables us to be counselors at all. Who we are needs to be revealed rather than hidden, exposed rather than protected, given outright to dying persons.

Dying persons speak symbolically. We must hone our sensitivity in order to catch their meanings as completely as possible. The symbols may be in gestures or in stories, or they may be tied up in the kinds of memories or reflections they choose to share with us. If we are aware that dying persons are not merely passing time but trying to spend it in getting across important messages, we will be more skilled at reading their communication. There is always a message waiting to be translated. Our principal function with the dying may be to give words to what they can only outline in symbols.

Dying persons are subjects, not objects. It is very easy to slip into treating the dying as objects, as somehow diminished and incapable of speaking for and about themselves. Sometimes other people, with the best of intentions, begin to make decisions about what is best for these dying persons. They may not be aware of how their taking over responsibility takes away from the sense of personhood that remains so important to the dying. People sometimes forget how much seriously ill people can hear and understand. Objects can be managed, but subjects must be listened to and allowed a voice in the matters connected with their treatment, their visitors, and all other matters relevant to them.

Counselors deal with more than thè dying person. Frequently those who counsel relate not only to the sick person but also to physicians, hospital staff, members of the family, and other friends. This is taxing but significant and important work because these parties also experience tangled emotions, and they can function much better if someone can respond to their often overlooked needs. Sensitivity that radiates out to all those connected with the dying person may put a strain on us but we manage it better by anticipating and planning our time so that we can respond when we find these demands being made on us.

What We Know

The research of some time ago, such as the work of Dr. Elisabeth Kübler-Ross, has taught us things about the experiences of dying patients that help enormously as we prepare to do our work more humanely and more effectively. An acquaintanceship with the literature on death and bereavement provides us with a base of reinforcing knowledge that improves our work while reducing its stress. Sherwin Nuland's *How We Die: Reflections on Life's Final Chapter* and Web-based resources such as the material provided by the Program on the Medical Encounter and Palliative Care at the Veterans Administration Hospital in Durham, North Carolina, are illustrative of information available for counselors working with dying persons.[3] Some of the things we have learned about dying include the following:

People want to live until they die. One of the functions of counseling is to help dying persons to do precisely this, to invest as much of themselves as possible in experiencing life fully even as they spend down their last weeks or days. They do not want to be treated as "dying." Many people who work closely with terminally ill patients observe how they begin to perceive the dying person as different from healthy persons. It resembles the way we occasionally talk louder to foreigners than we do to each other. If we find ourselves treating patients more as dying than as living, we should examine ourselves and find out why. It may be our way of denying the relevance of death to ourselves.

Dying persons pass through stages that, in various ways, have been repeatedly observed. They cannot skip any of the stages of coming to terms with death, and if we understand this progression, we increase our sensitivity to the real experience of dying persons. We can keep at-

---

What We Know
about Counseling the Dying

- People want to live until they die.
- Dying people pass through stages.

---

tuned to dying persons better if we sense the psychological map they are following. It also aids in interpreting the numerous symbolic gestures and other communications during these phases.

Although other experts have also witnessed stages in dying and conceptualize and even number them differently, Dr. Elisabeth Kübler-Ross is credited with first describing the stages of death and dying. She first mentions *denial* with some effort to carry on as usual. Patients may go from physician to physician trying to disprove the diagnosis, and they may avoid telling their families, just as they avoid telling themselves the truth about the situation.

The next stage is that of *anger* that the dying persons should be those chosen — the "why me?" phase. This is obviously a time for us not to take their anger personally.

Then follows what Dr. Ross describes as *bargaining* — individuals try to gain some stay of execution from God with promises of better behavior and other reforms. There are real efforts made at striking this kind of bargain before these persons can accept the fact that death is really coming.

The succeeding stage includes *depression*, in which dying persons mourn past losses and then begin to withdraw their interest from the world around them. The circle of those in whom interest is shown becomes smaller as dying persons experience preparatory grief.

The final stage is one of *acceptance*, in which persons meet death peacefully. Dr. Ross's book contains extensive descriptions and examples of these phases of the dying process.[4] As noted, others, including Avery Weisman, have observed that the stages vary considerably in number from individual to individual. There is no point in trying to make dying people go through the stages as we conceive them. They must be allowed to go in their own way, at their own rate. We can only accompany them.

The family members also pass through these same stages once they realize that someone is seriously ill. They do not pass through them at the same time as the dying person, and we must allow them to proceed as they will. We cannot hurry them or try artificially to have family members and dying persons pass through the same process at the same time. Nothing human works that way.

Our awareness that these stages are inevitable enables us to respond in a better informed manner to the grieving family as well as to the dying person. It allows us to omit the platitudes that hardly touch people when they are trying to work through the difficult realization of the death of someone close to them. It is a time for availability and presence rather than for words from the outside, no matter how supportive these may sound.

The Counselor

There are several things we may do to enlarge our capacity to respond to dying persons. First of all, we can acquaint ourselves with the growing sensible literature on the subject of dying. We may also attend seminars or take advantage of other educational experiences that help us perceive the issues associated with dying in a clearer and more humane fashion. There is no substitute for our actively trying to acquire a greater understanding of the human experience of death.

We may also deal seriously with our own self-knowledge. We need some reverence for ourselves, for our strong and weak points, and a genuine acceptance of our limitations. We expand ourselves if we can be part of a reflective team of persons who, as in a hospital or hospice program, work with dying patients. Working in a team allows us to handle our own emotions more clearly and to sort out our counter-transference feelings without being unnecessarily hard on ourselves for being human. A group setting also allows discussion of the serious questions that arise in relationship to any particular individual or family, providing human support for the difficult work of counseling the dying.

None of us should have a steady diet of working alone with the dying. We must respect our own needs and provide ourselves with the recreation or change in routine that keeps us fresh and able to enter more deeply and effectively into the lives of dying persons. Overworked and overwrought counselors don't see things clearly. If we become totally absorbed in death, we multiply stress and reduce our effectiveness. Working with the dying does not demand killing ourselves.

This work demands the simplest human responses we can give. These are the best. They are, in fact, all that we ever have to give. They are all that people seem really to be looking for: somebody to be there, somebody who can accept and understand their experience and sense their meaning. Dying people want other persons there who will accompany them on this last uncertain pilgrimage. The greatest thing we can do is to make this journey without being lost on it, to be able to stay with the dying persons even when we do not quite understand everything they are trying to say, to look steadily into the face of death rather than to turn away.

– 35 –

SUFFERING OUR LOSSES

L OSS, AS MAJESTIC AS DEATH or as mundane as taxes, is the sure
thing in every life, the experience that is as common as April rain
in almost every day, in some form or other, in our lives. The glories
of being human — our capacity for love, relationship, authorship, and
memory — are measured in the impact of their loss on us. We may
push the possibility of great losses to the far edge of our consciousness,
but we rehearse them in small ways all the time. There is a loss in
the response that does not come to our call, our e-mail, or the card
we sent to someone, the importance of whose answer does not strike
us until it does not come. That almost bloodless nick that depression
then makes in our spirits foreshadows the gash to the bone made by
later and larger losses. In a hundred ways — in misunderstandings,
rejections, postponements, autumn's coming, and defeats so personal
that we hardly admit them to ourselves — we sample the bitterness that
sweeps through us humans when we lose what defines us, our spouse,
our children, our health.

Nonprofessional counselors become experts at the blues, that American musical vetting of the everyday heartbreak of lost loves and lives.
The blues exist only because there is so much loss and so much need to
let the soul sing its own way about it. If, among many other callings,
we are pastors, doctors, nurses, police, emergency workers, or funeral
directors, we are triage officers for those who have their lives torn apart
by major losses. As such, we must understand the nature and effects of
loss and how to respond, within our skills and limitations, to help the
stricken cope with the stress of their worlds made desolate by loss.

Bereavement

We begin by acquainting ourselves with *bereavement,* the term that
allows us to distinguish the blues of profound human loss from those
of depression. "Bereavement" is a powerful word for our reactions to
the overwhelming way death attacks us in the loss of a spouse, a child,

or another loved one. Crack the word open and taste the bitter flavor of its origins. Its root *reup* means "to snatch," or, in Flemish, "to rip," and its aggressive energy pulsates in to plunder, to rob, to break, to usurp, to rupture, to interrupt, to bankrupt, and to corrupt.

Manifesting the genes of another rough ancestor, bereavement *rubs* us raw, assaulting us as a rapist might, bearing away by violence the kingdom of our souls. Bereavement *rips* us, leaving us, as the dictionary definition puts it, *desolate*. It is in itself depressing, but it is not itself depression in its clinical meaning

Distinguishing Grief and Depression

Psychiatry offers us an important distinction between *normal grief* and *depression*. *Grief* has been defined as "a complex constellation of psychological, physiological, and behavioral responses that accompany the human awareness of an irrevocable loss.... Bereavement is the term applied to loss specifically through death."[1] We experience depression during the siege of bereavement, but this must be differentiated, as noted, from clinical depression as defined in the literature.

Grieving is a process that we will shortly examine in greater depth but, for the moment, let us identify it as a *normal* experience. It is the blues that healthy people sing when they suffer a major loss. Major depression is never healthy and it is not a normal reaction to loss, even though elements of it may be observed during the bereavement period. Normal grief and depression are sometimes confounded, however, because of the overlap of their symptoms. Depression may be present before and may be made worse by the loss. Clinical depression may also be set off by the impact of a major loss.

Grief brings a harvest of reactions, ranging from somatic complaints, such as loss of sleep and appetite, to a broad range of physical complaints, often triggered by the pangs of grief that usually become less intense with time. We know that many factors, such as the closeness of the lost person, the health, maturity, resiliency, and spiritual resources of the bereaved individual, and even the manner of the lost person's death, may influence the course of this process. Most counselors have witnessed and perhaps offered support of one kind or another during the weeks or months of acute grieving. In addition to allowing the self-limiting process of normal grief to work itself out without our interfering with it by, for example, trying to organize it according to somebody's model of the "stages" of grief, we should be able to identify and respond to the signs of major depressive illness.

The *DSM-IV-TR* excludes "most persons whose depressions occur within the first 2 months of the death of a loved one from being diagnosed with a major depression...[using instead] the term bereavement."[2] If, however, the depression has begun before the loss is suffered, continues beyond two months, is thought abnormal by the one experiencing it, and is marked by such symptoms as "functional impairment, morbid preoccupation with worthlessness, suicidal ideation, psychotic symptoms, or psychomotor retardation," the distinction of bereavement yields to that of depression.[3]

Because of our main callings, we may be close witnesses to the course of the grieving of many individuals. If we observe the occurrence and persistence of such symptoms, we should entertain the notion that serious depression is present. While in all aspects of mourning, our support on the conscious level is important, it is critical, once we feel that serious depression is present, to consult and make a referral for the treatment of that syndrome according to the principles discussed in chapter 23.

Normal Grieving

Persons suffering bereavement turn first, of course, to us, the non-professional counselors always arrayed around significant life events. To stand with and respond to those who mourn can be a major source of pressure for us. The more we understand about the reactions of normal grief, as distinguished from major depression, and about our own emotional responses in attempting to help, the better will we manage ourselves and the more effective will we be in supporting others.

We may have complex feelings about grief that we are not eager to admit or to explore. Grieving is a subject somewhat like religion has become and as sex once was; powerful societal taboos make the search of one's own self and the integration of counseling principles in a practical response to the problems of others very difficult.

Here we experience, as Joyce put it, "all that is grave and constant" in our existence. In "The Person Confronting Death," Ned H. Cassem quotes psychiatrist George Engel's observation that, because of its enormous impact on our functioning, grief should be considered a disease.[4] But he also notes Rochlin's point that the "powerful dynamic produced by our losses is indispensable to emotional maturation. Mourning can lead to some of man's highest achievements as well as result in many pathological states when delayed or unresolved."[5] In short, we are, at this intersection of life and death, touching the essential mysteries of life.

That is why counselors who have an integrated philosophy or theology of their own — perhaps we should say, those who have preserved a sense of the tragic nature of life — bring that wisdom and spirituality to these telling encounters. Weisman reminds us that love and grief reflect each other in their intensity, thereby enhancing each other.[6] We cannot, therefore, approach this profound subject with automatic or easy prescriptions. Nor can we attempt to eliminate the edge of suffering that is necessarily an aspect of something so thoroughly human. It is especially important for pastoral counselors to understand their role, not as deathbed proselytizers but as those capable of bearing witness through their presence and understanding to the human majesty of mourning and grief. It has been noted that persons with well-internalized religious beliefs — those for whom faith is an integrating force rather than a grudging external custom — are better able to handle the challenges of these solemn yet common experiences. They are also less likely to suffer the complication of major depression.[7]

Grief provides a focus through which to examine what we are like as counselors in action. In its clear and unforgiving light we must face and come to terms with the interplay between our feelings and those of others. Grief also challenges us to read sensitively the symbolic expressions of those who mourn, for, although these may seem irrational, they contain significant messages. The classic studies of Murray Parkes are among those that are helpful in this regard.[8]

Fleshing Out Grief

Knowledge about these states comes to life vividly in our everyday work. Learning how to define and classify is very helpful, but things and people look different from textbook descriptions when we see them up close. We often remark on how some person looks different in real life than in photographs. Suffering looks different in life from the way it appears on the printed page. We get a better feeling for loss when we realize that grief is a process much like growth. Its determinants are complex. It responds not to abstractions but to our dynamic involvement in the person's working it through. Grief demands a special kind of growth because it confronts people with basic questions about their existential experience of themselves and others. What have they really done? What has really been done to them? Working through means that they must enter these relationships as miners do the earth, to find their living roots in time and place.

Parkes suggests four phases in the process of grief: *numbness, pin-*

ing, depression, and *recovery.* There is no way to predict, collapse or shorten these phases any more than one can control anything else connected with human growth. The grieving process, with the bereavement at death, is precipitated by loss, of course, but even when we speak of death, the definition of exactly what is lost is not easy. That is why it is truly said that a novel might emerge from even the most ordinary seeming life.

The person's own perception of the loss can be very complex, and there are many secondary factors that may be related to the initial experience of loss. Moreover, there may be related experiences that must also be appreciated by the sensitive helper. These include *stigma* and *deprivation.*

Although it may not be discussed very much, and although we may like to think we have advanced beyond it, some operational *stigma* remains attached to the person who loses a spouse. This is especially true for widows who, in some societies, are killed precisely because they no longer fit in. Western society prides itself on having moved away from such savagery, but its treatment of widows is still frequently quite harsh. Widows experience difficulty in finding a place socially and find it difficult to reincorporate themselves into the community. Some have suggested that the Western world treats mourning as though it were a weakness rather than a functional and necessary human experience. The remarkable work of Phillip Aries in studying burial customs over the centuries reveals our change in consciousness and attitude.[9] While a single death was once considered a loss that was suffered and mourned by an entire local community, it has now, especially in big cities, become something to be obscured, discreetly hidden from our common awareness, often to the detriment of those most intimately associated with it. The helper who does not appreciate this situation may badly misunderstand and perhaps, quite inadvertently, increase the suffering person's sense of being different and isolated from other people.

The problem for many women is intensified because social traditions have made them find so much of their identity as helpmate to a husband who was the possessor of the more significant identity role in society. If he is a teacher, a doctor, or a lawyer, these strong functional identities continue for him even if his wife dies. The woman who has, perhaps quite contentedly, surrendered the possibility of another identity in order to be a wife and mother finds herself extremely vulnerable when the children are grown and her husband dies. This is part of a general cultural concern of feminism that has battled for women's having enduring identities in their own right that not only offer them self-realization but a strong individual identity after the loss of their husbands through divorce or death.

Parkes distinguishes *deprivation* from *loss* by underscoring this as the result of the absence of the person who previously provided so many of life's necessities. The change in the social and financial status of a bereaved person gives them another dimension of vulnerability during an already difficult time. They are deprived not only of identity but of its strengthening effects. Those who understand and work effectively with the bereaved must appreciate the stress that is generated by this deprivation.

Many Faces / Many Phases

Losses other than death can also generate grief and mourning. People can lose a person who is very important to them in other ways as well. The loss is just as real, and the experience of working out its consequences is similar in its dynamics to that occasioned by death. An engaged person, for example, may suddenly lose the one he or she hoped to marry through a change of heart, a new love interest, or a sudden and unexplained rejection of the relationship. Loss can also occur through divorce or unexpected and prolonged separation. We can lose many things, such as our reputations, our innocence, our ability to create, a love relationship in which marriage was never possible. In all these situations counselors will be helpful — and will feel more confident — if they assist the person *to identify the loss that has occurred.* Grieving cannot take place — it cannot even begin — unless the loss is identified.

Whatever the loss, the first stage in the process of grief is frequently marked by a seeming absence of feelings, a sudden freezing of the emotions so that they seem locked away tightly within the bereaved person. This follows from the stressful impact of loss through death even when the death is something that has been expected for a long time. We humans have a way of selectively perceiving even the worst of news and of keeping our hopes up even when we have been told as explicitly as possible that the end is near. We all know that people often deny that a death has occurred. The news is just too much to absorb, and it must, for a while at least, be rejected while the person prepares really to hear and deal with it.

People may act in a panicky way under the first impact of this major stress. They have, after all, lost something that has defined them in relationship to themselves and to the rest of the world. Now they are exposed to that world and the alarm that they feel is much like that which people experience in times of some great natural calamity or sudden disaster.

During this stage, the bereaved individual suffers the most characteristic dimension of grief, the deep pangs of longing and anxiety that are associated with the loss that has been suffered. The bereaved person experiences an extremely painful wish for the restoration of the person who is gone.

The Search

It has been suggested that this painful pining is the way in which the bereaved person subjectively experiences something that is found during all periods of mourning — the search for the lost person. The grieving person knows that it is irrational to try to restore the dead person, but this urge is deep and frequently unconscious. This is why it is so painful and why it reveals itself in such indirect ways. Afflicted persons will be restless and almost obsessed with thoughts of the deceased person. They will be ready to see him or her on the street or in crowds, much as we are prepared to find a person we are expecting in an airport or bus terminal. Grieving persons lose interest in their appearance and in other things that were formerly quite important to them. They may direct their attention to those places and occasions associated with the lost person.

It is important for the counselor to understand the symbolic nature of this aspect of mourning. *There is a search going on*, even though it is one that cannot be admitted into consciousness. This behavior is not aimless; it is clearly directed toward finding the lost person. Because neither the mourners nor those around them can accept the search as a valid quest, it is often dismissed as aimless activity. Any effort to interfere or "be reasonable" with the person may frustrate one of the aspects of mourning that must be carried out. We cannot keep people from engaging symbolically in this search. As sensitive counselors, we can understand and allow this search to proceed, sensing in it an attempt to resolve the experience of loss.

In a later study, Parkes identified three patterns of abnormal or blocked grieving.[10] These are (1) unanticipated grief, (2) conflicted grief, (3) chronic grief. In the first, the loss is difficult to deal with because of its unexpected nature, while in the second, the problem arises because of ambivalent feelings in the relationship to the deceased. In chronic grief, the overly dependent quality of the relationship with the dead person interferes with the resolution of grief through the mourning process. These obstacles, as Cassem notes, work directly against "the three tasks of recovery: intellectual acceptance of the loss, emotional acceptance of the loss, and the new development of an independent identity."[11]

The Work of Grief

The search for the lost person may be an aspect of what Sigmund Freud termed "grief work." By this he suggests that mourning, far from being an inappropriate or mysterious reaction, is humanly appropriate and necessary if bereaved persons are to acknowledge, understand, and accept the losses they must face in life. There must be a mourning period if the person is to incorporate the loss and emerge once more into life with a successfully modified sense of identity. This is ditch-digging hard work, filled with pain; and those who stand with the grieving person may be so close that they cannot detect its meaningful and functional pattern. Counselors can facilitate it but they can also frustrate it by inappropriate interventions. Because it is so profoundly human, grief cannot be foreshortened but must proceed at its own pace and in its own time.

The work of grief involves individuals in looking back at the relationship before it ended or was interrupted by death. They explore and examine what took place over the years. Mourners may review the last illness or the last day of that illness and, with pain-filled wonder, question whether they did everything within their power for the dead person. Were they attentive enough and did they give the medicine properly? They also try to understand the significance of the relationship, to place it into perspective, and to see it in the light of their philosophy or religious faith.

Although it is not easy, there is no substitute for letting people face all of these difficulties directly. They deal with a drastic change in their identity; to exchange one's self-concept as a wife for one as a widow cannot be done in an instant. This demands major reorganization of the whole perceptual system. The person literally has to develop a new way of looking at the self. Again, this takes time and the freedom to be weak or depressed in the process. Grieving individuals may be preoccupied with the lost person and with the many memories of the past as they experience a deep loneliness. At the heart of all the range of feelings during grief, the bereaved is trying to come to terms with a major life experience. The concept of work — of needing slowly and thoroughly to process the many aspects of mourning — is appropriate for this struggle to come through on the other side of grief. We wisely recognize that it is inappropriate, ineffective, and often harmful to urge people, as if by an act of their will, to pass through the stages of mourning as they are described in some books. These stages may collapse on each other, assert their own sequence, or repeat themselves. The unconscious works as it will and we counselors must respect it.

Recovery follows on a period that may be marked with more experience of depressive symptoms, accompanied by occasional feelings of despair as the individual labors psychologically to overcome the loss and to develop a renewed identity. The pain lessens, according to researchers, as the person concludes the search that has marked the early stages of grief. The griever does this by finding the lost person again, not as a physical presence, but through sensing that person or that person's spirit as somehow very near.

Those who grieve resolve their relationship in a symbolic way, and this is often marked by statements about a new awareness of how the departed ones help or guide them in their lives and work. It is not surprising that the prolonged emotional search should end with a sense of discovery, making sense of the loss in a way that restores the other person in some degree. This is a time when religious support is important because it offers spiritual strength when individuals, out of whatever beliefs and faith they have, piece together a sense of life again. They must be allowed to do this themselves as we refrain from offering bromides or rational explanations that only obscure the symbolic nature of the process involved. Nor should we argue about the sense of restoration or psychological equilibrium that is achieved.

Things to Remember

We have sketched the process of grief as a living experience to provide a background of understanding across which we may formulate our ways of relating and responding to those who have suffered losses. Obviously we also have our own emotional reactions. Grief offers an interplay of transference and countertransference feelings.

The work of grief may be delayed or complicated precisely because people who want to help do not understand the importance of letting people work through the various phases of their mourning. It is not helpful to try to modify or in any way to deter individuals from carrying out the work of grief that only they can perform. We may inadvertently do this if we are unwilling to explore with the person the very feelings that must surface during this time of search and self-appraisal. We cannot permit our own inner stress reactions — whether of uneasiness, impatience, or revulsion — to dominate and possibly interfere with the process of mourning.

Counselors who ill-advisedly challenge other people's defenses will not be able to assist grieving people. Mourners need all of their defenses, especially at the earlier stages of grief, when they are emotionally unprepared to accept the death or to talk in utterly realistic terms about it. For people to be rational and undefended at a time of loss is unusual and cannot be forced on anyone. In mourning, we recognize the functional nature of defense mechanisms, especially in the way they permit individuals to buy time within which to readjust their perceptions of themselves and of the world in which they live. We must let the person deny or engage in other defensive behavior during the experience of grief.

In brief, if we face and deal with grief regularly, we need a good understanding of its dynamic nature and purposeful course. This removes the sense of stress that arises when we feel we are dealing totally with the unknown or the unpredictable. It also enables us to see individual expressions of grief in a psychologically significant context, to hear in them their inner meaning, and to see connections that would otherwise be obscure. When we can see the grieving experience as a whole we can also deal better with our own reactions.

Through a deepened appreciation of the dynamic character and function of mourning, we can lead others to a better understanding of the experience of grief. We thereby assist other members of the family, parish, or community to respond constructively to bereaved persons. A better grasp of the meaning of grief also frees counselors to enter into the sorrow of others with less fear that they will themselves be lost in the process. As a steadier presence, we give grieving persons increased freedom to mourn in their presence. By our very attitude, in other words, we can remove some of the stigma or sense of societal judgment that keeps people from the work of mourning they must inevitably carry out.

Side Effects

Stress is the ordinary weather of work with the bereaved. We never help relieve the pressure in others without feeling it rise within ourselves. We labor along with mourners as they do their grief work. Not the least of our stress is a function of the intense concentration we must give to interpreting and responding accurately to the extensive symbolic activity involved in the process. Good-heartedness, goodwill, and good instincts serve us well but so, too, does some anticipation of, and preparation for, accompanying others in their grief without losing ourselves in it. This is where we experience and must monitor what we have learned about the powerful invisible interplay of emotions that we term transference and countertransference reactions.

We must be ready for expressions of anger that are common during certain phases of the mourning process. The bereaved need to blame somebody for what has happened, for this calamity that has suddenly taken away their loved ones and left them seemingly helpless in the face of a complex world. The widow, for example, may be angry at the husband who has, as she experiences it, abandoned her, or at the supposedly loving God who seems to have treated her unfairly. Both widows and widowers may blame the doctors who attended their loved ones. Doctors are the most readily available targets for displaced anger that really has nothing to do with them but everything to do with the life history of the mourner. Our role is not to correct the anger but to allow them to get it out into the fresh air in which it dissipates and is no longer strongly displaced onto innocent bystanders.

It is common for people to experience ambivalent feelings toward others, even those closest to them, at one time or another in life. When death takes a loved one, they may feel quite guilty about these feelings and may try, in some way or other, to make up for what they judge as personal failings in the way they felt toward lost persons while they were alive. We may not like to hear it but we must anticipate this guilt and not try to avoid or to explain it away as though it were of no consequence. Part of the work of grief is to deal with this mixture of feelings, even when they seem shamefully inadmissible. This is profoundly human and we cannot wish it out of their lives, or our own, by any form of reassurance or distraction.

Also human is the highly charged emotional atmosphere that surrounds many bereavements, especially when people begin to exchange blame for various things connected with the dead person's life or last illness. Families sometimes become estranged or break up over the recriminations made at this stressful period. Whatever our principal calling is, we may function as sensible and sensitive intermediaries to help people to identify and express their feelings without destroying their relationships with each other. Family quarreling, in generally vain attempts to prove who is right and who is wrong, only adds to the burdens of the bereaved. We may shy away from such exchanges or find ourselves favoring one side over the other. We must manage our own feelings well if we are to intervene in an area to which a professional may have no access and in which we can do some of our most constructive and lasting counseling.

Are We Comforters or Controllers?

Our presence, as pastors, doctors, or lawyers, at these moments of privileged access to the pain of bereavement offers us important opportunities of which we should take disciplined advantage. We are there because we fill some other role, but we are also capable of providing understanding and counsel that will greatly help the bereaved. Are there limits to the ways in which we may involve ourselves?

Some experienced persons may feel that they are helping if, in some sense, they "take over" some of the difficult tasks or make some of the necessary decisions. How much should we manage and what, for example, should we tell people who have suffered a loss? We understand that it is not always a kindness to shield people from the death of those they love. Experience and research tell us that human beings may fulfill an important human function by viewing the body, even if in poor condition, of the deceased. Widows of military personnel killed in Vietnam report that viewing their remains on their return years after their deaths is an important element in completing their work of mourning. It is often very helpful if they can do something for the deceased, as, for example, when parents are allowed to help prepare their child's body for the funeral. We do not want to impose decisions that rule out what we think are difficult but which the bereaved experience as profound and helpful experiences.

We may help others greatly, as Cassem suggests, by asking them gently about the last days or hours of the dead person. We may also be able to supply useful information, such as the facts about Sudden Infant Death Syndrome, or to refer persons to support groups for survivors of such tragic events. Such special groupings, now multiplied in many churches and community organizations, have proved very helpful in assisting the bereaved to face and resolve the challenges of grief and mourning.

Many nonprofessional counselors already understand that there should be no effort, out of misplaced concern, to protect spouses or parents from participating in making the funeral preparations. This is an initial and important way for bereaved persons to deal with the work of grief. Grieving persons have a right and a need to do this.

Sometimes we do not want to involve them, not because we want to spare them but because we want to spare ourselves from their sadness at this poignant time. We may be tested by being with them in these moments, but there is no better place for us to be as we support them, even if we do or say little, as they carry out these obligations.

Most nonprofessional counselors also understand the importance of allowing the rituals of mourning to be carried out. Grieving persons need rituals the way they need light and air. It is psychologically important for persons to have a public and approved way in which to express their complex and deep feelings of grief. The rituals are, of course, for the living far more than they are for the dead, and they should not be oversimplified nor so blandly diluted that they fail to achieve their expressed purpose.

Bereaved persons need time and perspective in which to begin to absorb and deal with the impact of the loss. Common sense tells us that they need close friends, not to be doing everything for them but to be with them, or to be available during the weeks when they struggle to accept the varied feelings they have during the time of bereavement. It is not helpful to leave bereaved people alone, nor is it helpful to distract them with so many visitors and activities that they cannot get on with the grief that only they can and must experience. Nonprofessional counselors are often the ones who can continue to listen to them and to stand with them as they search themselves at this difficult time. Many hospice programs have bereavement counselors available after the death of a loved one. Counselors who are members of the clergy should not hesitate to keep contact after the funeral is over. Brief but regular visits are helpful.

Being There / Not Being There

We should not knowingly interrupt or interfere with their mourning by probing or reassuring people in a shallow way during this dynamic period. It is far more stressful for us to enter into mourning without knowing what we are doing than to have some sense of the process and the feelings associated with it. When we don't know what to say — or when we back off from entering into the mourning — we make ourselves and the grieving person uncomfortable. To substitute mannered concern for a genuine response to grief is to increase the burden for all parties concerned.

This is illustrated by the visits of Henry Adams to novelist Henry James after the death of a close friend of the latter. To a third person Adams wrote, "Even Henry James, with whom I lunch Sundays, is only a figure in the same old wall-paper, and really pretends to belong to a world which is as extinct as Queen Elizabeth. I enjoy it." Meanwhile, James wrote to a friend, "I like [Adams] but suffer from his monotonous, disappointed pessimism.... So what can I do for him? However, when the poor dear is in London, I don't fail to do what I can." Biographer Leon Edel adds: "Each thus seems to have believed he was comforting the other. In reality they made each other uncomfortable."[12]

We don't arrange things, then, but we must allow them to happen. It is not important to insist that the bereaved express themselves in some way we learned at a workshop. They will select the appropriate manner — the way right for them — in which to express themselves. These emotions must, however, be heard and accepted by someone else. That is the most important thing we can do for the grieving. When we can hear them despite the confusion of their grief they feel more understood, and this reduces their sense of isolation from the rest of the world.

Obviously this is not a time for pity or cliches, nor for the kind of stiff upper lip that prevents us from expressing our own feelings. Sometimes an expression of our own feelings of affection or concern can be healthy and helpful. Here again we do not plan to do this or to cast ourselves in a role more important than the one we have. If we do the right human thing, we will not do a wrong thing.

Our main work — to help other persons to find their own words for the meaning of their loss and to express a sense of a change in their own identity — is indispensable in assisting bereaved individuals to work through their grief. Our task, as Shakespeare put it, is to "give sorrow words." That requires a modest sense of our presence and a highly disciplined sense of when and how to speak.

Many counselors underestimate how much they may achieve by intervening in a measured way at the right moment in mourning. This may be related to a general cultural uneasiness about the subject of death and loss and a well-established tendency to deny both. As counselors we not only respond to the bereaved directly but also to the culture's general need for sensitive and sensible reeducation in this regard. As we are better informed and more confident in implementing our counseling skills in the work of grief, we reduce the stress of the experience for everybody, including ourselves. When we know what we can and cannot do, when we can read the symbols of mourning accurately, we transform a once mostly bewildering burden into a gift for offering real help to others.

EMERGENCIES:
BEING A STEADY PRESENCE

F OR MANY OF US, alarm bells ring regularly in the night. Whatever the actual severity of the situation, emergencies are perceived as serious by the persons directly involved in them. You are the one who comes immediately to their minds. You, they think, *you* will know just what to do.

Whatever our primary professional identification, those of us called upon for counsel during emergencies have ourselves as our first clients. We cannot enter an emergency situation, from which calm has fled and everything may be spinning out of control, unless we first have control of ourselves and our own reactions. Self-possession is indispensable if we are to be poised and ready to assume such command as may be necessary. It is therapeutic for everyone if we are a *steady presence* in unsteady circumstances. Whether we are physicians, pastors, school principals, or respected neighbors, we must understand two things: what *we* can do effectively and realistically and what the *others* involved in the situation can do as well.

One of our first tasks is to sort out the roles of those enmeshed in the crisis situation, reading them, their skills and their emotional states, to enlist them in the responses they are capable of making. This timely reorganization of the people clustered at the scene immediately changes the nature of the emergency, lessening its tension and freeing the involved people to use their own strengths — their own capacities to adapt — to improve things. This is not getting people out of our way, sending them off to boil water while a baby is being born. Such triage-like decisions are based on an appreciation of how persons function constructively with each other in an emergency whose initial confusion and fragmentation have been, in a real sense, healed by our integrating its scattered elements.

Bringing order reduces the anxiety that, as in all stressful encounters, can so easily paralyze or lessen the constructive potential of persons standing at the center or the edges of an emergency. Persons who remain calm and maintain self-control in a disaster become its natural leaders and can save many lives. The whole notion of a triage officer, one designated to make crucial decisions in *emergencies,* derives from this understanding of human reactions. Our ability to master ourselves and to telegraph confidence to others in an emergency calms the tempest, grounding the electric anxiety that crackles in the air, thereby decreasing the intensity of the emergency itself.

Life as a Crisis

Many of us nod in agreement at Lewis Mumford's observation that the human condition is "always desperate." Each day presents a fresh bounty of crises, some great, more small, but, whatever their dimension, bearing the same genetic code. Things and people break down all the time and, simply put, our task is to get them up and running again. Responding to crises or emergencies is, by its nature, short-term work. Crises are usually brief, limited by their nature, and they demand care that matches their structure. We do not enter emergencies to dig into the participants and rebuild their personalities. We do what, as nonprofessionals, we do best — offer them support so they can rally their own strengths to work their way through the crisis.

Some persons respond to a crisis and, failing to understand themselves or the character of crises, make things worse by extravagant and inappropriately emotional interventions. We must be wary of the crisis-needy, those persons, akin to do-gooders, who revel in the atmosphere of an emergency. As a rule of thumb, we should turn down the help of persons who need the crisis more than the crisis needs them. We need calm, self-possessed helpers who do not get a high on the vapors that drift off every emergency. Life may be a series of crises but it is not a feast of crises.

Crisis Styles

Emergencies may arise from within the *psychic structure* of individuals, as when they experience a breakdown in their psychological functioning. They may arise from their *physical structure,* when body systems fail, as in heart attacks or strokes. Crises may be *interpersonal,* as in marriages or between family members. We may also think about crises in other helpful ways.

Edwin Schneidman considers them in reference to life stages.[1] When the emergency is specific to some period, such as adolescence or old age, it is considered *intratemporal.* When it occurs at some juncture between

life stages, it is classified as *intertemporal*. As Schneidman sagely observes, in a remark that we can all apply to somebody we know, "Many
people can be adolescents quite successfully, but they have difficulty becoming adults." A crisis may indeed take place when a person cannot
give up a life stage, along with its fashions and activities, in order to
pass on to the next stage.

Many crises occur outside any discernible time frame. This kind of
crisis, seemingly untethered to time or incident, confronts us with the
mystery of our existence and the limitations on our being able to ana-
lyze and explain everything. Such crises, Schneidman suggests, explain
the otherwise "unaccountable suicides" that occur regularly. What is
the slender strand that might lead us back to the reason for this crisis at
this moment? We may not have the time to pursue that in our response
to support persons through the intense phase of the crisis.

While such classifications do not resolve crises in themselves, they
give us a way of thinking about them that can be very helpful in maintaining our objectivity, enough distance to be truly helpful, and a better
developed and less blurred picture of the situation with which we are
dealing.

As we respond to an emergency situation, we may ask *why* this event
has taken place *now,* that is, at this particular point in the person's
life. Even a provisional commonsense answer (They didn't want more
responsibility, they didn't want to get married, they are afraid of what
a physical exam may reveal, etc.) assists us in responding sensibly.

Understanding what is termed the "precipitating event" governs an
intervention that is ordered, as Schneidman says, to "undo the effects of
the precipitants." Identifying the precipitating stress follows the burned
powder trail back from the explosion to that place where the match
was struck and touched to it. There we find the circumstances that
unbalanced the person and gave rise to the symptoms now displayed.
Whether this window opens directly on psychological conflicts or on
the physiological level at which a physical symptom or illness stands
in for the conflict, we witness a symbolic revelation of the personality
structure of the individuals involved. Such knowledge allows us to help
these persons to use their own resources to adapt to the stress after we
have relieved the impact of the incident itself.

History's Lessons

The field of social work was associated with the first development
of crisis theory and technique. The acknowledged pioneer was Erich

Lindemann, who worked with the survivors of a disastrous 1942 fire at the Coconut Grove, a Boston night club. Along with Gerald Caplan and others, he developed fundamental principles with which we should be acquainted.[2]

First of all, crisis situations are episodic in the lives of people, families, groups, communities, and nations. They are ordinarily initiated by a blow from the outside or from internal pressures that can no longer be sustained. These may result in one catastrophic event or in a series of mishaps whose effect is cumulative.

Second, the basic human balance is disturbed and individuals are thereby rendered vulnerable. They go through a series of responses in an effort to restore their equilibrium. If these do not work, their anxiety builds up and they must seek new ways to regain their lost balance.

Third, if there is no resolution and the tension builds to a peak, then a *precipitating factor* may touch off the crisis so that, in an instant, so to speak, balance collapses and disorganization takes place. This is the state of *active crisis*.

Fourth, people may perceive the events under various rubrics: (1) threats to basic needs and independence; (2) a loss of self-identity or some ability; or (3) a challenge to survival, development, or mastery.

If the event is perceived as a loss, individuals will experience depression, deprivation, or mourning. If it is experienced as a threat, they will experience increasing anxiety. If it is seen as a challenge, we may observe a moderate increase in anxiety along with incipient hope and expectation.

Fifth, recall that the crisis situation is not essentially a sickness or a pathological experience. It is a realistic struggle in the true circumstances of the lives of affected persons. The emergency may revive conflicts that have been resolved or partially resolved, giving rise to inappropriate or exaggerated responses. Our task is (1) to resolve the *present* difficulty; (2) rework the *previous* struggle; (3) dissolve the *linkage* between the two.

We can usually follow the stages of response to a crisis, plot them imaginatively, and identify those points at which they may falter or stall. Careful observation allows us to understand why this is taking place and what is preventing the person from continuing the resolution of the process, from doing, as they say, their "crisis work."

We can be reasonably confident of the time limit built into active crisis states. With understandable variations between the first blow and the final resolution, the actual state of disequilibrium is limited by time and the outer limit is usually from four to six weeks. During the resolution of the crisis, people are typically ready to accept help. That is because their defenses are lowered and their previous methods of coping are not functioning well. Working with them at this time can have very beneficial results.

We must also remember an ironic final point. When people have gotten themselves together and are about to reenter life, they may learn new and better ways to cope with future crises. However, if they receive no help, they may learn maladaptive solutions or patterns that will not serve them well should future crises arise.

Knowing Ourselves

We prepare for emergencies every time we learn more about ourselves and our emotional reactions to stress, crises, or other equivalents of emergency. We cannot afford to address our vulnerabilities and to index our strengths only against the surprises that can be visited upon us when we are called into crisis situations. We wisely use the psychological device of *anticipation* to imagine or review our reactions to the contingencies of various stressful situations. *Anticipation* is a high order healthy defense, not just romantic Walter Mitty–like daydreaming through which we study our feelings when severe demands are made on us, as they are in emergencies.

Exploring the possibilities of our emotional behavior in an emergency informs us about our own stress-tolerance — I'm good at this, I need to monitor that — allowing us to manage ourselves and therefore the situations in which we become involved more securely. We play no idle game if, knowing that we will get that emergency call, we prepare by framing various questions beginning with, "What would I do if _____?" The knowledge yielded by such informal but searching surveys reduces our stress when we address the emergency itself.

With a good sense of ourselves, we may act in crises in ways that we might not choose in other situations. With a clear awareness of what we are doing, we may allow others to depend on us during the intense interval of crisis, letting them "lean" on us and telling them what to do. We take over the executive function of their lives to stabilize them psychologically and to prevent any unconscious conflicts from breaking through their defenses. We identify strong points in these persons — what we understand as their healthiest defenses — and encourage their use in their struggle to recapture their equilibrium.

Often neglected in times when religion was thought an inadmissible variable in psychology, faith and spirituality are now recognized as potent sources of personal integration and emotional well-being. In crisis, we may wisely call on the religious faith of those involved to support them during the time of stress.[3]

anticipate 預先預防的

The Critical Incident Stress Syndrome

With the development of what we might term a subculture of emergency workers, ranging from those who staff medical facilities to full- and part-time firefighters, police, nurses, EMS workers, and others, many organizations have developed programs to offer understanding and support to these people whose daily work is one unending emergency call. They have identified, for example, *Critical Incident Stress*, defined by Dr. Jeffrey Mitchell as "any situation faced by Emergency Services Personnel that causes them to experience unusually strong emotional reactions which have the potential to interfere with their ability at the scene or later, generates unusually strong feelings in the emergency service workers."[4] We can learn much from what these people have learned from their emergency work experience.

The purpose of such organizations is to <u>anticipate</u> the stress of emergency work, to develop ways to provide on-site support, to offer de-mobilization and debriefing services, and to assist the families and loved ones of emergency workers. Implementing such services mitigates the impact of critical incidents for victims, for secondary victims (those who are stressed in their attempts to <u>render</u> assistance), and for tertiary victims (the families and friends touched by the stress radiating out from the incident). These responses are directed toward lessening post-traumatic stress disorder, PTSD, a now not unfamiliar experience in our society.

render 給予

The Critical Incident Stress Syndrome is defined as (1) responding to a scene and becoming overwhelmed by what someone sees, hears, touches, or smells; or (2) experiencing *normal* reactions to an *abnormal* event. Common triggers include (1) the death of a co-worker; (2) mass casualty events; (3) death of a child; (4) death after a <u>prolonged</u> rescue effort; (5) victim reminding one of another; (6) highly dangerous event; (7) high media interest; (8) emergency service personnel causing an injury or death.

Experienced personnel emphasize that these are normal reactions for human beings, that they must be so accepted, that they are temporary, and that exploring these reactions with others will lessen their immediate and long-term effects. Common sense infuses their recommendations for helping those working at stressful emergencies. They include limiting the exposure of persons to the overwhelming sensory stimuli, providing rest breaks, encouraging talk about the experience, protecting the workers from bystanders and media representatives, using reassurance about the normal character of their reactions, and avoiding any remarks or reactions that may embarrass the affected persons. These may be wisely applied to ourselves and to those with whom we work at any point in the circles of stress that radiate out from a critical incident.

Classic Everyday Emergencies

Most of the emergencies will not make the evening news. They are no less poignant for their being so human and so common. The majority may be described as: (1) *intrapersonal*, in which individuals are moved by their own internal depression, anxiety, and confusion; (2) *somatic complaints*, the complex of physical symptoms perceived by persons as the cause of the emergency; (3) *interpersonal* problems, in which there is a significant player outside the self, as those situations in which persons are concerned or irritated by the behavior of others. Complaining persons are often those who bring those whose behavior concerns them to our attention.

The most common complaint in emergency situations is the experience of *depression*. This is usually related, as has been noted earlier, to some loss, real or imagined, in the individual's life. People may express very similar subjective feelings of depression and yet be very different inside. For example, there is the individual who may be truly suicidal in his state of depression and who comes to the helper precisely because of this. Another person may be reacting to the death of a loved one, and the depression is not suicidal but rather an understandable part of her overall dynamic process of mourning. Acute subjective pain is present but as the distillate of a very different pattern of reactions from those driving the suicidal individual. Both kinds of persons can appear at the counselor's door at times of emergency, and we ought to be able to distinguish one from the other so that we can respond appropriately.

Perhaps the clearest indicator that seriously depressed persons have a clear intention of committing suicide is found in their nonverbal signals. These telegraph their uncertain or conflicted feelings about living or dying. MacKinnon and Michels suggest that if individuals leave doors unlocked, spend money that would otherwise have been used for the necessities of life, or call distant friends with whom they have not been in contact in a long time, the ambivalence is clear.[5] So, too, if they seem unconcerned about time and place, as though they were already detached in some way from present existence.

As noted, a plan based on our awareness of what other help is available is our best preparation for such emergencies. Where, for example, can psychiatric or hospital assistance be obtained even at an awkward or difficult hour? It is frequently helpful for nonmedical persons to have some relationship already established with a competent medical colleague who will be able to be of assistance in these situations. It is clear that our stress will be reduced if we have at hand practical options for sensible action. It is not a time to improvise or to hunt frantically through the Yellow Pages for assistance, especially because such emergencies often occur over weekends or holidays when, unless it has been anticipated, it may be difficult to reach another professional colleague. That plan of action is a solid backing for the steady presence that is so important in alleviating such emergency situations.

The Cardinal Feature: Anxiety

Anxiety is a constant in emergencies. It may even be the major symptom cited by individuals seeking our help. Our task is to read the emergency carefully in order to tease out the significant roots of anxiety in the individual. When persons complain of an acute increase in anxiety, it is usually a sign that their ordinary internal balance between drives and defenses has been dislodged in some way. In response, they may attempt to build new defenses, the way a river city piles up sandbags against the flood, in an effort to maintain their sense of themselves. Patients whose fundamental defenses have been disturbed may, for example, begin to use the defense of projection — attributing their own motives to others — in an attempt to stabilize their internal difficulties.

Ordinarily we associate the expression of acute anxiety with one of the following factors: (1) some current event stirring to life fears that have been sleeping in the person's unconscious life; (2) patients feeling that they are losing control and may do something to act out their sexual or aggressive feelings. Their anxiety arises because they are terrified by the possible consequences of their losing control over their lives.

People in emergency situations are seldom aware of the specific fear affecting them and cannot easily give it a name. They present a more diffuse experience of panic and dread. We need to feel our way carefully into and beneath these complaints in order to grasp their true significance. Simple reassurance will not help when the roots of the problem are unconscious.

As we try to listen to the subtleties in the communications of others, we begin to appreciate something about the impulses or fantasies that cause them such discomfort. MacKinnon and Michels cite the common example of the adolescent boy who must share a room with another young man for the first time in college. "Homosexual feelings," they note, "become increasingly difficult to repress, and when he is under the influence of alcohol, his defenses are further weakened and he begins to panic."[6]

Such a panic may lead the individual to build a new line of defenses, and those are what we see on the surface. The use of projection, for example, leads him to express fears that his roommate is going to attack him. The real problem lies at a deeper level than this defensive accusation. This is a classic case of anxiety generated because of a sudden imbalance in a person's way of adjustment. It is precipitated by a new event — going to college and the need to relate with another man on a level of intimacy that has never been experienced before. When we understand this problem in the context of the interrelationship of these dynamic events, we are much better prepared to respond positively and constructively.

The same need to understand the deeper dynamics occurs when the individual is brought in by another person. A wife, for example, may bring in a disturbed husband because she is afraid he is going to hurt himself, the home, or the children. The breakdown she senses in him is more a source of anxiety for her and her family than it is for him. Again, the context of this situation allows us to understand and make a good response in the emergency.

Some people intervene in such emergencies by using reassurance or by trying to talk persons out of feeling the way they do. Nowhere is the fallacy of the "reasonable response" more obvious than in an emergency marked by quite irrational anxiety. In such instances, referral to a competent medical colleague or other professional resource is indicated.

Common Difficulties

Confusion is the symptom in individuals who seem mixed up and unable to locate themselves accurately in space and time. They are not easily able to manage their way through their environment, and they involve themselves in emergency situations through inadvertence. This is frequently a sign of dementia, an organic condition discussed in a previous chapter. Sensing their own confusion causes these people, who are sometimes elderly, to be bewildered and scared. Their actions are inappropriate and are noticed by others, and they are frequently brought for assistance by a friend or relative. In these situations our reading of the precipitating event in the context of the individual's life leads to the best management of the difficulty, which includes a referral for an accurate diagnosis of the underlying condition.

A major change in a person's life, for example, may burden a fragile personality with demands that it cannot meet. Persons who move to new surroundings after the death of a spouse, or any other major incident requiring great adjustment, may find that they are unable to make the transition easily or comfortably. They get confused, forget where they are, or cannot manage the basic essentials of their lives. It is obviously important to gather practical information about whether such confused individuals can cope with life on their own or whether they need some kind of assistance.

Several years ago an elderly couple from upstate New York were found dead in each other's arms. Their heat had been turned off because of their failure to pay their electric bills. There was money in the house and the local parish had, in fact, paid some of their bills for them. While people were angry at the utility company for its hardheartedness, it may be that friends and relatives had overestimated this elderly couple's capacity for managing their own environment. A sensible judgment, then, is obviously of the first order of importance in dealing with confused persons.

It is also important to include others in any emergency plan to deal with confused persons. These others should be introduced to the situation and helped to understand its dimensions. They need to grasp the practical limits to independent living by these confused people. Great complications can arise unless we recognize and respond to the feelings that friends and relatives have about the situation. Unless the problems can be seen with insight and comprehension, friends and relatives may not provide the kind of help that we think advisable. Good plans often fall apart because the persons we depend on to carry them out have not been sufficiently integrated into the situation. Such people need both information and emotional reassurance if we are to help them fill the roles that are theirs when an emergency situation affecting a relative comes to full term.

Somatic Problems

There is a cultural tendency to dismiss some physical complaints as meaningless and imaginary because we know that their origins are often psychological. Counselors responding to emergency situations in which

the complaint is somatic cannot quickly or confidently make such judgments. These need to be properly evaluated by a physician. In many
instances, a medical explanation for the symptoms is not found.

Quite often persons who have physical complaints deny their emotional problems and are unable to respond very well if we try to talk
to them in psychological terms about something they insist is quite
physical, even after a medical evaluation suggests otherwise. It is common, for example, to find persons experiencing hyperventilation during
a time of emergency. They are not satisfied by reassurances about the
common and relatively nonserious nature of their difficulty. It doesn't
help if we say, "It's all in your head." Psychological sensitivity enables
us to understand why the persons have these symptoms and why they
speak in a symbolic language of somatic illness. Their physical symptom is their language, and any abrupt dismissal of these persons may
only complicate what for them is already an acute emergency problem.

Difficulties with Others

Such crises arise over one individual's complaining about the behavior
of somebody else. Such an emergency situation has a courtroom air,
as though you were summoned to hand down an indictment. One person is brought by another who wants you to do something about his
or her behavior or the problems it is causing. The complexity of such
interpersonal emergencies is obvious. We have a special vulnerability
here if our main identity is not in psychology or psychiatry. Parents, for
example, may bring a son or a daughter whose behavior has generated
great anxiety. They avoid bringing their child to a psychiatrist or psychologist in the first instance because they do not want to interpret the
problem as an emotional one. They want somebody else — and we fit
the bill nicely — to "straighten out" the person's thinking, to get him
or her on the right road again.

Our instincts wisely warn us against taking on the Solomon role.
We are not judges, persuaders, or persons who can easily be enlisted
to do the bidding of one or the other party in such situations. We
respond to the emotional context of the event and this may not seem
to have much relationship to the symptoms first laid out. We want to
deal with the event in the perspective of the total relationship of the
persons involved. We do not react only to one individual but to the
overall dynamic governing the relationship of those before us.

We must approach emergencies well purged of our "rescue fantasies." We must come to terms with the limitations that emergencies

place on our capacity to solve the problems of others. We also monitor our own potential countertransference feelings toward the persons who are caught in the crisis. Emergencies, by their very nature, occur when we do not expect them or when we find responding to them inconvenient and uncomfortable. If, as suggested before, we can anticipate our own reactions, we can plan not only our mode of response but perhaps even our place of response as well. We should have some fairly comfortable office or room in which we can see people with minimal disturbance even in emergency situations. Beepers, telephones chirping, interruptions by secretaries or housekeepers interfere with the kind of concentration we need in emergency situations. Most of us have learned from experience to retire any ideas of trying to impress people by having important-sounding interruptions break into our work.

We must also expect to spend our time freely when emergencies arise. There is no way to contain emergencies within a schedule, no way to tidy them up by a certain hour. If we cannot live comfortably with letting our schedules go at times, we must either deal with these feelings or avoid emergency situations. There is enough anxiety connected with a crisis already. If we feel rushed, we will almost certainly compound the problem, adding to the difficulty rather than relieving it. These are basic ground rules that are simply footnotes to the foundation of self-possession, the strong point of all effective emergency treatment.

Do We Include Others?

Whether to include others in handling the emergency is a practical difficulty of the first magnitude. The answer is, as in so many other important questions: *It depends*. Other persons frequently accompany the one who is experiencing the emergency, and the question becomes whether they should be included in the interview with the person they have accompanied. Our healthy instincts are our best guide in these circumstances. Sometimes it is important to hold a joint interview with individuals and those who brought them, whether they are friends, roommates, or family members. Sometimes it is impossible for the persons to communicate without the assistance of some friend or relative, as, for example, in the case of elderly and confused patients.

Good instincts also tell us what to avoid. It is not good to talk privately to those who accompanied the one experiencing the emergency before talking first to the latter. These persons, already unsettled, may think that, having seen others, we are now enlisted against them or that we have accepted a version of their story other than theirs. We sensibly see the individuals before conferring with or bringing family members or others into the discussion.

In some situations, where the family is a problem in itself, it may be important to see all its members together to get some comprehension of how they function with each other and as a group. We may juggle the arrangements during the emergency situation when this seems called for. If we act straightforwardly, with some words of explanation, we may ask certain people to leave, or call in others, without disturbing the process.

We may ask ourselves some simple practical questions as we enter into the complicated relationships in which emergencies are swathed. Perhaps the most important question is: Whose idea is this? The right answer helps us both to appreciate the overall dynamics of the crisis and to respond to the person most in need. It may be, for example, that persons who have been referred by members of their family or by their teachers may be quite reluctant to talk about any problems. Help cannot be forced upon these persons and, if they do not perceive the situation as an emergency, they cannot be motivated to do so merely at our urging. We prudently avoid being manipulated into making the consultation work. We are not out to convince people that they are in trouble but to respond to them when they really are.

What Kind of a Referral?

The matter of referral remains the center of our concern and the center of gravity for understanding the context in which the emergency has taken place. It permits us to explore the definition that the concerned persons give to the problem, which may be presented in religious, legal, educational, or other terms. Whatever they seem on the surface, their roots may be quite different. Counselors in schools are familiar with these problems and realize that the academic emergency may signal some other emotional conflict that has not been addressed.

Our function is not to enforce the academic standards of the institution but to respond to the emotional needs of the persons referred for assistance. An associated question is: Why was I chosen as the person consulted in this emergency? Complex motivations may intersect in this regard, but if we can get some appreciation of how we were perceived in order to be chosen, this may lead us into the world of the persons with whom we must deal. Why were my skills deemed appropriate and what role am I expected to play? It is very helpful for us to answer these questions before overcommitting ourselves in an emergency situation.

What are the expectations? This central question offers us the opportunity to inquire with understanding about the recent past of the concerned parties. The information thus yielded is often very illuminating. The precipitating event may well be an anniversary, a move, or a holiday season. Or it may be a change of jobs, an imbalance in a marriage, or some frightening experience that the individual finds difficult to talk about.

Expectations are a part of every emergency situation. These exist both on the part of the individuals and on the part of those people who bring them to us. Some people expect magic, some expect us to take responsibility for everything, while others may want only reassurance from us about the way they are handling things. Some may seek absolution or some kind of permission from us to act in a particular way. Some persons ask us, in effect, to control their behavior, while others may actively try to get us to intervene on their behalf in some situation in school or at home. Still others may come to us because they want us to protect them from what they perceive as more serious psychiatric treatment.

It is sometimes necessary to urge treatment in a hospital or to make a referral to some other colleague, even when we wish that this were not the case. We may have to do this when the affected persons are unwilling to accept such a recommendation. This occurs when they complain of physical symptoms and when they can no longer care for themselves or when suicide is a serious risk and we are not able to manage helping them in any other way. These difficult decisions can be made only after careful thought and evaluation of all the elements and alternatives related to the situation. In deliberating on these, however, we should never try to trick their clients by, for example, making hospitalization sound palatable under some other name. We gain by being honest and straightforward and ready to explore the fears and unwillingness that people have about getting certain kinds of treatment. No one wants to hospitalize unwilling patients, but a far greater risk exists if we attempt to please them by avoiding it. We may make what is already an emergency into a tragedy.

Pain by Telephone

The telephone is a mode of communication that has certain limitations, but it is frequently the only medium available at times of emergency. Brief, constructive contacts can be very helpful even over the telephone. We wisely remember that there is a person on the other end of the phone testing us in some way to see whether we are trustworthy or approachable. The phone can be a potent instrument for communicating our understanding and informed concern, and it should be used as skillfully as possible. It may be very helpful to try to personalize the conversation by finding something out about the individuals so that they are not just a detached voice on the other end of the line. It may also be practical to find out where they are, their age, and whether they have been getting help from anyone else.

All too often, the phone contact is the best that persons can manage when they are under severe pressure. It may be the last thing, as in the case of Marilyn Monroe, that certain people use in an effort to make contact with the world around them. We must make the most of it, sometimes settling for at least another appointment on the phone if a face-to-face meeting cannot be arranged. Sometimes people announce their suicides to us by phone, telling us that they have just taken so many pills of this kind or that, and by such a gesture dramatically reach out for some kind of help. We should get the facts about the situation, including the name of the drug, as well as the address and telephone number of the caller. It is useful to tell them that we are going to summon help and that they should leave their door open so that there will be no problem when help arrives. It is also wise to tell them that we will call back to confirm the imminent arrival of help. If there is time, it is advisable to get the name and phone number of a neighbor who may be able to be of assistance in the emergency.

– 37 –

TAKING COUNSEL WITH OURSELVES

W HAT CAN WE LEARN about ourselves if we really think about our experiences in helping other persons? Perhaps the first deep insight is that these others are persons, individual human beings, more than "cases," "clients," or "patients." Identifying them consistently in this manner renews and refreshes us, for it keeps our focus on the humanity to which we want to relate even though it may be masked and shrouded by the hundred disguises of psychological problems.

That perspective allows us to see ourselves as persons, too, reminding us to draw on what is healthy and human in us, rather than using artificial constructions, such as that men are from Mars and women from Venus, as we search for that contact point of the human and healthy in others. We do not want to reenact the myth of Sisyphus, laboriously bearing the stones of our work up the hill, only to see them roll down, putting our shoulders to them at first light only to spend that next day, and the next and all that lie beyond, in worn-down frustration.

Lessening our stress is a by-product of knowing how to use ourselves in a mature, professional manner in our work. We seldom rid ourselves of stress by a direct, frontal attack. Stress is decreased, however, when we learn to enter more fully and more confidently into our work with other persons. How can we use ourselves even more sensitively so that our talents are used fully and our effectiveness with others increased? We answer this not abstractly but personally in and through our work with others.

Winging It

We live in the age of improvisation and make-do. "Winging it" has become in many occupations almost the accustomed way of performing. There are many rationalizations for doing things without adequate preparation. Some speak, for example, of freshness and spontaneity, of "playing it by ear," but may in fact be explaining away carelessness instead of describing creativity. There is a peculiar misunderstanding abroad that creative persons are undisciplined. Nothing is further from the truth. In creative people, according to all observations and studies, there exists an intense inner discipline that governs them in their work. Only pseudocreative people lack discipline and, although they may call themselves poets or artists, their shoddiness is revealed clearly in what they produce.

We have all witnessed the chaos and unnecessary suffering that are harvested from improvisation and lack of discipline in helping relationships. Unfortunately, winging it in the helping professions not only harms other persons but induces a great deal of stress in counselors. Tension is connected with any self-discipline, but it is not the grinding and destructive agency that stress becomes in an unplanned and uncertain situation.

Whether we work at helping others full- or part-time, our most important objective is to develop a professional attitude toward ourselves and our work. This is not only the best protection against stress but it defines us clearly in terms of work situations, goals to be achieved, people to work with, and the limits and organization of therapeutic work. This sense of professionalism also enables cooperation with other professional helpers in an intelligent and productive manner. When we function as nonprofessionals who hold themselves to professional standards, we do not float around like protoplasm, snagging now on one thing and now on another, or drifting away on the latest stream of fashionable activity.

This professional attitude increases our self-confidence and self-esteem, strengths that enable us to face difficult situations, even those in which we are not quite sure what to do, and to work through them in a constructive manner. Counseling is an activity in which being an amateur is really not good enough. Unfortunately, in counseling, as in other responsible professions, some people can know just enough to do a lot of harm to themselves and to others. To organize our sense of self around a professional definition does not necessarily make us impersonal or somehow part of the "establishment" or "institution." True professionalism gives us a healthy sense of independence as it allows us to define where we stand and what we can do. Operating on goodwill, or merely the desire to be helpful, does not deliver this sense of competence to us.

Elements of Professionalism

Some of the important features of developing this professional sense include the following:

We need time for regular study. Surprisingly enough, many people who engage in counseling activity almost every day seldom consult the literature or even their own textbooks. They feel, perhaps because they went through an educational system that confined learning to the length of the school term, that they have completed their formal study because they have passed certain courses. But all professionals go on learning throughout their lives. And, no matter how much experience we may have, it is always helpful to study again the particular psychological dynamics that may be involved in a current counseling responsibility.

Most counselors recognize that ongoing education is the natural state of things for all professionals at the present time. The heart of this is the desire to continue educating ourselves, to continue learning more about ourselves and the subject matter of our counseling work.

For example, as we hypothesize that a person has an obsessive-compulsive personality disorder, we may turn back to some book that deals with this subject. It will read differently after clinical experience because we will have seen new facets of the obsessive style that we had not previously noticed. We will have a personal feel for it. A thorough reading of at least one treatment of the obsessive-compulsive personality, for example, will bring out added dimensions in our current counseling experience. Such reading resembles research. It takes time and care; it is helpful to make notes and, when we finish, to draw up a brief resume of the important insights gained from this exercise. Add reflection on the person who prompted our study and we not only see better the road we have taken but we will see farther down the way we must yet go with them.

Such study does not give us information as if for an exam, but helps us grow into a more informed sense of ourselves as counselors. We do not just learn about a certain subject; we penetrate it so that we have knowledge, not merely to answer questions, but to integrate within ourselves operational professional knowledge that issues into better helping relationships. In short, we are different, more fully grown, because we continue to study in this way.

Professionals make a habit of reading professional journals and reviews. These enable counselors to understand the important developments in the field and offer them an opportunity to appreciate changes in training and psychological techniques. These can also be provided by attendance at professional meetings or other continuing education seminars. Counselors can do a great deal on their own, however, especially with the variety of materials available in print, in various media, and through Internet sites.

Personality Theory

Some counselors may not immediately see how mastering a personality theory is related to psychotherapeutic technique and practice. Without it, however, we lack a context for our work or a framework for thinking about it. To deepen as much as possible our appreciation of at least one personality theory, we should constantly refine our appreciation of its elements and meaning. In a sense that must be understood carefully, it does not make any difference what personality theory we follow as long as we follow it consistently. Professionals increase self-confidence by operating in reference to a well-understood set of principles about personality development. When we grasp a particular theory in depth, we can use it constructively and also relate it more readily to the work of others.

It has been noted that professionals with very different orientations are able to communicate without too much difficulty even though their personality theories may be different. What enables this to happen is their thorough grasp of the underlying notions that guide their work. Real professionals can talk across differing schools of thought because they can make the translations necessary for understanding others when they are familiar with their own first principles.

We should run for cover should anyone urge us to be "eclectic." There are ways of understanding this notion properly, of course, but often enough it suggests a hodgepodge of notions about psychological functioning with no clear or consistent theory to hold it all together. A firm grasp of personality theory enables us to integrate our experience in a systematic fashion, providing us with a way of reflecting on what takes place between ourselves and others in counseling. This becomes a base for us to stand on and a source of therapeutic communication. Being "eclectic" may sound charming, but it may mean that a person knows a little of some things and not a great deal of any one thing. "Eclectic" sounds impartial and vaguely wise, but it can represent an outlook that has never been thought through seriously. Counselors who wish to serve sensitively and professionally begin with mastering a guiding theoretical framework.

When we continue to read and to work at understanding personality theory, we have an unusual but healthy recurring experience. We feel that we are always just beginning really to understand human personality and are always discovering something we did not know before. Such discoveries might alarm amateurs, but professionals who are always moving deeper in counseling work experience them on many occasions. This sense of discovery comes regularly to people who keep themselves open to learning at every stage in their lives. Their work never becomes boring because their attitude toward it disposes them to seeing it always in a fresh manner. It is as simple as that. When we don't think we know everything we place ourselves in the ever renewing position of still being able to learn. Such an attitude not only lessens stress but makes life and work more deeply enjoyable.

A further sign of professionalism is found in our readiness to seek out continuing supervision. We should value it enough to be willing to pay for it in order to get it on a regular basis. This experience is probably more important than any other in assisting us to see ourselves and how we work in a fresh and more accurate perspective. Supervision is in itself a process of continuing education. Sometimes we may feel that we cannot afford to pay for supervision but, in certain instances, we may be able to group together with other counselors to get supervisory assistance in a seminar style. It may sometimes happen that supervision cannot be obtained. Some approximation of this, even if it is just talking one's case over with a colleague, is of great value. This enables us to express our own feelings, to explore them, and to get a look at ourselves and those with whom we work from new angles. Such self-examination is considered a professional necessity.

Time

What everybody needs, of course, is more time, as the ticking clock is a major cause of stress. Time, in fact, dominates many aspects of our counseling activity. Despite its pressure, we must learn to take some time for ourselves. Some of us skip this because we feel guilty if we are not out helping people all the time. When we feel that we cannot take sufficient time, for example, to study about a certain problem with which we are dealing, we have a signal that we are overcommitted or poorly organized. We have let the cargo move so that the vessel of our lives lists badly.

If we feel guilty if we do not put in X number of hours every day seeing people directly, we have a problem with our self-image that needs investigation. As we allow ourselves some time for reflection and reading, we may find that we function more effectively in our actual counseling work. A great deal of unnecessary stress is traceable to un-acknowledged feelings, such as the driving power of our own guilt, in ourselves.

Only as we take time to listen to ourselves can we sense, understand, and monitor the emergence of countertransference feelings in the course of counseling. Some of us may be afraid to discover such feelings. We may think that we are not supposed to have them and we may be upset because they seem inconsistent with our idea of ourselves as counselors. Experience of countertransference feelings is not, of course, a bad thing. It is a sign that something is going on in the counseling work, so such feelings need to be heard and understood properly. To discover that we are human is to learn what makes it possible for us to help other people at all.

Counselors who give themselves no leeway in their schedule — are we numbered among them? — may be trapped, and sometimes badly hurt, by their failure to understand their own psychological processes. Time for ourselves is a simple human need we should acknowledge and provide without feeling less of ourselves for it.

The Economy of the Helper

This phrase has at times been used by certain psychologists to describe the counselors' own resources in relationship to the demands made upon them. No one has an infinitely expandable economy of the self. We can be effective only if we respect the limitations, both human and professional, under which we operate. Understanding our psycholog-ical economy does not mean drawing up a balance sheet about it. It means rather that we appreciate the rhythm of our lives and have a sensible appreciation of what, as ordinary human beings, we can and cannot do. A healthy psychological economy includes an understanding that we always make mistakes.

One of the remarkable things about counseling is that it works even when the helper is imperfect. It is more like friendship or love than golf. Doing some of the right things in counseling makes up for doing a lot of the wrong things. If we get the main sense of things — and that centers on a true understanding of other persons and their dynamics — then there is a large margin for error. We need not worry or be ashamed of the human truth that errors will always be with us.

We can also say *no*. There may be times when we cannot help people, or must turn them away or refer them to somebody else. Sometimes we may need to say no in order to preserve enough time for our continued professional development. This may be one of the hardest lessons for some of us to learn but learn it we must if we want to help others without destroying ourselves.

Nor need we feel guilty as we identify persons who try to give rise to these feelings in us. These people may want to be dependent on us, may want to be treated only according to their own whim, or may have mastered the manipulative arts of making others feel sorry for them. Such persons, and a wide variety of others, can tax our adjustment severely. When we feel free to let people be mad at us or disappointed in us, we are free indeed.

If, after all our best efforts, we feel that we do not function well as counselors — and some of us may feel this way at times — we should not be discouraged but at least learn from our mistakes as we try to avoid some of our bigger ones. There is nothing wrong in refusing to represent ourselves as possessing psychological skills if we find that our personalities keep us from mastering the discipline that is required in good therapists. We can call ourselves advice-givers, philosophers, or whatever, but we must not delude ourselves into claiming that we are counselors if we know that we really are not. Such a decision is much better for ourselves and for those with whom we work. There is no shame in this as we may reveal our better skills in education, religious teaching, or pastoral work without apologies. For most of us, maybe all of us, becoming professional is a noble and never-ending quest.

NOTES

Preface: A Changed Book for a Changed Time

1. American Psychiatric Association, *Diagnostic and Statistical Manual of Mental Disorders,* 4th ed., text revision (henceforth *DSM-IV-TR*) (Washington, D.C.: American Psychiatric Association, 2000).

1. Guiding Principles

1. For a discussion of psychological mindedness and defense mechanisms see Paul A. Dewald, *Psychotherapy: A Dynamic Approach,* 2d ed. (New York: Basic Books, 1971); first softcover edition published as *The Supportive and Active Psychotherapies: A Dynamic Approach* (Northvale, N.J.: Jason Aronson, 1994).

4. What Other People Do to Us

1. M. H. Stone, "Cluster C Personality Disorders," in *Current Psychiatric Therapy II,* ed. D. L. Dunner (Philadelphia: W. B. Saunders, 1997), 441; emphasis added.

2. *DSM-IV-TR,* 789.

3. Ibid., 790.

6. Revelations about Ourselves in Relationship with Others

1. R. A. MacKinnon and R. Michels, *The Psychiatric Interview in Clinical Practice* (Philadelphia: W. B. Saunders, 1971), 27; see also R. A. MacKinnon and S. C. Yudofsky, *Principles of the Psychiatric Evaluation* (Philadelphia: Lippincott, 1991).

2. Paul A. Dewald, *Psychotherapy: A Dynamic Approach,* 2d ed. (New York: Basic Books, 1971), 188.

7. What Is It Like to Be Real?

1. S. Freud, *The Psychopathology of Everyday Life* (New York: Norton, 1971).

9. Are We Friends or Counselors?

1. W. E. Henry, J. H. Sims, and S. L. Spray, *Public and Private Lives of Psychotherapists* (San Francisco: Jossey-Bass Publishers, 1973), 218–19.

2. H. H. Strupp, *Psychotherapy and Behavior Change 1973* (Chicago: Aldine Publishing, 1974), vii.

3. C. Rogers, *On Becoming a Person* (Boston: Houghton Mifflin, 1961, 1995).

4. W. Schofield, *Psychotherapy: The Purchase of Friendship* (New York: Prentice Hall, 1964; New Brunswick, N.J.: Transaction Books, 1986).

5. C. B. Truax and R. B. Carkhuff, *Toward Effective Counseling and Psychotherapy: Training and Practice* (Chicago: Aldine Press, 1967).

6. H. H. Strupp, "On the Basic Ingredient of Psychotherapy," *Journal of Consulting and Clinical Psychology* 43 (1973): 1–8.

7. R. Felder, in *Counseling and Psychotherapy, Overview,* ed. D. S. Arbuckle (New York: McGraw-Hill, 1967), 109.

8. J. M. Reismann and T. Yamakoski, "Psychotherapy and Friendship: An Analysis of the Communication of Friends," *Journal of Counseling Psychology* 21 (1974): 269–73.

9. Paul A. Dewald, *Psychotherapy: A Dynamic Approach,* 2d ed. (New York: Basic Books, 1971), 179–80.

10. N. Gartrell, J. Herman, S. Olarte, M. Feldstein, et al., "Psychiatrist-Patient Sexual Contact: Results of a National Survey," *American Journal of Psychiatry* 143 (1986): 1126–31.

11. N. Gartrell, J. Herman, S. Olarte, R. Localio, et al., "Psychiatric Residents' Sexual Contact with Educators and Patients: Results of a National Survey," *American Journal of Psychiatry* 145 (1988): 690–94.

12. American Psychiatric Association, *Code of Ethics* (Washington, D.C.: American Psychiatric Association, 2001).

13. T. G. Gutheil and G. O. Gabbard, "Misuses and Misunderstandings of Boundary Theory in Clinical and Regulatory Settings," *American Journal of Psychiatry* 155 (1998): 409–14.

Chapter 11. This Wasn't My Idea

1. W. Glasser, *Reality Therapy* (New York: Harper & Row, 1965). See also W. Glasser, *Reality Therapy in Action* (New York: HarperCollins Publishers, 2000).

2. M. S. Swartz, J. W. Swanson, H. R. Wagner, et al., "Can Involuntary Outpatient Commitment Reduce Hospital Recidivism? Findings from a Randomized Trial with Severely Mentally Ill Individuals," *American Journal of Psychiatry* 156 (1999): 1968–75.

3. S. K. Paulson, "Colorado Bill Would Delay Divorce a Year for Counseling," *Naples Daily News,* February 25, 2001, 14A.

4. Paul A. Dewald, *Psychotherapy: A Dynamic Approach,* 2d ed. (New York: Basic Books, 1971), 307.

Chapter 12. I Won't Dance, You Can't Make Me

1. Paul A. Dewald, *Psychotherapy: A Dynamic Approach,* 2d ed. (New York: Basic Books, 1971), 224.

2. Ibid., 225.

3. Ibid., 231.

Chapter 14. Diagnosis: Goals and Resources

1. *DSM-IV-TR,* xxxi.

2. Ibid., 685.

Chapter 15. Listening to the Lives of Others

1. G. Greene, *A Sort of Life* (New York: Pocket Books, 1973), 160.

2. R. A. Gardner, *Therapeutic Communication with Children: The Mutual Storytelling Technique* (New York: Science House, 1971). See also R. A. Gardner, *Storytelling in Psychotherapy with Children* (Northvale, N.J.: J. Aronson, 1993).

Chapter 17. When Can I Say What I Feel?

1. R. A. MacKinnon and R. Michels, *The Psychiatric Interview in Clinical Practice* (Philadelphia: W. B. Saunders, 1971), 30.

Chapter 18. Supportive Psychotherapy

1. Paul A. Dewald, *Psychotherapy: A Dynamic Approach,* 2d ed. (New York: Basic Books, 1971), 171.

Chapter 19. Reading the Signs / Working with Families

1. American Psychiatric Association, "Practice Guideline for the Treatment of Patients with Alzheimer's Disease and other Dementias of Late Life," in *Practice Guidelines for the Treatment of Psychiatric Disorders,* Compendium 2000, (Washington, D.C.: American Psychiatric Press, 2000), 91–92.

Chapter 20. Drugs: Use and Abuse

1. E. H. Adams and J. C. Groerer, "Elevated Risk of Cocaine Use in Adults," *Psychiatric Annals* (September 1988).

2. American Psychiatric Association, "Practice Guideline for the Treatment of Patients with Substance Use Disorders: Alcohol, Cocaine, Opioids," in *Practice Guidelines for the Treatment of Psychiatric Disorders,* Compendium 2000 (Washington, D.C.: American Psychiatric Press, 2000), 154.

3. Ibid., 154–55.

4. 1999 National Household Survey on Drug Abuse funded by the Substance Abuse and Mental Health Services Administration (SAMHSA).

5. *DSM-IV-TR,* 248.

6. "Practice Guideline for the Treatment of Patients with Substance Use Disorders," 194.

7. K. Verby and M. S. Gold, "From Coca Leaves to Crack," *Psychiatric Annals* (September 1988).

8. Ibid., 517.

9. Ibid.

10. Drug Abuse Warning Network (DAWN) survey: Substance Abuse and Mental Health Service Administration (SAMHSA), Washington, D.C., 1999.

11. "Practice Guidelines for the Treatment of Patients with Substance Use Disorders," 200.

12. G. Belkin, *Practical Counseling in the Schools* (Dubuque, Iowa: W. C. Brown Co. Publishers, 1975).

13. Community Epidemiology Workgroup: NIDA INFOFAX, Nationwide Trends, National Institute on Drug Abuse, 2001.

14. J. Randall, "Ecstasy-Fueled 'Rave' Parties Become Dances of Death for English Youths," *JAMA* 268 (1992): 1505–6.

15. B. Vastag, "Talking with Alan I. Lesher PhD, National Institute on Drug Abuse Director," *JAMA* 285 (2001): 1141–43.

16. "Practice Guideline for the Treatment of Patients with Substance Use Disorders," 156.

Chapter 21. Drink, Drank, Drunk

1. American Psychiatric Association, "Practice Guideline for the Treatment of Patients with Substance Use Disorders: Alcohol, Cocaine, Opioids," in *Practice Guidelines for the Treatment of Psychiatric Disorders,* Compendium 2000 (Washington, D.C.: American Psychiatric Press, 2000), 182.

2. *DSM-IV-TR,* 217, 220.

3. National Highway Transportation Safety Administration (NHTSA): Traffic Safety Facts 1999, National Center for Statistics and Analysis.

4. "Practice Guideline for the Treatment of Patients with Substance Use Disorders," 183.

5. J. A. Renner, "Alcoholism and Alcohol Abuse," in *Psychiatry Update and Board Preparation,* ed. T. A. Stern and J. B. Herman (New York: McGraw-Hill, 2000), 76.

6. C. A. Prescott and K. S. Kendler, "Genetic and Environmental Contributions to Alcohol Abuse and Dependence in a Population-Based Sample of Male Twins," *American Journal of Psychiatry* 156 (1999): 34–40.

7. R. C. Kessler, R. M. Crum, L. S. Warner, et al., "Lifetime Co-occurrence of DSM-III-R Alcohol Abuse and Dependence with Other Psychiatric Disorders in the National Comorbidity Survey," *Archives of General Psychiatry* 54 (1997): 313–21.

8. Renner, "Alcoholism and Alcohol Abuse," 82.

9. Ibid., 79.

10. "Practice Guideline for the Treatment of Patients with Substance Use Disorders," 187.

11. N. E. Noel, B. S. McCrady, R. L. Stout, et al., "Predictors of Attrition from an Outpatient Alcoholism Treatment Program for Couples," *Journal for the Study of Alcohol* 48 (1987): 229–35.

12. "Practice Guidelines of the Treatment of Patients with Substance Use Disorders," 157.

13. E. Nace, "Alcoholics Anonymous," in *Substance Abuse: A Comprehensive Textbook,* ed. J. H. Lowinson, P. Ruiz, R. B. Millman, and J. G. Langrod (Baltimore: Williams and Wilkins, 1992), 486–95; 3d ed., 1997.

14. "Practice Guidelines for the Treatment of Patients with Substance Use Disorders," 183.

Chapter 22. The Language of the Seriously Disturbed

1. *DSM-IV-TR,* 297.

2. W. R. Yates and G. R. Bergus, "Psychotic Disorders," in *Psychiatry for the Primary Care Physician,* ed. L. S. Goldman, T. N. Wise, and D. S. Brody (American Medical Association, 1998), 120.

3. American Psychiatric Association, "Practice Guidelines for the Treatment of Patients with Schizophrenia," in *Practice Guidelines for the Treatment of*

Patients with Psychiatric Disorders, Compendium 2000 (Washington, D.C.: American Psychiatric Association, 2000), 306.

4. National Institute of Mental Health (NIMH), *The Numbers Count: Mental Disorders in America,* publication no. 01-4584, January 2001.

5. D. C. Henderson and D. C. Goff, "Psychosis and Schizophrenia," in *Psychiatry Update and Board Preparation,* ed. T. A. Stern and J. B. Herman (New York: McGraw-Hill, 2000), 99.

6. "Guidelines for the Treatment of Patients with Schizophrenia," 377.

7. H. Green, *I Never Promised You a Rose Garden* (New York: Holt, Rinehart & Winston, 1964).

8. "Guidelines for the Treatment of Patients with Schizophrenia," 305.

9. Ibid., 310.

Chapter 23. Everyperson's Illness: Depression

1. *DSM-IV-TR,* 353.

2. H. Wechsler, S. Levine, R. K. Idelson, E. L. Schor, and E. Coakley, "The Physician's Role in Health Promotion Revisited: A Survey of Primary Care Practitioners," *New England Journal of Medicine* 334 (1996): 996–98.

3. R. A. MacKinnon and R. Michels, *The Psychiatric Interview in Clinical Practice* (Philadelphia: W. B. Saunders, 1971), 177.

4. *DSM-IV-TR,* 371.

5. American Psychiatric Association, "Practice Guideline for the Treatment of Patients with Major Depressive Disorder (revised)," *American Journal of Psychiatry* (supplement) 157, no. 4 (April 2000): 12.

6. J. F. Greden and J. F. Lopez, "Treatment of Major Depressive Disorder," in *Current Psychiatric Therapy II,* ed. D. L. Dunner (Philadelphia: W. B. Saunders, 1993), 221.

7. *DSM-IV-TR,* 373.

8. Ibid., 386.

9. National Institute of Mental Health, *Helping the Depressed Person Get Treatment,* DHHS publication no. (ADM) 90-1675, 1990.

Chapter 24. Stressed Out and Anxious

1. S. Freud, *Inhibitions, Symptoms and Anxieties,* ed. J. Strachey (New York: W. W. Norton, 1977).

2. I. Janis, *Psychological Stress* (New York: Wiley, 1958; New York: Academic Press, 1974).

3. *DSM-IV-TR,* 472.

4. American Psychiatric Association, "Practice Guideline for the Treatment of Patients with Panic Disorder," in *Practice Guidelines for the Treatment of Patients with Psychiatric Disorders,* Compendium 2000 (Washington, D.C.: American Psychiatric Association, 2000), 574.

5. Ibid., 603.

6. J. L. Herman, *Trauma and Recovery* (New York: Basic Books, 1992; rev. ed., 1997).

7. R. D. Ornstein, "Trauma and Post-traumatic Stress Disorder," in *Psychia-*

try Update and Board Preparation, ed. T. A. Stern and J. B. Herman (New York: McGraw-Hill, 2000), 130.

8. M. J. Horowitz, "Disaster Stress Studies," in *Conclusions in Disaster Stress Studies: New Methods and Findings,* ed. J. H. Shore (Washington, D.C.: American Psychiatric Press, 1986), 148.

9. J. G. Allen, *Coping with Trauma: A Guide to Self-Understanding* (Washington, D.C.: American Psychiatric Press, 1995), 244.

10. Ornstein, "Trauma and Post-traumatic Stress Disorder," 133–34.

11. J. E. Carr and M. E. Addis, "Specific and Social Phobia," in *Current Psychiatric Therapy II,* ed. D. L. Dunner (Philadelphia: W. B. Saunders, 1997), 316.

12. Ibid., 319.

Chapter 25. The Problems of Healthy People

1. *DSM-IV-TR,* 683.

2. T. H. Holmes and R. H. Rahe, "The Social Readjustment Rating Scale," in *Journal of Psychosomatic Research* 11, no. 2 (1967): 213–18.

3. M. Masuda and T. H. Holmes, "Life Events: Perceptions and Frequencies," *Psychosomatic Medicine* 40, no. 3 (1978): 236–61.

Chapter 26. Introductory Notes on Personality Disorders

1. *DSM-IV-TR,* 685–86.

2. P. Smallwood, "Personality Disorders," in *Psychiatry Update and Board Preparation,* ed. T. A. Stern and J. B. Herman (New York: McGraw-Hill, 2000), 189.

Chapter 27. Personality Disorders: Cluster A

1. *DSM-IV-TR,* 694.

2. M. Figment, "Road Rage versus Reality," *Atlantic Monthly* (August 1998), digital edition.

3. C. F. Zale, M. M. O'Brien, R. L. L. Trestman, et al., "Cluster A Personality Disorders," in *Current Psychiatric Therapy II,* ed. D. L. Dunner (Philadelphia: W. B. Saunders, 1997), 430.

4. *DSM-IV-TR,* 697.

5. Ibid., 701.

6. Ibid., 699.

7. Ibid.

8. Zale et al., "Cluster A Personality Disorders," 433.

Chapter 28. Personality Disorders: Cluster B

1. *DSM-IV-TR,* 686.

2. Ibid., 706.

3. N. Mailer, *The Executioner's Song* (Boston: Little Brown, 1979; New York: Vintage International, 1998).

4. H. Cleckley, *The Mask of Sanity* (St. Louis: Mosby, 1964).

5. *DSM-IV-TR,* 703.

6. P. Smallwood, "Personality Disorders," in *Psychiatry Update and Board Preparation,* ed. T. A. Stern and J. B. Herman (New York: McGraw-Hill, 2000), 193.

7. J. Coleman, *Abnormal Psychology and Modern Life* (Glenview, Ill.: Scott Foresman, 1964).

8. Ibid., 364.

9. D. E. McGee and M. M. Lineman, "Cluster B Personality Disorders," in *Current Psychiatric Therapy II,* ed. D. L. Dunner (Philadelphia: W. B. Saunders, 1997), 434.

10. *DSM-IV-TR*, 710.

11. K. A. Phillips and J. G. Gunderson, "Personality Disorders," in *The American Psychiatric Press Textbook of Psychiatry,* ed. R. E. Hales, M. C. Zanarini, and J. A. Talbott (Washington, D.C.: American Psychiatric Press, 1998).

12. McGee and Lineman, "Cluster B Personality Disorders," 435.

13. American Psychiatric Association, *Practice Guideline for the Treatment of Patients with Borderline Personality Disorder* (in press, 2001).

14. M. M. Lineman, D. A. Tutek, and H. L. Heard, et al., "Interpersonal Outcome of Cognitive Behavioral Treatment for Chronically Suicidal Borderline Patients," *American Journal of Psychiatry* 151 (1994): 1771–76.

15. Ibid.

16. R. A. MacKinnon and R. Michels, *The Psychiatric Interview in Clinical Practice* (Philadelphia: W. B. Saunders, 1971), 129.

17. *DSM-IV-TR*, 714.

18. Ibid., 717.

19. L. C. Groopman and A. M. Cooper, "Narcissistic Personality Disorder," in *Treatment of Psychiatric Disorders,* 2d ed., ed. G. O. Gabbard (Washington, D.C.: American Psychiatric Press, 1995), 2327–43.

Chapter 29. Personality Disorders: Cluster C

1. *DSM-IV-TR*, 721.

2. Ibid., 729.

3. L. Salzman, *The Obsessive Personality* (New York: Science House, 1968), 16.

4. R. A. MacKinnon and R. Michels, *The Psychiatric Interview in Clinical Practice* (Philadelphia: W. B. Saunders, 1971), 99.

5. *DSM-IV-TR*, 725.

Chapter 30. Marriage Counseling

1. G. Birchler and W. Fals-Stewart, "Considerations for Clients with Marital Dysfunction," in *Effective Brief Therapies: A Clinician's Guide,* ed. M. Herson and M. Biaggio (San Diego: Academic Press, 2000), 393.

2. Ibid., 394ff.

Chapter 31. Counseling Persons with Sexual Problems

1. Centers for Disease Control and Prevention, Trends by Disease, 2000. www.cdc.nlhstp.

2. H. S. Kaplan, *The Sexual Desire Disorders: Dysfunctional Regulation of Sexual Motivation* (New York: Brunner/Mazel, 1995); E. O. Laumann, A. Paik, and R. C. Rosen, "Sexual Dysfunction in the United States: Prevalence and Predictors," *Journal of the American Medical Association* 281 (1999): 537–44.

3. L. Shafer, "Sexual Disorders and Sexual Dysfunction," in *Psychiatry Update and Board Preparation,* ed. T. A. Stern and J. B. Herman (New York: McGraw-Hill, 2000), 157–66.

4. *DSM-IV-TR,* 535.

5. Shafer, "Sexual Disorders and Sexual Dysfunction," 157.

6. *DSM-IV-TR,* 535.

7. Shafer, "Sexual Disorders and Sexual Dysfunction," 164.

8. *DSM-IV-TR,* 571.

Chapter 32. Counseling the HIV/AIDS Patient

1. American Psychiatric Association, *Practice Guideline for the Treatment of Patients with HIV/AIDS* (Washington, D.C.: American Psychiatric Association, 2000), 6.

2. Centers for Disease Control and Prevention: HIV/AIDS Surveillance Report 1999, 1(11).

3. J. A. Cheong, S. G. Silva, J. M. Petitto, M. J. Herkow, and D. L. Evans, "Human Immunodeficiency Virus-Related Psychopathology and Treatment," in *Current Psychiatric Therapy II,* ed. D. L. Dunner (Philadelphia: W. B. Saunders, 1997), 521.

4. Ibid., 522.

5. *Practice Guideline for the Treatment of Patients with HIV/AIDS,* 62.

6. J. J. Wallack, "AIDS Anxiety among Health Care Professionals," *Hospital and Community Psychiatry* 40, no. 5 (1989): 507–10.

7. *Practice Guideline for the Treatment of Patients with HIV/AIDS,* 27.

8. T. J. Mayne, M. Acree, M. A. Chesney, and S. Folkman, "HIV Sexual Risk Behavior Following Bereavement in Gay Men," *Health Psychology* 17 (1998): 403–11.

9. P. M. Marzuk, H. Tierney, K. Tardiff, et al., "Increased Risk of Suicide in Persons with AIDS," *JAMA* 259 (1988): 1333–37.

10. P. M. Marzuk, K. Tardiff, A. C. Leon, et al., "HIV Seroprevalence among Suicide Victims in New York City, 1991–1993," *America Journal of Psychiatry* 154 (1997): 1720–25.

Chapter 33. Suicide: Weighing the Risk

1. American Academy of Child and Adolescent Psychiatry, *Practice Parameters for the Assessment and Treatment of Children and Adolescents with Suicidal Behavior* (Washington, D.C., 2000), 6.

2. Ibid., 7.

3. Ibid.

4. Ibid., 8.

5. E. S. Shneidman and N. L. Farberow, eds., *Clues to Suicide* (New York: McGraw-Hill, 1957, 1963).

6. American Foundation for Suicide Prevention: www.afsp.org. American Psychiatric Association: www.psych.org. American Academy of Child and Adolescent Psychiatry: www.aacap.org.

7. American Academy of Child and Adolescent Psychiatry, *Practice Parameters,* 52.

Chapter 34. Death in Our Culture

1. B. DeMott, *The Atlantic Monthly* (June 1974): 99.

2. C. K. Cassel, "Introduction," in *Pioneer Programs in Palliative Care: Nine Case Studies* (New York: Robert Wood Johnson Foundation, Milbank Memorial Fund, 2000), v.

3. S. B. Nuland, *How We Die: Reflections on Life's Final Chapter* (New York: Vintage Books, 1995); Institute for Clinical and Epidemiologic Medicine: Program on the Medical Encounter and Palliative Care. hsrd.durham.med.va.gov/pmepc/teach.htm.

4. E. K. Ross, *On Death and Dying* (New York: Macmillan, 1969).

Chapter 35. Suffering Our Losses

1. S. Zisook and S. R. Schucter, "Bereavement," in *Current Psychiatric Therapy II,* ed. D. L. Dunner (Philadelphia: W. B. Saunders, 1997), 248.

2. Ibid., 250.

3. Ibid.

4. N. H. Cassem, "The Person Confronting Death," in *The New Harvard Guide to Psychiatry,* ed. A. M. Nicholi Jr. (Cambridge: Belknap Press of Harvard University Press, 1988; 3d ed., 1999), 728–58.

5. Ibid., 752.

6. A. Weisman, "Is Mourning Necessary?" in *Anticipatory Grief* (New York: Columbia University Press, 1974).

7. H. G. Koenig, M. E. McCullough, and D. B. Larson, eds., *Handbook of Religion and Health* (New York: Oxford University Press, 2001). Refer to chapter 7, "Depression," 118–35, for a thorough review of religious affiliation and depression.

8. C. M. Parkes, *Bereavement: Studies of Grief in Adult Life,* 3d ed. (Madison, Conn.: International Universities Press, 1998).

9. P. Aries, *Western Attitudes toward Death: From the Middle Ages to the Present* (Baltimore: Johns Hopkins University Press, 1974; London: Marion Boyars, 1994).

10. C. M. Parkes and R. S. Weiss, *Recovery from Bereavement* (New York: Basic Books, 1983; 1st softcover ed.: Northvale, N.J.: J. Aronson, 1995).

11. Cassem, "The Person Confronting Death," 750.

12. L. Edel, *Henry James, The Treacherous Years: 1895–1902* (Philadelphia: J. B. Lippincott, 1969), 57.

Chapter 36. Emergencies: Being a Steady Presence

1. E. S. Schneidman, "Crisis Intervention: Some Thoughts and Perspectives," in *Crisis Intervention,* ed. G. A. Specter and W. C. Claiborn (New York: Behavioral Publications, 1973; 2d ed.: New York: Human Sciences Press, 1983); E. S.

Shneidman, N. L. Farberow, and R. E. Litman, *The Psychology of Suicide* (New York: Science House, 1970; rev. ed.: Northvale, N.J.: J. Aronson, 1994).

2. E. Lindemann, "Symptomatology and Management of Acute Grief, 1944 (classic article)," *American Journal of Psychiatry* 151 (1994) [6 Suppl]: 155–60; G. Caplan, "Loss, Stress, and Mental Health," *Community Mental Health Journal* 26 (1990): 27–48.

3. H. G. Koenig, M. E. McCullough, and D. B. Larson, eds., *Handbook of Religion and Health* (New York: Oxford University Press, 2001).

4. Critical Incident Stress Web Site, New Jersey PBA CISM, geocities.com/CapitolHill/Lobby/3082/.

5. R. A. MacKinnon and R. Michels, *The Psychiatric Interview in Clinical Practice* (Philadelphia: W. B. Saunders, 1971), 414.

6. Ibid., 404.

INDEX

abnormal grieving, 378–79
Abnormal Psychology and Modern Life
(Coleman), 279
abuse, distinguished from dependence,
185–86, 192
acceptance
importance of, 108–9
stage of dying, 369
ACoA. *See* Adult Children of Alcoholics
acquired immunodeficiency syndrome. *See*
AIDS
acting out, form of resistance, 118
acute stress disorder, 241–42
Adams, Henry, 384–85
addiction, 180–81, 182
address, form of in helping relationship,
93–94
adjustment disorders, 140–41, 248–49,
250–51, 252–53, 350
adolescence
deferring maturity during, 183–84
work of, 182–83
Adult Children of Alcoholics, 196
affective disorder, 195–96
aggression
in antisocial personalities, 280
in helping relationship, 96–97
agnosia, 177
agoraphobia, 239, 245
AIDS, 187, 332, 336, 340, 341. *See also*
HIV
Al-Anon, 198
Alateen, 198
alcohol, 182, 184
physiological dependence on, 192
rate of dependence, 193
alcohol abuse
Fetal Alcohol Syndrome, 197
identified in behavioral changes, 193
signs of, 197
alcohol dependence, signs of, 197
Alcoholics Anonymous, 157, 191, 198–99
alcoholism
children of alcoholic patients, 196–97
comorbid disorders, 195–96

complications of, 200–201
genetic vulnerability toward, 195
keeping person rather than problem in
focus during treatment, 193–95
personal relationships in context of,
197–98
prevalence of, 192
psychiatric evaluation and treatment,
200
relapse, 194–95
treatment, 198–200
alcohol use
American ambivalence toward, 194
assessing public health dimensions of,
192–93
legal means of addressing, 194
Alzheimer's Association, 138, 179
Alzheimer's disease, 177, 178
ambivalence, in time of grief, 382
American Academy of Child and Adolescent Psychiatry, 197, 354,
360
American Foundation for Suicide
Prevention, 354
American Medical Association, 158
American Psychiatric Association, vii, 134,
158, 214, 345
Code of Ethics, 80
schizophrenia treatment guidelines, 213
American Psychological Association, xiii,
158, 214, 319
amnestic disorder, 137–38
amphetamines, 184, 186
analysis
misunderstanding nature of
interpretation in, 53
overconfidence in, 53
Anderson, Robert, 364
anger
among depressed persons, 227
diversionary tactic, 117
in helping relationship, 33–35, 36–37
phase of mourning process, 382
stage of dying, 369
anorexia nervosa, 140

anticipation, 390
antidepressant medication, 225
antipsychotic medication, 204
antisocial personalities, 119
    reasons for entering counseling, 281
    unsocialized behavior, 276
antisocial personality disorder, 34, 195,
    256
    behaviors indicating, 276–78, 279–81
    characteristics of, 278–81, 289
    demographics of, 278, 279
    difficulty in identifying, 275–76
    factors in diagnosis, 276
    gender prevalence, 278
    innocents affected by, 277–78, 281–83
    lack of emotion in, 280
    personalities of, 276–78
    secondary complications of life, 280–81
anxiety
    acute, 235–36
    dangers of advice for, 236–37
    diagnosing, 235–37
    among helpers, 237
    reaction to adjustment disorder, 250
    reaction to emergencies, 393–94
    related to fear, 244–45
    signals and symptoms of, 234–35
    symptoms similar to physical conditions,
        236
anxiety disorders, 140, 195–96, 238–46
anxiety management techniques, 238
anxiety neurosis, 238
anxiolytics, 184
aphasia, 177
appetite, change in, 219
appointments, 88–90
    importance of beginnings and endings,
        301–2
    switching times for, 118
approval, need for, 49–50
apraxia, 177
Aries, Phillip, 376
Ars Morendi (Art of Dying), 362
ascetic practices, 9
authority, reacting against, 106
aversive techniques, treatment for sexual
    problems, 339
avoidant disorder, 34, 256
avoidant personality disorder
    characteristics of, 295–96
    similarity with social phobias, 296, 297
    treatment, 297
Axis I–V, 137

bargaining, stage of dying, 369
behavioral couple therapy, 7 Cs of, 319
behavioral techniques, with paranoid
    personality disorder, 271
behavior therapy
    for phobic disorders, 245
    for sexual problems, 339
    See also cognitive behavioral therapy
Bellow, Saul, 301
bereavement, 249, 349, 372–73
    allowing emotions of, 383–85
    counselor's role during, 383–85
    emotional atmosphere surrounding,
        382–83
    literature about, 368–70
biofeedback, 238
bipolar disorder, 139, 205, 227
bipolar illness, 206, 222
blended families, 312
blocked grieving, 378–79
borderline personalities
    distrust of counselors, 286
    effect on helpers, 286
borderline personality disorder, 34, 256,
    257, 305
    characteristics of, 284, 289
    features of, 285–86
    gender prevalence, 285
    manipulative pressures of, 283–84
    misdiagnosis and underdiagnosis of, 284
    treatment for, 287
    unknown origin, 285
boundary crossing, 80–81
boundary issues, 80–81
boundary violation, 80–81
Brawley, Tawana, 264
Breslin, Jimmy, 282
Bringing Out the Dead, 363
bug chasing, 349
bulimia nervosa, 140

Cameron, Norman, 264
cannabis, 184. *See also* marijuana
Caplan, Gerard, 389
caring, expression of, 165
Cassem, Ned H., 374, 379, 383
CBT. *See* cognitive behavioral techniques
Centers for Disease Control and Prevention,
    333, 341, 353
CEWG. *See* Community Epidemiology
    Work Group
change
    accepting inability to, 69, 70–71
    helper's need for, 108

charmer, 276–77
Cheever, John, 319
chronic grief, 378–79
chronic mental illness, 205–8. *See also* schizophrenia
Churchill, Winston, 215
clarification, 7–8
claustrophobia, 245
Cleckley, Hervey, 278
clinical depression, 196, 218, 373
clinical disorders, 137
clinical judgment, 125
Clinton, Bill, 76
closed-end questions, danger of, 114
cocaine, 182, 184, 186–88
cognitive behavioral therapy
    for avoidant personality disorder, 297
    for generalized anxiety disorder, 238
    for panic disorder, 239
    for obsessive-compulsive personality disorder, 304
    for paranoid personality disorder, 271
    for personality disorder, 259
    for schizotypal personality disorder, 274
    for scruples, 241
    for social phobia, 245–46
cognitive disorder, 137–38
cognitive disturbance, 215
command hallucination, 214
common sense, importance of, vii, ix, xiv
communication
    responding to essentials in, 147–48
    sensitivity toward, 60–61
    signals in, 20–23, 29, 85, 113, 131–32
    totality of, 60
community, counselors for, 71–72
community-based treatment, 204–5, 214
Community Epidemiology Work Group, 190
community resources, 138
comorbid disorders, 195–96
compensation, symbolism of, 93
competition, in counseling relationship, 118–19
compulsion, 185, 240
concentration, diminished ability for, 221
condensation, 299
conditioning processes, treatment for sexual problems, 339
conduct disorder, 276
confidence, loss of, 29–30
conflicted grief, 378

conflict resolution, 168
confusion, 113, 394–95
conspiracy theories, 261, 264
contamination fears, 241
context, appreciating in storytelling, 146
continuing education, 158
controlling authoritarianism, 74–75
counseling
    changes in, vii
    confusing with ministry, 94–95
    democratization of, x–xi, 74, 134
    as different relationship, 76–77
    do's and don'ts, 15
    forced, 103–5
    freeing oneself in helping relationship, 45–47
    human contact as principal objective, 302
    manipulation of relationship, 42
    for others, 44
    with others, 44–47
    related to friendship, 75–81
    See also counseling relationship
counseling-become-friendship, 79
counseling relationship
    with antisocial persons, 281
    breakdown and stagnation, 29–30, 38
    mistaken goal of, 63
    revealing patterns of other behavior, 61–62
    stressing cooperation over competition, 60–61
counselors
    as authority figures, 95
    decreasing stress, 401
    expressing feelings of, 159–60
    impact of feelings on helping relationship, 40–47
    problems with improvising in helping, 401–2
    professional attitude, importance of, 402
    viewing selves as persons, 401
counselors, nonprofessional, vii–xiv, 3–4
    avoiding techniques, 7
    emotional involvement, 11–19
    personality as chief asset, 28
    psychological mindedness, 5–6
    restraint by, 12
    self-assessment, 13–14, 16, 18–19
    self-confidence, 4–5
    self-restraint of, 26
    supportive therapy, 6–9
    See also nonprofessional helpers

countertransference, 15, 16–17, 18
  with borderline personality disorder,
    286, 287
  in counseling for sexual problems,
    329–30
  dealing with stress of, 62
  with dependent personality disorder, 33,
    307
  in emergency situations, 397
  empathy as method of dealing with, 256
  gauging emergence of, 406
  with grief, 380, 382
  with histrionic personality disorder,
    291–92
  with HIV counseling, 343, 346
  in listening to stories, 145, 148
  managing challenges of, 67
  with marriage counseling, 311–12, 314
  with narcissistic personality disorder,
    294
  with obsessive-compulsive personality
    disorder, 303–4
  referrals bringing out feelings of, 149–52
  related to treatment of alcoholics, 193
  signs of, 161–63
  sorting out from transference, 38–39
  unconscious aspects of, 81
  unrecognized, 160–64
couples therapy
  for borderline personality disorder, 287
  for histrionic personality disorder, 292
crack, 186, 187–88
crisis
  stages of, 388–89
  styles of, 387–88
  time span of effects, 389–90
  viewed as loss, 389
crisis management, 170
crisis theory and technique, 388–89
crisis work, 389
critical incident stress syndrome, 391–92
cultural differences, in describing somatic
    problems, 217

Daley, Richard J., ix
DAWN. *See* Drug Abuse Warning Network
death
  anticipating and preparing for with
    AIDS, 351
  avoiding superficial treatment of, 362–64
  challenge of facing, 364–65
  children facing, 365
  common attitudes about, 366–68
  counseling challenges of, 364–65

counseling the dying, 368–69
  interest in, 361
  interwoven with sex, 362
  literature about, 368–70
  as management problem, 361–62
  palliative care, 366
  recurring thoughts, 221–22
  responding to dying persons, 362
  stigma surrounding, 376
debriefing, 243
defeats, accepting, 68
defenses, 8, 9–10
  building new lines of, 394
  encouraging the healthiest, 390
  ill-advised challenge to at time of grief,
    381
  limited among persons with personality
    disorder, 259
  with obsessive-compulsive personality
    disorder, 304
  purposes of, 62
  strengthening the healthiest, 170, 172
  used in counseling, 61–62
  used in marriage counseling, 324
defensiveness, 53
deinstitutionalization, 204–5, 206, 214
delirium, 137–38, 175–76, 350
delusional disorder, 262
Demara, Ferdinand, Jr., 279
dementia, 137–38, 175, 177–79, 206, 350,
    394
demoralization, 239, 350–51
DeMott, Benjamin, 363
denial, 247–48
  with HIV/AIDS, 348–49
  with paranoid personality disorder, 268
  stage of dying, 369
dependence
  distinguished from abuse, 185–86, 192
  in schizophrenics, 209–10
  useful tool in crisis management, 172
dependent disorder, 256
dependent personality, 32–33
dependent personality disorder, 34
  characteristics of, 305–7
  counseling difficulties, 306
  overlap with other disorders, 305–6
  treatment for, 307
depression, 141, 206
  actions of depressed individuals, 216–17
  associated with panic disorder, 239
  bereavement distinguished from, 372–73
  coexistence with marital distress, 312
  diagnosing from mild to severe, 224–25

double, 222
familiar pattern for, 227
grief distinguished from, 373, 374
in helping relationship, 36–37
listening to persons with, 223–24
naming the problem, 224–25
overlooking or undiagnosed, 217–18
periodicity of, 226
postcrisis, 389
range of, 215
reaction to adjustment disorder, 250
resulting from emergency situation, 392
self-punishment with, 228–29
somatic problems, 217–18
stage of dying, 369
style of counseling for, 229–31
symptoms, 217–23, 226
taking on characteristics of subject of
    loss, 227
from threats to self-image, 252
treating, 225, 226
See also major depression
depressive disorders, 139, 218–19
deprivation, 376, 377, 389
desensitization therapy
    for avoidant personality disorder, 297
    for sexual problems, 339
despondency, 350–51
detachment, 272
Dewald, Paul
    on cornerstones of treatment, 171
    on dealing with reluctant, 110
    on insight-oriented treatment, 168
    on interpretation, 54
    on resistance, 111, 112, 120
    on therapeutic relationship, 77
diagnosis, 121–22
    developing skills for, 134
    development and refinement, 141
    employing and applying guidelines, 136
    extension of understanding, 131
    helpfulness of, 124
    leading to referral, 126
    persons subject to, 126–27
    practical issues, 123, 128–31
    principal, 136–37
    provisional, 136
    respecting individuality in, 131
    understanding true personality, 125–26,
        127
    unhelpfulness of, 123
    using *DSM-IV-TR* language, 133
    watching for disturbances and
        abnormalities, 132

*Diagnostic and Statistical Manual of
    Mental Disorders, 4th edition. See
    DSM-IV-TR*
dialectical behavioral therapy, for
    borderline personality disorder,
    287
disaster response. *See* frontline work
displacement, 299
distance, maintaining when treating
    paranoid personality disorder, 269–70
distancing, in helping relationship, 41–42,
    43–44
distortion, 347
distracting behavior, 105
distractions, counselors', 165
disturbance, manifestations of, 132
divorce, 312–13
do-gooding, 24–26, 66, 144
doing well, 144
    destructiveness of attempting, 27–28
    trap of, 85
domination, helper's need for, 79
double depression, 222
dream analysis, 7
drug abuse
    counselor's approach to, 189–91
    signs and symptoms, 184–86
    survey of symptoms, 189
Drug Abuse Warning Network, 188
drug use
    adolescent rite of passage, 181–82
    generational differences in approach to,
        181
    historical perspective, 180
    in youths, 181–82
DSM-III, 238
DSM-IV-TR, vii
    bereavement and depression, 374
    categorizing sexual disorders, 335,
        338
    cocaine information, 186
    current classification, 136–41
    familiarity with, 3
    history of "psychotic" classification,
        202–3
    inadequacy of clustering system, 275
    mental disorder defined, 135–36
    multiaxial approach, 136–37
    passive aggression recategorized, 34
    purpose of, 134–35
    schizophrenia, diagnostic criteria for,
        207
    substance use classifications, 185

dying
  role of counselor in, 370–71
  stages of, 369–70
dysthymic disorder, 195, 196, 221–22

eating disorders, 140
ECA. *See* Epidemiological Catchment Area
    Study
eclecticism, dangers of, 404
economy of the helper, 406–7
ecstasy, 182, 190–91
Edel, Leon, 385
education, 8, 403–4
emergencies, 87–88
  anxiety as constant reaction to, 393
  common difficulties in, 394–95
  counselors' role in, 386–87
  difficulties with others, 396–97
  everyday, 392–93
  expectations in situation, 399
  involving others in handling of, 397–98
  precipitating events, 388, 389
  referrals in, 398–99
  somatic problems in, 395–96
  sources of, 387
  stages of, 387–88
emergency, use of telephone during,
    399–400
emergency workers, 391–92
emotional dependence, counselor's, 160–
    61
emotional depth, assessing, 124–26
emotional involvement
  avoiding, 40
  challenges of, xii–xiii
emotions, appropriateness of, 132
empathy, 5–6, 8, 75
  in frontline work, 243
  lacking for psychosis, 203–4
  in treating adjustment disorders, 253
  in treating phobic disorders, 246
  in treating schizophrenia, 209, 212
energy, loss of, 220
Engel, George, 374
enlistment syndrome, 314
environmental problems, 137
envoi, 110
Epidemiological Catchment Area Study,
    193, 244
Erikson, Erik, 182
etiology, 135, 136
Executioner's Song, The (Mailer), 277–78
executive function, 177, 390
exhibitionism, 338

expectations, 94–96, 102–3
experience
  learning from, 20
  processing of, 142–43
exploration of problems, 7, 8
extra time, pattern of requiring, 90
extratherapeutic contact, 81

face-to-face meeting, preferred goal of
    initial communication, 86
faith
  crisis of, 241
  source of well-being, 390–91
FAL. *See* Fetal Alcohol Syndrome
fallacy of the reasonable response, 394
fallacy of the reasonable solution, 317–18
family therapy, not recommended for
    borderline personality disorder, 287
fatigue, 220
fear
  in helping relationship, 35–36
  management, 233–34
  pathological, 244–45
feeling tone, 145–46
Felder, Richard, 76
fetal alcohol syndrome, 197
fetishism, 338
finances, and counseling relationship, 92
forced counseling, 103–5
Forster, E. M., 75
free association, 7
free-floating anxiety, 237
Freud, Sigmund
  on anxiety, 232, 234–35
  Freudian slips, 59–60, 61
  grief work, 379
  purpose of life, 58
  types of resistance, 112
  usefulness of theories in understanding
    obsessive-compulsive personality
    disorder, 298–99
Freudian slip, 59–60, 61
friends
  communication between, compared with
    therapeutic relationship, 77
  danger of acting like therapists with,
    77–79
friendship
  different from helping relationship, 78
  related to counseling, 75–81
frontline work, 242–44
Frost, Robert, 7, 80, 319
frotteurism, 338

Gabbard, Glen, 80–81
GAF. *See* Global Assessment of Functioning Scale
Gardner, Richard A., 143
gateway drugs, 182
gender identity disorders, 140, 335
generalized anxiety disorder, 238
generalizing, form of resistance, 116
general medical conditions, mental disorders due to, 137, 138
generative authority, 74–75
genital herpes, 332–33
genuineness, 75
Gilmore, Gary, 277–78
Glasser, William, 102
global assessment of functioning, 137
Global Assessment of Functioning Scale, 137
Greene, Graham, 142–43
grief
    counselors' philosophy/theology as aid in helping, 375
    depression distinguished from, 373, 374
    growth process of, 375–76
    from loss other than death, 377–78
    resolution of relationship, 380
    side effects, 381–83
    work of, 379–80
grieving
    abnormal (blocked), 378–79
    normal, 373, 374–75
ground rules, 87, 88
group therapy, 272
    not appropriate for histrionic personality disorder, 292
    for dependent personality disorder, 307
guilt
    from treating depressed persons, 228
    inappropriate feelings of, 220–21
Gutheil, Thomas, 80–81

HAD. *See* HIV-associated dementia, 350
hallucinogens, 184
H.C.E., 283
Health Maintenance Organizations, vii
help
    counselor's need to, 66
    naming of person receiving, xiii
helpers, frustration among, 255
helping, setting end point for, 89–90
Helping the Depressed Person Get Treatment (National Institute of Mental Health), 230

helping relationships
    counselor's agenda in, 51–52
    mutuality of, 42, 43, 44–47
    styles of, 41–44
helplessness, 32–33, 216
heroin, 180–81
historical information, 129–30
histrionic personalities, attracted to obsessive personalities, 292
histrionic personality disorder, 34, 256, 306
    characteristics of, 288–90
    emotional difficulties, 290–91
    gender prevalence, 289
    in men, 291
    narcissistic qualities of, 292
    sharing traits of other personality disorders, 288
    treatment of, 292
Hitchcock, Alfred, 245
HIV, 177, 332
    avoiding unconscious material and defenses in counseling, 346–47
    common reactions to, 348–51
    confidentiality issues, 345
    counseling challenges, 341–43
    counseling pre- and post-testing, 345
    description of disease, 340–41
    extent of problem, 341
    frequency of mental disorders in population, 350
    importance of team approach to, 346
    legal issues, 344–45
    reactions to diagnosis, 344
    recent therapies for, 348
    testing for, 343, 344–45
HIV-associated dementia, 350
homelessness, 71–72, 206
hopelessness, reaction to adjustment disorder, 250
Hospice Movement, 367, 384
hospitalization, 70–71, 214, 225, 358, 399
hostility, 105, 113
    handling in interviews, 96–99
    with paranoid personality disorder, 262, 265–67, 269
    in schizophrenics, 210
How We Die: Reflections on Life's Final Chapter (Nuland), 368
human condition
    living in, 126–27
    stressors in, 253–54
human immunodeficiency virus. *See* HIV
hypnotics, 184, 188–89

hypochondria, with paranoid personality
    disorder, 263
hypomanic disorders, 139
hypoxyphilia, 338

identity, development during adolescence,
    182–83
imperfection, accepting, 65–67
impulse disorders, 141
impulse gratification, 278
indecisiveness, 221
indirection, style of expression, 235
individuality, achieving, 58
individual-vs.-institution dilemma, 107–8
I Never Promised You a Rose Garden,
    208
initial meeting, laying ground rules, 87
insight-directed therapy, 119–20
insight-oriented treatment, 168–69,
    171–72
institutionalization, 204
institution-vs.-individual dilemma, 107–8
intellectualization, form of resistance,
    115–16
intellectual lethargy, with depression, 222
interest
    expression of, 165
    loss of, 218–19
internal life, assessing, 124–26
interpersonal emergencies, 392, 396–97
interpretation
    careful use of, 53
    rush to, 52–54
interruptions, 91, 95
interviewing
    addressing parties in, 93–94
    allowing interruptions, 91
    appointments, 88–90
    as chief tool for depression diagnosis,
        221
    ending, 99–100
    expectations of, 94–96
    hostility in, 96–99
    opening and closing moments,
        importance of, 85, 96–100
    overeagerness of helper, 98–99
    physical arrangements, 90–93
    with schizophrenia, 208
    subsequent meeting planning, 100
    telephone, 86–88
intimacy, inexperience counselors and, 161
intoxication, 185, 186
intrapersonal emergencies, 392
isolation, 299

James, Henry, 384–85
Janis, Irving, 233–34
jargon, 116
Joyce, James, 283, 374
judging others, 50–51, 54
judging without condemning, 122

Kübler-Ross, Elisabeth, 363, 368, 369

Landers, Ann, vii
Lasch, Christopher, 76
laughing, form of resistance, 114–15
Lean, David, 252
Lesher, Alan, 190–91
lethality scale, for suicide, 352–53
Levant, Oscar, xi
life changes, in context of emergencies, 395
limitations
    accepting, 68
    acknowledging, 67
Lincoln, Abraham, 215
Lindemann, Erich, 388–89
listening, 20–23, 113
    benefits of, 37–39
    to depressed persons, 223–24
    hearing through one's own reactions,
        30–32, 37–39
    for lifelong character of personality
        disorder, 259–60
loners, 272
Los Angeles Suicide Prevention Center, 352
loss
    perceptions of, 376–77
    types of, 372, 377–78

MacKinnon, R. A.
    on ambivalence toward life, 392
    on countertransference, 162
    on depression, 220
    on hysterical patients, 288
    on questioning, 51–52
    strategies for dealing with obsessive-
        compulsive personality disorder,
        303
    on weakened defenses, 394
MADD. *See* Mothers Against Drunk
    Drivers
Mailer, Norman, 232, 277–78
major depression, 195, 205, 251, 350,
    373–74
    less likely in people with well-internalized
        religious beliefs, 375
    in schizotypal personality disorder, 274

maladaptive behavior, reaction to
  adjustment disorder, 250–51
mania, 141, 222
manic-depressive illness. *See* bipolar
  disorder
manic disorders, 139
manipulation, 281, 285
marijuana, 182. *See also* cannabis
marriage counseling
  avoiding choosing sides, 313–15
  confidence about, 311
  cultural context for, 312–13, 323–25
  defenses in, 324
  different growth rates for spouses, 322
  goals of, 316–17
  mandatory, 104
  mediators used in, 319–20
  preparing for, 313–14, 316–17, 320–21,
    323–25
  problems brought to, 317–18
  questioning attraction of spouses,
    311–12
  seeing spouses alone or together, 314–15
  7 Cs of behavioral couple therapy, 319
  shortcuts ineffective for, 318–19, 320
  surprises in, 321–22, 325–26
  tips for, 322
  transference and countertransference
    issues, 311–12, 314
Mask of Sanity, The (Cleckley), 278
masochism, 228–29. *See also* sexual
  masochism
master therapist, acting the role of, 163–64
maturity, deferred, 183–84
MDMA. *See* ecstasy
MEDEM, 157
mediators, 319–20
medical condition, mental disorders due to,
  179
medication, vii
  for anxiety, 238
  for avoidant personality disorder, 297
  for borderline personality disorder, 287
  for dealing with stress, 232
  for obsessive-compulsive personality
    disorder, 304
  for panic disorder, 239
  for paranoid personality disorder, 271
  for personality disorder, 259
  for phobic disorders, 245
  for post-traumatic stress disorder, 242
  for schizotypal personality disorder, 274
  for scruples, 241

  for sexual problems, 339
  for symptoms of adjustment disorder,
    254
meditation, 232
Menninger, Karl, 81
mental disorders, 205
  defining, 135–36
  due to general medical condition, 179
  overlap of symptoms, 136
  psychoanalytic viewpoint toward, 135
  psychodynamic viewpoint toward, 135
  types of, 136–41
  unknown cause, 135
mental retardation, 137
methamphetamine, 182
Michels, R.
  on ambivalence toward life, 392
  on countertransference, 162
  on depression, 220
  on hysterical patients, 288
  on questioning, 51–52
  strategies for dealing with obsessive-
    compulsive personality disorder,
    303
  on weakened defenses, 394
ministry, confusing with counseling, 94–95
mistrust, with paranoid personality
  disorder, 269
Mitchell, Jeffrey, 391
Monroe, Marilyn, 400
mood changes, 218–19, 221–22
mood disorders, 139, 215
moral imbeciles, 275
Mothers Against Drunk Drivers, 194
mourning
  allowing rituals of, 384
  need for defenses, 381
  postcrisis, 389
  as search for object of loss, 378
Mumford, Lewis, 387
mutual aid centers, 157
"My Fair Lady" complex, 79

narcissism, American preoccupation with,
  292
narcissistic personality disorder, 256
  characteristics of, 293
  difficulties in counseling, 293–94
  gender prevalence, 293
Narcotics Anonymous, 191
narratives, abnormalities in, 132
National Alliance for the Mentally Ill, 214
National Highway Transportation Safety
  Administration, 194

National Institute of Drug Abuse, 190
National Institute of Mental Health, 230
National Mental Health Association, 214
"Necessary and Sufficient Conditions for
    Therapeutic Personality Change, The"
    (Rogers), 75
negativistic personality disorder, 33–35
neurotic, 222
neurotic anxiety, 232
neutrality, 7, 40
NIDA. *See* National Institute of Drug
    Abuse
nonprofessional helpers
    counseling by, vii–x
    guiding principles for, 3–10
    human assets of, xi–xii
    See also counselors, nonprofessional
nonverbal communication, 131–32
Nuland, Sherwin, 368

obsessions, 240, 241
obsessive-compulsive disorder, 140, 205,
    240, 256, 299
obsessive-compulsive personality disorder
    challenge of counseling, 297, 300–303
    characteristics of, 298–99
    gender prevalence, 298
    instructiveness of beginnings and endings
        of appointments, 301–2
    likelihood of seeking treatment, 304
    personality structure of, 298–300
    treatment for, 304–5
On Becoming a Person (Rogers), 75
On Death and Dying (Kübler-Ross), 363
opening up, misguided goal of, 62–63
opioid disturbance, 180–81
opioids, 184, 188
optimism, 66
organic mental disorders, reclassification,
    138
outpatient treatment, 104
overdiagnosis, 251
overeagerness, dangers of, 114
overidentification, 162
overreacting, with potential suicides, 355

panic attacks, 141, 238, 239
panic disorder, 140, 238–39
pan-therapeutic approach, 76
paranoia, 124, 228, 237, 261
paranoid personality, 256
paranoid personality disorder, 34, 35–36
    challenge of referral, 271–72
    characteristics of people with, 262–64

communications of people with, 263–64
denial with, 268
features of, 261–62
hostility with, 262, 265–67
manifestations of humor with, 266
mistrust with, 269
projection with, 268
in public life, 264
reaction-formation with, 268
rejection with, 269
related psychotic conditions, 262
relations with counselors, 269–72
source of distortions, 264–65
targets of in need of counseling, 267–68
treatment for, 271–72
paraphilias, 140, 335, 337–38, 339
Parkes, Murray, 375–76, 377, 378–79
participant-observers, 38–39, 301
passive aggressive personality disorder,
    33–34
passivity, 114
pastoral counseling, 171
patients' rights, 70–71
payments, related to counseling
    relationship, 92
pedophilia, 338, 339
peer counselors, 242
people, focusing on, 23–24
perfection, quest for, 67
perfectionism, 298, 299
performance, counselor's expectations,
    102–3
"Person Confronting Death, The"
    (Cassem), 374
personality, reorganizing through insight-
    oriented treatment, 169
personality disorders, 137, 141
    in children, 258–59
    Cluster A, 256, 261–74
    Cluster B, 256, 275–94
    Cluster C, 256, 295–307
    difficulty in determining etiology, 258–59
    DSM-IV-TR classification, 256
    lack of symptoms with, 256–57
    not otherwise specified, 256
    prevalence of, 257–60
    vigilance in addressing when treating
        alcoholism, 195–96
    See also specific personality disorders:
        antisocial, avoidant, borderline,
        dependent, histrionic, narcissistic,
        obsessive-compulsive, paranoid,
        passive aggressive, schizoid,
        schizotypal

personality theory, 404–5
perspective, clarifying in storytelling, 146
perversions, 337
phencyclidine, 184
phobias, 195, 244–46
physical arrangement, helping session, 90–93
post-traumatic stress disorder, 141, 241–42, 243, 391
post-traumatic stress syndrome, 232
power, prizing, 146
Practice Guideline for the Treatment of Schizophrenia (American Psychiatric Association), 213
preplanned outcomes, trouble of, 25
prescription drug abuse, 188–89, 190
problems, overfocusing on, 23–24
professional forums, 158
professionalism, 75, 403–4, 405, 407
Program on the Medical Encounter and Palliative Care, 368
projection
  with paranoid personality disorder, 268
  reaction to emergency, 393
pseudo-communities, 264
psychiatric assessment, for suspected drug disorders, 191
psychiatric treatment, for depression, 225, 226
psychoactive substances, 184
psychoanalysis, for dependent personality disorder, 307
psychoanalytic theory, understanding personality disorder, 259
psychodynamic psychotherapy, 222
psychological issues, 69–71
psychological mindedness, 5–6
psychological structure, importance of determining, 122
psychomotor changes, 219–20
Psychopathology of Everyday Life, The (Freud), 59
psychopaths, 119, 275
psychosis
  counselor's need for understanding, 204–5
  defining, 202–3
  shifts in attitude toward, 204–6
  unfamiliarity with language of, 202
psychosocial problems, 137
psychotherapies, distinction between, 169
psychotherapy, 238
  for avoidant personality disorder, 297
  for borderline personality disorder, 287

democratization of, 159
  for dependent personality disorder, 307
  for depression, 225
  for histrionic personality disorder, 292
  ineffectiveness for antisocial personalities, 279
  for narcissistic personality disorder, 294
  for post-traumatic stress disorder, 242
  for schizotypal personality disorder, 274
  treatment for obsessive-compulsive personality disorder, 304
  treatment for sexual problems, 339
Psychotherapy: The Purchase of Friendship (Schofield), 75
psychotic disorders, 139
psychotic symptoms, in schizotypal personality disorder, 273
PTSD. *See* post-traumatic stress disorder
"Pygmalion" complex, 79

questioning, necessity of proper approach, 128, 129–30
questionnaires, 123
questions
  avoiding "why," 116, 130, 336
  excessiveness, 51–52

rage, 267–68, 294
rapport, 49–50
rationalization, 9, 54, 347
  with alcohol use, 200, 201
  with personality disorder, 258
  with substance abuse, 182
reaction-formation, 268, 299
reality principles, 59–64
Reality Therapy (Glasser), 102
reassurance, 8
  false, 54–56
  problems with, 251
reconstructive therapy, avoiding, 346–47
recovery, three tasks of, 379
recreational drugs, 182
recrimination, 69
referrals, 70
  for adjustment disorders, 254
  for antisocial personality disorder, 283
  for borderline personality disorder, 287
  challenge with paranoid personality disorder, 271–72
  completing, 155–56
  in counseling for sexual problems, 330–31, 336–37, 338–39
  countertransference in context of, 149–52

referrals (continued)
for depression, 221, 226, 230
developing relationships for, 155, 157
difficulties with, 156–57
elements of quality in, 155
in emergency situations, 393, 398–99
for generalized anxiety disorder, 238
guilt over, 150
human process of, 153–54
impressions of rejection with, 151
to lawyers for targets of paranoid
persons, 268
for mania, 222
manner of, 130–31
for narcissistic personality disorder, 294
need for, 132–33
for panic disorder, 239–40
preparing for, 149–50, 154
to psychiatrists for targets of paranoid
persons, 268
reasons for, 154
resulting from diagnosis, 126
for schizophrenia, 213
for scruples, 241
for sexual problems, 334–35
sources for, 155, 157
for suicide risks, 357–58
telling the truth about, 153–54
timing of, 130
transference in context of, 150, 152, 153
when needs go beyond supportive
treatment, 172
regret, 69
Reismann, John M., 77
rejection
fear of, 296
projected reluctance, 106
self-inflicted for depressed persons,
223–24
relationships
being in, 14–17
checklist for, 18
for depressed persons, 223–24
reacting to, 17–19
structuring, 88–90
relaxation therapy, 238
religious faith, vii
reluctance, 98, 101–2
dealing with mutually, 109
emotional context, 102
handling, 106–7, 108–9
motives for, 105–8
projecting, 106
reluctant, characteristics of, 103–4

repetition, in storytelling, 147
repetition-compulsion resistance, 112
repression resistance, 112
rescue fantasies, 25–26, 46, 66, 396
resistance, 98, 101, 102, 111–20
acknowledging, 119
attack on, 113–14
characteristics of, 111–12
counselor's involvement in, 118–19
recognizing as form of defense, 119
recognizing and responding to, 113–14
signs of, 114–18
silence, 112–14
types of, 112
working through, 119
responding, need to, 78
responses, focusing on others, 63–64
responsibility, helping people accept for
themselves, 24, 26
revenge, in HIV-positive people, 349
ritualization, 300
Rogers, Carl, 26, 74, 75
role, observing in storytelling, 147
Ronald McDonald homes, 365

SAMHSA. *See* Substance Abuse and Mental
Health Service Administration
Saunders, Cicely, 366
savior complex, 68
scene-making, form of resistance, 117
scheduling
admitting need to modify, 95–96
building in time for reflection, 130
schizoid personality, 256
capability for relationships, 209, 211
disorganization of, 211, 212
hostility in, 210
schizoid personality disorder, 272–73, 296
schizophrenia, 139, 141, 205–6
challenges for counselors, 208–11
classification for, 206–8
paranoid type, 262
relation to schizotypal personality
disorder, 274
treatment basics, 211–14
schizotypal personality disorder, 256,
273–74
Schneidman, Edwin, crises in reference to
life stages, 387–88
Schofield, William, 75
Scorsese, Martin, 363
scruples, 241
second substance disorder, 195
secondary gain, 229

secondary-gain resistance, 112
sedatives, 184
seduction, reciprocal process of, 79–80
seductive behavior
  form of resistance, 117
  with histrionic personality disorder, 290,
    291
self
  instrument in helping others, 65–72
  submergence of, 77–78
  utilizing in psychotherapy, 76
self-assessment, 68–70
  counselor's expectations, 102–3
  in counseling obsessive-compulsive
    personality disorder, 302
self-awareness, 48
  freeing helpers of emotional involvement,
    131
  importance in marriage counseling,
    311–12, 320–21
self-confidence, reluctance eroding
    counselor's, 106
self-counseling, 68–69
self-discipline, 78
self-disclosure, 81
self-esteem
  enhanced by professionalism, 402
  loss of underlying counseling
    relationship, 106
self-expression, helper's, 159
self-help groups, 157, 191
self-image, threats to, 252
self-knowledge
  being oneself, importance of, 57–64
  practical themes in, 67–71
  regarding emergency preparation,
    390–91
self-perception, 68–70
self-punishment, among depressed persons,
    228–29
self-reflection, post-interview, 100
self-revelations, counselors', 164–66
separations, in counseling relationship,
    154
sex, interwoven with death, 362
"sex out of context," 127–28
sex therapists, 330–31, 334
sexual deviations, 337
sexual disorders, 140, 335
sexual dysfunctions, 334, 335–36
sexuality
  expressions of, 331–33
  politicization of, 327
  relational nature of, 43

sexual masochism, 338
sexual problems
  decoding expressions of sexuality,
    331–33
  determining healthy vs. unhealthy
    sexuality, 333
  objective of people seeking help for,
    328–29
  physical aspects, 335–36
  remaining approachable for counseling
    of, 327
  responding to reports of, 338–39
  treating people, not problems, 327
  treatment for, 339
sexual relations, in helping relationships,
    79–80
sexual sadism, 338
Shostrom, Everett, 74
silence, 52
  form of resistance, 112–14
  helper's tactic, 98
  among reluctant, 104–5
skills training
  for avoidant personality disorder, 297
  for schizotypal personality disorder,
    274
sleep patterns, change in, 219
social phobias, 244
  similarity with avoidant personality
    disorder, 296, 297
  treatment for, 245, 297
Social Readjustment Rating Scale, 249
social skills training, 272
sociopaths, 275
soldiers' sickness, 180
somatic problems
  with depression, 217–18
  in emergencies, 395–96
  related to grief, 373
  relating to emergencies, 392
  varying cultural expressions, 217
somatoform disorders, 140
Sort of Life, A (Greene), 142–43
specific phobia, 244
spirituality, source of well-being, 390–91
spiritual problems, 127–28
split treatment, 225
splitting, 257, 285–86, 287, 305
spontaneity, 59, 77–78
stigma, 376–77
Stockholm Syndrome, 282–83
Stone, Michael, 32–33

storytelling
  focusing on teller, 144–45
  methods for proper listening, 145–48
  missing the point of, 143–45
  relevance of, 142–43
stress, 11–14
  adjustment disorders related to, 248–49
  in anticipating role demands of
    counseling, 57
  from attempts to control counseling
    relationship, 63
  of counseling-ministry confusion, 95
  death and challenge of facing, 364–65
  divorce as source of, 312–13
  from failure to appreciate individuality,
    63
  function of working with bereaved,
    381–82
  of helpers, 247
  from helpers' inability to help, 255
  from helpers' need for accomplishment,
    46
  histrionic persons as source of, 292
  induced from improvisation in helping
    professions, 402
  institutional, 107–8
  interview's initial moments, 97–98
  lessened through genuineness of
    relations, 59
  of marriage counseling, 313
  positive effects of, 247
  referrals as source of, 153, 156
  relationship dragging out, 89
  reluctance as cause of, 101
  rescue fantasies leading to, 25, 27
  resulting from power contests, 96
  role in onset and exacerbation of
    schizophrenic symptoms, 206
  scoring the stressors, 249–50
  self-forgetfulness increasing, 68
  side effect of well-lived life, 248
  silence as source of, 52
  telephone as source of, 86
  from threats to self-image, 252
  tolerance, 390
  from treating depressed persons, 228
  universal concern, 232, 236
  universal effects of, 247
  vague arrangements as cause of, 100
  from working with dying, 361
  See also anxiety
stressors, rating, 249
structured interviews, 123
Strupp, Hans, 74, 76

Styron, William, 215
substance abuse, 137, 177, 185
  consequences of, 185–86
  development of, 182
  second substance disorder, 195
  See also alcohol, drug *entries*
Substance Abuse and Mental Health Service
    Administration, 188
substance abuse disorders, 350
substance dependence, 185
substance-induced disorders, 185
substance intoxication, 185, 186
substance-related disorders, 138–39,
    184–85
substance withdrawal, 185, 186
success, expectations of, 67–68
suggestion, 8
suicide
  adolescent, 353–54
  alcohol's role in, 196
  announced by phone, reactions to, 400
  attempts, 358–59
  among borderline personalities, 284, 286
  counseling challenges, 355–56
  danger of emotional unresponsiveness
    to, 356
  with depression, 216
  determination to commit, 352
  evaluation of risk, 352–55
  history of panic attacks, 239
  with HIV, 350
  ideation, 221–22
  improper responses to threats of, 356
  lethality scale, 352–53
  nonverbal signaling, 392
  prevention, 359–60
  proper responses to threats of, 356–58
  reactivation of urge, 358–59
  among schizophrenics, 214
  three phases of therapy for attempts,
    358–59
  unaccountable, 388
Sullivan, Harry Stack, viii
supportive therapy, 6–9, 119–20, 169,
    170–72
  avoiding subconscious material, 329,
    330
  for dependent personality disorder, 307
  for depression, 225, 226
  effective management, 122
  foundation of, 54–55
  interpretation in, 53, 54
  therapist's role in, 171–72

symbolization, 299
sympathy, 5, 6

talking, form of resistance, 115
tardiness, 90
team approach, to counseling the dying, 370
telephone, 86–88
    use during emergency, 399–400
theme, identifying in storytelling, 147
"Therapeutic Society," 76
therapeutic alliance, 329, 330
therapeutic relationships
    examining style of, 78–79
    prevailing model for, 73–74
    qualities and characteristics, 75–76
therapy
    equality of participants in, 74–75
    prevailing model for, 73–74
    special form of friendship, 75–76
time, stress of, 405–6
tolerance, 185, 192
transference, 15, 16, 18, 118, 160, 163
    avoiding with supportive treatment, 171
    in context of referrals, 150, 152
    in counseling for sexual problems, 329–30
    dealing with stress of, 62
    with grief, 380, 382
    with marriage counseling, 311–12, 314
    with narcissistic personality disorder, 294
    related to treatment of alcoholics, 193
    resistance, 112
    unconscious aspects of, 81
transvestic fetishism, 338
Travelers' Aid, 157
truth, expression of, 59–61
Turner, Ted, 222

twelve-step program, 198–99. *See also* Alcoholics Anonymous; Narcotics Anonymous
twin studies, 195, 206, 227

unanticipated grief, 378
unconditional love, 75
unconditional positive regard, 75
unconscious
    avoiding risk of probing, 8, 167, 169, 170, 346–47
    entering through insight-oriented treatment, 169, 171
uncovering, 6
uncovering therapy, 119–20
    avoiding, 346–47
    interpretation in, 53
underreacting, with potential suicides, 355–56
understanding, 56
    counselor's lack of, 164–65
    diagnosis as extension of, 131
    importance of, vii, ix, xiv
undoing, 299
unsocialized behavior, 276

ventilation, 7, 8
viral set-point, 340–41
Virginia Twin Registry Study, 195
voyeurism, 338

Wallace, Mike, 215
Waugh, Evelyn, 215
WEBMD, 157
weight, change in, 219
Weisman, Avery, 369, 375
"why" questions, avoiding, 116, 130, 336
withdrawal, 53, 185, 186, 192
work, helper's overinvestment in, 78
worthlessness, feelings of, 220–21

Yamakoski, Tom, 77